THE GREAT FLOOD
and
OTHER MYTHS AND LEGENDS
of
THE OLD TESTAMENT

by

Sir James George Frazer

GLOBAL COMMUNICATIONS
EX LIBRIS
POST OFFICE BOX 753
NEW BRUNSWICK, NJ 08903

The Great Flood And Other Myths And Legends Of The Old Testament:
Studies in Comparative Religion, Legend & Law
by Sir James George Frazer

Original © 1918 by McMillan, London

New Version © 2008 by Timothy G. Beckley

First Edition

ISBN 978-60611-003-4
ISBN 1-60611-003-9

Published by   Timothy Green Beckley
                     P. O. Box 753
                     New Brunswick, New Jersey
                     08903

                     Timothy Green Beckley, Publisher
                     Carol Ann Rodriguez, Assistant to the Publisher
                     Wm Kern, Cover and graphics and general editing
                     Sean Casteel, Associate Editor

Printed in the United States of America

The Truth About The Great Flood And Other Biblical Mysteries
By Timothy Green Beckley

I do not consider myself a Biblical scholar.

I am not even what you would call a "true believer." I don't take what I read in the Bible at face value. I am not an athiest, but I don't go around preaching hellfire and brimstone either.

On the other hand, I have always been interested in Biblical history and the ancient world where the events described in both the Old and New Testaments take place.

I even remember going to a class on Bible stories when I was maybe ten years old. In my hazy recollection, it was not even a class given by the church my parents attended. But the stories of the Bible always were intriguing to me. After all, they are supernatural — it's like reading an ancient edition of "Fate Magazine."

My main interest, as most readers of Inner Light Publications will immediately recognize, gravitate around the subject of UFOs. I have witnessed three sightings, and can honestly testify that UFOs are as real as the day is long, although I admit I don't know what they are or from whence they originate. I even edited a book, "Flying Saucers In The Holy Bible," which discusses the connection between UFOs and the Tower of Babel, as well as how the real "Star Wars" is taking place in the universe between the forces of good and evil — the negative forces being directed, some theorize, by the fallen angel, Lucifer.

Some might consider the book you are now holding in your hands to be provocative. It is, nevertheless, "down-to-earth" and logical — and certainly well-documented.

This book offers proof that the stories of the Great Flood are universal, and that the Tower of Babel really existed and was the scene where different languages sprang up and spread throughout the world as punishment for man's arrogance. The subject matter is altogether fascinating and I think it will appeal to scholars, believers, nonbelievers and those generally interested in the truth about Biblical accounts.

Bless you all and may this book bring peace into your world.

—Timothy Beckley, Publisher
Inner Light/Global Communications

The Great Flood And Other Myths And Legends Of The Old Testament:
Studies in Comparative Religion, Legend & Law
by Sir James George Frazer

CONTENTS
Introduction

Introduction

Introductory comments by Paul Abramson, Editor

Sir James George Frazer wrote an impressive 3 volume set of *negative* commentaries on Genesis. This book (published in 1918, by McMillan, London, England) is the first volume (from Creation to the Tower of Babel). He was a proud scoffer, but the evidence that he assembled in order to try to attack Scriptural integrity is simply great. So ignore Frazer's temporal theorizing about "Jehovistic" vs. "Priestly" documents; unrepentant scoffers like him later had to abandon such spurious attacks.

By the beginning of the 20th Century, most of the world had been "discovered," mapped, and the "Civilized World" had been successively introduced (over the course of the previous 300 years or so) to the wide variety of life and heritages from around the globe. From staid scientific publications to the sensationalist popular media of the modern era an array of new and exotic discoveries had been heralded and duly discussed by kings and emperors, along with theologians and philosophers as well as by the common man.

The "Christian World" tried to assimilate all of the new knowledge flowing into the generally understood historical conventions of The Creation, Man's Fall From Grace, the Great Flood and the Tower of Babel as generally accepted historical events, particularly since the Bible is very clear on their humankind encompassing scope and precise sequence. ***All of humankind shares the same origins heritage until breaking up during the dispersion at Babel. Therefore, all of humankind should still retain remnants of these stories in their diverse cultures.***

In 1918 Sir James George Frazer brought much of the compendium of world legends as related to biblical accounts together into this well researched volume. The carefully catalogued recollections in these five long chapters (the printed book is 400 pages) had been slowly brought back to the "Civilized World" by many different ship captains, traders, missionaries, historians and other inquisitive travelers to distant lands. Men had tried to compare and contrast these various beliefs against their own "Christian" knowleddge of the distant past.

The longest single chapter (#4; about 250 pages) concerns the many surviving records of the Great Flood in the world. They're found on every continent. ***The Global Flood of about 5,000 years ago left the strongest single historical imprint upon all of humanity, no matter where on the globe folks had later moved to and resettled.***

Yet in spite of all the evidence supporting the Bible's accounts of our early history (of about 6,000 years ago), we're increasingly in danger of losing our true common history. Skeptics and modern false teachers have proclaimed that the Flood of Noah was merely "regional" in scope, even though the Bible is quite clear: (Genesis 7:19b) "*...all the high hills, that (were) under the whole heaven, were covered.*" In Frazer's time, just as today, doubts of the Bible's absolute accuracy abounded, as you will see in his commentaries throughout this volume. But when we look at it today, we can see how well these foundational events of humanity's origins were still remembered around the world, even up until less than 100 years ago.

(from Chapter IV—The Flood) "*...the calamity which their traditions say once befell them, **destroying the whole human race,** excepting one man, who landed from his canoe on a high mountain in the West. This tradition, however, was not peculiar to the Mandan tribe, for **amongst one hundred and twenty different tribes** that I have vvisited in North and South and Central America, **not a tribe exists that has not related to me distinct or vague traditions of such a calamity,** in which one, or three, or eight persons were saved above the water... .*"

Painter and traveler, George Catlin, 1830s

CHAPTER I
THE CREATION OF MAN

Two different accounts of the creation of man in Genesis
The Priestly and the Jehovistic narratives
The Jehovistic the more primitive
Babylonian and Egyptian parallels
Greek legend of the creation of man out of clay
Australian and Maori stories of the creation of man out of clay
Tahitian tradition: creation of woman out of man's rib
Similar stories of the creation of woman in Polynesia
Similar Karen and Tartar stories
Other stories of the creation of man in the Pacific
Melanesian legends of the creation of men out of clay
Stories of the creation of man in Celebes
Stories told by the Dyaks of Borneo
Legend told by the natives of Nias
Stories told by the natives of the Philippines
Indian legends of the creation of man
Cheremiss story of the creation of man
African stories of the creation of man
American stories of the creation of man
Our first parents moulded out of red clay
Belief of savages in the evolution of man out of lower animals
American Indian stories of the evolution of men out of animals
African and Malagasy stories of the evolution of men
Evolution of men out of fish in Africa and Borneo
Descent of men from trees and animals in the Indian Archipelago
Descent of men from animals in New Guinea
Descent of men from fish and grubs in the Pacific
Evolution of men out of animals in Australia
Evolutionary hypothesis of Empedocles
Creation or evolution?

CHAPTER II
THE FALL OF MAN

CHAPTER III
THE MARK OF CAIN

The theory that the mark was a tribal badge Homicides shunned as infected
Attic law concerning homicides
Seclusion of murderers in Dobu
Belief in the infectiousness of homicides in Africa
Earth supposed to spurn the homicide
Wanderings of the matricide Alcmaeon
Earth offended by bloodshed and appeased by sacrifice
The homicide's mark perhaps a danger-signal to others
The mark perhaps a protection against the victim's ghost
Ceremonies to appease the ghosts of the slain
Seclusion of murderer through fear of his victim's ghost
Fear of ghosts of the murdered, a motive for executing murderers
Protection of executioners against the ghosts of their victims
Bodily marks to protect people against ghosts of the slain
Need of guarding warriors against the ghosts of the slain
Various modes of guarding warriors against the ghosts of the slain
Faces or bodies of manslayers painted in diverse colours
The mark of Cain perhaps a disguise against the ghost of Abel
Advantage of thus interpreting the mark
The blood rather than the ghost of Abel prominent in the narrative
Fear of leaving blood of man or beast uncovered
Superstition a crutch of morality

CHAPTER IV
THE GREAT FLOOD

§ 1. Introduction
Huxley on the Great Flood
The present essay a study in folk-lore
Bearing of flood stories on problems of origin and diffusion

§ 2. The Babylonian Story of a Great Flood
Babylonian tradition recorded by Berosus
Nicolaus of Damascus on the flood
Modern discovery of the original Babylonian story
The Gilgamesh epic
Journey of Gilgamesh to Ut-napishtim
Ut-napishtim's story of the Great Flood
The building of the ship—the embarkation—the storm
The sending forth of the dove and the raven—the landing
Other fragmentary versions of the Babylonian story
Sumerian version of the flood story
The flood story borrowed by the Semites from the Sumerians
The scene of the story laid at Shurippak on the Euphrates

§ 3. The Hebrew Story of a Great Flood
The story in Genesis The story compounded of two different narratives
The Priestly Document and the Jehovistic Document
Late date and ecclesiastical character of the Priestly Document
Its contrast with the Jehovistic Document
Verbal differences between the Priestly and the Jehovistic Documents
Material differences between the documents in the flood story
The Jehovistic document the older of the two
Dependence of the Hebrew on the Babylonian story of the flood
Fanciful additions made to the flood story in later times

§ 4. Ancient Greek Stories of a Great Flood
Deucalion and Pyrrha The grounding of the ark on Parnassus
Aristotle and Plato on Deucalion's flood

Stories as to the origin of the diversity of tongues in Greece, Africa, Assam, Australia, and America

§ 19. The Origin of Stories of a Great Flood
Old theory of a universal deluge supported by evidence of fossils
Survivals of the theory of a universal deluge in the nineteenth century
Stories of a Great Flood interpreted as solar, lunar, or stellar myths
Evidence of geology against a universal deluge
Philosophical theories of a universal primeval ocean
Many flood stories probably reminiscences of real events
Memorable floods in Holland
Floods caused by earthquake waves in the Pacific
Some flood stories in the Pacific probably reminiscences of earthquake waves
Inundations caused by heavy rains
Babylonian story explained by annual inundation of the Euphrates valley
Suess's theory of a flood caused by an earthquake and a typhoon
Objections to the theory
Diluvial traditions partly legendary, partly mythical
Myths of observation based on geological configuration and fossils
All flood stories probably comparatively recent

ATTENTIVE readers of the Bible can hardly fail to remark a striking discrepancy between the two accounts of the creation of man recorded in the first and second chapters of Genesis. In the first chapter, we read how, on the fifth day of creation, God created the fishes and the birds, all the creatures that live in the water or in the air; and how on the sixth day he created all terrestrial animals, and last of all man, whom he fashioned in his own image, both male and female. From this narrative we infer that man was the last to be created of all living beings on earth, and incidentally we gather that the distinction of the sexes, which is characteristic of humanity, is shared also by the divinity; though how the distinction can be reconciled with the unity of the Godhead is a point on which the writer vouchsafes us no information. Passing by this theological problem, as perhaps too deep for human comprehension, we turn to the simpler question of chronology and take note of the statements that God created the lower animals first and human beings afterwards, and that the human beings consisted of a man and a woman, produced to all appearance simultaneously, and each of them reflecting in equal measure the glory of their divine original. So far we read in the first chapter. But when we proceed to peruse the second chapter, it is somewhat disconcerting to come bolt on a totally different and, indeed, contradictory account of the same momentous transaction. For here we learn with surprise that God created man first, the lower animals next, and woman last of all, fashioning her as a mere afterthought out of a rib which he abstracted from man in his sleep. The order of merit in the two narratives is clearly reversed. In the first narrative the deity begins with fishes and works steadily up through birds and beasts to man and woman. In the second narrative he begins with man and works downwards through the lower animals to woman, who apparently marks the nadir of the divine workmanship. And in this second version nothing at all is said about man and woman being made in the image of God. We are simply told that "the Lord God formed man of the dust of the ground, and breathed into his nostrils the breath of life; and man became a living soul." 1 Afterwards, to relieve the loneliness of man, who wandered without a living companion in the beautiful garden which had been created for him, God fashioned all the birds and beasts and brought them to man, apparently to amuse him and keep him company. Man looked at them and gave to them all their names; but still he was not content with these playmates, so at last, as if in despair, God created woman out of an insignificant portion of the masculine frame, and introduced her to man to be his wife.2

The flagrant contradiction between the two accounts is explained very simply by the circumstance that they are derived from two different and originally independent documents which were afterwards combined into a single book by an editor, who pieced the two narratives together without always taking pains to soften or harmonize their discrepancies. The account of the creation in the first chapter is derived from what is called the Priestly Document, which was composed by priestly writers during or after the Babylonian captivity. The account of the creation of man and the animals in the second chapter is derived from what is called the Jehovistic Document, which was written several hundred years before the other, probably in the ninth or eighth century before our era.3 The difference between the religious standpoints of the two writers is manifest. The later or priestly writer conceives God in an abstract form as withdrawn from human sight, and creating all things by a simple fiat. The earlier or Jehovistic writer conceives God in a very concrete form as acting and speaking like a man, modeling a human being out of clay, planting a garden, walking in it at the cool of the day, calling to the man and woman to come out from among the trees behind which they had hidden themselves, and making coats of skin to replace the too scanty garments of fig-leaves with which our abashed first parents sought to conceal their nakedness.1 The charming naivety, almost the gaiety, of I the earlier narrative contrasts with the high seriousness of the later; though we cannot but be struck by a vein of sadness and pessimism running under the brightly coloured picture of life in the age of innocence, which the great Jehovistic artist has painted for us. Above all, he hardly attempts to hide his deep contempt for woman. The lateness of her creation, and the irregular and undignified manner of it—made out of a piece of her lord and master, after all the lower animals had been created in a regular and decent manner—sufficiently mark the low opinion he held of her nature; and in the sequel his misogynism, as we may fairly call it, takes a still darker tinge, when he ascribes all the misfortunes and sorrows of the human race to the credulous folly and unbridled appetite of its first mother.2

Of the two narratives, the earlier or Jehovistic is not only the more picturesque but also the richer in folk-lore, retaining many features redolent of primitive simplicity which have been carefully effaced by the later writer, the two. Accordingly, it offers more points of comparison with the childlike stories by which men in many ages and countries have sought to explain the great mystery of the beginning of life on earth. Some of these simple tales I will adduce in the following pages.

The Jehovistic writer seems to have imagined that God Babylonian moulded the first man out of clay, just as a potter might do, Egyptian or as a child moulds a doll out of mud; and that having parallels, kneaded and patted the clay into the proper shape, the deity animated it by breathing into the mouth and nostrils of the figure, exactly as the prophet Elisha is said to have restored to life the dead child of the Shunammite by lying on him, and putting his eyes to the child's eyes and his mouth to the child's mouth, no doubt to impart his breath to the corpse; after which the child sneezed seven times and opened its eyes.1 To the Hebrews this derivation of our species from the dust of the ground suggested itself all the more naturally because, in their language, the word for "ground" (adamah) is in form the feminine of the word for "man" (adam)2

From various allusions in Babylonian literature it would seem that the Babylonians also conceived man to have been moulded out of clay.3 According to Berosus, the

Babylonian priest, whose account of creation has been preserved in a Greek version, the god Bel cut off his own head, and the other gods caught the flowing blood, mixed it with earth, and fashioned men out of the bloody paste; and that, they said, is why men are so wise, because their mortal clay is tempered with blood divine.4 In Egyptian mythology Khnoumou, the Father of the Gods, is said to have moulded men out of clay on his potter's wheel.5 So in Greek legend the sage Prometheus is said to have moulded the first men out of clay at Panopeus in Phocis. When he had done his work, some of the clay was left over, and might be seen on the spot long afterwards in the shape of two large boulders lying at the edge of a ravine. A Greek traveler, who visited the place in the second century of our era, thought that the boulders had the color of clay, and that they smelt strongly of human flesh.6 I, too, visited the spot some seventeen hundred and fifty years later. It is a forlorn little glen, or rather hollow, on the southern side of the hill of Panopeus, below the long line of ruined but still stately walls and towers which crowns the gray rocks of the summit. It was a hot day in late autumn—the first of November—and after the long rainless summer of Greece the little glen was quite dry; no water trickled down its bushy sides, but in the bottom I found a reddish crumbling earth, perhaps a relic of the clay out of which Prometheus modeled our first parents. The place was solitary and deserted: not a human being, not a sign of human habitation was to be seen; only the line of moldering towers and battlements on the hill above spoke of the busy life that had long passed away.

The whole scene, like so many else in Greece, was fitted to impress the mind with a sense of the transitoriness of man's little bustling existence on earth compared with the permanence and, at least, the outward peace and tranquility of nature. The impression was deepened when I rested, in the heat of the day, on the summit of the hill under the shade of some fine holly-oaks, and surveyed the distant prospect, rich in memories of the past, while the sweet perfume of the wild thyme scented all the air. To the south the finely cut peak of Helicon peered over the low intervening ridges. In the west loomed the mighty mass of Parnassus, its middle slopes darkened by pine-woods like shadows of clouds brooding on the mountain side; while at its skirts nestled the ivy-mantled walls of Daulis overhanging the deep glen, whose romantic beauty accords so well with the loves and sorrows of Procne and Philomela, which Greek legend associated with the spot. Northwards, across the broad plain to which the steep bare hill of Panopeus descends, the eye rested on the gap in the hills through which the Cephissus winds his tortuous way to flow under grey willows, at the foot of barren stony hills, till his turbid waters lose themselves, no longer in the vast reedy swamps of the now vanished Copaic Lake, but in a dark cavern of the limestone rock. Eastward, clinging to the slopes of the bleak range of which the hill of Panopeus forms part, were the ruins of Chaeronea, the birthplace of Plutarch; and out there in the plain was fought the fatal battle which laid Greece at the feet of Macedonia. There, too, in a later age, East and West met in deadly conflict, when the Roman armies under Sulla defeated the Asiatic hosts of Mithridates. Such was the landscape spread out before me on one of those farewell autumn days of almost pathetic splendor, when the departing summer seems to linger fondly, as if loath to resign to winter the enchanted mountains of Greece. Next day the scene had changed: summer was gone. A grey November mist hung low on the hills which only yesterday had shone resplendent in the sun, and under its melancholy curtain the dead flat of the Chaeronea plain, a wide, treeless expanse shut in by desolate slopes, wore an aspect of chilly sadness befitting the battlefield where a nation's freedom was lost.

We cannot doubt that such rude conceptions of the origin of mankind, common to Greeks, Hebrews, Babylonians, and Egyptians, were handed down to the civilized peoples of antiquity by their savage or barbarous forefathers. Certainly stories of the same sort have been recorded among the savages and barbarians of to-day or yesterday. Thus the Australian blacks in the neighborhood of Melbourne said that Pund-jel, the Creator, cut three large sheets of bark with his big knife. On one of these he placed some clay and worked it up with his knife into a proper consistence. He then laid a portion of the clay on one of the other pieces of bark and shaped it into a human form; first he made the feet, then the legs, then the trunk, the arms, and the head. Thus he made a clay man on each of the two pieces of bark; and being well pleased with his handiwork, he danced round them for joy. Next he took stringy bark from the eucalyptus tree, made hair of it, and stuck it on the heads of his clay men. Then he looked at them again, was pleased with his work, and again danced round them for joy. He then lay down on them, blew his breath hard into their mouths, their noses, and their navels; and presently they stirred, spoke, and rose up as full-grown men.1 The Maoris of New Zealand say that a certain god, variously named Tu, Tiki, and Tane, took red riverside clay, kneaded it with his own blood into a likeness or image of himself, with eyes, legs, arms, and all complete, in fact, an exact copy of the deity; and having perfected the model, he animated it by breathing into its mouth and nostrils, whereupon the clay effigy at once came to life and sneezed. "Of all these things," said a Maori, in relating the story of man's creation, "the most important is the fact that the clay sneezed, forasmuch as that sign of the power of the gods remains with us even to this day in order that we may be reminded of the great work Tu accomplished on the altar of the Kauhanga-nui, and hence it is that when men sneeze the words of Tu are repeated by those who are present;" for they say, "Sneeze, O spirit of life." 1 So like himself was the man whom the Maori Creator Tiki fashioned that he called him Tiki-ahua, that is, Tiki's likeness.2

A very generally received tradition in Tahiti was that the first human pair was made by Taaroa, the chief god. They say that after he had formed the world he created man out of red earth, which was also the food of mankind until bread-fruit was produced. Further, some say that one day Taaroa called for the man by name, and when he came he made him fall asleep. As he slept, the Creator took out one of his bones (ivi) and made of it a woman, whom he gave to the man to be his wife, and the pair became the progenitors of mankind. This narrative was taken down from the lips of the natives in the early years of the mission to Tahiti. The missionary who records it observes: "This always appeared to me a mere recital of the Mosaic account of creation, which they had heard from some European, and I never placed any reliance on it, although they have repeatedly told me it was a tradition among them before any foreigner arrived. Some have also stated that the woman's name was Ivi, which would be by them pronounced as if written Eve. Ivi is an aboriginal word, and not only signifies a bone, but also a widow, and a victim slain in war. Notwithstanding the assertion of the natives, I am disposed to think that Ivi, or Eve,

15

is the only aboriginal part of the story, as far as it respects the mother of the human race."
1 However, the same tradition has been recorded in other parts of Polynesia besides
Tahiti. Thus the natives of Fakaofo or Bow-ditch Island say that the first man was produced out of a stone. After a time he bethought him of making a woman. So he gathered
earth and moulded the figure of a woman out of it, and having done so he took a rib out of
his left side and thrust it into the earthen figure, which thereupon started up a live woman.
He called her Ivi (Eevee) or "rib" and took her to wife, and the whole human race sprang
from this pair.2 The Maoris also are reported to believe that the first woman was made
out of the first man's ribs.3 This wide diffusion of the story in Polynesia raises a doubt
whether it is merely, as Ellis thought, a repetition of the Biblical narrative learned from
Europeans.

However, the story of the creation of the first woman out of a rib of the first man meets
us elsewhere in forms so closely resembling the Biblical account that they can hardly be
independent of it. Thus the Karens of Burma say that God "created man, and of what did
he form him? He created man at first from the earth, and finished the work of creation. He
created woman, and of what did he form her? He took a rib from the man and created the
woman." Again they say, "He created spirit or life. How did he create spirit? Father God
said : 'I love these my son and daughter. I will bestow my life upon them.' He took a
particle of his life, and breathed it into their nostrils, and they came to life and were men.
Thus God created man. God made food and drink, rice, fire and water, cattle, elephants
and birds." 1 The suspicion that we have here to do with missionary or at all events European influence, is confirmed, if not raised to a certainty, by other traditions current among
the Ghaikos, a branch of the Karens. For the Ghaikos trace their genealogy to Adam, and
count thirty generations from him to the building of a great tower and the confusion of
tongues. According to them "in the days of Pan-dan-man, the people determined to build
a pagoda that should reach up to heaven. The place they suppose to be somewhere in
the country of the Red Karens, with whom they represent themselves as associated until
this event. When the pagoda was half way up to heaven, God came down and confounded
the language of the people, so that they could not understand each other. Then the people
scattered, and Than-mau-rai, the father of the Ghaiko tribe, came west, with eight chiefs,
and settled in the valley of the Sitang." 2 Again, the Bedel Tartars of Siberia have a tradition that God at first made a man, who lived quite alone on the earth. But once, while this
solitary slept, the devil touched his breast; then a bone grew out from his ribs, and falling to the ground it grew long and became the first woman.3 Thus these Tartars have
deepened the cynicism of the writer in Genesis by giving the devil a hand in the creation
of our common mother.4 But to return to the Pacific.

In Nui, or Netherland Island, one of the Ellice Islands, they say that the god Aulialia
made models of a man and a woman out of earth, and when he raised them up they came
to life. He called the man Tepapa and the woman Tetata.5 The Pelew Islanders relate that
a brother and sister made men out of clay kneaded with the blood of various animals,
and that the characters of these first men and of their descendants were determined by
the characters of the animals whose blood had been mingled with the primordial clay ;
for instance, men who have rat's blood in them are thieves, men who have serpent's

blood in them are sneaks, and men who have cock's blood in them are brave.1 According to a Melanesian legend, told in Mota, one of the Banks' Islands, the hero Qat moulded men of clay, the red clay from the marshy riverside at Vanua Lava. At first he made men and pigs just alike, but his brothers remonstrated with him, so he beat down the pigs to go on all fours and made man walk upright. Qat fashioned the first woman out of supple twigs, and when she smiled he knew she was a living woman.2 A somewhat different version of the Melanesian story is told at Lakona, in Santa Maria. There they say that Qat and another spirit (vui) called Marawa both made men. Qat constructed them out of the wood of dracaena-trees. Six days he worked at them, carving their limbs and fitting them together. Then he allowed them six days to come to life. Three days he hid them away, and three days more he worked to make them live. He set them up and danced to them and beat his drum, and little by little they stirred, till at last they could stand all by themselves. Then Qat divided them into pairs and called each pair husband and wife. Marawa also constructed men out of the wood of a tree, but it was a different tree, the tavisoviso. He likewise worked at them six days, beat his drum, and made them live, just as Qat did. But when he saw them move, he dug a pit and buried them in it for six days, and then, when he scraped away the earth to see what they were doing, he found them all rotten and stinking. That was the origin of death.3 The natives of Malekula, one of the New Hebrides, give the name of Bokor to the great being who kneaded the first man and woman out of clay.4

The inhabitants of Noo-hoo-roa, in the Kei Islands, say that their ancestors were fashioned out of clay by the supreme god, Dooadlera, who breathed life into the clay figures.1 According to the Bare'e-speaking Toradjas of Central Celebes there were at first no human beings on the earth. Then i Lai, the god of the upper world, and i Ndara, the goddess of the under world, resolved to make men. They committed the task to i Kombengi, who made two models, one of a man and the other of a woman, out of stone or, according to others, out of wood. When he had done his work, he set up his models by the side of the road which leads from the upper to the under world, so that all spirits passing by might see and criticize his workmanship. In the evening the gods talked it over, and agreed that the calves of the legs of the two figures were not round enough. So Kombengi went to work again, and constructed another pair of models which he again submitted to the divine criticism. This time the gods observed that the figures were too pot-bellied, so Kombengi produced a third pair of models, which the gods approved of, after the maker had made a slight change in the anatomy of the figures, transferring a portion of the male to the female figure. It now only remained to make the figures live. So the god Lai returned to his celestial mansion to fetch eternal breath for the man and woman; but in the meantime the Creator himself, whether from thoughtlessness or haste, had allowed the common wind to blow on the figures, and they drew their breath and life from it. That is why the breath returns to the wind when a man dies.2

The aborigines of Minahassa, in the north of Celebes, say that two beings called Wailan Wangko and Wangi were alone on an island, where grew a coco-nuttree. Said Wailan Wangko to Wangi, "Remain on earth while I climb up the tree." Said Wangi to Wailan Wangko, "Good." But then a thought occurred to Wangi, and he climbed up the tree to ask Wailan Wangko why he, Wangi, should remain down there all alone. Said Wailan Wangko to Wangi, "Return and take earth and make two images, a man and a woman." Wangi did so, and both images were men who could move but not speak. So Wangi swarmed up the tree again to ask Wailan Wangko, "How now? The two images are made, but they cannot speak." Said Wailan Wangko to Wangi, "Take this ginger and go and blow it on the skulls and the ears of these two images, that they may be able to speak; call the man Adam and the woman Ewa." 1 In this narrative the names of the man and woman betray Christian or Mohammedan influence, but the rest of the story may be aboriginal.

The Dyaks of Sakarran in British Borneo say that the first man was made by two large birds. At first they tried to make men out of trees, but in vain. Then they hewed them out of rocks, but the figures could not speak. Then they moulded a man out of damp earth and infused into his veins the red gum of the kumpang-tree. After that they called to him and he answered; they cut him and blood flowed from his wounds, so they gave him the name of Tannah Kumpok or "moulded earth." 2 Some of the Sea Dyaks, however, are of a different opinion. They think that a certain god named Salampandai is the maker of men. He hammers them into shape out of clay, thus forming the bodies of children who are to be born into the world. There is an insect which makes a curious clinking noise at night, and when the Dyaks hear it, they say that it is the clink of Salampandai's hammer at his work. The story goes that he was commanded by the gods to make a man, and he made one of stone ; but the figure could not speak and was therefore rejected. So he set to work again, and made a man of iron ; but neither could he speak, so the gods would have none of him. The third time Salampandai made a man of clay, and he had the power of speech. Therefore the gods were pleased and said, "The man you have made will do well. Let him be the ancestor of the human race, and you must make others like him." So Salampandai set about fashioning human beings, and he is still fashioning them at his anvil, working away with his tools in unseen regions. There he hammers out the clay babies, and when one of them is finished he brings it to the gods, who ask the infant, "What would you like to handle and use? "If the child answers, "A sword," the gods pronounce it a male; but if the child replies, "Cotton and a spinning-wheel," they pronounce it a female. Thus they are born boys or girls, according to their own wishes.1

The natives of Nias, an island to the south-west of Sumatra, have a long poem descriptive of the creation, which they recite at the dances performed at the funeral of a chief. In this poem, which is arranged in couplets after the style of Hebrew poetry, the second verse repeating the idea of the first in somewhat different language, we read how the supreme god, Luo Zaho, bathed at a celestial spring which reflected his figure in its clear water as in a mirror, and how, on seeing his image in the water, he took a handful of earth as large as an egg, and fashioned out of it a figure like one of those figures of ancestors which the people of Nias construct. Having made it, he put it in the scales and weighed it; he weighed also the wind, and having weighed it, he put it on the lips of the figure which he had made; so the figure spoke like a man or like a child, and God gave him the name of Sihai. But though Sihai was like God in form, he had no offspring; and the world was dark, for as yet there was neither sun nor moon. So God meditated, and sent Sihai down to earth to live there in a house made of tree-fern. But while as yet he had neither wife nor child, he one day died at noon. However, out of his mouth grew two trees, and the trees budded and blossomed, and the wind shook the blossoms from the trees, and blossoms fell to the ground and from them arose diseases. And from Sihai's throat grew a tree, from which gold is derived; and from his heart grew another tree, from which men are descended. Moreover, out of his right eye came the sun, and out of his left eye came the moon.2 In this legend the idea of creating man in his own image appears to have been suggested to the Creator by the accident of seeing his own likeness reflected in a crystal spring.

The Bila-an, a wild tribe of Mindanao, one of the Philippine Islands, relate the creation of man as follows. They say that in the beginning there was a certain being named Melu, of a size so huge that no known thing can give any idea of it; he was white in color, and had golden teeth, and he sat upon the clouds, occupying all the space above. Being of a very cleanly habit, he was constantly rubbing himself in order to preserve the whiteness of his skin unsullied. The scurf which he thus removed from his person he laid on one side, till it gathered in such a heap as to fidget him. To be rid of it he constructed the earth out of it, and being pleased with his work he resolved to make two beings like himself, only much smaller in size. He fashioned them accordingly in his own likeness out of the leavings of the scurf whereof he had moulded the earth, and these two were the first human beings. But while the Creator was still at work on them, and had finished one of them all but the nose, and the other all but the nose and one other part, Tau Dalom Tana came up to him and demanded to be allowed to make the noses. After a heated argument with the Creator, he got his way and made the noses, but in applying them to the faces of our first parents he unfortunately placed them upside down. So warm had been the discussion between the Creator and his assistant in regard to the noses, that the Creator quite forgot to finish the other part of the second figure, and went away to his place above the clouds, leaving the first man or the first woman (for we are not told which) imperfect; and Tau Dalom Tana also went away to his place below the earth. After that a heavy rain fell, and the two first of human kind nearly perished, for the rain ran off the tops of their heads into their upturned nostrils. Happily the Creator perceived their plight and coming down from the clouds to the rescue he took off their noses and replaced them right end up.1

A variant of the foregoing legend told by the Bila-an runs thus. In the beginning four beings, two male and two female, lived on a small island no bigger than a hat. Neither trees nor grass grew on the island, but one bird lived on it. So the four beings sent the bird to fetch some earth, the fruit of the rattan, and the fruit of trees. When it brought the articles, Melu, who was one of the two male beings, took the earth and moulded it into land, just as a woman moulds pots; and having fashioned it he planted the seeds in it, and they grew. But after a time he said, "Of what use is land without people?" The others said, "Let us make wax into people." They did so, but when the waxen figures were set near the fire, they melted. So the Creators perceived that they could not make man out of wax. Not to be baffled, they resolved to make him out of dirt, and the two male beings accordingly addressed themselves to the task. All went well till it came to fashioning the noses.

19

The Creator who was charged with this operation put the noses on upside down, and though his colleague Melu pointed out his mistake, and warned him that the people would be drowned if they went about with their noses in that position, he refused to repair his blunder and turned his back in a huff. His colleague seized the opportunity and the noses at the same instant, and hastily adjusted these portions of the human frame in the position which they still occupy. But on the bridge of the nose you can see to this day the print left by the Creator's fingers in his hurry.1

The Bagobos, a pagan tribe of South-Eastern Mindanao, say that in the beginning a certain Diwata made the sea and the land, and planted trees of many sorts. Then he took two lumps of earth, shaped them like human figures, and spat on them; so they became man and woman. The old man was called Tuglay, and the old woman, Tugli-bung. They married and lived together, and the old man made a great house and planted seeds of different kinds, which the old woman gave him.2

The Kumis, who inhabit portions of Arakan and the Chittagong hill tracts in eastern India, told Captain Lewin the following story of the creation of man. God made the world and the trees and the creeping things first, and after that he made one man and one woman, forming their bodies of clay; but every night, when he had done his work, there came a great snake, which, while God was sleeping, devoured the two images. This happened twice or thrice, and God was at his wits' end, for he had to work all day, and could not finish the pair in less than twelve hours; besides, if he did not sleep, "he would be no good," as the native narrator observed with some show of probability. So, as I have said, God was at his wits' end. But at last he got up early one morning and first made a dog and put life into it; and that night, when he had finished the images, he set the dog to watch them, and when the snake came, the dog barked and frightened it away. That is why to this day, when a man is dying, the dogs begin to howl; but the Kumis think that God sleeps heavily nowadays, or that the snake is bolder, for men die in spite of the howling of the dogs. If God did not sleep, there would be neither sickness nor death; it is during the hours of his slumber that the snake comes and carries us off.1 A similar tale is told by the Khasis of Assam. In the beginning, they say, God created man and placed him on earth, but on returning to look at the work of his hands he found that the man had been destroyed by the evil spirit. This happened a second time, whereupon the deity created first a dog and then a man; and the dog kept watch and prevented the devil from destroying the man. Thus the work of the deity was preserved.2 The same story also crops up, with a slight varnish of Hindu mythology, among the Korkus, an aboriginal tribe of the Central Provinces of India. According to them, Rawan, the demon king of Ceylon, observed that the Vindhyan and Satpura ranges were uninhabited, and he besought the great god Mahadeo to people them. So Mahadeo, by whom they mean Siva, sent a crow to find for him an ant-hill of red earth, and the bird discovered such an ant-hill among the mountains of Betul. Thereupon the god repaired to the spot, and taking a handful of the red earth he fashioned out of it two images, in the likeness of a man and a woman. But no sooner had he done so than two fiery horses, sent by Indra, rose from the earth and trampled the images to dust. For two days the Creator persisted in his attempts, but as often as the images were made they were dashed in pieces by the horses. At last the god made an image of a dog, and breathed into it the breath of life, and the animal kept off the fiery steeds of Indra. Thus the god was able to make the two images of man and woman undisturbed, and bestowing life upon them, he called them Mula and Mulai. These two became the ancestors of the Korku tribe.1

A like tale is told, with a curious variation, by the Mundas, a primitive aboriginal tribe of Chota Nagpur. They say that the Sun-god, by name Singbonga, first fashioned two clay figures, one meant to represent a man and the other a woman. But before he could endow the figures with life, the horse, apprehensive of what in future he might endure at their hands, trampled them under its hoofs. In those days the horse had wings and could move about much faster than now. When the Sun-god found that the horse had destroyed his earthen figures of men, he first created a spider and then fashioned two more clay figures like those which the horse had demolished. Next he ordered the spider to guard the effigies against the horse. Accordingly the spider wove its web round the figures in such a way that the horse could not break them again. After that, the Sun-god imparted life to the two figures, which thus became the first human beings.2

A story of the same sort, in fuller form and with material variations, is told by the Santals of Bengal. They say that in the beginning there was a certain Thakur Jiu. There was no land visible, all was covered with water. Then Thakur Jiu's servants said to him, "How shall we create human beings?" He replied, "If it be so desired, we can create them."

They then said, "If you give us a blessing (or the gift), we shall be able to do so." Thakur Jiu then said, "Go, call Malin Budhi. She is to be found in a rock cave under the water." When she came, she received the order to form two human beings. Some say ‘ she made them of a kind of froth which proceeded from a supernatural being who dwelt at the bottom of the sea, but others say she made them of a stiff clay. Thakur Jiu was a spectator of what was being done. At length Malin Budhi made the bodies of two human beings, and laid them out to dry. In the meantime Day-horse (Singh Sadom) passed that way, and trampling them under foot destroyed them. After an interval Thakur Jiu demanded of Malin Budhi whether she had prepared the figures. She replied, "I made them, but I have many enemies." Thakur Jiu inquired who they were, and she answered, "Who but Day-horse?" Thakur Jiu then said, "Kick the pieces into the Sora Nai and the Samud Nai." At this point the reciter of the story chants the following staves :—

"Oh! the Day-horse.

Oh! the Day-horse,

The Day-horse has gone to the river Gang,

The Day-horse has floated to the Sora Sea,

Oh! the Day-horse."

Thakur Jiu then said to Malin Budhi, "I again give you a blessing; go, make two human beings." Having prepared them, she went to Thakur Jiu, who said, "Well, have you got them ready?" She replied, "They are ready; give them the gift of life." He said, "Above the door-frame is the life (or spirit) of birds; do not bring that. Upon the cross-beam is the life of human beings; bring it." So she went, but being low of stature she could not reach the cross-beam; hence she brought the birds' life from above the door. No sooner had she given the birds' life to the figures than they flew up into the heavens, where they continued to course about, whether for twelve years or for twelve months is doubtful. The names of the birds were Has and Hasin. At length the desire to breed came upon them, and they went to Thakur Jiu and said, "You gave us being, but we cannot find a place on which to rest." He answered, "I will prepare a place for you."

Living in the water were Sole-fish, Crab, Prince Earthworm, and Lendom Kuar. Thakur Jiu called them and ordered them to raise the earth above the water. Sole-fish said, "I will raise the earth above the water," but though he tried and tried again, he could not do it. Then Crab came and said, "I will do it," but he also failed. Prince Earth-worm then came and undertook to accomplish it. So he ducked his head under water and swallowed earth, and the earth passed through him and came out at the other end; but when it fell on the surface of the water, it immediately sank to the bottom again. Then Prince Earthworm said, "Within the water resides Prince Tortoise; if we fasten him at the four corners with chains, and then raise the earth on his back, it will remain and not fall into the water again." So Prince Earth-worm secured Prince Tortoise with chains and raised the earth on his back, and in a short time there was an island in the midst of the waters. Thakur Jiu then caused a karam tree1 to spring up, and at the foot of the karam tree he caused sirom grass2 to grow. He then caused dhobi grass3 to spring up, after which he covered the earth with all kinds of trees and herbs. In this manner the earth became firm and stable.

Then the birds Has and Hasin came and alighted on the karam tree, and afterwards made their nest among the sirom grass at its foot. There the female laid two eggs, and Raghop Buar came and ate them. Again she laid other two eggs, and again Raghop Buar came and devoured them. Then Has and Hasin went to Thakur Jiu and informed him that Raghop Buar had twice eaten their eggs. On hearing this Thakur Jiu said, "I shall send some one to guard your eggs." So, calling Jaher-era, he committed the eggs of the two birds to her care. So well did she perform her task that the female was allowed to hatch her eggs, and from the eggs emerged two human beings, a male and a female; their names were Pilchu Haram and Pilchu Budhi. These were the parents of man-kind. Here the reciter of the story bursts out into song as follows:

"Hae, hae, two human beings,

Hae, hae, are born in the water,

Hae, hae, how can I bring them up ?

Hae, hae, where can I place them ?

My mother gave me birth among the sirom grass,

My father had his dwelling at the karma tree foot."

This Santal story of the origin of man combines the principles of creation and evolution, for according to it mankind is ultimately derived from two images, which were modeled in human form out of froth or damp clay, but were afterwards accidentally transformed into birds, from whose eggs the first man and woman of flesh and blood were hatched.

The Cheremiss of Russia, a Finnish people, tell a story of the creation of man which recalls episodes in the Toradjan and Indian legends of the same event. They say that God moulded man's body of clay and then went up to heaven to fetch the soul, with which to animate it. In his absence he set the dog to guard the body. But while he was away the Devil drew near, and blowing a cold wind on the dog he seduced the animal by the bribe of a fur-coat to relax his guard. Thereupon the fiend spat on the clay body and beslavered it so foully, that when God came back he despaired of ever cleaning up the mess and saw himself reduced to the painful necessity of turning the body outside in. That is why a man's inside is now so dirty. And God cursed the dog the same day for his culpable neglect of duty.2

Turning now to Africa, we find the legend of the creation of mankind out of clay among the Shilluks of the White Nile, who ingeniously explain the different complexions of the various races by the differently colored clays out of which they were fashioned. They say that the creator Juok moulded all men out of earth, and that while he was engaged in the work of creation he wandered about the world. In the land of the whites he found a pure white earth or sand, and out of it he shaped white men. Then he came to the land of Egypt and out of the mud of the Nile he made red or brown men. Lastly, he came to the land of the Shilluks, and finding there black earth he created black men out of it. The way in which he modeled men was this. He took a lump of earth and said to himself, "I will make man, but he must be able to walk and run and go out into the fields, so I will give him two long legs, like the flamingo." Having done so, he thought again, "The man must be able to cultivate his millet, so I will give him two arms, one to hold the hoe, and the other to tear up the weeds." So he gave him two arms. Then he thought again, "The man must be able to see his millet, so I will give him two eyes." He did so accordingly. Next he thought to himself, "The man must be able to eat his millet, so I will give him a mouth." And a mouth he gave him accordingly. After that he thought within himself, "The man must be able to dance and speak and sing and shout, and for these purposes he must have a tongue." And a tongue he gave him accordingly. Lastly, the deity said to himself, "The man must be able to hear the noise of the dance and the speech of great men, and for that he needs two ears." So two ears he gave him, and sent him out into the world a perfect man.1 The Fans of West Africa say that God created man out of clay, at first in the shape of a lizard, which he put in a pool of water and left there for seven days. At the end of the seven days God cried, "Come forth," and a man came out of the pool instead of a lizard.2 The Ewe-speaking tribes of Togo-land, in West Africa, think that God still makes men out of clay. When a little of the water with which he moistens the clay remains over, he pours it on the ground, and out of that he makes the bad and disobedient people. When he wishes to make a good man he makes him out of good clay; but when he wishes to make a bad man, he employs only bad clay for the purpose. In the beginning God fashioned a man and set him on the earth ; after that he fashioned a woman, The two looked at each other and began to laugh, whereupon God sent them into the world.3

The story of the creation of mankind out of clay occurs also in America, both among the Eskimo and the Indians, from Alaska to Paraguay. Thus the Eskimo of Point Barrow, in Alaska, tell of a time when there was no man in the land, till a certain spirit named á sê lu, who resided at Point Barrow, made a clay man, set him up on the shore to dry, breathed into him, and gave him life.1 Other Eskimo of Alaska relate how the Raven made the first woman out of clay, to be a companion to the first man; he fastened water-grass to the back of the head to be hair, flapped his wings over the clay figure, and it arose, a beautiful young woman.2 The Acagchemem Indians of California said that a powerful being called Chinigchinich created man out of clay which he found on the banks of a lake; male and female created he them, and the Indians of the present day are the descendants of the clay man and woman.3

According to the Maidu Indians of California the first man and woman were created by a mysterious personage named Earth-Initiate, who descended from the sky by a rope made of feathers. His body shone like the sun, but his face was hidden and never seen. One afternoon he took dark red earth, mixed it with water, and fashioned two figures, one of them a man and the other a woman. He laid the man on his right side and the woman on his left side, in his house. He lay thus and sweated all that afternoon and all that night. Early in the morning the woman began to tickle him in the side. He kept very still and did not laugh. By and by he arose, thrust a piece of pitch-wood into the ground, and fire burst out. The two people were very white. No one to-day is so white as they were. Their eyes were pink, their hair was black, their teeth shone brightly, and they were very handsome. It is said that Earth-Initiate did not finish the hands of the people, because he did not know how best to do it. The coyote, or prairie-wolf, who plays a great part in the myths of the Western Indians, saw the people and suggested that they ought to have hands like his. But Earth-Initiate said, "No, their hands shall be like mine." Then he finished them. When the coyote asked why their hands were to be like that, Earth-Initiate answered, "So that, if they are chased by bears, they can climb trees." The first man was called Kuksu, and the first woman was called Morning-Star Woman.1

The Diegueño Indians or, as they call themselves, the Kawakipais, who occupy the extreme south-western corner of the State of California, have a myth to explain how the world in its present form and the human race were created. They say that in the beginning there was no earth or solid land, nothing but salt water, one vast primeval ocean. But under the sea lived two brothers, of whom the elder was named Tcaipakomat. Both of them kept their eyes shut, for if they had not done so, the salt water would have blinded them. After a while the elder brother came up to the surface and looked about him, but he could see nothing but water. The younger brother also came up, but on the way to the surface he incautiously opened his eyes, and the salt water blinded him; so when he emerged he could see nothing at all, and therefore he sank back into the depths. Left alone on the face of the deep, the elder brother now undertook the task of creating a habitable earth out of the waste of waters. First of all he made little red ants, which produced land by filling up the water solid with their tiny bodies. But still the world was dark, for as yet neither sun nor moon had been created. Tcaipakomat now caused certain black birds with flat bills to come into being ; but in the darkness the birds lost their way and could not find where to roost. Next Tcaipakomat took three kinds of clay, red, yellow, and black, and thereof he made a round flat thing, which he took in his hand and threw up against the sky. It stuck there, and beginning to shed a dim light became the moon. Dissatisfied with the faint illumination of this pallid orb, Tcaipakomat took more clay, moulded it into another round flat disc, and tossed it up against the other side of the sky. It stuck there and became the sun, lighting up everything with his beams. After that Tcaipakomat took a lump of light-colored clay, split it partly up, and made a man of it. Then he took a rib from the man and made a woman of it. The woman thus created out of the man's rib was called Sinyaxau or First Woman (from siny, "woman," and axau, "first"). From this first man and woman, modeled by the Creator out of clay, mankind is descended. At first people lived at a great mountain called Wikami. If you go there and put your ear to the ground, you will hear the sound of dancing; it is made by the spirits of all the dead people footing it away. For when people die, they go back to the place where all things were at first created, and there they dance, just as live folks do here.1

The Hopi or Moqui Indians of Arizona similarly believe that in the beginning there was nothing but water everywhere, and that two deities, apparently goddesses, both named Huruing Wuhti, lived in houses in the ocean, one of them in the east, and the other in the west; and these two by their efforts caused dry land to appear in the midst of the water. Nevertheless the sun, on his daily passage across the newly created earth, noticed that there was no living being of any kind on the face of the ground, and he brought this radical defect to the notice of the two deities. Accordingly the divinities met in consultation, the eastern goddess passing over the sea on the rainbow as a bridge to visit her western colleague. Having laid their heads together they resolved to make a little bird; so the goddess of the east made a wren of clay, and together they chanted an incantation over it, so that the clay bird soon came to life. Then they sent out the wren to fly over the world and see whether he could discover any living being on the face of the earth; but on his return he reported that no such being existed anywhere. Afterwards the two deities created many sorts of birds and beasts in like manner, and sent them forth to inhabit the world. Last of all the two goddesses made up their mind to create man. Thereupon the eastern goddess took clay and moulded out of it first a woman and afterwards a man; and the clay man and woman were brought to life just as the birds and beasts had been so before them.1

The Pima Indians, another tribe of Arizona, allege that the Creator took clay into his hands, and mixing it with the sweat of his own body, kneaded the whole into a lump.

Then he blew upon the lump till it began to live and move and became a man and a woman.2 A priest of the Natchez Indians in Louisiana told Du Pratz "that God had kneaded some clay, such as that which potters use, and had made it into a little man; and that after examining it, and finding it well formed, he blew upon his work, and forthwith that little man had life, grew, acted, walked, and found himself a man perfectly well shaped." As to the mode in which the first woman was created, the priest frankly confessed that he had no information, the ancient traditions of his tribe being silent as to any difference in the creation of the sexes ; he thought it likely, however, that man and woman were made in the same way. So Du Pratz corrected his erroneous ideas by telling him the tale of Eve and the rib, and the grateful Indian promised to bruit it about among the old men of his tribe.3

The Michoacans of Mexico said that the great god Tucapacha first made man and woman out of clay, but that when the couple went to bathe in a river they absorbed so much water that the clay of which they were composed all fell to pieces. To remedy this inconvenience the Creator applied himself again to his task and moulded them afresh out of ashes, but the result was again disappointing. At last, not to be baffled, he made them of metal. His perseverance was rewarded. The man and woman were now perfectly watertight; they bathed in the river without falling in pieces, and by their union they became the progenitors of mankind.4

According to a legend of the Peruvian Indians, which was told to a Spanish priest in Cuzco about half a century after the conquest, it was in Tiahuanaco that the human race was restored after the great flood which had destroyed them all, except one man and woman. There in Tiahuanaco, which is about seventy leagues from Cuzco, "the Creator began to raise up the people and nations, that are in that region, making one of each nation of clay, and painting the dresses that each one was to wear. Those that were to wear their hair, with hair, and those that were to be shorn, with hair cut; and to each nation was given the language that was to be spoken, and the songs to be sung, and the seeds and food that they were to sow. When the Creator had finished painting and making the said nations and figures of clay, he gave life and soul to each one, as well men as women, and ordered that they should pass under the earth. Thence each nation came up in the places to which he ordered them to go." 1 The Lengua Indians of Paraguay believe that the Creator, in the shape of a beetle, inhabited a hole in the earth, and that he formed man and woman out of the clay which he threw up from his subterranean abode. At first the two were joined together, "like the Siamese twins," and in this very inconvenient posture they were sent out into the world, where they contended, at great disadvantage, with a race of powerful beings whom the beetle had previously created. So the man and woman besought the beetle to separate them. He complied with their request and gave them the power to propagate their species. So they became the parents of mankind. But the beetle, having created the world, ceased to take any active part or interest in it.2 We are reminded of the fanciful account which Aristophanes, in the Symposium of Plato, gives of the original condition of mankind; how man and woman at first were knit together in one composite being, with two heads, four arms, and four legs, till Zeus cleft them down the middle and so separated the sexes.3

It is to be observed that in a number of these stories the clay out of which our first parents were moulded is said to have been red. The color was probably intended to explain the redness of blood. Though the Jehovistic writer in Genesis omits to mention the color of the clay which God used in the construction of Adam, we may perhaps, without being very rash, conjecture that it was red. For the Hebrew word for man in general is adam, the word for ground is adamah, and the word for red is adorn; so that by a natural and almost necessary concatenation of causes we arrive at the conclusion that our first parent was modeled out of red earth. If any lingering doubt could remain in our mind on the subject, it would be dissipated by the observation that down to this day the soil of Palestine is of a dark reddish brown, "suggesting," as the writer who notices it justly remarks, "the connection between Adam and the ground from which he was taken; especially is this color noticeable when the soil is newly turned, either by the plough or in digging." 1 So remarkably does nature itself bear witness to the literal accuracy of Holy Writ.

However, it is noteworthy that in regard to the origin of the human species many savages reject the hypothesis of creation in favour of the theory of evolution. They believe, in fact, that men in general, or their own tribespeople in particular, have been developed out of lower forms of animal life. The theory of evolution is particularly popular among totemic tribes who imagine that their ancestors sprang from their totemic animals or plants, but it is by no means confined to them. For example, some of the Californian Indians, in whose mythology the coyote or prairie-wolf is a leading personage, think that they are descended from coyotes. At first they walked on all fours; then they began to have some members of the human body, one finger, one toe, one eye, one ear, and so on; then they got two fingers, two toes, two eyes, two ears, and so forth; till at last, progressing from period to period, they became perfect human beings. The loss of their tails, which they still deplore, was produced by the habit of sitting upright.2 Similarly Darwin thought that "the tail has disappeared in man and the anthropomorphous apes, owing to the terminal portion having been injured by friction during a long lapse of time; the basal and embedded portion having been reduced and modified, so as to become suitable to the erect or semi-erect position." 1

The Turtle clan of the Iroquois think that they are descended from real mud turtles which used to live in a pool. One hot summer the pool dried up, and the mud turtles set out to find another. A very fat turtle, waddling after the rest in the heat, was much incommoded by the weight of his shell, till by a great effort he heaved it off altogether. After that he gradually developed into a human being and became the progenitor of the Turtle clan.2 The Crawfish clan of the Choctaws are in like manner descended from real crawfish, which used to live underground, only coming up occasionally through the mud to the surface. Once a party of Choctaws smoked them out, taught them to speak the Choctaw language and to walk on two legs, and made them cut off their toe nails and pluck the hair from their bodies, after which they adopted them into the tribe. But the rest of their kindred, the crawfish, are crawfish under the ground to this day.3 The Osage Indians universally believed that they were descended from a male snail and a female beaver. A flood swept the snail down to the Missouri and left him high and dry on the bank, where the sun ripened him into a man. He met and married a beaver maid, and from the pair the tribe of the Osages is descended. For a long time these Indians retained a pious reverence for their animal ancestors and refrained from hunting beavers, because in killing a beaver they killed a brother of the Osages. But when white men came among them and offered high prices for beaver skins, the Osages yielded to the temptation and took the lives of their furry brethren.4 The Carp clan of the Ootawak (Ottawa) Indians are descended ' from the eggs of a carp which had been deposited by the fish on the banks of a stream and warmed by the sun.1 The Crane clan of the Ojibways are sprung originally from a pair of cranes, which after long wanderings settled on the rapids at the outlet of Lake Superior, where they were changed by the Great Spirit into a man and woman.2 The members of two Omaha clans were at first buffaloes and lived under water, which they splashed about, making it muddy. And at death all the members of these clans went back to their ancestors the buffaloes. So when one of them lay a-dying, his friends used to wrap him up in a buffalo skin with the hair outside and say to him, "You came hither from the animals and you are going back thither. Do not face this way again. When you go, continue walking." 3

The Haida Indians of the Queen Charlotte Islands believe that long ago the raven, who is the chief figure in the mythology of North-Western America, took a cockle from the beach and married it; the cockle gave birth to a female child, whom the raven took to wife, and from their union the Indians were produced.4 Speaking of these Indians, a writer who lived among them tells us that "their descent from the crows is quite gravely affirmed and steadfastly maintained. Hence they never will kill one, and are always annoyed, not to say angry, should we whites, driven to desperation by the crow-nests on every side of us, attempt to destroy them. This idea likewise accounts for the coats of black paint with which young and old in all those tribes constantly besmear themselves. The crow-like color affectionately reminds the Indians of their reputed forefathers, and thus preserves the national tradition." 5 The Delaware Indians called the rattlesnake their grandfather and would on no account destroy one of these reptiles, believing that were they to do so the whole race of rattlesnakes would rise up and bite them. Under the influence of the white man, however, their respect for their grandfather the rattlesnake gradually died away, till at last they killed him without compunction or ceremony whenever they met him. The writer who records the old custom observes that he had often reflected on the curious connection which appears to subsist in the mind of an ndian between man and the brute creation ; "all animated nature," says he, "in whatever degree, is in their eyes a great whole, from which they have not yet ventured to separate themselves." 1 However, the title of grandfather, which these Indians bestowed on the rattlesnake, hardly suffices to prove that they believed themselves to be actually descended from the creature; it may have only been a polite form of address intended to soothe and gratify the formidable reptile. Some of the Indians of Peru boasted of being descended from the puma or American lion; hence they adored the lion as a god, and appeared at festivals, like Hercules, dressed in the skins of lions with the heads of the beasts fixed over their own. Others claimed to be descended from condors and attired themselves in great black and white wings, like that huge bird.2

28

The Wanika of East Africa look upon the hyena as one of their ancestors or as associated in some way with their origin and destiny. The death of a hyena is mourned by the whole people, and the greatest funeral ceremonies which they perform are performed for this brute. The wake held over a chief is as nothing compared to the wake held over a hyena ; one tribe alone mourns the death of its chief, but all the tribes unite to celebrate the obsequies of a hyena.3 Some Malagasy families claim to be descended from the babacoote (Lichanotus brevicaudatus), a large lemur of grave-appearance and staid demeanor which lives in the depth of the forest. When they find one of these creatures dead, his human descendants bury it solemnly, digging a grave for it wrapping it in a shroud, and weeping and lamenting over its carcass. A doctor who had shot a babacoote was accused by the inhabitants of a Betsimisaraka village of having killed "one of their grandfathers in the forest," and to appease their indignation he had to promise not to skin the animal in the village but in a solitary place where nobody could see him.1 Many of the Betsimisaraka believe that the curious nocturnal animal called the aye-aye (Cheiromys madagascariensis) "is the embodiment of their forefathers, and hence will not touch it, much less do it an injury. It is said that when one is discovered dead in the forest, these people make a tomb for it and bury it with all the forms of a funeral. They think that if they attempt to entrap it, they will surely die in consequence."2 Some Malagasy tribes believe themselves descended from crocodiles and accordingly they deem the ferocious reptiles their brothers. If one of these scaly brothers so far forgets the ties of kinship as to devour a man, the chief of the tribe, or in his absence an old man familiar with the tribal customs, repairs at the head of the people to the edge of the water, and summons the family of the culprit to deliver him up to the arm of justice. A hook is then baited and cast into the river or lake. Next day the guilty brother, or one of his family, is dragged ashore, formally tried, sentenced to death, and executed. The claims of justice being thus satisfied, the erring brother is lamented and buried like a kinsman; a mound is raised over his grave, and a stone marks the place of his head.3

Amongst the Tshi-speaking tribes of the Gold Coast in West Africa the Horse-mackerel family traces its descent from a real horse-mackerel whom an ancestor of theirs once took to wife. She lived with him happily in human shape on shore, till one day a second wife, whom the man had married, cruelly taunted her with being nothing but a fish. That hurt her so much that, bidding her husband farewell, she returned to her old home in the sea, with her youngest child in her arms, and never came back again. But ever since the Horse-mackerel people have refrained from eating horse-mackerels because the lost wife and mother was a fish of that sort.1 Some of the Land Dyaks of Borneo tell a similar tale to explain a similar custom. "There is a fish which is taken in their rivers called a puttin, which they would on no account touch, under the idea that if they did they would be eating their relations. The tradition respecting it is, that a solitary old man went out fishing and caught a puttin, which he dragged out of the water and laid down in his boat. On turning round, he found it had changed into a very pretty little girl. Conceiving the idea she would make, what he had long wished for, a charming wife for his son, he took her home and educated her until she was fit to be married. She consented to be the son's wife, cautioning her husband to use her well. Some time after their marriage, however, being out of temper, he struck her, when she screamed, and rushed away into the water ; but not without leaving behind her a beautiful daughter, who became afterwards the mother of the race."2 The Kayans of Borneo think that the first man and woman were born from a tree, which had been fertilized by a creeper swaying backwards and forwards in the wind. The man was named Kaluban Gai and the woman Kalubi Angai. However, they were incomplete, for they had no legs, and even the lower half of their trunks was wanting, so that their entrails protruded. Nevertheless they married and became the progenitors of mankind.3 Thus the Kayans suppose the human race to have been directly evolved from plants without passing through the intermediate stage of animals.

Members of a clan in Mandailing, on the west coast of Sumatra, allege that they are descended from a tiger, and at the present day, when a tiger is shot, the women of the clan are bound to offer betel to the dead beast. When members of this clan come upon the tracks of a tiger, they must, as a mark of homage, enclose them with three little sticks. Further, it is believed that the tiger will not attack or lacerate his kinsmen, the members of the clan.1 The Battas or Bataks of Central Sumatra are divided into a number of clans which have for their totems white buffaloes, goats, wild turtle-doves, dogs, cats, apes, tigers, and so forth ; and one of the explanations which they give of their totems is that these creatures were their ancestors, and that their own souls after death can transmigrate into the animals.2

Some of the natives of Minahassa, a district at the northeastern extremity of Celebes, believe that they are descended from apes, and that the parent stock of these animals still inhabits the woods of Menado toowah, or Old Menado, an island which rises out of the sea in the shape of a conical mountain. The old inhabitants of Menado, a town on the mainland of Celebes, stoutly affirmed that the apes on that island were their forefathers. In former times they used to send offerings of rice, bananas, and so forth, every year to their simian ancestors in the woods, but afterwards they found it more convenient to place their offerings on a raft of bamboo stems and then, in the darkness of night, illuminated by the glare of torches, to let the frail bark drift down the river amid a hubbub of noises and the clamor of multitudinous voices wishing it good speed. A similar belief in their descent from these apes is cherished by the inhabitants of Tanawangko, another town of Minahassa distant somewhat farther from the ancestral island. These people sometimes repair to the island for the purpose of felling timber, and it is said that, rather than chase away or injure the apes which infest the forest, they suffer the thievish animals to steal their rice, bananas, and clothes, believing that sickness or death would be the inevitable consequence of any attempt to defend their property against the monkeys.1

In Amboyna and the neighboring islands the inhabitants of some villages aver that they are descended from trees, such as the Capellenia moluccana, which had been fertilized by the Pandion Haliaetus. Others claim to be sprung from pigs, octopuses, crocodiles, sharks, and eels. People will not bum the wood of the trees from which they trace their descent, nor eat the flesh of the animals which they regard as their ancestors. Sicknesses of all sorts are believed to result from disregarding these taboos.2 Similarly in Ceram persons who think they are descended from crocodiles, serpents, iguanas, and sharks will not eat the flesh of these animals.3 Many other peoples of the Molucca Islands entertain similar beliefs and observe similar taboos.4

The Bukaua of North-Eastern New Guinea appear to trace their descent from their totemic animals. Thus the inhabitants of one village will not eat a certain sea-fish (ingot) because they allege that they are all descended from it. Were one of them to eat the fish, they believe that the doom of all the villagers would be sealed. Another clan revere white parrots as their totems, and never eat the bird, though they are glad to deck themselves with its feathers. If they see other people eating a white parrot, they are grieved, sprinkle themselves with ashes in token of sorrow for the death of the bird, and expect compensation from the murderers. If one of themselves ate a white parrot, he would suffer from sore eyes. The members of a particular family refuse to eat pig, because they owe their existence to a sow, which farrowed babies and little pigs at the same birth.5

Similarly some of the natives of Astrolabe Bay in Northern New Guinea believe that they are descended from a crocodile, which a human ancestress of theirs brought forth along with a twin girl. Hence they refuse to eat the flesh of crocodiles, and they tell a long story about the vicious behavior of their crocodile forefather.1

A somewhat different account of the origin of man is given by the Marindineeze, a tribe who occupy the dreary, monotonous treeless flats on the southern coast of Dutch New Guinea, not far from the border of the British territory. They say that one day a crane or stork (dik) was busy picking fish out of the sea. He threw them on the beach, where the clay covered and killed them. So the fish were no longer anything but shapeless lumps of clay. They were cold and warmed themselves at a fire of bamboos. Every time that a little bamboo burst with a pop in the heat, the lumps of clay assumed more and more the shape of human beings. Thus the apertures of their ears, eyes, mouth, and nostrils were opened, but as yet they could not speak, they could only utter a murmuring sound. Their fingers were still joined by membranes like those in the wings of bats. However, with a bamboo knife they severed the membranes and threw them into the sea, where they turned into leeches. When the nature spirit (dema) saw the human beings, he was wroth, and enviously asked the crane, why he had bestowed life on these creatures. So the crane ceased to peck at the fish and pecked at a log of wood instead; and that is why his beak has been bent ever since. At last, while the first men were sitting round the fire, a big bamboo burst with a louder crack than usual, which frightened the people so that they gave a loud shriek, and that was the beginning of human speech. You may still hear shrieks of the same sort at the present day, when in time of sickness the descendants of these first parents are sitting by the fire and throwing bamboos into it, in order that the crackling and popping of the bamboos in the flames may put the spirit of disease to flight. Every time a bamboo bursts with a pop, all the people shout and load the demon with curses. And this Papuan narrative of the descent of man usually winds up with the words, "So the stork or crane (dik) bestowed life on us." 1

A somewhat different version of the story is told by other members of the tribe. They say that before the first human pair appeared on earth, there were spirits (demas) resid-

31

ing at Wegi, near Kondo-miraaf which is near the extreme south-eastern corner of the tribal territory. Now the spirits owned a dog and a bird (diegge), which may be presumed to be the same crane or stork (dik, diek) which figures in the former version. One day the dog, snuffing about, was attracted by the scent to a certain spot, and there with his paws he scraped a hole in the ground, from which the first human pair, a man and a woman, came forth. They possessed all animal instincts, but their minds were very imperfectly developed. They lived like beasts, without experience and without feeling the need of communicating with each other by speech. As for the necessaries of life, they received them from the spirits. Roaming about one day they came to a river, and in their ignorance of the nature of water they walked straight into it and might have been drowned, if the bird had not flown to their rescue and drawn them out of the stream. That is how they came to be acquainted with water; but still they were ignorant of fire. Their knowledge of that element they acquired from watching a fire which the spirits had kindled to warm themselves at in cold weather; and it was the astonishment our first parents felt at the sight of the devouring flames, and the alarm they experienced at the loud crackling of the bamboos in the heat, which elicited from them the first cry of fear and wonder and so unloosed their tongues. Henceforth they could speak. The hole from which these ancestors of mankind emerged on that memorable day has continued to be a hole ever since; but water has gathered in it, and it is now the sacred pool of Wegi. Even in seasons of the greatest drought the water in that pool never fails; and all the animals and plants about it, every thing that runs or flies or grows there, is holy.[1]

The legend which in one or other of these versions the Marindineeze tell to account for the origin of the human species is said to be represented dramatically by them at the mysteries or rites of initiation which they celebrate every year, and on the celebration of which they apparently believe the fertility of the land, of man, and of beast to be dependent. Thus the story that the bird picked the first human beings from the water in the likeness of fish and threw them on the beach, is acted by an initiated man who comes hopping along on two sticks, picks up the novices one by one and throws them into the sacred enclosure. There they must lie motionless; they are stripped of all their ornaments, and coated from head to foot with a thick layer of clay; more than that, lumps of clay are thrust into their mouths by initiated men, and these they have afterwards to spit out into holes dug in the ground. This scene of the mysteries seems to recall either the clay which is said to have covered our fishy ancestors when they were first cast on the beach, or the earth from which they emerged when the dog had scraped away the soil from above them. The subsequent stages of the mysteries consist for the most part in a series of lessons designed to initiate the novices successively into the various occupations of ordinary life, of which, like newborn babes or their ancestors when they first emerged from the water or the earth, they are presumed to be entirely ignorant.[2]

Again, in Ponape, one of the Caroline Islands, "the different families suppose themselves to stand in a certain relation to animals, and especially to fishes, and believe in their descent from them. They actually name these animals ' mothers'; the creatures are sacred to the family and may not be injured. Great dances, accompanied with the offering of prayers, are performed in their honor. Any person who killed such an animal would expose himself to contempt and punishment, certainly also to the vengeance of the insulted deity." Blindness is commonly supposed to be the consequence of such a sacrilege.1 The Samoans have a tradition that the first two men were developed out of two grubs, which were produced through the rotting of a convolvulus torn up by its roots. But the transformation of the grubs into men was carried out by two divine beings under the direction of Tuli (a species of plover), who was himself the son of the great god Tangaloa of the Skies. When the two men had received all their human limbs and features complete at the hands of the deities, they dwelt in the land where they had been formed, but being both males they could not continue the species. However, it chanced that one day, while he was fishing, one of the two men received a mortal hurt from a little fish and died ; whereupon the great god Tangaloa caused the dead man to be changed into a woman and to be brought to life again. So the man and the woman married and became the parents of mankind.2 This Samoan story of the origin of man combines the processes of evolution and creation; for while it represents the first men as developed out of grubs, it attributes their final perfection to the formative action of divine beings.

Some of the aborigines of Western Australia believe that their ancestors were swans, ducks, or various other species of water-fowl before they were transformed into men.1 The Dieri tribe of Central Australia, who are divided into totemic clans, explain their origin by the following legend. They say that in the beginning the earth opened in the midst of Perigundi Lake, and the totems (murdus or madas) came trooping out one after the other. Out came the crow, and the shell parakeet, and the emu, and all the rest. Being as yet imperfectly formed and without members or organs of sense, they laid themselves down on the sand hills which surrounded the lake then, just as they do now. It was a bright day, and the totems lay basking in the sunshine, till at last, refreshed and invigorated by it, they stood up as human beings and dispersed in all directions. That is why people of the same totem are now scattered all over the country. You may still see the island in the lake out of which the totems came trooping long ago.2 Another Dieri legend relates how Paralina, one of the Mura-Muras or mythical predecessors of the Dieri, perfected mankind. He was out hunting kangaroos, when he saw four incomplete beings cowering together. So he went up to them, smoothed their bodies, stretched out their limbs, slit up their fingers and toes, formed their mouths, noses, and eyes, stuck ears on them, andblew into their ears in order that they might hear. Having perfected their organs and so produced mankind out of these rudimentary beings, he went about making men everywhere.3 Yet another Dieri tradition sets forth how the Mura-Mura produced the race of man out of a species of small black lizards, which may still be met with under dry bark. To do this he divided the feet of the lizards into fingers and toes, and, applying his forefinger to the middle of their faces, created a nose; likewise he gave them human eyes, mouths, and ears. He next set one of them upright, but it fell down again because of its tail; so he cut off its tail, and the lizard then walked on its hind legs. That is the origin of mankind.1

The Arunta tribe of Central Australia similarly tell how in the beginning mankind was developed out of various rudimentary forms of animal life. They say that in those days two beings called Ungambikula, that is, "out of nothing," or "self-existing," dwelt in the western sky. From their lofty abode they could see, far away to the east, a number of inapertwa creatures, that is, rudimentary human beings or incomplete men, whom it was their mission to make into real men and women. For at that time there were no real men and women; the rudimentary creatures (inapertwa) were of various shapes and dwelt in groups along the shore of the salt water which covered the country. These embryos, as we may call them, had no distinct limbs or organs of sight, hearing, and smell ; they did not eat food, and they presented the appearance of human beings all doubled up into a rounded mass, in which only the outline of the different parts could be vaguely perceived. Coming down from their home in the western sky, armed with great stone knives, the Ungambikula took hold of the embryos, one after the other. First of all they released the arms from the bodies, then making four clefts at the end of each arm they fashioned hands and fingers; afterwards legs, feet, and toes were added in the same way. The figure could now stand; a nose was then moulded and the nostrils bored with the fingers. A cut with the knife made the mouth, which was pulled open several times to render it flexible.

A slit on each side of the face separated the upper and lower eyelids, disclosing the eyes, which already existed behind them ; and a few strokes more completed the body. Thus out of the rudimentary creatures were formed men and women. These rudimentary creatures or embryos, we are told, "were in reality stages in the transformation of various animals and plants into human beings, and thus they were naturally, when made into human beings, intimately associated with the particular animal or plant, as the case may be, of which they were the transformations—in other words, each individual of necessity belonged to a totem the name of which was of course that of the animal or plant of which he or she was a transformation." However, it is not said that all the totemic clans of the Arunta were thus developed ; no such tradition, for example, is told to explain the origin of the important Witchetty Grub clan. The clans which are known, or said, to have originated out of embryos in the way described are the Plum Tree, the Grass Seed, the Large Lizard, the Small Lizard, the Alexandra Parakeet, and the Small Rat clans. When the Ungambikula had thus fashioned people out of these totems, they circumcised them all, except the Plum Tree men, by means of a fire-stick. After that, having done the work of creation or evolution, the Ungambikula turned themselves into little lizards which bear a name meaning "snappers-up of flies." 1

This Arunta tradition of the origin of man, as Messrs. Spencer and Gillen, who have recorded it, justly observe, "is of considerable interest; it is in the first place evidently a crude attempt to describe the origin of human beings out of non-human creatures who were of various forms; some of them were representatives of animals, others of plants, but in all cases they are to be regarded as intermediate stages in the transition of an animal or plant ancestor into a human individual who bore its name as that of his or her totem." 2 In a sense these speculations of the Arunta on their own origin may be said, like a similar myth of the Samoans,3 to combine the theory of creation with the theory of evolution; for while they represent men as developed out of much simpler forms of life, they at the same time assume that this development was effected by the agency of two powerful beings, whom so far we may call creators. It is well known that at a far higher stage of culture a crude form of the evolutionary hypothesis was propounded by the Greek philosopher Empedocles. He imagined that shapeless lumps of earth and water, thrown up by the subterranean fires, developed into monstrous animals, bulls with the heads of men, men with the heads of bulls, and so forth; till at last, these hybrid forms being gradually eliminated, the various existing species of animals and men were evolved.1 The theory of the civilized Greek of Sicily may be set beside the similar theory of the savage Arunta of Central Australia. Both represent gropings of the human mind in the dark abysses of the past; both were in a measure grotesque anticipations of the modern theory of evolution.

The foregoing examples may serve to illustrate two very different views which primitive man has taken of his own origin. They may be distinguished as the theory of creation and the theory of evolution. According to the one, the human race was fashioned in its present form by a great artificer, whether a god or a hero; according to the other, it was evolved by a natural process out of lower forms of animal or even vegetable life. Roughly speaking, these two theories still divide the civilized world between them. The partisans of each can appeal in support of their view to a large consensus of opinion; and if truth were to be decided by weighing the one consensus against the other, with Genesis in the one scale and The Origin of Species in the other, it might perhaps be found, when the scales were finally trimmed, that the balance hung very even between creation and evolution.

Chapter 2 - The Fall of Man

§ 1.   The Narrative in Genesis
The temptation and the fall, the woman and the serpent
The two trees
The Tree of Life and the Tree of Death
The Creator's good intention frustrated by the serpent
The serpent's selfish motive for deceiving the woman
Widespread belief in the immortality of serpents
Story of the Fall, a story of the origin of death

§ 2. The Story of the Perverted Message
Hottentot story of the Moon and the hare
Bushman story of the Moon and the hare
Nandi story of the Moon and the dog
Hottentot story of the Moon, the insect, and the hare
Bushman story of the Moon, the tortoise, and the hare
Louyi story of the Sun and Moon, the chameleon and the hare
Ekoi story of God, the frog, and the duck
Gold Coast story of God, the sheep, and the goat
Ashantee story of God, the sheep, and the goat
Akamba story of God, the chameleon, and the thrush
Togoland story of God, the dog, and the frog
Calabar story of God, the dog, and the sheep
Bantu story of God, the chameleon, and the lizard
The miscarriage of the message of immortality

§ 3. The Story of the Cast Skin
Supposed immortality of animals that cast their skins
How men missed immortality and serpents, etc., obtained it
Belief that men formerly cast their skins and lived for ever
Belief that men used to rise from the dead after three days
How men missed immortality and the Moon obtained it
Bahnar story how men used to rise from the dead
Rivalry between men and serpents, etc., for immortality

§ 4. The Composite Story of the Perverted Message and the Cast Skin
Galla story of God, the blue bird, and the serpent Stories of the Good Spirit, men, and serpents

§ 5. Conclusion

Original form of the story of the Fall of Man

1. The Narrative in Genesis

WITH a few light but masterly strokes the Jehovistic writer depicts for us the blissful life of our first parents in the happy garden which God had created for their abode. There every tree that was pleasant to the sight and good for food grew abundantly; there the animals lived at peace with man and with each other; there man and woman knew no shame, because they knew no ill: it was the age of innocence.1 But this glad time was short, the sunshine was soon clouded. From his description of the creation of Eve and her introduction to Adam, the writer passes at once to tell the sad story of their fall, their loss of innocence, their expulsion from Eden, and the doom of labor, of sorrow, and of death pronounced on them and their posterity. In the midst of the garden grew the tree of the knowledge of good and evil, and God had forbidden man to eat of its fruit, saying, "In the day that thou eatest thereof thou shalt surely die." But the serpent was cunning, and the woman weak and credulous: he persuaded her to eat of the fatal fruit, and she gave of it to her husband, and he ate also. No sooner had they tasted it than the eyes of both of them were opened, they knew that they were naked, and filled with shame and confusion they hid their nakedness under aprons of fig-leaves: the age of innocence was gone for ever. That woeful day, when the heat of noon was over and the shadows were growing long in the garden, God walked there, as was his wont, in the cool of the evening. The man and woman heard his footsteps,1 perhaps the rustling of the fallen leaves (if leaves could fall in Eden) under his tread, and they hid behind the trees, ashamed to be seen by him naked. But he called them forth from the thicket, and learning from the abashed couple how they had disobeyed his command by eating of the tree of knowledge, he flew into a towering passion. He cursed the serpent, condemning him to go on his belly, to eat dust, and to be the enemy of mankind all the days of his life: he cursed the ground, condemning it to bring forth thorns and thistles: he cursed the woman, condemning her to bear children in sorrow and to be in subjection to her husband : he cursed the man, condemning him to wring his daily bread from the ground in the sweat of his brow, and finally to return to the dust out of which he had been taken. Having relieved his feelings by these copious maledictions, the irascible but really kind-hearted deity relented so far as to make coats of skins for the culprits to replace their scanty aprons of fig-leaves, and clad in these new garments the shamefaced pair retreated among the trees; while in the west the sunset died away, and the shadows deepened on Paradise Lost.2

In this account everything hinges on the tree of the knowledge of good and evil: it occupies, so to say, the centre of the stage in the great tragedy, with the man and woman and the talking serpent grouped round it. But when we look closer we perceive a second tree standing side by side with the other in the midst of the garden. It is a very remarkable tree, for it is no less than the tree of life, whose fruit confers immortality on all who eat of it. Yet in the actual story of the fall this wonderful tree plays no part. Its fruit hangs there on the boughs ready to be plucked; unlike the tree of knowledge, it is hedged about by no divine prohibition, yet no one thinks it worth while to taste of the luscious fruit and live for ever. The eyes of the actors are all turned on the tree of knowledge; they appear not to see the tree of life. Only, when all is over, does God bethink himself of the wondrous tree standing there neglected, with all its infinite possibilities, in the midst of the garden ; and fearing lest man, who has become like him in knowledge by eating of the one tree, should become like him in im-mortality by eating of the other, he drives him from the garden and sets an angelic squadron, with flaming swords, to guard the approach to the tree of life, that none henceforth may eat of its magic fruit and live for ever. Thus, while throughout the moving tragedy in Eden our attention is fixed exclusively on the tree of knowledge, in the great transformation scene at the end, where the splendors of Eden fade for ever into the light of common day, the last glimpse we catch of the happy garden shows the tree of life alone lit up by the lurid gleam of brandished angelic falchions.1

It appears to be generally recognized that some confusion has crept into the account of the two trees, and that in the original story the tree of life did not play the purely passive and spectacular part assigned to it in the existing narrative. Accordingly, some have thought that there were originally two different stories of the fall, in one of which the tree of knowledge figured alone, and in the other the tree of life alone, and that the two stories have been unskillfully fused into a single narrative by an editor, who has preserved the one nearly intact, while he has clipped and pared the other almost past recognition.2 It may be so, but perhaps the solution of the problem is to be sought in another direction. The gist of the whole story of the fall appears to be an attempt to explain man's mortality, to set forth how death came into the world. It is true that man is not said to have been created immortal and to have lost his immortality through disobedience ; but neither is he said to have been created mortal. Rather we are given to understand that the possibility alike of immortality and of mortality was open to him, and that it rested with him which he would choose; for the tree of life stood within his reach, its fruit was not forbidden to him, he had only to stretch out his hand, take of the fruit, and eating of it live for ever. Indeed, far from being prohibited to eat of the tree of life, man was implicitly permitted, if not encouraged, to partake of it by his Creator, who had told him expressly, that he might eat freely of every tree in the garden, with the single exception of the tree of the knowledge of good and evil.1 Thus by planting the tree of life in the garden and not prohibiting its use, God apparently intended to give man the option, or at least the chance, of immortality, but man missed his chance by electing to eat of the other tree, which God had warned him not to touch under pain of immediate death. This suggests that the forbidden tree was really a tree of death, not of knowledge, and that the mere taste of its deadly fruit, quite apart from any question of obedience or disobedience to a divine command, sufficed to entail death on the eater. The inference is entirely in keeping with God's warning to man, "Thou shalt not eat of it: for in the day that thou eatest thereof thou shalt surely die."2 Accordingly we may suppose that in the original story there were two trees, a tree of life and a tree of death; that it was open to man to eat of the one and live for ever, or to eat of the other and die; that God, out of good will to his creature, advised man to eat of the tree of life and warned him not to eat of the tree of death; and that man, misled by the serpent, ate of the wrong tree and so forfeited the immortality which his benevolent Creator had designed for him.

At least this hypothesis has the advantage of restoring the balance between the two trees and of rendering the whole narrative clear, simple, and consistent it dispenses with the necessity of assuming two original and distinct stories which have been clumsily stitched together by a botching editor. But the hypothesis is further recommended by another and deeper consideration. It sets the character of the Creator in a far more amiable light: it clears him entirely of that suspicion of envy and jealousy, not to say malignity and cowardice, which, on the strength of the narrative in Genesis, has so long rested like a dark blot his reputation. For according to that narrative, God grudged man the possession both of knowledge and of immortality; he desired to keep these good things to himself, and feared that if man got one or both of them, he would be the equal of his maker, a thing not to be suffered at any price. Accordingly he forbade man to eat of the tree of knowledge, and when man disregarded the command, the deity hustled him out of the garden and closed the premises, to prevent him from eating of the other tree and so becoming immortal. The motive was mean, and the conduct despicable. More than that, both the one and the other are utterly inconsistent with the previous behavior of the deity, who, far from grudging man anything, had done all in his power to make him happy and comfortable, by creating a beautiful garden for his delectation, beasts and birds to play with, and a woman to be his wife. Surely it is far more in harmony both with the tenor of the narrative and with the goodness of the Creator to suppose, that he intended to crown his kindness to man by conferring on him the boon of immortality, and that his benevolent intention was only frustrated by the wiles of the serpent.

But we have still to ask, why should the serpent practise this deceit on man? what motive had he for depriving the human race of the great privilege which the Creator had planned for them? Was his interference purely officious? or had he some deep design behind it? To these questions the narrative in Genesis furnishes no answer. The serpent gains nothing by his fraud; on the contrary he loses, for he is cursed by God and condemned thenceforth to crawl on his belly and lick the dust. But perhaps his conduct was not so wholly malignant and purposeless as appears on the surface. We are told that he was more subtle than any beast of the field; did he really show his sagacity by-blasting man's prospects without improving his own? We may suspect that in the original story he justified his reputation by appropriating to himself the blessing of which he deprived our species; in fact, that while he persuaded our first parents to eat of the tree of death, he himself ate the tree of life and so lived for ever. The supposition is not so extravagant as it may seem. In not a few savage stories of the origin of death, which I will relate immediately, we read that serpents contrived to outwit or intimidate man and so to secure for themselves the immortality which was meant for him; for many savages believe that by annually casting their skins, serpents and other animals renew their youth and live for ever.

The belief appears to have been shared by the Semites; for, according to the ancient Phoenician writer Sanchuniathon, the serpent was the longest-lived of all animals, because it cast its skin and so renewed its youth.1 But if the Phoenicians held this view of the serpent's longevity and the cause of it, their neighbors and kinsfolk the Hebrews may well have done the same. Certainly the Hebrews seem to have thought that eagles renew their youth by molting their feathers;2 and if so, why not serpents by casting their skins? Indeed, the notion that the serpent cheated man of immortality by getting possession of a life-giving plant which the higher powers had destined for our species, occurs in the famous Gilgamesh epic, one of the oldest literary monuments of the Semitic race and far more ancient than Genesis. In it we read how the deified Ut-napishtim revealed to the hero Gilgamesh the existence of a plant which had the miraculous power of renewing youth and bore the name "the old man becomes young"; how Gilgamesh procured the plant and boasted that he would eat of it and so renew his lost youth; how before he could do so, a serpent stole the magic plant from him, while he was bathing in the cool water of a well or brook; and how, bereft of the hope of immortality, Gilgamesh sat down and wept.1 It is true that nothing is here said about the serpent eating the plant and so obtaining immortality for himself; but the omission may be due merely to the state of the text, which is obscure and defective, and even if the poet were silent on this point, the parallel versions of the story, which I shall cite, enable us to supply the lacuna with a fair degree of probability. These parallels further suggest, though they cannot prove, that in the original of the story, which the Jehovistic writer has mangled and distorted, the serpent was the messenger sent by God to bear the glad tidings of immortality to man, but that the cunning creature perverted the message to the advantage of his species and to the ruin of ours. The gift of speech, which he used to such ill purpose, was lent him in his capacity of ambassador from God to man.

To sum up, if we may judge from a comparison of the versions dispersed among many peoples, the true original story of the Fall of Man ran somewhat as follows. The benevolent Creator, after modeling the first man and woman out of mud and animating them by the simple process of blowing into their mouths and noses, placed the happy pair in an earthly paradise, where, free from care and toil, they could live on the sweet fruits of a delightful garden, and where birds and beasts frisked about them in fearless security. As a crowning mercy he planned for our first parents the great gift of immortality, but resolved to make them the arbiters of their own fate by leaving them free to accept or reject the proffered boon. For that purpose he planted in the midst of the garden two wondrous trees that bore fruits of very different sorts, the fruit of the one being fraught with death to the eater, and the other with life eternal. Having done so, he sent the serpent to the man and woman and charged him to deliver this message: "Eat not of the Tree of Death, for in the day ye eat thereof ye shall surely die ; but eat of the Tree of Life and live for ever." Now the serpent was more subtle than any beast of the field, and on his way he bethought him of changing the message; so when he came to the happy garden and found the woman alone in it, he said to her, "Thus saith God : Eat not of the Tree of Life, for in the day ye eat thereof ye shall surely die ; but eat of the Tree of Death, and live for ever." The foolish woman believed him, and ate of the fatal fruit, and gave of it to her husband, and he ate also. But the sly serpent himself ate of the Tree of Life. That is why men have been mortal and serpents immortal ever since, for serpents cast their skins every year and so renew their youth. If only the serpent had not perverted God's good message and deceived our first mother, we should have been immortal instead of the serpents; for like the serpents we should have cast our skins every year and so renewed our youth perpetually.

That this, or something like this, was the original form of the story is made probable by a comparison of the following tales, which may conveniently be arranged under two heads, "The Story of the Perverted Message" and "The Story of the Cast Skin."

§ 2. The Story of the Perverted Message

Like many other savages, the Namaquas or Hottentots associate the phases of the moon with the idea of immortality, the apparent waning and waxing of the luminary being understood by them as a real process of alternate disintegration and reintegration, of decay and growth repeated perpetually. Even the rising and setting of the moon is interpreted by them as its birth and death.1 They say that once on a time the Moon wished to send to mankind a message of immortality, and the hare undertook to act as messenger. So the Moon charged him to go to men and "As I die and rise to life again, so shall you die and rise to life again." Accordingly the hare went to men, but either out of forgetfulness or malice he reversed the message and said, "As I die and do not rise to life again, so you shall also die and not rise to life again." Then he went back to the Moon, and she asked him what he had said. He told her, and when she heard how he had given the wrong message, she was so angry that she threw a stick at him which split his lip. That is why the hare's lip is still cloven. So the hare ran away and is still running to this day. Some people, however, say that before he fled he clawed the Moon's face, which still bears the marks of the scratching, as anybody may see for himself on a clear moonlight night. But the Namaquas are still angry with the hare for robbing them of immortality. The old men of the tribe used to say, "We are still enraged with the hare, because he brought such a bad message, and we will not eat him." Hence from the day when a youth comes of age and takes his place among the men, he is forbidden to eat hare's flesh, or even to come into contact with a fire on which a hare has been cooked. If a man breaks the rule, he is not infrequently banished the village. However, on the payment of a fine he may be readmitted to the community.1

A similar tale, with some minor differences, is told by the Bushmen. According to them, the Moon formerly said to men, "As I die and come to life again, so shall ye do; when ye die, ye shall not die altogether but shall rise again." But one man would not believe the glad tidings of immortality, and he would not consent to hold his tongue. For his mother had died, he loudly lamented her, and nothing could persuade him that she would come to life again. A heated altercation ensued between him and the Moon on this painful subject. "Your mother's asleep," says the Moon. "She's dead," says the man, and at it they went again, hammer and tongs, till at last the Moon lost patience and struck the man on the face with her fist, cleaving his mouth with the blow. And as she did so, she cursed

41

him saying, "His mouth shall be always like this, even when he is a hare. For a hare he shall be. He shall spring away, he shall come doubling back. The dogs shall chase him, and when they have caught him they shall tear him in pieces. He shall altogether die. And all men, when they die, shall die outright. For he would not agree with me, when I bid him not to weep for his mother, for she would live again. 'No,' says he to me, 'my mother will not live again.' Therefore he shall altogether become a hare. And the people, they shall altogether die, because he contradicted me flat when I told him that the people would do as I do, returning to life after they were dead." So a righteous retribution overtook the skeptic for his skepticism, for he was turned into a hare, and a hare he has been ever since. But still he has human flesh in his thigh, and that is why, when the Bushmen kill a hare, they will not eat that portion of the thigh, but cut it out, because it is human flesh. And still the Bushmen say, "It was on account of the hare that the Moon cursed us, so that we die altogether. If it had not been for him, we should have come to life again when we died. But he would not believe what the Moon told him, he contradicted her flat." l In this Bushman version of the story the hare is not the animal messenger of God to men, but a human skeptic who, for doubting the gospel of eternal life, is turned into a hare and involves the whole human race in the doom of mortality. This may be an older form of the story than the Hottentot version, in which the hare is a hare and nothing more.

The Nandi of British East Africa tell a story in which the origin of death is referred to the ill-humor of a dog, who brought the tidings of immortality to men, but, not being received with the deference due to so august an embassy, he changed his tune in a huff and doomed mankind to the sad fate to which they have ever since been subject. The story runs thus. When the first men lived upon the earth a dog came to them one day and said, "All people will die like the Moon, but unlike the Moon you will not return to life again unless you give me some milk to drink out of your gourd and beer to drink through your straw. If you do this, I will arrange for you to go to the river when you die and to come to life again on the third day." But the people laughed at the dog, and gave him some milk and beer to drink off a stool. The dog was angry at not being served in the same vessels as a human being, and though he put his pride in his pocket and drank the milk and beer from the stool, he went away in high dudgeon, saying, "All people will die, and the Moon alone will return to life." That is why, when people die, they stay away, whereas when the Moon goes away she comes back again after three days' absence. If only people had given that dog a gourd to drink milk out of, and a straw to suck beer through, we should all have risen from the dead, like the moon, after three days.l In this story nothing is said as to the personage who sent the dog with the message of immortality to men; but from the messenger's reference to the Moon, and from a comparison with the parallel Hottentot story, we may reasonably infer that it was the Moon who employed the dog to run the errand, and that the unscrupulous animal misused his opportunity to extort privileges for himself to which he was not strictly entitled.

In these stories a single messenger is engaged to carry the momentous message, and the fatal issue of the mission is set down to the carelessness or malice of the missionary. However, in some narratives of the origin of death, two messengers are dispatched, and the cause of death is said to have been the dilatoriness or misconduct of the messenger who bore the glad tidings of immortality. There is a Hottentot story of the origin of death which is cast in this form; They say that once the Moon sent an insect to men with this message, "Go thou to men and tell them, 'As I die, and dying live, so ye shall also die, and dying live.' "The insect set off with this message, but as he crawled along, the hare came leaping after him, and stopping beside him asked, "On what errand art thou bound?"

The insect answered, "I am sent by the Moon to men, to tell them that as she dies, and dying lives, they also shall die, and dying live."

The hare said, "As thou art an awkward runner, let me go." And away he tore with the message, while the insect came creeping slowly behind. When he came to men, the hare perverted the message which he had officiously taken upon himself to deliver, for he said, "I am sent by the Moon to tell you, 'As I die, and dying perish, in the same manner ye shall also die and come wholly to an end.'" Then the hare returned to the Moon, and told her what he had said to men. The Moon was very angry and reproached the hare, saying, "Darest thou tell the people a thing which I have not said?" With that she took a stick and hit him over the nose. That is why the hare's nose is slit down to this day.1

The same tale is told, with some slight variations, by the Tati Bushmen or Masarwas, who inhabit the Bechuanaland Protectorate, the Kalahari desert, and portions of Southern Rhodesia. The men of old time, they say, told this story. The Moon wished to send a message to the men of the early race, to tell them that as she died and came to life again, so they would die, and dying come to life again. So the Moon called the tortoise and said to him, "Go over to those men there, and give them this message from me. Tell them that as I dying live, so they dying will live again." Now the tortoise was very slow, and he kept repeating the message to himself, so as not to forget it. The Moon was very vexed with his slowness and with his forgetfulness; so she called the hare and said to her, "You are a swift runner. Take this message to the men over yonder: 'As I dying live again, so you will dying live again.'" So off the hare started, but in her great haste she forgot the message, and as she did not wish to show the Moon that she had forgotten, she delivered the message to men in this way, "As I dying live again, so you dying will die for ever." Such was the message delivered by the hare. In the meantime the tortoise had remembered the message, and he started off a second time. "This time," said he to himself, "I won't forget." He came to the place where the men were, and he delivered his message. When the men heard it they were very angry with the hare, who was sitting at some distance. She was nibbling the grass after her race. One of the men ran and lifted a stone and threw it at the hare. It struck her right in the mouth and cleft her upper lip; hence the lip has been cleft ever since. That is why every hare has a cleft upper lip to this day, and that is the end of the story.1

In a story told by the A-Louyi tribe of the Upper Zambesi, the messengers of death and of life respectively are the chameleon and the hare. They say that Nyambe, whom they identify with the sun, used to dwell on earth with his wife Nasilele, whom they identify with the moon. But Nyambe retired to heaven from fear of men. Whenever he carved wood, men carved it also; when he made a wooden plate, so did they. After he had withdrawn to the sky, it happened that Nyambe's dog died. He loved the animal, and said, "Let the dog live." But his wife said, "No, I won't have it. He's a thief." Nyambe still persisted. "For my part," said he, "I love my dog." But his wife said, "Throw him out." So they threw him out. By and by Nyambe's mother-in-law died, and his wife said to him, "Let her live," just as Nyambe himself had said to her about his dog. But Nyambe answered, "No, let her die and be done with it. I said to you that my dog should live, and you refused. It is my wish that your mother should die for good and all." So die she did for good and all. After that the husband and wife sent two messengers, a chameleon and a hare, to men on the earth. To the chameleon they said, "When thou art come to men, say to them, 'Ye shall live'; but as for thee, O hare, when thou art come to men, say to them, 'Ye shall die once for all.'" The chameleon and the hare set off with their messages. Now the chameleon, as he went, kept constantly turning about, but the hare ran. So the hare arrived first, and said that men should die once for all. Having delivered his message, the hare returned. That is why, when men die, they die once for all.1 From this Louyi legend it would appear that human mortality resulted from a domestic war in heaven, the deity falling out with his wife over his dead dog and mother-in-law. From such seemingly trivial causes may flow such momentous consequences.

The Ekoi of Southern Nigeria, on the border of the Cameroons, attribute human mortality to the gross misconduct of a duck. It happened in this way. The sky-god Obassi Osaw one day thought to himself, "Men fear to die. They do not know that perhaps they may come to life again. I will tell them that sometimes such a thing may happen, then they will have less dread of death." So he stood up in his house in the sky, and called a frog and a duck before him. To the frog he said, "Go to earth and say to the people, 'When a man dies, it is the end of all things; he shall never live again.' To the duck he said, "Go tell the earth folk that if a man dies he may come to life again." He then led them a little way and showed them the road, saying, "Take my message. Duck, you may go to the left hand. Frog, keep to the right." So the frog kept on to the right, and when he came to the earth he delivered his message of death to the first men he met, telling them that when they died it would be an end of them. In due time the duck also reached the earth, but happening to arrive at a place where the people were making palm oil, she fell to gobbling it up and forgot all about the message of immortality which the good god had charged her to deliver to mankind. That is why we are all mortal down to this day. We are bound to go by the message of the frog; we cannot go by the message of the duck, which never reached us.2

The story of the two messengers is related also by the Negroes of the Gold Coast, and in their version the two messengers are a sheep and a goat. The following is the form in which the tale was told by a native to a Swiss missionary at Akropong. In the beginning, when sky and earth existed, but there were as yet no men on earth, there fell a great rain, and soon after it had ceased a great chain was let down from heaven to earth with seven men hanging on it. These men had been created by God, and they reached the earth by means of the chain. They brought fire with them and cooked their food at it. Not long afterwards God sent a goat from heaven to deliver the following message to the

44

seven men, "There is something that is called Death; it will one day kill some of you; but though you die, you will not perish utterly, but you will come to me here in heaven." The goat went his way, but when he came near the town he lit on a bush which seemed to him good to eat; so he lingered there and began to browse. When God saw that the goat lingered by the way, he sent a sheep to deliver the same message. The sheep went, but did not say what God had commanded her to say; for she perverted the message and said, "When you once die, you perish, and have no place to go to." Afterwards the goat came and said, "God says, you will die, it is true, but that will not be the end of you, for you will come to me." But the men answered, "No, goat, God did not say that to you. What the sheep first reported, by that we shall abide." 1 In another version of the story, also told at Akropong, the parts of the goat and the sheep are inverted; it is the sheep that bears the good tidings and loiters by the way to browse, and it is the goat that bears the evil tidings, and is the first to deliver them. The story ends with the melancholy reflection that "if only the sheep had made good speed with her message, man would have died but returned after death; but the goat made better speed with the contrary message, so man returns no more." 2

In an Ashantee version of the story the two messengers are also a sheep and a goat, and the perversion of the message of immortality is ascribed sometimes to the one animal and sometimes to the other. The Ashantees say that long ago men were happy, for God dwelt among them and talked with them face to face. However, these blissful days did not last for ever. One unlucky day it chanced that some women were pounding a mash with pestles in a mortar, while God stood by looking on. For some reason they were annoyed by the presence of the deity and told him to be off; and as he did not take himself off fast enough to please them, they beat him with their pestles. In a great huff God retired altogether from the world and left it to the direction of the fetishes; and still to this day people say, "Ah, if it had not been for that old woman, how happy we should be!" However, God was very good-natured, and even after he had gone up aloft, he sent a kind message by a goat to men on earth, saying, "There is something which they call Death. He will kill some of you. But even if you die, you will not perish completely. You will come to me in heaven." So off the goat set with this cheering intelligence. But before he came to the town, he saw a tempting bush by the wayside, and stopped to browse on it. When God looked down from heaven and saw the goat loitering by the way, he sent off a sheep with the same message to carry the joyful news to men without delay. But the sheep did not give the message aright. Far from it: she said, "God sends you word that you will die, and that will be an end of you." When the goat had finished his meal, he also trotted into the town and delivered his message, saying, "God sends you word that you will die, certainly, but that will not be the end of you, for you will go to him." But men said to the goat, "No, goat, that is not what God said. We believe that the message which the sheep brought us is the one which God sent to us." That unfortunate misunderstanding was the beginning of death among men.1

However, in another Ashantee version of the tale the parts played by the sheep and goat are reversed. It is the sheep who brings the tidings of immortality from God to men, but the goat overruns him, and offers them death instead. In their innocence men accepted death with enthusiasm, not knowing what it was, and naturally they have died ever since.2 In British East Africa the two gospel messengers are a chameleon and a thrush, whom God sent out together to find people who died one day and came to life the next, and to bear the glad tidings of immortality to men. So off they set, the chameleon leading the way, for in those days he was a very high and mighty person indeed. As they went along, what should they see but some people lying like dead by the wayside. The chameleon went up to them and said softly, "Niwe, niwe, niwe" But the thrush asked him testily what he was making that noise for. The chameleon mildly answered, "I am only calling the people who go forward and then come back," and he explained to the thrush that these seemingly dead folk would rise from the dead, just as he himself in walking lurches backward and forward before he takes a step. This argument from analogy, which might have satisfied a Butler, had no effect on the skeptical thrush. He derided the idea of the resurrection. Undeterred by this blatant infidelity the chameleon persisted in calling to the dead people, and sure enough they opened their eyes and listened to him. But the thrush rudely interrupted him and told the dead people that dead they were and dead they would remain, nothing could bring them to life. With that he flew away, and though the chameleon stayed behind and preached to the corpses, telling them that he had come from God on purpose to bring them to life again, and that they were not to believe the lies of that shallow skeptic the thrush, they turned a deaf ear to his message; not one of those dead corpses would so much as budge. So the chameleon returned crestfallen to God and reported the failure of his mission, telling him how, when he preached the glad tidings of resurrection to the corpses, the thrush had roared him down, so that the corpses could not hear a word he said. Thereupon God cross-questioned the thrush, who stated that the chameleon had so bungled the message that he, the thrush, felt it to be his imperative duty to interrupt him. The simple-minded deity believed the lying thrush, and being very angry with the honest chameleon he degraded him from his high position and made him walk very slow, lurching this way and that, as he does down to this very day. But the thrush he promoted to the office of wakening men from their slumber every morning, which he still does punctually at 2 A.M. before the note of any other bird is heard in the tropical forest.1

In all these versions of the story the message is sent from God to men, but in another version, reported from Togoland in West Africa, the message is dispatched from men to God. They say that once upon a time men sent a dog to God to say that when they died they would like to come to life again. So off the dog trotted to deliver the message. But on the way he felt hungry and turned into a house, where a man was boiling magic herbs. So the dog sat down and thought to himself, "He is cooking food." Meantime the frog had set off to tell God that when men died they would prefer not to come to life again. Nobody had asked him to give that message; it was a piece of pure officiousness and impertinence on his part. However, away he tore. The dog, who still sat hopefully watching the hell-broth brewing, saw him hurrying past the door, but he thought to himself, "When I have had something to eat, I will soon catch froggy up." However, froggy came in first, and said to the deity, "When men die, they would prefer not to come to life again." After that, up comes the dog, and says he, "When men die, they would like to come to life again." God was naturally puzzled, and said to the dog, "I really do not understand these two messages. As I heard the frog's request first, I will comply with it. I will not do what you said." That is the reason why men die and do not come to life again. If the frog had only minded his own business instead of meddling with other people's, the dead would all have come to life again to this day. But frogs come to life again when it thunders at the beginning of the rainy season, after they have been dead all the dry season while the Har-mattan wind was blowing. Then, while the rain falls and the thunder peals, you may hear them quacking in the marshes.2 Thus we see that the frog had his own private ends to serve in distorting the message. He gained for himself the immortality of which he robbed mankind.

In Calabar a somewhat different version of the same widespread story is told. The messengers are a dog and a sheep, and they go backwards and forwards between God and men. They say that for a long time after the creation of the world there was no death in it. At last, however, a man sickened and died. So the people sent a dog to God to ask him what they should do with the dead, man. The dog stayed so long away that the people grew tired of waiting and sent off a sheep to God with the same question. The sheep soon returned, and reported that God said, "Let the dead man be buried." So they buried him. Afterwards the dog returned also and reported that God said, "Put warm ashes on the dead man's belly, and he will rise again." However, the people told the dog that he came too late; the dead man was already buried according to the instructions of the sheep. That is why men are buried when they die. But as for the dog, he is driven from men and humiliated, because it is through his fault that we all die.1

In these stories the origin of death is ascribed to the blunder or willful deceit of one of the two messengers. However, according to another version of the story, which is widely current among the Bantu tribes of Africa, death was caused, not by the fault of the mes-senger, but by the vacillation of God himself, who, after deciding to make men immortal, changed his mind and resolved to make or leave them mortal; and unluckily for man-kind the second messenger, who bore the message of death, overran the first messen-ger, who bore the message of immortality. In this form of the tale the chameleon figures as the messenger of life, and the lizard as the messenger of death. Thus the Zulus say that in the beginning Unkulunkulu, that is, the Old Old One, sent the chameleon to men with a message, saying, "Go, chameleon, go and say, Let not men die." The chameleon set out, but it crawled very slowly and loitered by the way to eat the purple berries of the ubukwebezane shrub or of a mulberry tree; however, some people say that it climbed up a tree to bask in the sun, filled its belly with flies, and fell fast asleep. Meantime the Old Old One had thought better of it and sent a lizard post-haste after the chameleon with a very different message to men, for he said to the animal, "Lizard, when you have arrived, say, Let men die." So the lizard ran, passed the dawdling chameleon, and arriv-ing first among men delivered his message of death, saying, "Let men die." Then he turned and went back to the Old Old One who had sent him. But after he was gone, the chameleon at last arrived among men with his joyful news of immortality, and he shouted, saying, "It is said, Let not men die !" But men answered, "Oh ! we have heard the word of the lizard; it has told us the word, ' It is said, Let men die.' We cannot hear your word. Through the word of the lizard, men will die." And died they have ever since from that day to this. So the Zulus hate the lizard and kill it whenever they can, for they say, " This is the very piece of deformity which ran in the beginning to say that men should die." But others hate and hustle or kill the chameleon, saying, "That is the little thing which delayed to tell the people that they should not die. If he had only told us in time, we too should not have died; our ancestors also would have been still living; there would have been no diseases here on earth. It all comes from the delay of the chameleon."1

The same story is told in nearly the same form by other Bantu tribes such as the Bechuanas,1 the Basutos,2 the Baronga,8 the Ngoni,4 and apparently by the Wa-Sania of British East Africa.5 It is found, in a slightly altered form, even among the Hausas, who are not a Bantu people.6 To this day the Baronga and the Ngoni owe the chameleon a grudge for having brought death into the world by its dilatoriness. Hence, when they find a chameleon slowly climbing on a tree, they tease it till it opens its mouth, whereupon they throw a pinch of tobacco on its tongue, and watch with delight the creature writhing and changing color from orange to green, from green to black in the agony of death; for so they avenge the great wrong which the chameleon did to mankind.7

Thus the belief is widespread in Africa, that God at one time purposed to make mankind immortal, but that the benevolent scheme miscarried through the fault of the messenger to whom he had entrusted the gospel message.

§ 3. The Story of the Cast Skin

Many savages believe that, in virtue of the power of periodically casting their skins, certain animals and in particular serpents renew their youth and never die. Holding this belief, they tell stories to explain how it came about that these creatures obtained, and men missed, the boon of immortality.

Thus, for example, the Wafipa and Wabende of East Africa say that one day God, whom they name Leza, came down to earth, and addressing all living creatures said, "Who wishes not to die?" Unfortunately man and the other animals were asleep; only the serpent was awake and he promptly answered, "I do." That is why men and all other animals die. The serpent alone does not die of himself. He only dies if he is killed. Every year he changes his skin, and so renews his youth and his strength.1 In like manner the Dusuns of British North Borneo say that when the Creator had finished making all things, he asked, "Who is able to cast off his skin? If any one can do so, he shall not die." The snake alone heard and answered, "I can." For that reason down to the present day the snake does not die unless he is killed by man. The Dusuns did not hear the Creator's question, or they also would have thrown off their skins, and there would have been no death.2 Similarly the Todjo-Toradjas of Central Celebes relate that once upon a time God summoned men and animals for the purpose of determining their lot. Among the various lots proposed by the deity was this, "We shall put off our old skin." Unfortunately mankind on this momentous occasion was represented by an old woman in her dotage, who did not hear the tempting proposal. But the animals which slough their skins, such as serpents and shrimps, heard it and closed with the offer.3 Again, the natives of Vuatom,

48

an island in the Bismarck Archipelago, say that a certain To Konokonomiange bade two lads fetch fire, promising that if they did so they should never die, but that, if they refused, their bodies would perish, though their shades or souls would survive. They would not hearken to him, so he cursed them, saying, "What! you would all have lived! Now you shall die, though your soul shall live. But the iguana (Goniocephalus) and the lizard (Varanus indicus) and the snake (Enygrus), they shall live, they shall cast their skin and they shall live for evermore." When the lads heard that, they wept, for bitterly they rued their folly in not going to fetch the fire for To Konokono-miange.1

The Arawaks of British Guiana relate that once upon a time the Creator came down to earth to see how his creature man was getting on. But men were so wicked that they tried to kill him; so he deprived them of eternal life and bestowed it on the animals which renew their skin, such as serpents, lizards, and beetles.2 A somewhat different version of the story is told by the Tamanachiers, an Indian tribe of the Orinoco. They say that after residing among them for some time the Creator took a boat to cross to the other side of the great salt water from which he had come. Just as he was shoving off from the shore, he called out to them in a changed voice, "You will change your skins," by which he meant to say, "You will renew your youth like the serpents and the beetles." But unfortunately an old woman, hearing these words, cried out "Oh!" in a tone of skepticism, if not of sarcasm, which so annoyed the Creator that he changed his tune at once and said testily, "Ye shall die." That is why we are all mortal.3

The people of Nias, an island to the west of Sumatra, say that, when the earth was created, a certain being was sent down from above to put the finishing touches to the work. He ought to have fasted, but, unable to withstand he pangs of hunger, he ate some bananas. The choice of food was very unfortunate, for had he only eaten river crabs, men would have cast their skins like crabs, and so, renewing their youth perpetually, would never have died. As it is, death has come upon us all through the eating of those bananas.1 Another version of the Niasian story adds that "the serpents on the contrary ate the crabs, which in the opinion of the people of Nias cast their skins but do not die; therefore serpents also do not die but merely cast their skin." 2

In this last version the immortality of serpents is ascribed to their having partaken of crabs, which by casting their skins renew their youth and live for ever. The same belief in the immortality of shell-fish occurs in a Samoan story of the origin of death. They say that the gods met in council to determine what should be the end of man. One proposal was that men should cast their skins like shellfish, and so renew their youth. The god Palsy moved, on the contrary, that shellfish should cast their skins, but that men should die. While the motion was still before the meeting a shower of rain unfortunately interrupted the discussion, and as the gods ran to take shelter, the motion of Palsy was carried unanimously. That is why shellfish still cast their skins and men do not.3

Thus not a few peoples appear to believe that the happy privilege of immortality, obtainable by the simple process of periodically shedding the skin, was once within reach of our species, but that through an unhappy chance it was transferred to certain of the lower creatures, such as serpents, crabs, lizards, and beetles. According to others, how-ever, men were at one time actually in possession of this priceless boon, but forfeited it through the foolishness of an old woman. Thus the Melanesians of the Banks' Islands and the New Hebrides say that at first men never died, but that when they advanced in life they cast their skins like snakes and crabs, and came out with youth renewed. After a time a woman, growing old, went to a stream to change her skin; according to some, she was the mother of the mythical or legendary hero Qat, according to others, she was Ulta-marama, Change-skin of the world. She threw off her old skin in the water, and observed that as it floated down it caught against a stick. Then she went home, where she had left her child. But the child refused to recognize her, crying that its mother was an old woman, not like this young stranger. So to pacify the child she went after her cast integument and put it on. From that time mankind ceased to cast their skins and died.1 A similar story of the origin of death is told in the Shortlands Islands 2 and by the Kai, a Papuan tribe of north-eastern New Guinea. The Kai say that at first men did not die but renewed their youth. When their old brown skin grew wrinkled and ugly, they stepped into water and, stripping it off, got a new, youthful white skin instead. In those days there lived an old grandmother with her grandchild. One day the old woman, weary of her advanced years, bathed in the river, cast off her withered old hide, and returned to the village, spick and span, in a fine new skin. Thus transformed, she climbed up the ladder and entered her house. But when her grandchild saw her, he wept and squalled, and refused to believe that she was his granny. All her efforts to reassure and pacify him proving vain, she at last went back in a rage to the river, fished her wizened old skin out of the water, put it on, and returned to the house a hideous old hag again. The child was glad to see his granny come back, but she said to him, "The locusts cast their skins, but ye men shall die from this day forward." And sure enough, they have done so ever since.3 The same story, with some trivial variations, is told by natives of the Admiralty Islands. They say that once on a time there was an old woman, and she was frail. She had two sons, and they went a-fishing, while she herself went to bathe. She stripped off her wrinkled old skin and came forth as young as she had been long ago. When her sons came from the fishing they were astonished to see her. The one said, "It is our mother;" but the other said, "She may be your mother, but she shall be my wife." Their mother overheard them and said, "What were you two saying? "The two said, "Nothing! We only said that you are our mother."

"You are liars," she retorted, "I heard you both. If I had had my way, we should have grown to be old men and women, and then we should have cast our skin and been young men and young women. But you have had your way. We shall grow old men and old women, and then we shall die." With that she fetched her old skin, and put it on, and became an old woman again. As for us, her descendants, we grow up and we grow old. But if it had not been for those two young scapegraces, there would have been no end of our days, we should have lived for ever and ever.1

Still farther away from the Banks Islands the very same story is repeated by the To Koolawi, a mountain tribe of Central Celebes. As reported by the Dutch missionaries who discovered it, the Celebes version of this widely diffused tale runs thus. In the olden time men had, like serpents and shrimps, the power of casting their skin, whereby they became young again. Now there was an old woman who had a grandchild. Once upon a time she went to the water to bathe, and thereupon laid aside her old skin and hung it up on a tree. With her youth quite restored she returned to the house. But her grandchild did not know her again, and would have nothing to do with his grandmother; he kept on saying, "You are not my grandmother; my grandmother was old, and you are young." Then the woman went back to the water and drew on her old skin again. But ever since that day men have lost the power of renewing their youth and must die.2

A variant form of the Melanesian story is told in Anei-tyum, one of the New Hebrides. There they say that once an old man took off his skin before he began to work in his garden. He then looked young. But one day his two grandchildren, finding his skin folded away, pierced it through, making many holes therein. When the old man put it on again he shivered with cold, and seeing the holes in his skin he said to his grandchildren, "I thought we should live for ever and cast our skins and become young again; but as you have done this we shall all die." Thus death came into the world.1

Another Melanesian tradition ascribes the introduction of death to purely economic causes. In the days when men changed their skins and lived for ever, the permanence of property in the same hands was found to be a great inconvenience; it bore very hard on the heirs, who were perpetually tantalized by the prospect of an inheritance to which it was legally and physically impossible that they should ever succeed. All this time Death had resided either in a shadowy underground region called Panoi or by the side of a volcanic vent in Santa Maria, it is not quite certain which; but now in answer to the popular demand he was induced to come abroad and show himself. He was treated to a handsome funeral of the usual sort; that is to say, he was laid out on a board and covered with a pall, a pig was killed, and the mourners enjoyed a funeral feast and divided the property of the deceased. Afterwards, on the fifth day, the conch shell was blown to drive away the ghost. In short, nothing was left undone to soothe and gratify the feelings of the departed. So Death returned down the road to the underground region from which he had emerged; and all mankind have since followed him thither.2

While some peoples have supposed that in the early ages of the world men were immortal in virtue of periodically casting their skins, others have ascribed the same high privilege to a certain lunar sympathy, in consequence of which mankind passed through alternate states of growth and decay, of life and death, corresponding to the phases of the moon, without ever coming to an end. On this view, though death in a sense actually occurred, it was speedily repaired by resurrection, generally, it would seem, by resurrection after three days, since three days is the period between the disappearance of the old moon and the reappearance of the new. Thus the Mentras or Mantras, a shy tribe of savages in the jungles of the Malay Peninsula, allege that in the early ages of the world men did not die, but only grew thin at the waning of the moon and then waxed fat again as she waxed to the full. Thus there was no check whatever on the population, which increased to an alarming extent. So a son of the first man brought this state of things to his father's notice, and asked him what was to be done. The first man, a good easy soul, said, "Leave things as they are;" but his younger brother, who took a more Malthusian view of the matter, said, "No, let men die like the banana, leaving their offspring behind." The question was submitted to the Lord of the Underworld, and he decided in favour of death. Ever since then men have ceased to renew their youth like the moon and have died like the banana.1 In the Caroline Islands it is said that in the olden time death was unknown, or rather it was only a short sleep. Men died on the last day of the waning moon and came to life again on the appearance of the new moon, just as if they had wakened from a refreshing slumber. But an evil spirit somehow contrived that when men slept the sleep of death they should wake no more.2 The Wotjobaluk, a tribe of south-eastern Australia, related that when all animals were men and women, some of them died and the moon used to say, "You up again," whereupon they came to life again. But once on a time an old man said, "Let them remain dead;" and since then nobody has ever come to life again, except the moon, which still continues to do so down to this very day.3

The Unmatjera and Kaitish, two tribes of central Australia, say that their dead used to be buried either in trees or underground, and that after three days they regularly rose from the dead. The Kaitish tell how this happy state of things came to an end. It was all the fault of a man of the Curlew totem, who found some men of the Little Wallaby totem in the act of burying a man of that ilk. For some reason the Curlew man flew into a passion and kicked the corpse into the sea. Of course after that the dead man could not come to life again, and that is why nowadays nobody rises from the dead after three days, as everybody used to do long ago.1 Though nothing is said about the moon in this narrative of the origin of death, the analogy of the preceding stories makes it probable that the three days, during which the dead used to lie in the grave, were the three days during which the moon lay "hid in her vacant interlunar cave." The Fijians also associated the possibility, though not the actual enjoyment, of human immortality with the phases of the moon. They say that of old two gods, the Moon and the Rat, discussed the proper end of man. The Moon said, "Let him be like me, who disappear awhile and then live again." But the Rat said, "Let man die as a rat dies." And he prevailed.2

The Upotos of the Congo tell how men missed and the Moon obtained the boon of immortality. One day God, whom they call Libanza, sent for the people of the moon and the people of the earth. The people of the moon hastened to the deity, and were rewarded by him for their alacrity. "Because," said he, addressing the moon, "thou earnest to me at once when I called thee, thou shalt never die. Thou shalt be dead for but two days each month, and that only to rest thee; and thou shalt return with greater splendor." But when the people of the earth at last appeared before Libanza, he was angry and said to them, "Because you came not at once to me when I called you, therefore you will die one day and not revive, except to come to me." 3

The Bahnars of eastern Cochin China explain the immortality of primitive man neither by the phases of the moon nor by the custom of casting the skin, but apparently by the recuperative virtue of a certain tree. They say that in the beginning, when people died, they used to be buried at the foot of a tree called Long Blo, and that after a time they always rose from the dead, not as infants, but as full-grown men and women. So the earth was peopled very fast, and all the inhabitants formed but one great town under the presidency of our first parents. In time men multiplied to such an extent that a certain lizard could not take his walks abroad without somebody treading on his tail. This vexed him, and the wily creature gave an insidious hint to the gravediggers. "Why bury the dead at the foot of the Long Blo tree?" said he; "bury them at the foot of Long Khung, and they will not come to life again. Let them die outright and be done with it." The hint was taken, and from that day men have not come to life again.1

In this last story, as in many African tales, the instrument of bringing death among men is a lizard. We may conjecture that the reason for assigning the invidious office to a lizard was that this animal, like the serpent, casts its skin periodically, from which primitive man might infer, as he infers with regard to serpents, that the creature renews its youth and lives forever. Thus all the myths which relate how a lizard or a serpent became the maleficent agent of human mortality may perhaps be referred to an old idea of a certain jealousy and rivalry between men and creatures which cast their skins, notably serpents and lizards; we may suppose that in all such cases a story was told of a contest between man and his animal rivals for the possession of immortality, a contest in which, whether by mistake or guile, the victory always remained with the animals, who thus became immortal, while mankind was doomed to mortality.

§ 4. The Composite Story of the Perverted Message and the Cast Skin

In some stories of the origin of death the incidents of the perverted message and the cast skin are combined. Thus the Gallas of East Africa attribute the mortality of man and the immortality of serpents to the mistake or malice of a certain bird which falsified the message of eternal life entrusted to him by God. The creature which did this great wrong to our species is a black or dark blue bird, with a white patch on each wing and a crest on its head. It perches on the tops of trees and utters a wailing note like the bleating of a sheep; hence the Gallas call it holawaka or "the sheep of God," and explain its apparent anguish by the following tale. Once upon a time God sent that bird to tell men that they should not die, but that when they grew old and weak they should slip off their skins and so renew their youth. In order to authenticate the message God gave the bird a crest to serve as the badge of his high office. Well, off the bird set to deliver the glad tidings of immortality to man, but he had not gone far before he fell in with a snake devouring carrion in the path. The bird looked longingly at the carrion and said to the snake, "Give me some of the meat and blood, and I will tell you God's message."

"I don't want to hear it," said the snake tartly, and continued his meal. But the bird pressed him so to hear the message that the snake rather reluctantly consented. "The message," then said the bird, "is this. When men grow old they will die, but when you grow old you will cast your skin and renew your youth." That is why people grow old and die, but snakes crawl out of their old skins and renew their youth. But for this gross perversion of the message God punished the heedless or wicked bird with a painful internal malady, from which he suffers to this day; that is why he sits wailing on the tops of trees.1

Again, the Melanesians, who inhabit the coast of the Gazelle Peninsula in New Britain, say that To Kambinana, the Good Spirit, loved men and wished to make them immortal. So he called his brother To Korvuvu and said to him, "Go to men and take them the secret of immortality. Tell them to cast their skin every year. So will they be protected from death, for their life will be constantly renewed. But tell the serpents that they must thenceforth die." However, To Korvuvu acquitted himself badly of his task; for he commanded men to die, and betrayed to the serpents the secret of immortality. Since then all men have been mortal, but the serpents cast their skins every year and never die.2

A similar story of the origin of death is told in Annam. They say that Ngoc hoang sent a messenger from heaven to men to say that when they reached old age they should change their skins and live for ever, but that when serpents grew old they must die. The messenger came down to earth and said, rightly enough, "When man is old he shall cast his skin; but when serpents are old they shall die and be laid in coffins." So far so good. But unluckily there happened to be a brood of serpents within hearing, and when they learned the doom pronounced on their kind, they fell into a fury and said to the messenger, "You must say it over again and just the contrary, or we will bite you." That frightened the messenger, and he repeated his message, changing the words thus, "When the serpent is old he shall cast his skin; but when man is old he shall die and be laid in the coffin." That is why all creatures are now subject to death, except the serpent, who, when he is old, casts his skin and lives for ever.1

§ 5. Conclusion

Thus, arguing from the analogy of the moon or of animals which cast their skins, the primitive philosopher has inferred that in the beginning a perpetual renewal of youth was either appointed by a benevolent being for the human species or was actually enjoyed by them, and that but for a crime, an accident, or a blunder it would have been enjoyed by them for ever. People who pin their faith in immortality to the cast skins of serpents, lizards, beetles, and the like, naturally look on these animals as the hated rivals who have robbed us of the heritage which God or nature intended that we should possess; consequently they tell stories to explain how it came about that such low creatures contrived to oust us from the priceless possession. Tales of this sort are widely diffused throughout the world, and it would be no matter for surprise to find them among the Semites. The story of the Fall of Man in the third chapter of Genesis appears to be an abridged version of this savage myth. Little is wanted to complete its resemblance to the similar myths still told by savages in many parts of the world. The principal, almost the only, omission is the silence of the narrator as to the eating of the fruit of the tree of life by the serpent, and the consequent attainment of immortality by the reptile. Nor is it difficult to account for the lacuna. The vein of rationalism, which runs through the Hebrew account of creation and has stripped it of many grotesque features that adorn or disfigure the corresponding Babylonian tradition, could hardly fail to find a stumbling-block in the alleged immortality of serpents; and the redactor of the story in its final form has removed this stone of offence from the path of the faithful by the simple process of blotting out the incident entirely from the legend. Yet the yawning gap left by his sponge has not escaped the commentators, who look in vain for the part which should have been played in the narrative by the tree of life. If my interpretation of the story is right, it has been left for the comparative method, after thousands of years, to supply the blank in the ancient canvas, and to restore, in all their primitive crudity, the gay barbaric colors which the skilful hand of the Hebrew artist had softened or effaced.

Chapter 3 - The Mark of Cain

The theory that the mark was a tribal badge
Homicides shunned as infected
Attic law concerning homicides
Seclusion of murderers in Dobu
Belief in the infectiousness of homicides in Africa
Earth supposed to spurn the homicide
Wanderings of the matricide Alcmaeon
Earth offended by bloodshed and appeased by sacrifice
The homicide's mark perhaps a danger-signal to others
The mark perhaps a protection against the victim's ghost
Ceremonies to appease the ghosts of the slain
Seclusion of murderer through fear of his victim's ghost
Fear of ghosts of the murdered, a motive for executing murderers
Protection of executioners against the ghosts of their victims
Bodily marks to protect people against ghosts of the slain
Need of guarding warriors against the ghosts of the slain
Various modes of guarding warriors against the ghosts of the slain
Faces or bodies of manslayers painted in diverse colours
The mark of Cain perhaps a disguise against the ghost of Abel
Advantage of thus interpreting the mark
The blood rather than the ghost of Abel prominent in the narrative
Fear of leaving blood of man or beast uncovered
Superstition a crutch of morality

We read in Genesis that when Cain had murdered his brother Abel, he was driven out from society to be a fugitive and a vagabond on earth. Fearing to be slain by any one who might meet him, he remonstrated with God on the hardness of his lot, and God had so far compassion on him that he "set a mark upon Cain, lest any finding him should kill him." 1 What was the mark that God put on the first murderer? or the sign that he appointed for him?

That we have here a reminiscence of some old custom observed by manslayers is highly probable; and, though we cannot hope to ascertain what the actual mark or sign was, a comparison of the customs observed by manslayers in other parts of the world may help us to understand at least its general significance. Robertson Smith thought that the mark in question was the tribal mark, a badge which every member of the tribe wore on his person, and which served to protect him by indicating that he belonged to a community that would avenge his murder.2 Certainly such marks are common among peoples who have preserved the tribal system. For example, among the Bedouins of today one of the chief tribal badges is a particular mode of wearing the hair.1 In many parts of the world, notably in Africa, the tribal mark consists of a pattern tattooed or incised on some part of the person.2 That such marks might serve as a protection to the tribesman in the way supposed by Robertson Smith seems probable; though on the other hand it is to be remembered that in a hostile country they might, on the contrary, increase his danger by advertising him as an enemy. But even if we concede the protective value of a tribal mark, still the explanation thus offered of the mark of Cain seems hardly to fit the case. It is too general. Every member of a tribe was equally protected by such a mark, whether he was a manslayer or not. The whole drift of the narrative tends to show that the mark in question was not worn by every member of the community, but was peculiar to a murderer. Accordingly we seem driven to seek for an explanation in another direction.

From the narrative itself we gather that Cain was thought to be obnoxious to other dangers than that of being slain as an outlaw by any one who met him. God is represented saying to him, "What hast thou done? the voice of thy brother's blood crieth unto me from the ground. And now cursed art thou from the ground, which hath opened her mouth to receive thy brother's blood from thy hand; when thou tillest the ground, it shall not henceforth yield unto thee her strength; a fugitive and a wanderer shalt thou be in the earth." 3 Here it is obvious that the blood of his murdered brother is regarded as constituting a physical danger to the murderer; it taints the ground and prevents it from yielding its increase. Thus the murderer is thought to have poisoned the sources of life and thereby jeopardized the supply of food for himself, and perhaps for others. On this view it is intelligible that a homicide should be shunned and banished the country, to which his presence is a continual menace. He is plague-stricken, surrounded by a poisonous atmosphere, infected by a contagion of death; his very touch may blight the earth. Hence we can understand a certain rule of Attic law. A homicide who had been banished, and against whom in his absence a second charge had been brought, was allowed to return to Attica to plead in his defense; but he might not set foot on the land, he had to speak from a ship, and even the ship might not cast anchor or put out a gangway. The judges avoided all contact with the culprit, for they judged the case sitting or standing on the shore.1 Clearly the intention of this rule of law was to put the manslayer in quarantine, lest by touching Attic earth even indirectly through the anchor or the gangway he should blast it. For the same reason, if such a man, sailing the sea, had the misfortune to be cast away on the country where his crime had been perpetrated, he was allowed indeed to camp on the shore till a ship came to take him off, but he was expected to keep his feet in sea water all the time, 2 evidently in order to counteract, or at least dilute, the poison which he was supposed to instill into the soil.

The quarantine which Attic law thus imposed on the manslayer has its counterpart in the seclusion still enforced on murderers by the savages of Dobu, an island off the south-eastern extremity of New Guinea. On this subject a missionary, who resided for seventeen years in the island, writes as follows: "War may be waged against the relatives of the wife, but the slain must not be eaten. The person who kills a relation by marriage must never after partake of the general food or fruit from his wife's village. His wife alone must cook his food. If his wife's fire goes out she is not allowed to take a fire-stick from a house in her village. The penalty for breaking this tabu is that the husband dies of blood-poisoning! The slaying of a blood relation places an even stricter tabu on the slayer. When the chief Gaganumore slew his brother (mother's sister's son) he was not allowed to return to his own village, but had to build a village of his own. He had to have a separate lime-gourd and spatula; a water-bottle and cup of his own; a special set of cooking pots; he had to get his drinking cocoanuts and fruit elsewhere; his fire had to be kept burning as long as possible, and if it went out it could not be relit from another fire, but by friction. If the chief were to break this tabu, his brother's blood would poison his blood so that his body would swell, and he would die a terrible death." 1

In these Dobuan cases the blood of the slain man is supposed to act as a physical poison on the slayer, should he venture to set foot in, or even to hold indirect communication with, the village of his victim. His seclusion is therefore a precaution adopted in his own interest rather than in that of the community which he avoids; and it is possible that the rules of Attic law in the matter of homicide ought to be similarly interpreted. However, it is more probable that the danger was believed to be mutual; in other words, that both the homicide and the persons with whom he came into contact were thought liable to suffer from blood-poisoning caused by contagion. Certainly the notion that a manslayer can infect other people with a malignant virus is held by the Akikuyu of British East Africa. They think that if a man who has killed another comes and sleeps at a village and eats with a family in their hut, the persons with whom he has eaten contract a dangerous pollution (thahu), which might prove fatal to them, were it not removed in time by a medicine-man. The very skin on which the homicide slept has absorbed the taint and might infect any one else who slept on it. So a medicine-man is called in to purify the hut and its inmates.1

Similarly among the Moors of Morocco a manslayer "is considered in some degree unclean for the rest of his life. Poison oozes out from underneath his nails; hence anybody who drinks the water in which he has washed his hands will fall dangerously ill. The meat of an animal which he has killed is bad to eat, and so is any food which is partaken of in his company. If he comes to a place where people are digging a well, the water will at once run away. In the Hiáina, I was told, he is not allowed to go into a vegetable garden or an orchard, nor to tread on a threshing-floor or enter a granary, nor to go among the sheep. It is a common, although not universal, rule that he must not perform the sacrifice at the Great Feast with his own hands; and in some tribes, mostly Berber-speaking ones, there is a similar prohibition with reference to a person who has killed a dog, which is an unclean animal. All blood which has left the veins is unclean and haunted by jnun" 2 (jinn).

But in the Biblical narrative of the murder of Abel the blood of the murdered man is not the only inanimate object that is personified. If the blood is represented as crying aloud, the earth is represented as opening her mouth to receive the blood of the victim.3 To this personification of the earth Aeschylus offers a parallel, for he speaks of the ground drinking the blood of the murdered Agamemnon.4 But in Genesis the attribution of personal qualities to the earth seems to be carried a step further, for we are told that the murderer was "cursed from the ground;" and that when he tilled it, the land would not yield him her strength, but that a fugitive and a wanderer should he be in the world. The implication apparently is that the earth, polluted by blood and offended by his crime, would refuse to allow the seed sown by the murderer to germinate and bear fruit; nay, that it would expel him from the cultivated soil on which he had hitherto prospered, and drive him out into the barren wilderness, there to roam a houseless and hungry vagabond. The conception of earth as a personal being, who revolts against the sin of the dwellers upon it and spurns them from her bosom, is not foreign to the Old Testament. In Leviticus we read that, defiled by human iniquity, "the land vomiteth out her inhabitants;"1 and the Israelites are solemnly warned to keep God's statutes and judgments, "that the land vomit not you out also, when ye defile it, as it vomited out the nation that was before you." 2

The ancient Greeks apparently entertained similar notions as to the effect of polluting earth by the shedding of human blood, or, at all events, the blood of kinsfolk; for tradition told how the matricide Alcmaeon, haunted by the ghost of his murdered mother Eriphyle, long wandered restlessly over the world, till at last he repaired to the oracle at Delphi, and the priestess told him, that "the only land whither the avenging spirit of Eriphyle would not dog him was the newest land, which the sea had uncovered since the pollution of his mother's blood had been incurred;"3 or, as Thucydides puts it, "that he would never be rid of his terrors till he had found and settled in a country which, when he slew his mother, the sun had not yet shone on, and which at that time was not yet dry land; for all the rest of the earth had been polluted by him." 4 Following the directions of the oracle, he discovered at the mouth of the Achelous the small and barren Echinadian Islands which, by washing down the soil from its banks, the river was supposed to have created since the perpetration of his crime; and there he took up his abode.5 According to one version of the legend, the murderer had found rest for a time in the bleak upland valley of Psophis, among the solemn Arcadian mountains, but even there the ground refused to yield its increase to the matricide, and he was forced, like Cain, to resume his weary wanderings.1

The belief that the earth is a powerful divinity, who is defiled and offended by the shedding of human blood and must be appeased by sacrifice, prevails, or prevailed till lately, among some tribes of Upper Senegal, who exact expiation even for wounds which have merely caused blood to flow without loss of life. Thus at Laro, in the country of the Bobos, "the murderer paid two goats, a dog, and a cock to the chief of the village, who offered them in sacrifice to the Earth on a piece of wood stuck in the ground. Nothing was given to the family of the victim. All the villagers, including the chief, afterwards partook of the flesh of the sacrificial victims, the families of the murderer and his victim alone being excluded from the banquet. If it was an affair of assault and wounds, but blood had not been shed, no account was taken of it. But when blood had been spilt, the Earth was displeased at the sight, and therefore it was necessary to appease her by a sacrifice. The culprit gave a goat and a thousand cowries to the chief of the village, who sacrificed the goat to the Earth and divided the cowries among the elders of the village. The goat, after being offered to the Earth, was also divided among the village elders. But the injured party throughout the affair was totally forgotten and received nothing at all, and that, too, logically enough. For the intention was not to compensate the injured party for his wrong at the cost of the wrongdoer, but to appease the Earth, a great and redoubtable divinity, who was displeased at the sight of bloodshed. In these circumstances there was nothing for the injured party to get. It sufficed that the Earth was pacified by eating the soul of the goat that had been sacrificed to her;" 2 for "among the Bobos, as among the other blacks, the Earth is esteemed a great goddess of justice." 3

Among the Nounoumas, another tribe of Upper Senegal, the customs and beliefs in regard to bloodshed were similar. A murderer was banished for three years and had to pay heavy fine in cowries and cattle, not as a blood-wit to the family of his victim, but to appease the Earth and the other local divinities, who had been offended by the sight of spilt blood. The ox or oxen were sacrificed to the angry Earth by a priest who bore the title of the Chief of the Earth, and the flesh together with the cowries, was divided among the elders of the village, the family of the murdered man receiving nothing, or at most only a proportionate share of the meat and money. In the case of brawls where no life had been taken, but blood had flowed, the aggressor had to pay an ox, a sheep, a goat, and four fowls, all of which were sacrificed to pacify the anger of the local deities at the sight of bloodshed. The ox was sacrificed to the Earth by the Chief of the Earth in presence of all the elders of the village; the sheep was sacrificed to the River; and the fowls to the Rocks and the Forest. As for the goat, it was sacrificed, by the chief of the village to his private fetish. If these expiatory sacrifices were not offered, it was believed that the gods in their wrath would slay the culprit and all his family. The Chief of the Earth received as his due the intestines, hide, head, horns, and one shoulder of the sacrificial ox ; the rest of the ox and the remaining victims were divided between the chief of the village, the headmen of the various wards, and the elders. Every one carried off his portion of flesh to his own house and ate it there. In some places the assailant had also to pay a fine in cowries proportioned to the seriousness of the wound which he had inflicted.1

The foregoing facts suggest that a mark put on a homicide might be intended primarily, not for his protection, but for the protection of the persons who met him, lest by contact with his pollution they should defile themselves and incur the wrath of the god whom he had offended, or of the ghost by whom he was haunted; in short, the mark might be a danger-signal to warn people off, like the special garb prescribed in Israel for lepers.2

However, there are other facts which tend to show that the murderer's mark was designed, as the story of Cain implies, for the benefit of the murderer alone, and further that the real danger against which it protected him was not the anger of his victim's kinsfolk, but the wrath of his victim's ghost. Here again, as in the Athenian customs already mentioned, we seem to touch the bed-rock of superstition in Attica. Plato tells us that according to a very ancient Greek belief the ghost of a man who had just been killed was angry with his slayer and troubled him, being enraged at the sight of the homicide stalking freely about in his, the ghost's, old familiar haunts; hence it was needful for the homicide to depart from his country for a year until the wrath of the ghost had cooled down, nor might he return before sacrifices had been offered and ceremonies of purification performed. If the victim chanced to be a foreigner, the slayer had to shun the native land of the dead man as well as his own, and in going into banishment he had to follow a prescribed road; l for clearly it would never do to let him rove about the country with the angry ghost at his heels. Again, we have seen that among the Akikuyu a murderer is believed to be tainted by a dangerous pollution (thahu) which he can communicate to other people by contact. That this pollution is connected with his victim's ghost appears from one of the ceremonies which are performed to expiate the deed. The elders of the village sacrifice a pig beside one of those sacred fig-trees which play a great part in the religious rites of the tribe. There they feast on the more succulent parts of the animal, but leave the fat, intestines, and some of the bones for the ghost, who is supposed to come that very night and devour them in the likeness of a wild cat; his hunger being thus stayed, he considerately refrains from returning to the village to trouble the inhabitants. It deserves to be noticed that a Kikuyu homicide incurs ceremonial pollution (thahu) only through the slaughter of a man of his own clan; there is no ceremonial pollution incurred by the slaughter of a man of another clan or of another tribe.2

Among the Bagesu of Mount Elgon, in British East Africa, when a man has been guilty of manslaughter and his victim was a member of the same clan and village, he must leave the village and find a new home elsewhere, even though he may settle the matter amicably with the relations of the deceased. Further, he must kill a goat, smear the contents of its stomach on his chest, and throw the remainder upon the roof of the house of the murdered man "to appease the ghost." l In this tribe very similar ceremonies of expiation are performed by a warrior who has slain a man in battle; and we may safely assume that the intention of the ceremonies is to appease the ghost of his victim. The warrior returns to his village, but he may not spend the first night in his own house, he must lodge in the house of a friend. In the evening he kills a goat or sheep, deposits the contents of the stomach in a pot, and smears them on his head, chest, and arms. If he has any children, they must be smeared in like manner. Having thus fortified himself and his progeny, the warrior proceeds boldly to his own house, daubs each door-post with the stuff, and throws the rest on the roof, probably for the benefit of the ghost who may be supposed to perch, if not to roost, there. For a whole day the slayer may not touch food with the hands which shed blood; he conveys the morsels to his mouth with two sticks cut for the purpose. On the second day he is free to return home and resume his ordinary life. These restrictions are not binding on his wife; she may even go and mourn over the slain man and take part in his obsequies.2 Such a pretence of sorrow may well mollify the feelings of the ghost and induce him to spare her husband.

Again, among the Nilotic Kavirondo, another tribe of British East Africa, a murderer is separated from the members of his village and lives in a hut with an old woman, who attends to his wants, cooks for him, and also feeds him, because he may not touch his food with his hands. This separation lasts for three days, and on the fourth day a man, who is himself a murderer, or who has at some time killed a man in battle, takes the murderer to a stream, where he washes him all over. He then kills a goat, cooks the meat, and puts a piece of it on each of four sticks ; after which he gives the four pieces to the murderer to eat in turn. Next he puts four balls of porridge on the sticks, and these also the murderer must swallow. Finally, the goat-skin is cut into strips, and one strip is put on the neck, and one strip round each of the wrists of the homicide. This ceremony is performed by the two men alone at the river. After the performance the murderer is free to return home. It is said that, until this ceremony is performed, the ghost cannot take its departure for the place of the dead, but hovers about the murderer.1

Among the Boloki of the Upper Congo a homicide is not afraid of the ghost of the man whom he has killed, when his victim belongs to any of the neighboring towns, because the area within which Boloki ghosts can travel is extremely limited; but murder, which in that case he might commit with an easy mind, assumes a much more serious complexion when it is perpetrated on a man of the same town, for then he knows himself to be within striking distance of the ghost. The fear of ghostly vengeance now sits heavy on him. There are unfortunately no rites by the observance of which he could allay these terrors, but in default of them he mourns for his victim as though he were a brother, neglecting his toilet, shaving his head, fasting, and lamenting with torrents of crocodile tears.2 Thus the symptoms of sorrow, which the ingenuous European might take for signs of genuine repentance and remorse of conscience, are nothing but shams intended to deceive the ghost.

Once more among the Omaha Indians of North America a murderer, whose life was spared by the kinsmen of his victim, had to observe certain stringent regulations for a period which varied from two to four years. He must walk barefoot, and he might eat no warm food, nor raise his voice, nor look around. He had to pull his robe about him and to keep it tied at the neck, even in warm weather; he might not let it hang loose or fly open. He might not move his hands about, but had to keep them close to his body. He might not comb his hair, nor allow it to be blown about by the wind. No one would eat with him, and only one of his kindred was allowed to remain with him in his tent. When the tribe went hunting, he was obliged to pitch his tent about a quarter of a mile from the rest of the people, "lest the ghost of his victim should raise a high wind which might cause damage." 1 The reason here alleged for banishing the murderer from the camp probably gives the key to all the similar restrictions laid on murderers and manslayers among primitive peoples; the seclusion of such persons from society is dictated by no moral aversion to their crime: it springs purely from prudential motives, which resolve themselves into a simple dread of the dangerous ghost by which the homicide is supposed to be pursued and haunted.

This fear of the wrathful ghost of the slain is probably at the root of many ancient customs observed in connection with homicide; it may well have been one of the principal motives for inflicting capital punishment on murderers. For if such persons are dogged by a powerful and angry spirit, which makes them a danger to their fellows, society can obviously protect itself very simply by sacrificing the murderer to the ghost; in other words, by putting him to death. But then it becomes necessary to guard the executioners in their turn against the ghosts of their victims, and various precautions are adopted for this purpose. For example, among the Bakongo, of the Lower Congo, when a man has been executed for murder, his body is burnt to ashes. "By reducing the body to ashes they believe that they thereby destroy his spirit, and thus prevent the spirit from seeking revenge by bewitching his executioners." 2 At Porto Novo, on the coast of Guinea, the public executioner used to decorate the walls of his house with the jawbones of his victims in order to prevent their ghosts from troubling him at night.3 At Issini, on the Gold Coast, executioners used to remain in seclusion for three days after doing their office; during that time they lived in a hut built for the purpose at a distance from the village. When the three days were up, they proceeded to the place of execution, and there called thrice by name on the criminal whom they had put to death.1 The invocation was probably supposed to protect the executioners against the ghost of their victim.

Another mode of effecting the same purpose is to taste of his blood; this has been customary with executioners on the Lower Niger in West Africa, and among the Shans ofBurma. The alleged intention of the custom is to prevent the executioner from being affected by a kind of homicidal madness or otherwise contracting a fatal illness;2 but these effects are in all probability believed to be wrought by the ghost of the slain man, who has entered into and taken possession of the body of his slayer, and the motive for tasting of his blood is to bring about a reconcilement between the slayer and the slain by establishing a blood covenant between them.3

Among the Tupi Indians of Brazil a man who had publicly executed a prisoner had to fast and lie in his hammock for three days, without setting foot on the ground; further, he had to make incisions in his breast, arms, and other parts of his body, and a black powder was rubbed into the wounds, which left indelible scars so artistically arranged that they presented the appearance of a tight-fitting garment. It was believed that he would die if he did not observe these rules and draw blood from his own body after slaughtering the captive.4 The fear of his victim's ghost is not indeed mentioned by our authorities as the motive for practising these customs; but that it was the real motive is not only suggested by the analogy of the West African customs, but is practically proved by a custom which these same Brazilian Indians observed before the execution. They formally invited the doomed man to avenge his death, and for this purpose they supplied him with stones or potsherds, which he hurled at his guards, while they protected themselves against the missiles with shields made of hide.1 The form of the invitation, which ran thus, "Avenge your death before your deceased," clearly implies a hope that if a man had thus satisfied his thirst for vengeance in his lifetime, his ghost would not trouble them after death. But to make assurance doubly sure the executioner secluded himself, and observed the curious precautions which I have described. The drawing of blood from his own body, which was regarded as essential to the preservation of his life,2 may have been intended to satisfy the ghost's demand of blood for blood, or possibly to form a blood covenant with him, while the permanent marks left on the slayer's body would be a standing evidence that he had given satisfaction to his victim and made his peace with him. Could any reasonable ghost ask for more?

This interpretation of the marks on the executioner's body is confirmed by the following custom. Among the Yabim, on the north-eastern coast of New Guinea, when the kinsmen of a murdered man have accepted a blood-wit instead of avenging his death, they take care to be marked with chalk on the forehead by the relatives of the murderer, "... lest the ghost should trouble them for failing to avenge his death, and should carry off their pigs or loosen their teeth."3

In this custom it is not the murderer but the kinsmen of his victim who are marked, but the principle is the same. The ghost of the murdered man naturally turns in fury on his heartless relatives who have not exacted blood for his blood. But just as he is about to swoop down on them to loosen their teeth, or steal their pigs, or make himself unpleasant in other ways, he is brought up short by the sight of the white mark on their black or coffee-colored brows. It is the receipt for the payment in full of the blood-wit; it is the proof that his kinsfolk have exacted a pecuniary, though not a sanguinary, compensation for his murder; with this crumb of consolation he is bound to be satisfied, and to spare his family any molestation in future. The same mark might obviously be put for the same purpose on the murderer's brows to prove that he had paid in cash, or whatever may be the local equivalent for cash, for the deed he had done, and that the ghost therefore had no further claim upon him. Was the mark of Cain a mark of this sort? Was it a proof that he had paid the blood-wit? Was it a receipt for cash down?

It may have been so, but there is still another possibility to be considered. On the theory which I have just indicated it is obvious that the mark of Cain could only be put on a homicide when his victim was a man of the same tribe or community as himself, since it is only to men of the same tribe or community that compensation for homicide is paid. But the ghosts of slain enemies are certainly not less dreaded than the ghosts of slain friends; and if you cannot pacify them with a sum of money paid to their kinsfolk, what are you to do with them? Many plans have been adopted for the protection of warriors against the spirits of the men whom they have sent out of the world before their due time. Apparently one of these precautions is to disguise the slayer so that the ghost may not recognize him; another is to render his person in some way so formidable or so offensive that the spirit will not meddle with him. One or other of these motives may explain the following customs, which I select from a large number of similar cases.1

Among the Ba-Yaka, a Bantu people of the Congo Free State "a man who has been killed in battle is supposed to send his soul to avenge his death on the person of the man who killed him; the latter, however, can escape the vengeance of the dead by wearing the red tail-feathers of the parrot in his hair, and painting his forehead red."1 The Thonga of south-eastern Africa believe that a man who has killed an enemy in battle is exposed to great danger from his victim's ghost, who haunts him and may drive him mad. To protect himself from the wrath of the ghost, the slayer must remain in a state of taboo at the capital for several days, during which he may not go home to his wife, and must wear old clothes and eat with special spoons off special plates. In former times it was customary to tattoo such a man between the eyebrows, and to rub in medicines into the incisions, so as to raise pimples and to give him the appearance of a buffalo when it frowns.2 Among the Basutos "warriors who have killed an enemy are purified. The chief has to wash them, sacrificing an ox in the presence of the whole army. They are also anointed with the gall of the animal, which prevents the ghost of the enemy from pursuing them any farther." 3

Among the Wawanga, of the Elgon district in British East Africa, a man on returning from a raid, on which he has killed one of the enemy, may not enter his hut until he has taken cow's dung and rubbed it on the cheeks of the women and children of the village, and has purified himself by the sacrifice of a goat, from whose forehead he cuts a strip of skin and wears it round his right wrist for the next four days.4 Among the Bantu tribes of Kavirondo, in British East Africa, when a man has killed a foe in battle he shaves his head on his return home, and his friends rub a medicine, which generally consists of cow's dung, over his body to prevent the spirit of the slain man from troubling him.1 In these cases the cow's dung may serve either to wipe off the ghost or to disgust and repel him. Among the Ja-Luo, a Nilotic tribe of Kavirondo, the warrior who has slain a foe in battle shaves his head three days after his return from the fight; and before he enters his village he must hang a live fowl, head uppermost, round his neck; then the bird is decapitated and its head left hanging round his neck. Soon after his return a feast is made for the slain man, in order that his ghost may not haunt his slayer.2

According to another account the ceremonies observed on such occasions by the Nilotic tribes of Kavirondo are as follows. "When a warrior kills another in battle, he is isolated from his village, lives in a separate hut some four days, and an old woman cooks his food and feeds him like a child because he is forbidden to touch any food. On the fifth day he is escorted to the river by another man, who washes him; a white goat is killed and cooked by the attendant, who feeds the man with the meat; the goat-skin is cut into strips and put upon the man's wrists and round his head, and he returns to his temporary home for the night. The next day he is again taken to the river and washed, and a white fowl is presented to him. He kills it and it is cooked for him, and he is again fed with the meat. He is then pronounced to be clean and may return to his home. It sometimes happens that a warrior spears another man in battle, and the latter dies from the wound some time after. When death takes place, the relatives go to the warrior and tell him of the death, and he is separated at once from the community until the ceremonies above described have been performed. The people say that the ceremonies are necessary in order to release the ghost of the dead man, which is bound to the warrior who slew him, and is only released on the fulfillment of the ceremonies. Should a warrior refuse to fulfill the ceremonies, the ghost will ask, 'Why don't you fulfill the ceremonies and let me go?' Should a man still refuse to comply, the ghost will take him by the throat and strangle him. 3

We have seen that among the Nilotic tribes of Kavirondo a very similar ceremony is observed by a murderer for the avowed purpose of freeing himself from the ghost of his victim, which otherwise haunts him.1 The close resemblance of the ritual in both cases, together with the motives expressly assigned for it, set in the clearest light the essential purpose of the purificatory ceremonies observed by a homicide, whether he is a warrior or a murderer: that purpose is simply to rid the man of his victim's ghost, which will otherwise be his undoing. The intention of putting strips of goat-skin round his head and wrists may be to disguise him from the ghost.

A similar custom is observed by other tribes of East Africa on a variety of occasions, which will be noticed later on.2 Even when no mention is made of the ghosts of the slain by our authorities, we may still safely assume that the purificatory rites performed by or for warriors after bloodshed are intended to appease or repel or deceive these angry spirits. Thus among the Ngoni of British Central Africa, when a victorious army approaches the royal village, it halts by the bank of a stream, and all the warriors who have killed enemies smear their bodies and arms with white clay, but those who were not the first to dip their spears in the blood of the victims, but merely helped to dispatch them, whiten their right arms only. That night the manslayers sleep in the open pen with the cattle, and do not venture near their own homes. In the early morning they wash off the white clay from their bodies in the river. The witch-doctor attends to give them a magic potion, and to smear their persons with a fresh coating of clay. This process is repeated on six successive days, till their purification is complete. Their heads are then shaved, and being pronounced clean they are free to return to their own homes.3 Among the Borâna Gallas, when a war-party has returned to the village, the victors who have slain a foe are washed by the women with a mixture of fat and butter, and their faces are painted red and white.4

Masai warriors, who have killed barbarians in a fight, paint the right half of their bodies red and the left half white.1 Similarly a Nandi, who has slain a man of another tribe, paints one side of his body red, and the other side white; for four days after the slaughter he is deemed unclean and may not go home. He must build a small shelter by the river and live there; he may not associate with his wife or sweetheart, and he may only eat porridge, beef, and goat's flesh. At the end of the fourth day he must purify himself by drinking a strong purge made from the segetet tree, and by drinking goat's milk mixed with bullock's blood.2 Among the Wagogo, of German East Africa, a man who has killed an enemy in battle paints a red circle round his right eye and a black circle round his left eye.3

Among the Thompson Indians of British Columbia it used to be customary for men who had slain enemies to blacken their faces. If this precaution were neglected, it was believed that the spirits of their victims would blind them.4 A Pima Indian who slew one of his hereditary foes, the Apaches, had regularly to undergo a rigid seclusion and purification, which lasted sixteen days. During the whole of that time he might not touch meat or salt, nor look at a blazing fire, nor speak to a human being. He lived alone in the woods attended by an old woman, who brought him his scanty dole of food. He kept his head covered almost the whole time with a plaster of mud, and he might not touch it with his fingers.5

A band of Tinneh Indians, who had massacred a helpless party of Eskimo at the Copper River, considered themselves to be thereby rendered unclean, and they observed accordingly a number of curious restrictions for a considerable time afterwards. Those who had actually shed blood were strictly prohibited from cooking either for themselves or for others; they might not drink out of any dish nor smoke out of any pipe but their own; they might eat no boiled flesh, but only flesh that was raw or had been broiled at a fire or dried in the sun; and at every meal, before they would taste a morsel, they had to paint their faces with red ochre from the nose to the chin and across the cheeks almost to the ears.1

Among the Chinook Indians of Oregon and Washington a man who had killed another had his face painted black with grease and charcoal, and wore rings of cedar bark round his head, his ankles, knees, and wrists. After five days the black paint was washed off his face and replaced by red. During these five days he might not sleep nor even lie down; he might not look at a child nor see people eating. At the end of his purification he hung his head-ring of cedar bark on a tree, and the tree was then supposed to dry up.2 Among the Eskimo of Langton Bay the killing of an Indian and the killing of a whale were considered to be equally glorious achievements. The man who had killed an Indian was tattooed from the nose to the ears; the man who had killed a whale was tattooed from the mouth to the ears. Both heroes had to refrain from all work for five days, and from certain foods for a whole year; in particular, they might not eat the heads nor the intestines of animals.3

Among the Southern Massim of British New Guinea a warrior who has slain a man remains secluded in his house for six days. During the first three days he may eat only roasted food and must cook it for himself. Then he bathes and blackens his face for the remaining three days.4 When a party of Arunta, in Central Australia, are returning from a mission of vengeance, on which they have taken the life of an enemy, they stand in fear of the ghost of their victim, who is believed to pursue them in the likeness of a small bird, uttering a plaintive cry. For some days after their return they will not speak of their deed, and continue to paint themselves all over with powdered charcoal, and to decorate their foreheads and noses with green twigs. Finally, they paint their bodies and faces with bright colors, and become free to talk of the affair; but still of nights they must lie awake listening for the plaintive cry of the bird in which they fancy they hear the voice of their victim.1

In Fiji any one who had clubbed a human being to death in war was consecrated or tabooed. He was smeared red by the king with turmeric from the roots of his hair to his heels. A hut was built, and in it he had to pass the next three nights, during which he might not lie down, but must sleep as he sat. Till the three nights had elapsed he might not change his garment, nor remove the turmeric, nor enter a house in which there was a woman.2 That these rules were intended to protect the Fijian warrior from his victim's ghost is strongly suggested, if not proved, by another Fijian custom. When these savages had buried a man alive, as they often did, they used at nightfall to make a great uproar by means of bamboos, trumpet-shells, and so forth, for the purpose of frightening away his ghost, lest he should attempt to return to his old home. And to render his house unattractive to him they dismantled it and clothed it with everything that to their thinking seemed most repulsive.3 So the North American Indians used to run through the village with hideous yells, beating on the furniture, walls, and roofs of the huts to drive away the angry ghost of an enemy whom they had just tortured to death.4 A similar custom is still observed in various parts of New Guinea and the Bismarck Archipelago.5

Thus the mark of Cain may have been a mode of disguising a homicide, or of rendering him so repulsive or formidable in appearance that his victim's ghost would either not know him or at least give him a wide berth. Elsewhere I have conjectured that mourning costume in general was originally a disguise adopted to protect the surviving relatives from the dreaded ghost of the recently departed.1 Whether that be so or not, it is certain that the living do sometimes disguise themselves to escape the notice of the dead. Thus in the western districts of Timor, a large island of the Indian Archipelago, before the body of a man is coffined, his wives stand weeping over him, and their village gossips must also be present, "all with loosened hair in order to make themselves unrecognizable by the nitu (spirit) of the dead." 2 Again, among the Herero of South-West Africa, when a man is dying he will sometimes say to a person whom he does not like, "Whence do you come? I do not wish to see you here," and so saying he presses the fingers of his left hand together in such a way that the tip of the thumb protrudes between the fingers. "The person spoken to, now knows that the other has decided upon taking him away (okutuaerera) after his death, which means that he must die. In many cases, however, he can avoid this threatening danger of death. For this purpose he hastily leaves the place of the dying man, and looks for an onganga (i.e. 'doctor,' 'magician'), in order to have himself undressed, washed, and greased again, and dressed with other clothes. He is now quite at ease about the threatening of death caused by the deceased; for, says he, 'Now, our father does not know me' (Nambano tate ke ndyi i). He has no longer any reason to fear the dead." 3

In like manner we may suppose that, when Cain had been marked by God, he was quite easy in his mind, believing that the ghost of his murdered brother would no longer recognize and trouble him. What the mark exactly was which the divinity affixed to the first murderer for his protection, we have no means of knowing; at most we can hazard a conjecture on the subject. If it is allowable to judge from the similar practices of savages at the present day, the deity may have decorated Cain with red, black, or white paint, or perhaps with a tasteful combination of these colors. For example, he may have painted him red all over, like a Fijian; or white all over, like a Ngoni ; or black all over, like an Arunta; or one half of his body red and the other half white, like the Masai and the Nandi. Or if he confined his artistic efforts to Cain's countenance, he may have painted a red circle round his right eye and a black circle round his left eye, in the Wagogo style; or he may have embellished his face from the nose to the chin, and from the mouth to the ears, with a delicate shade of vermilion, after the manner of the Tinneh Indians. Or he may have plastered his head with mud, like the Pimas, or his whole body with cow's dung, like the Kavirondo. Or again, he may have tattooed him from the nose to the ears, like the Eskimo, or between the eyebrows, like the Thonga, so as to raise pimples and give him the appearance of a frowning buffalo. Thus adorned the first Mr. Smith—for Cain means Smith 1 —may have paraded the waste places of the earth without the least fear of being recognized and molested by his victim's ghost.

This explanation of the mark of Cain has the advantage of relieving the Biblical narrative from a manifest absurdity. For on the usual interpretation God affixed the mark to Cain in order to save him from human assailants, apparently forgetting that there was nobody to assail him, since the earth was as yet inhabited only by the murderer himself and his parents. Hence by assuming that the foe of whom the first murderer went in fear was a ghost instead of a living man we avoid the irreverence of imputing to the deity a crave lapse of memory little in keeping with the divine omniscience. Here again, therefore, the comparative method approves itself a powerful advocatus Dei.

To this explanation of the mark of Cain it may be objected, with some show of reason, that the ghost of the murdered Abel is nowhere alluded to in the Biblical narrative, according to which it was not the ghost, but the blood, of his victim which endangered the murderer by calling aloud from the ground for vengeance. It is true that the conception of blood thus endowed with a voice and with a thirst for vengeance differs from the conception of a ghost, being a simpler and possibly a more primitive idea; yet in practice it perhaps made little material difference to the manslayer whether he believed himself to be pursued by the bloody phantom or only by the dolorous voice of his victim's blood shrieking after him. Still it cannot be denied that in the Old Testament it is the actual blood, and not the ghost, of the murdered person which figures prominently in the references to manslaughter and to the retribution which should overtake the slayer.

Thus in the Priestly Document we read, with regard to homicide, that "blood, it polluteth the land: and no expiation can be made for the land for the blood that is shed therein, but by the blood of him that shed it." 1 The notion seems to have been, that so long as the blood lay exposed to the air and had not run away or soaked into the ground, it continued to call aloud for vengeance on the murderer, but that its mouth could be stopped and its voice stifled by a handful of earth. Hence Job, looking for death and passionately appealing against the injustice of his fate, cries out in his agony, "O earth, cover not my blood, and let my cry have no resting place." 2 And in denouncing the wrath of God on Jerusalem for all the innocent blood shed in the city, the prophet Ezekiel ex-claims, "Woe to the bloody city, to the caldron whose rust is therein, and whose rust is not gone out of it! bring it out piece by piece; no lot is fallen upon it. For her blood is in the midst of her; she set it upon the bare rock; she poured it not on the ground to cover it with dust; that it might cause fury to come up to take vengeance, I have set her blood upon the bare rock, that it should not be covered." 1 Here it is mentioned as a great aggravation alike of the guilt and of the danger of Jerusalem, that the blood shed in her midst still weltered in clotted pools, like rust, on her rocky surface instead of being mercifully covered with dust or allowed to soak into the ground; for so long as it lay there festering in the sun, the multitudinous voices of the slain would ascend up to heaven, clamoring in a doleful chorus for vengeance on their slayers.2

The belief that unavenged human blood cries aloud from the ground is still held by the Arabs of Moab. A Bedouin of that country told a preaching friar that "the blood cries from the earth, and it continues to cry until the blood of an enemy has been shed."3 So scrupulous indeed were the ancient Hebrews about leaving blood of any sort exposed to the air, that the Levitical law commands the hunter or fowler to cover up with dust the blood of the beast or fowl which he has poured out on the ground.4 The precept may well embody a traditional usage based on an ancient belief that animals, like men, acknowledged the obligation of avenging the death of their kind on their murderer or his kinsfolk, and that consequently if their blood was left uncovered, it would cry aloud to all beasts or birds of the same sort to exact retribution from the guilty hunter or fowler who had spilt it on the ground.

At all events similar notions as to the practice of blood revenge by animals and birds are common among savages in modern times, 5 and they may well have prevailed among the Semites in antiquity, though we need not suppose that they were consciously present to the mind of the author or editor of Leviticus. It would appear that in the opinion of some savages not only may the blood of animals cry to heaven for vengeance, but if its cry is not answered, the slayer of the beast may be compelled, like Cain, to roam an outlaw from land to land for the rest of his life. Thus in a legend of the Waboungou, a tribe of German East Africa, we hear of a skilful hunter who one day killed an elephant with his arrows. Thereupon a mysterious personage called the Great Sultan appeared to him and said, "The smell of spilt blood has reached even to me. That blood calls for vengeance. If you do not bring me the bones of the elephant, there can be no peace between us. I will tell all the Sultans to drive you from their countries, so that you will henceforth find no place where to build a hut." But the obstinate hunter refused to bring the bones of the elephant to the Great Sultan. Therefore the Sultan drove him from his kingdom, and the wretch went roving from land to land till the day of his death.1

We may smile if we please at these quaint fancies of vengeful ghosts, shrieking gore, and Earth opening her mouth to drink blood or to vomit out her guilty inhabitants; nevertheless it is probable that these and many other notions equally unfounded have served a useful purpose in fortifying the respect for human life by the adventitious aid of superstitious terror. The venerable framework of society rests on many pillars, of which the most solid are nature, reason, and justice; yet at certain stages of its slow and laborious construction it could ill have dispensed with the frail prop of superstition.2 If the day should ever come when the great edifice has been carried to completion and reposes in simple majesty on adamantine foundations, it will be possible, without risk to its stability, to cut away and destroy the rotten timbers that shored it up in the process of building.

Chapter 4 - The Great Flood

§ 1. Introduction
Huxley on the Great Flood
The present essay a study in folk-lore
Bearing of flood stories on problems of origin and diffusion

§ 2. The Babylonian Story of a Great Flood
Babylonian tradition recorded by Berosus Nicolaus of Damascus on the flood
Modern discovery of the original Babylonian story
The Gilgamesh epic
Journey of Gilgamesh to Ut-napishtim
Ut-napishtim's story of the Great Flood
The building of the ship—the embarkation—the storm
The sending forth of the dove and the raven—the landing
Other fragmentary versions of the Babylonian story
Sumerian version of the flood story
The flood story borrowed by the Semites from the Sumerians
The scene of the story laid at Shurippak on the Euphrates

§ 3. The Hebrew Story of a Great Flood
The story in Genesis
The story compounded of two different narratives
The Priestly Document and the Jehovistic Document
Late date and ecclesiastical character of the Priestly Document
Its contrast with the Jehovistic Document
Verbal differences between the Priestly and the Jehovistic Documents
Material differences between the documents in the flood story
The Jehovistic document the older of the two
Dependence of the Hebrew on the Babylonian story of the flood
Fanciful additions made to the flood story in later times

§ 4. Ancient Greek Stories of a Great Flood
Deucalion and Pyrrha
The grounding of the ark on Parnassus
Aristotle and Plato on Deucalion's flood

THE GREAT FLOOD AND OTHER MYTHS AND LEGENDS OF THE OLD TESTAMENT

Stories as to the origin of the diversity of tongues in Greece, Africa, Assam, Australia, and America

§ 1. Introduction

WHEN the Council of the Royal Anthropological Institute invited me to deliver the annual Huxley lecture, I gratefully accepted the invitation, esteeming it a high honour to be thus associated with one for whom, both as a thinker and as a man, I entertain a deep respect, and with whose attitude towards the great problems of life I am in cordial sympathy. His own works will long keep his memory green; but it is fitting that our science should lay, year by year, a wreath on the grave of one of the most honoured of its exponents.

Casting about for a suitable subject, I remembered that in his later life Huxley devoted some of his well-earned leisure to examining those traditions as to the early ages of the world which are recorded in the Book of Genesis; and accordingly I thought that I might appropriately take one of them for the theme of my discourse. The one which I have chosen is the familiar story of the Great Flood. Huxley himself discussed it in an instructive essay written with all the charm of his lucid and incisive style.2 His aim was to show that, treated as a record of a deluge which overwhelmed the whole world, drowning almost all men and animals, the story conflicts with the plain teaching of geology and must be rejected as a fable. I shall not attempt either to reinforce or to criticize his arguments and his conclusions, for the simple reason that I am no geologist, and that for me to express an opinion on such a matter would be a mere impertinence. I have approached the subject from a different side, namely, from that of tradition. It has long been known that legends of a great flood, in which almost all men perished, are widely diffused over the world; and accordingly what I have tried to do is to collect and compare these legends, and to inquire what conclusions are to be deduced from the comparison. In short, my discussion of the stories is a study in comparative folk-lore. My purpose is to discover how the narratives arose, and how they came to be so widespread over the earth; with the question of their truth or falsehood I am not primarily concerned, though of course it cannot be ignored in considering the problem of their origin. The inquiry thus defined is not a novel one. It has often been attempted, especially in recent years, and in pursuing it I have made ample use of the labours of my predecessors, some of whom have discussed the subject with great learning and ability. In particular, I would acknowledge my debt to the eminent German geographer and anthropologist, the late Dr. Richard Andree, whose monograph on diluvial traditions, like all his writings, is a model of sound learning and good sense, set forth with the utmost clearness and conciseness.1

Apart from the intrinsic interest of such legends as professed records of a catastrophe which destroyed at a blow almost the whole human race, they deserve to be studied for the sake of their bearing on a general question which is at present warmly debated among anthropologists. That question is, How are we to explain the numerous and striking similarities which obtain between the beliefs and customs of races inhabiting distant parts of the world? Are such resemblances due to the transmission of the customs and beliefs from one race to another, either by immediate contact or through the medium of intervening peoples? Or have they arisen independently in many different races through the similar working of the human mind under similar circumstances? Now, if I may presume to offer an opinion on this much-debated problem, I would say at once that, put in the form of an antithesis between mutually exclusive views, the question seems to me absurd.

So far as I can judge, all experience and all probability are in favour of the conclusion, that both causes have operated extensively and powerfully to produce the observed similarities of custom and belief among the various races of mankind; in other words, many of these resemblances are to be explained by simple transmission, with more or less of modification, from people to people, and many are to be explained as having originated independently through the similar action of the human mind in response to similar environment. If that is so—and I confess to thinking that this is the only reasonable and probable view—it will follow that in attempting to account for any particular case of resemblance which may be traced between the customs and beliefs of different races, it would be futile to appeal to the general principle either of transmission or of independent origin; each case must be judged on its own merits after an impartial scrutiny of the facts and referred to the one or the other principle, or possibly to a combination of the two, according as the balance of evidence inclines to the one side or to the other, or hangs evenly between them.

This general conclusion, which accepts the two principles of transmission and independent origin as both of them true and valid within certain limits, is confirmed by the particular investigation of diluvial traditions. For it is certain that legends of a great flood are found dispersed among many diverse peoples in distant regions of the earth, and so far as demonstration in such matters is possible, it can be demonstrated that the similarities which undoubtedly exist between many of these legends are due partly to direct transmission from one people to another, and partly to similar, but quite independent, experiences either of great floods or of phenomena which suggested the occurrence of great floods, in many different parts of the world. Thus the study of these traditions, quite apart from any conclusions to which it may lead us concerning their historical credibility, may serve a useful purpose if it mitigates the heat with which the controversy has sometimes been carried on, by convincing the extreme partisans of both principles that in this as in so many other disputes the truth lies wholly neither on the one side nor on the other, but somewhere between the two.

§ 2. The Babylonian Story of a Great Flood

Of all the legends of a Great Flood recorded in literature, by far the oldest is the Babylonian or rather the Sumerian; for we now know that, ancient as was the Babylonian version of the story, it was derived by the Babylonians from their still more ancient predecessors, the Sumerians, from whom the Semitic inhabitants of Babylonia appear to have derived the principal elements of their civilization.

The Babylonian tradition of the Great Flood has been known to Western scholars from the time of antiquity, since it was recorded by the native Babylonian historian Berosus, who composed a history of his country in the first half of the third century before our era. Berosus wrote in Greek and his work has not come down to us, but fragments of it have been preserved by later Greek historians, and among these fragments is fortunately his account of the deluge. It runs as follows :

The tenth king of Babylon. Now the god Cronus appeared to him in a dream and warned him that all men would be destroyed by a flood on the fifteenth day of the month Daesius, which was the eighth month of the Macedonian calendar.1 Therefore the god enjoined him to write a history of the world from the beginning and to bury it for safety in Sippar, the city of the Sun.2 Moreover, he was to build a ship and embark in it with his kinsfolk and friends, and to lay up in it a store of meat and drink, and to bring living things, both fowls and four-footed beasts, into the ship, and when he had made all things ready he was to set sail. And when he asked, "And whither shall I sail?" the god answered him, "To the gods; but first thou shalt pray for all good things to men." So he obeyed and built the ship, and the length of it was five furlongs,1 and the breadth of it was two furlongs; and when he had gathered all things together he stored them in the ship and embarked his children and friends. And when the flood had come and immediately abated, Xisuthrus let fly some of the birds. But as they could find no food nor yet a place to rest, they came back to the ship. And again after some days Xisuthrus let fly the birds ; and they returned again to the ship with their feet daubed with clay. A third time he let them fly, and they returned no more to the vessel.

Then Xisuthrus perceived that the land had appeared above the water; so he parted some of the seams of the ship, and looking out he saw the shore, and drove the ship aground on a mountain, and stepped ashore with his wife, and his daughter, and the helmsman. And he worshipped the ground, and built an altar, and when he had sacrificed to the gods, he disappeared with those who had disembarked from the ship. And when those who had remained in the ship saw that he and his company returned not, they disembarked likewise and sought him, calling him by name. But Xisuthrus himself was nowhere to be seen. Yet a voice from the air bade them fear the gods, for that he himself for his piety was gone to dwell with the gods, and that his wife, and his daughter, and the helmsman partook of the same honour. And he commanded them that they should go to Babylon, and take up the scriptures which they had buried, and distribute them among men. Moreover, he told them that the land in which they stood was Armenia. And when they heard these things, they sacrificed to the gods and journeyed on foot to Babylon. But of the ship that grounded on the mountains of Armenia a part remains to this day,2 and some people scrape the bitumen off it and use it in charms. So when they were come to Babylon they dug up the scriptures in Sippar, and built many cities, and restored the sanctuaries, and repeopled Babylon.

According to the Greek historian Nicolaus of Damascus, a contemporary and friend of Augustus and of Herod the Great, "there is above Minyas in Armenia a great mountain called Baris, to which, as the story goes, many people fled for refuge in the flood and were saved; they say too that a certain man, floating in an ark, grounded on the summit, and that remains of the timbers were preserved for a long time. The man may have been he who was recorded by Moses, the legislator of the Jews." 1 Whether Nicolaus of Damascus drew this information from Babylonian or Hebrew tradition, may be doubted; the reference to Moses seems to show that he was acquainted with the narrative in Genesis, which he may easily have learned through his patron, Herod.

For many centuries the Babylonian tradition of a great flood was known to Western scholars only through its preservation in the Greek fragments of Berosus; it was reserved for modern times to recover the original Babylonian version from the long-lost archives of Assyria. In the course of those excavations at Nineveh, which were one of the glories of the nineteenth century and which made an epoch in the study of ancient history, the English explorers were fortunate enough to discover extensive remains of the library of the great king Ashurbanipal, who reigned from 668 to 626 B.C. in the splendid sunset of the Assyrian empire, carrying the terror of his arms to the banks of the Nile, embellishing his capital with magnificent structures, and gathering within its walls from far and near a vast literature, historical, scientific, grammatical and religious, for the enlightenment of his people.2

The literature, of which a great part was borrowed from Babylonian originals, was inscribed in cuneiform characters on tablets of soft clay, which were afterwards baked hard and deposited in the library. Apparently the library was arranged in an upper story of the palace, which, in the last sack of the city, collapsed in the flames, shattering the tablets to pieces in its fall. Many of them are still cracked and scorched by the heat of the burning ruins. In later ages the ruins were ransacked by antiquaries of the class of Dousterswivel, who sought among them for the buried treasures not of learning but of gold, and by their labours contributed still further to the disruption and disintegration of the precious records. To complete their destruction, the rain, soaking through the ground

79

every spring, saturates them with water containing chemicals, which form in every crack and fissure crystals that by their growth split the already broken tablets into minute fragments. Yet by laboriously piecing together a multitude of these fragments George Smith, of the British Museum, was able to recompose the now famous epic of Gilgamesh in twelve cantos, or rather tablets, the eleventh of which contains the Babylonian story of the deluge. The great discovery was announced by Mr. Smith at a meeting of the Society of Biblical Archaeology on December the 3rd, 1872.1

It was ingeniously conjectured by Sir Henry Rawlinson that the twelve cantos of the Gilgamesh epic corresponded to the twelve signs of the zodiac, so that the course of the poem followed, as it were, the course of the sun through the twelve months of the year. The theory is to some extent confirmed by the place assigned to the flood legend in the eleventh canto; for the eleventh Babylonian month fell at the height of the rainy season, it was dedicated to the storm-god Ramman, and its name is said to signify "month of the curse of rain." 2 Be that as it may, the story as it stands is an episode or digression destitute of all organic connection with the rest of the poem. It is introduced as follows:—1

The hero of the poem, Gilgamesh, has lost his dear friend Engidu 2 by death, and he himself has fallen grievously sick. Saddened by the past and anxious for the future, he resolves to seek out his remote ancestor Ut-napishtim, 3 son of Ubara-Tutu, and to inquire of him how mortal man can attain to eternal life. For surely, he thought, Ut-napishtim must know the secret, since he has been made like to the gods and now dwells somewhere far away in blissful immortality. A weary and a perilous journey must Gilgamesh accomplish to come at him. He passes the mountain, guarded by a scorpion man and woman, where the sun goes down: he traverses a dark and dreadful road never trodden before by mortal man: he is ferried across a wide sea: he crosses the Water of Death by a narrow bridge, and at last he enters the presence of Ut-napishtim.1 But when he puts to his great ancestor the question, how man may attain to eternal life, he receives a discouraging reply: the sage tells him that immortality is not for man. Surprised at this answer from one who had been a man and was now himself immortal, Gilgamesh naturally asks his venerable relative to explain how he had contrived to evade the common doom. It is in answer to this pointed question that Ut-napishtim tells the story of the great flood, which runs as follows:—

Ut-napishtim spoke to him, to Gilgamesh: "I will reveal to thee, O Gilgamesh, a hidden word, and the purpose 2 of the gods will I declare to thee. Shurippak, a city which thou knowest, which lies on the bank of the Euphrates, that city was old; 3 and the gods within it, their heart prompted the great gods to send a flood. 4 There was their father Anu, their counsellor the warrior Enlil, 5 their messenger Ninib, their prince Ennugi. The Lord of Wisdom, Ea, sat also with them, he repeated their word to the hut 6 of reeds, saying, 'O reed hut, reed hut, O wall, wall, O reed hut hearken, O wall attend. O man of Shurippak, son of Ubara-Tutu, pull down thy house, build a ship, forsake thy possessions, take heed for thy life! Thy gods abandon, save thy life, bring living seed of every kind into the ship. As for the ship which thou shalt build, well planned must be its dimensions, its breadth and its length shall bear proportions each to each, and thou shalt launch it in the ocean.'1 I took heed and spake unto Ea, my lord, saying, 'The command, O my lord, which thou hast given, I will honour and will fulfil. But how shall I make answer unto the city, the people and the elders thereof? 'Ea opened his mouth and spake, and he said unto me his servant, 'Thus shalt thou answer and say unto them: Because Enlil hates me, no longer may I abide in your city nor lay my head on Enlil's earth. Down into the deep sea must I go with Ea, my lord, to dwell.'"

So Ut-napishtim obeyed the god Ea and gathered together the wood and all things needful for the building of the ship, and on the fifth day he laid down the hull. In the shape of a barge he built it, and on it he set a house a hundred and twenty cubits high, and he divided the house into six stories, and in each story he made nine rooms. Water-plugs he fastened within it; the outside he daubed with bitumen, and the inside he caulked with pitch. He caused oil to be brought, and he slaughtered oxen and lambs. He filled jars with sesame-wine and oil and grape-wine; he gave the people to drink like a river and he made a feast like to the feast of the New Year. And when the ship was ready he filled it with all that he had of silver, and all that he had of gold, and all that he had of living seed. Also he brought up into the ship all his family and his household, the cattle of the field likewise and the beasts of the field, and the handicraftsmen: all of them he brought in. A fixed time the sun-god Shamash had appointed, saying, "'At eventide the lord of darkness will send a heavy rain. Then enter thou into the ship and shut thy door.' The time appointed drew near, and at eventide the lord of darkness sent a heavy rain. Of the storm, I saw the beginning, to look upon the storm I was afraid. I entered into the ship and shut the door. To the pilot of the ship, even to Puzur-Amurri, the sailor, I committed the (floating) palace l and all that therein was.

> When the early dawn appeared there came up from the horizon a black cloud
> Ramman thundered in the midst thereof, the gods
> Mujati and Lugal went before
> Like messengers they passed over mountain and land;
> Irragal 5 tore away the ship's post
> There went Ninib and he made the storm to burst
> The Anunnaki lifted up flaming torches,
> with the brightness thereof they lit up the earth
> The whirlwind of Ramman mounted up into the heavens,
> and all light was turned into darkness."

A whole day the tempest raged, and the waters rose on the mountains. "No man beheld his fellow, no more could men know each other. In heaven the gods were afraid of the deluge, they drew back, they climbed up into the heaven of Anu. The gods crouched like dogs, they cowered by the walls. Ishtar cried out like a woman in travail, loudly lamented the queen of the gods with her beautiful voice: 'Let that day be turned to clay, when I commanded evil in the assembly of the gods! Alas, that I commanded evil in the assembly of the gods, that for the destruction of my people I commanded battle! That which I brought forth, where is it? Like the spawn of fish it filleth the sea.' The gods of the Anunnaki wept with her, the gods were bowed down, they sat down weeping. Their lips were pressed together.

For six days and six nights the wind blew, and the deluge and the tempest overwhelmed the land. When the seventh day drew nigh, then ceased the tempest and the deluge and the storm, which had fought like a host. Then the sea grew quiet, it went down; the hurricane and the deluge ceased. I looked upon the sea, there was silence come,1 and all mankind was turned back into clay. Instead of the fields a swamp lay before me. 2 I opened the window and the light fell upon my cheek; I bowed myself down, I sat down, I wept, over my cheek flowed my tears. I looked upon the world, and behold all was sea. After twelve (days?)8 an island arose, to the land Nisir the ship made its way. The mount of Nisir 4 held the ship fast and let it not slip.

The first day, the second day, the mountain Nisir held the ship fast: the third day, the fourth day, the mountain Nisir held the ship fast: the fifth day, the sixth day, the mountain Nisir held the ship fast. When the seventh day drew nigh, I sent out a dove, and let her go forth. The dove flew hither and thither, but there was no resting-place for her, and she returned. Then I sent out a swallow and let her go forth. The swallow flew hither and thither, but there was no resting-place for her, and she returned. Then I sent out a raven and let her go forth. The raven flew away, she beheld the abatement of the waters, she ate, 5 she waded, she croaked, but she did not return. Then I brought all out unto the four winds, I offered an offering, I made a libation on the peak of the mountain. By sevens I set out the vessels, under them I heaped up reed, and cedar-wood, and myrtle.1 The gods smelt the savour, the gods smelt the sweet savour. The gods gathered like flies about him that offered up the sacrifice. Then the Lady of the gods drew nigh, she lifted up the great jewels which Anu had made according to her wish. She said, 'Oh ye gods here, as truly as I will not forget the jewels of lapis lazuli which are on my neck, so truly will I remember these days, never shall I forget them! Let the gods come to the offering, but Enlil 2 shall not come to the offering, for he took not counsel and sent the deluge, and my people he gave to destruction.'

Now when Enlil drew nigh, he saw the ship; then was Enlil wroth.
He was filled with anger against the gods, the Igigi (saying),
'Who then hath escaped with his life? No man shall live after the destruction.'
Then Ninib opened his mouth and spake, he said to the warrior Enlil,
'Who but Ea could have done this thing? For Ea knoweth every matter.'
Then Ea opened his mouth and spake, he said to the warrior Enlil,
'Thou art the governor of the gods,
O warrior, but thou wouldst not take counsel and thou hast sent the deluge!
On the sinner visit his sin, and on the transgressor visit his transgression.

But hold thy hand, that all be not destroyed! and forbear, that all be not confounded! Instead of sending a deluge, let a lion come and minish mankind! Instead of sending a deluge, let a leopard come and minish mankind! Instead of sending a deluge, let a famine come and waste the land! Instead of sending a deluge, let the Plague-god come and slay mankind! I did not reveal the purpose of the great gods. I caused

Atrakhasis to see a dream, and thus he heard the purpose of the gods.' Thereupon Enlil arrived at a decision, and he went up into the ship. He took my hand and brought me forth, he brought my wife forth, he made her to kneel at my side, he turned towards us, he stood between us, he blessed us (saying), 'Hitherto hath Ut-napishtim been a man, but now let Ut-napishtim and his wife be like unto the gods, even us, and let Ut-napishtim dwell afar off at the mouth of the rivers!' Then they took me, and afar off, at the mouth of the rivers, they made me to dwell."

Such is the long story of the deluge interwoven into the Gilgamesh epic, with which, to all appearance, it had originally no connection. A fragment of another version of the tale is preserved on a broken tablet, which, like the tablets of the Gilgamesh epic, was found among the ruins of Ashurbanipal's library at Nineveh. It contains a part of the conversation which is supposed to have taken place before the flood between the god Ea and the Babylonian Noah, who is here called Atrakhasis, a name which, as we saw, is incidentally applied to him in the Gilgamesh epic, though elsewhere in that version he is named not Atrakhasis but Ut-napishtim. The name Atrakhasis is said to be the Babylonian original which in Berosus's Greek version of the deluge legend is represented by Xisuthrus.1 In this fragment the god Ea commands Atrakhasis, saying, "Go in and shut the door of the ship. Bring within thy corn, thy goods and thy possessions, thy (wife?), thy family, thy kinsfolk, and thy craftsmen, the cattle of the field, the beasts of the field, as many as eat grass." 2 In his reply the hero says that he has never built a ship before, and he begs that a plan of the ship be drawn for him on the ground, which he may follow in laying down the vessel.3

Thus far the Babylonian versions of the flood legend date only from the time of Ashurbanipal in the seventh century before our era, and might therefore conceivably be of later origin than the Hebrew version and copied from it. However, conclusive evidence of the vastly greater antiquity of the Babylonian legend is furnished by a broken tablet, which was discovered at Abu-Habbah, the site of the ancient city of Sippar, in the course of excavations undertaken by the Turkish Government. The tablet contains a very mutilated version of the flood story, and it is exactly dated; for at the end there is a colophon or note recording that the tablet was written on the twenty-eighth day of the month Shabatu (the eleventh Babylonian month) in the eleventh year of King Ammizaduga, or about 1966 B.C. Unfortunately the text is so fragmentary that little information can be extracted from it; but the name of Atrakhasis occurs in it together with references to the great rain and apparently to the ship and the entrance into it of the people who were to be saved.1

Yet another very ancient version of the deluge legend came to light at Nippur in the excavations conducted by the University of Pennsylvania. It is written on a small fragment of unbaked clay, and on the ground of the style of writing and of the place where the tablet was found it is dated by its discoverer, Professor H. V. Hilprecht, not later than 2100 B.C. In this fragment a god appears to announce that he will cause a deluge which will sweep away all mankind at once; and he warns the person whom he addresses to build a great ship, with a strong roof, in which he is to save his life, and also to bring into it the beasts of the field and the birds of heaven.2

All these versions of the flood story are written in the Semitic language of Babylonia and Assyria; but another fragmentary version, found by the American excavators at Nippur and recently deciphered, is written in Sumerian, that is, in the non-Semitic language of the ancient people who appear to have preceded the Semites in Babylonia and to have founded in the lower valley of the Euphrates that remarkable system of civilization which we commonly call Babylonian.1 The city of Nippur, where the Sumerian version of the deluge legend has been discovered, was the holiest and perhaps the oldest religious centre in the country, and the city-god Enlil was the head of the Babylonian pantheon. The tablet which records the legend would seem, from the character of the script, to have been written about the time of the famous Hammurabi, king of Babylon, that is about 2100 B.C. But the story itself must be very much older; for by the close of the third millennium before our era, when the tablet was inscribed, the Sumerians as a separate race had almost ceased to exist, having been absorbed in the Semitic population, and their old tongue was already a dead language, though the ancient literature and sacred texts embalmed in it were still studied and copied by the Semitic priests and scribes.2

Hence the discovery of a Sumerian version of the deluge legend raises a presumption that the legend itself dates from a time anterior to the occupation of the Euphrates valley by the Semites, who after their immigration into the country appear to have borrowed the story from their predecessors the Sumerians. It is of interest to observe that the Sumerian version of the flood story formed a sequel to an account, unfortunately very fragmentary, of the creation of man, according to which men were created by the gods before the animals. Thus the Sumerian story agrees with the Hebrew account, in Genesis, in so far as both of them treat the creation of man and the great flood as events closely connected with each other in the early history of the world; and further the Sumerian narrative agrees with the Jehovistic against the Priestly Document in representing the creation of man as antecedent to the creation of the animals.1

Only the lower half of the tablet on which this Sumerian Genesis was inscribed has as yet come to light, but enough remains to furnish us with the main outlines of the flood story. From it we learn that Ziugiddu, or rather Ziudsuddu,2 was at once a king and a priest of the god Enki, the Sumerian deity who was the equivalent of the Semitic Ea; 3 daily he occupied himself in the god's service, prostrating himself in humility and constant in his observance at the shrine. To reward him for his piety Enki informs him that at the request of Enlil it has been resolved in the council of the gods to destroy the seed of mankind by a rain-storm. Before the holy man receives this timely warning, his divine friend bids him take his stand beside a wall, saying, "Stand by the wall on my left side, and at the wall I will speak a word with thee." These words are evidently connected with the curious passage in the Semitic version, where Ea begins his warning to Ut-napishtim, "O reed hut, reed hut, O wall, wall, O reed hut hearken, O wall attend."4 Together the parallel passages suggest that the friendly god, who might not directly betray the resolution of the gods to a mortal man, adopted the subterfuge of whispering it to a wall of reeds, on the other side of which he had first stationed Ziudsuddu. Thus by eavesdropping the good man learned the fatal secret, while his divine patron was able afterwards to protest that he had not revealed the counsel of the gods. The subterfuge reminds us of the well-known story, how the servant of King Midas detected the ass's ears of his master, and unable to contain himself, whispered the secret into a hole in the ground and filled up the hole with earth; but a bed of reeds grew up on the spot, and rustling in the wind, proclaimed to all the world the king's deformity.1

The part of the tablet which probably described the building of the ship and Ziudsuddu's embarkation is lost, and in the remaining portion we are plunged into the midst of the deluge. The storms of wind and rain are described as raging together. Then the text continues: "When for seven days, for seven nights, the rain-storm had raged in the land, when the great boat had been carried away by the wind-storms on the mighty waters, the Sun-god came forth, shedding light over heaven and earth." When the light shines into the boat, Ziudsuddu prostrates himself before the Sun-god and sacrifices an ox and a sheep. Then follows a gap in the text, after which we read of Ziudsuddu, the King, prostrating himself before the gods Anu and Enlil. The anger of Enlil against men appears now to be abated, for, speaking of Ziudsuddu, he says, "Life like that of a god I give to him," and "an eternal soul like that of a god I create for him," which means that the hero of the deluge legend, the Sumerian Noah, receives the boon of immortality, if not of divinity. Further, he is given the title of "Preserver of the Seed of Mankind," and the gods cause him to dwell on a mountain, perhaps the mountain of Dilmun, though the reading of the name is uncertain. The end of the legend is wanting.

Thus in its principal features the Sumerian version of the deluge legend agrees with the much longer and more circumstantial version preserved in the Gilgamesh epic. In both a great god (Enlil or Bel) resolves to destroy mankind by flooding the earth with rain; in both another god (Enki or Ea) warns a man of the coming catastrophe, and the man, accepting the admonition, is saved in a ship; in both the flood lasts at its height for seven days; in both, when the deluge has abated, the man offers a sacrifice and is finally raised to the rank of the gods. The only essential difference is in the name of the hero, who in the Sumerian version is called Ziudsuddu, and in the Semitic version Ut-napishtim or Atrakhasis. The Sumerian name Ziudsuddu resembles the name Xisuthrus, which Berosus gives as that of the hero who was saved from the flood; if the two names are really connected, we have fresh ground for admiring the fidelity with which the Babylonian historian followed the most ancient documentary sources.

The discovery of this very interesting tablet, with its combined accounts of the creation and the deluge, renders it highly probable that the narratives of the early history of the world which we find in Genesis did not originate with the Semites, but were borrowed by them from the older civilized people whom, some thousands of years before our era, the wild Semitic hordes, swarming out of the Arabian desert, found in possession of the fat lands of the lower Euphrates valley, and from whom the descendants of these primitive Bedouins gradually learned the arts and habits of civilization, just as the northern barbarians acquired a varnish of culture through their settlement in the Roman empire.

The various fragmentary versions, Babylonian and Sumerian, of the deluge story confirm the conclusion that the legend circulated independently of the Gilgamesh epic, into which the poet loosely inserted it as an episode. In the epic the original scene of the disaster is laid, as we saw, at the city of Shurippak on the Euphrates. Recent excavations of the German Oriental Society have revealed the site of the ancient city. The place is at the hill of Fara, to the north of Uruk; and the remains which have come to light there seem to show that Shurippak was among the very oldest Sumerian settlements yet discovered; for the inscribed clay tablets which have been excavated on the spot are of a very archaic character, and are believed to have been written not much later than 3400 B.C.1 The site is now a long way from the sea and at some distance from the Euphrates; but we know that in the course of ages the river has repeatedly changed its bed, and that the sea has retreated, or rather that the land has advanced, in consequence of the vast quantities of soil annually washed down by the Euphrates and the Tigris.2 Apparently the ancient city perished, not by water, but by fire; for the ruins are buried under a thick layer of ashes. After the conflagration the greater part of the hill seems to have remained desolate, though a small town existed on the spot during the Sumerian and Accadian periods. From about the time of Hammurabi, that is, from about 2100 B.C. onward, the very name of Shurippak vanishes from Babylonian history.3 Thus the story of the great flood which destroyed the city cannot have originated later than the end of the third millennium before Christ, and it may well have been very much older. In the Sumerian version of the deluge legend Shurippak is named, along with Eridu, Larak, and Sippar, as cities before the flood; but in the fragmentary state of the text it is impossible to say whether or not it was the city of Ziudsuddu, the Sumerian Noah.4

§ 3. The Hebrew Story of a Great Flood

The ancient Hebrew legend of a great flood, as it is recorded in the book of Genesis, runs thus :—

"And the Lord saw that the wickedness of man was great in the earth, and that every imagination of the thoughts of his heart was only evil continually. And it repented the Lord that he had made man on the earth, and it grieved him at his heart. And the Lord said, I will destroy man whom I have created from the face of the ground; both man, and beast, and creeping thing, and fowl of the air; for it repenteth me that I have made them. But Noah found grace in the eyes of the Lord.

"These are the generations of Noah. Noah was a righteous man and perfect in his generations: Noah walked with God. And Noah begat three sons, Shem, Ham, and Japheth. And the earth was corrupt before God, and the earth was filled with violence. And God saw the earth, and, behold, it was corrupt; for all flesh had corrupted his way upon the earth. And God said unto Noah, The end of all flesh is come before me; for the earth is filled with violence through them; and, behold, I will destroy them with the earth. Make thee an ark of gopher wood; rooms shalt thou make in the ark, and shalt pitch it within and without with pitch. And this is how thou shalt make it: the length of the ark three hundred cubits, the breadth of it fifty cubits, and the height of it thirty cubits. A light shalt thou make to the ark, and to a cubit shalt thou finish it upward; and the door of the ark shalt thou set in the side thereof; with lower, second, and third stories shalt thou make it. And I, behold, 1 do bring the flood of waters upon the earth, to destroy all flesh, wherein is the breath of life, from under heaven; every thing that is in the earth shall die. But I will establish my covenant with thee; and thou shalt come into the ark, thou, and thy sons, and thy wife, and thy sons' wives with thee. And of every living thing of all flesh, two of every sort shalt thou bring into the ark, to keep them alive with thee; they shall be male and female. Of the fowl after their kind, and of the cattle after their kind, of every creeping thing of the ground after its kind, two of every sort shall come unto thee, to keep them alive. And take thou unto thee of all food that is eaten, and gather it to thee; and it shall be for food for thee, and for them. Thus did Noah; according to all that God commanded him, so did he.

"And the Lord said unto Noah, Come thou and all thy house into the ark; for thee have I seen righteous before me in this generation. Of every clean beast thou shalt take to thee seven and seven, the male and his female; and of the beasts that are not clean two, the male and his female; of the fowl also of the air, seven and seven, male and female: to keep seed alive upon the face of all the earth. For yet seven days, and I will cause it to rain upon the earth forty days and forty nights; and every living thing that I have made will I destroy from off the face of the ground. And Noah did according unto all that the Lord commanded him. And Noah was six hundred years old when the flood of waters was upon the earth.

"And Noah went in, and his sons, and his wife, and his sons' wives with him, into the ark, because of the waters of the flood. Of clean beasts, and of beasts that are not clean, and of fowls, and of every thing that creepeth upon the ground, there went in two and two unto Noah into the ark, male and female, as God commanded Noah. And it came to pass after the seven days, that the waters of the flood were upon the earth. In the six hundredth year of Noah's life, in the second month, on the seventeenth day of the month, on the same day were all the fountains of the great deep broken up, and the windows of heaven were opened. And the rain was upon the earth forty days and forty nights. In the selfsame day entered Noah, and Shem, and Ham, and Japheth, the sons of Noah, and Noah's wife, and the three wives of his sons with them, into the ark; they, and every beast after its kind, and all the cattle after their kind, and every creeping thing that creepeth upon the earth after its kind, and every fowl after its kind, every bird of every sort.

"And they went in unto Noah into the ark, two and two of all flesh, wherein is the breath of life. And they that went in, went in male and female of all flesh, as God commanded him: and the Lord shut him in. And the flood was forty days upon the earth; and the waters increased, and bare up the ark, and it was lift up above the earth. And the waters prevailed, and increased greatly upon the earth; and the ark went upon the face of the waters. And the waters prevailed exceedingly upon the earth; and all the high mountains that were under the whole heaven were covered. Fifteen cubits upward did the waters prevail; and the mountains were covered. And all flesh died that moved upon the earth, both fowl, and cattle, and beast, and every creeping thing that creepeth upon the earth, and every man: all in whose nostrils was the breath of the spirit of life of all that was in the dry land, died. And every living thing was destroyed which was upon the face of the ground, both man, and cattle, and creeping thing, and fowl of the heaven; and they were destroyed from the earth: and Noah only was left, and they that were with him in the ark. And the waters prevailed upon the earth an hundred and fifty days.

"And God remembered Noah, and every living thing, and all the cattle that were with him in the ark: and God made a wind to pass over the earth, and the waters assuaged; the fountains also of the deep and the windows of heaven were stopped, and the rain from heaven was restrained; and the waters returned from off the earth continually: and after the end of an hundred and fifty days the waters decreased. And the ark rested in the seventh month, on the seventeenth day of the month, upon the mountains of Ararat. And the waters decreased continually until the tenth month: in the tenth month, on the first day of the month, were the tops of the mountains seen. And it came to pass at the end of forty days, that Noah opened the window of the ark which he had made: and he sent forth a raven, and it went forth to and fro, until the waters were dried up from off the earth. And he sent forth a dove from him, to see if the waters were abated from off the face of the ground; but the dove found no rest for the sole of her foot, and she returned unto him to the ark, for the waters were on the face of the whole earth: and he put forth his hand, and took her, and brought her in unto him into the ark. And he stayed yet other seven days; and again he sent forth the dove out of the ark; and the dove came in to him at eventide; and, lo, in her mouth an olive leaf pluckt off: so Noah knew that the waters were abated from off the earth. And he stayed yet other seven days; and sent forth the dove; and she returned not again unto him any more. And it came to pass in the six hundred and first year, in the first month, the first day of the month, the waters were dried up from off the earth: and Noah removed the covering of the ark, and looked, and, behold, the face of the ground was dried. And in the second month, on the seven and twentieth day of the month, was the earth dry.

"And God spake unto Noah, saying, Go forth of the ark, thou, and thy wife, and thy sons, and thy sons' wives with thee. Bring forth with thee every living thing that "is with thee of all flesh, both fowl, and cattle, and every creeping thing that creepeth upon the earth; that they may breed abundantly in the earth, and be fruitful, and multiply upon the earth.

"And Noah went forth, and his sons, and his wife, and his sons' wives with him: every beast, every creeping thing, and every fowl, whatsoever moveth upon the earth, after their families, went forth out of the ark. And Noah builded an altar unto the Lord; and took of every clean beast, and of every clean fowl, and offered burnt offerings on the altar. And the Lord smelled the sweet savour; and the Lord said in his heart, I will not again curse the ground any more for man's sake, for that the imagination of man's heart is evil from his youth; neither will I again smite any more every thing living, as I have done. While the earth remaineth, seedtime and harvest, and cold and heat, and summer and winter, and day and night shall not cease. And God blessed Noah and his sons, and said unto them, Be fruitful, and multiply, and replenish the earth. And the fear of you and the dread of you shall be upon every beast of the earth, and upon every fowl of the air; with all wherewith the ground teemeth, and all the fishes of the sea, into your hand are they delivered. Every moving thing that liveth shall be food for you; as the green herb have I given you all. But flesh with the life thereof, which is the blood thereof, shall ye not eat. And surely your blood, the blood of your lives, will I require; at the hand of every beast will I require it: and at the hand of man, even at the hand of every man's brother, will I require the life of man. Whoso sheddeth man's blood, by man shall his blood be shed: for in the image of God made he man. And you, be ye fruitful, and multiply; bring forth abundantly in the earth, and multiply therein.

"And God spake unto Noah, and to his sons with him, saying, And I, behold, I establish my covenant with you, and with your seed after you; and with every living creature that is with you, the fowl, the cattle and every beast of the earth with you; of all that go out of the ark, even every beast of the earth. And I will establish my covenant with you; neither shall all flesh be cut off any more by the waters of the flood; neither shall there any more be a flood to destroy the earth. And God said, This is the token of the covenant which I make between me and you and every living creature that is with you, for perpetual generations: I do set my bow in the cloud, and it shall be for a token of a covenant between me and the earth. And it shall come to pass, when I bring a cloud over the earth, that the bow shall be seen in the cloud, and I will remember my covenant, which is between me and you and every living creature of all flesh; and the waters shall no more become a flood to destroy all flesh. And the bow shall be in the cloud; and I will look upon it, that I may remember the everlasting covenant between God and every living creature of all flesh that is upon the earth. And God said unto Noah, This is the token of the covenant which I have established between me and all flesh that is upon the earth."

In this account of the deluge Biblical critics are now agreed in detecting the presence of two originally distinct and partially inconsistent narratives, which have been combined so as to present the superficial appearance of a single homogeneous story. Yet the editorial task of uniting them has been performed so clumsily that the repetitions and inconsistencies left standing in them can hardly fail to attract the attention even of a careless reader. In reproducing the text of the legend from the English Revised Version I have distinguished the two strands of the composite narrative by printing them in different types; the analysis thus exhibited is the one now generally accepted by critics.1

Of the two versions of the legend thus artificially combined, the one, printed in ordinary Roman type, is derived from what the critics call the Priestly Document or Code (usually designated by the letter P); the other, printed in italic type, is derived from what the critics call the Jehovistic or Jahwistic Document (usually designated by the letter J), which is characterized by the use of the divine name Jehovah (Jahweh, or rather Yahweh). The two documents differ conspicuously in character and style, and they belong to different ages; for while the Jehovistic narrative is probably the oldest, the Priestly Code is now generally admitted to be the latest, of the four principal documents which have been united to form the Hexateuch.

The Jehovistic document is believed to have been written in Judea in the early times of the Hebrew monarchy, probably in the ninth or eighth century before our era; the Priestly Code dates from the period after the year 586 B.C., when Jerusalem was taken by Nebuchadnezzar, king of Babylon, and the Jews were carried away by him into captivity. Both documents are in their form historical, but while the Jehovistic writer displays a genuine interest in the characters and adventures of the men and women whom he describes, the Priestly writer appears to concern himself with them only so far as he deemed them instruments in the great scheme of Providence for conveying to Israel a knowledge of God and of the religious and social institutions by which it was his gracious will that the Chosen People should regulate their lives.

The history which he writes is sacred and ecclesiastical rather than secular and civil; his preoccupation is with Israel as a church rather than as a nation. Hence, while he dwells at comparative length on the lives of the patriarchs and prophets to whom the deity deigned to reveal himself, he hurries over whole generations of common mortals, whom he barely mentions by name, as if they were mere links to connect one religious epoch with another, mere packthread on which to string at rare intervals the splendid jewels of revelation. His attitude to the past is sufficiently explained by the circumstances of the times in which he lived.

The great age of Israel was over; its independence was gone, and with it the hopes of worldly prosperity and glory. The rosy dreams of empire, which the splendid reigns of David and Solomon had conjured up in the hearts of the people, and which may have lingered for a while, like morning clouds, even after the disruption of the monarchy, had long ago faded in the clouded evening of the nation's day, under the grim reality of foreign domination. Barred from all the roads of purely mundane ambition, the irrepressible idealism of the national temperament now found a vent for itself in another direction. Its dreams took a different cast. If earth was shut upon it, heaven was still open; and like Jacob at Bethel, with enemies behind him and before, the dreamer beheld a ladder stretching up beyond the clouds, by which angelic hosts might descend to guard and comfort the forlorn pilgrim.

In short, the leaders of Israel sought to console and compensate their nation for the humiliations she had to endure in the secular sphere by raising her to a position of supremacy in the spiritual. For this purpose they constructed or perfected an elaborate system of religious ritual designed to forestall and engross the divine favour, and so to make Zion the holy city, the joy and centre of God's kingdom on earth. With these aims and ambitions the tone of public life became more and more clerical, its interests ecclesiastical, its predominant influence priestly. The king was replaced by the high priest, who succeeded even to the purple robes and golden crown of his predecessor.1 The revolution which thus substituted a line of pontiffs for a line of temporal rulers at Jerusalem, was like that which converted the Rome of the Cæsars into the Rome of the mediæval Popes.

It is this movement of thought, this current of religious aspirations setting strongly in the direction of ecclesiasticism, which is reflected, we may almost say arrested and crystallized, in the Priestly Code. The intellectual and moral limitations of the movement are mirrored in the corresponding limitations of the writer. It is the formal side of religion in which alone he is really interested; it is in the details of rites and ceremonies, of ecclesiastical furniture and garments, that he revels with genuine gusto. The deeper side of religion is practically a sealed book for him; its moral and spiritual aspects he barely glances at; into the profound problems of immortality and the origin of evil, which have agitated inquiring spirits in all the ages, he never enters. With his absorption in the minutiæ of ritual, his indifference to purely secular affairs, his predilection for chronology and genealogy, for dates and figures, in a word, for the dry bones rather than the flesh and blood of history, the priestly historian is like one of those monkish chroniclers of the Middle Ages who looked out on the great world through the narrow loophole of a cloistered cell or the many-tinted glass of a cathedral window. His intellectual horizon was narrowed, the atmosphere in which he beheld events was coloured, by the medium through which he saw them.

Thus the splendours of the Tabernacle in the wilderness, invisible to all eyes but his, are as if they had loomed on his heated imagination through the purple lights of a rose-window or the gorgeous panes of some flamboyant oriel. Even in the slow processes or sudden catastrophes which have fashioned or transformed the material universe he discerned little more than the signs and wonders vouchsafed by the deity to herald new epochs of religious dispensation. For him the work of creation was a grand prelude to the institution of the sabbath.1 The vault of heaven itself, spangled with glorious luminaries, was a magnificent dial-plate on which the finger of God pointed eternally to the correct seasons of the feasts in the ecclesiastical calendar.2 The deluge, which swept away almost the whole of mankind, was the occasion which the repentant deity took to establish a covenant with the miserable survivors; and the rainbow, glowing in iridescent radiance against the murky storm-cloud, was nothing but the divine seal appended to the covenant as a guarantee of its genuine and irrevocable character.3

For the priestly historian was a lawyer as well as an ecclesiastic, and as such he took great pains to prove that the friendly relations of God to his people rested on a strictly legal basis, being authenticated by a series of contracts into which both parties entered with all due formality. He is never so much in his element as when he is expounding these covenants; he never wearies of recalling the long series of Israel's title-deeds. Nowhere does this dry-as-dust antiquary, this rigid ritualist, so sensibly relax his normal severity, nowhere does he so nearly unbend and thaw, as when he is expatiating on the congenial subject of contracts and conveyances. His masterpiece of historical narrative is acknowledged to be his account of the negotiations into which the widowed Abraham entered with the sons of Heth in order to obtain a family vault in which to bury his wife.1 The lugubrious nature of the transaction does not damp the professional zest of the narrator; and the picture he has drawn of it combines the touches of no mean artist with the minute exactitude of a practised conveyancer. At this distance of time the whole scene still passes before us, as similar scenes may have passed before the eyes of the writer, and as they may still be witnessed in the East, when two well-bred Arab sheikhs fence dexterously over a point of business, while they observe punctiliously the stately forms and courtesies of Oriental diplomacy. But such pictures are rare indeed in this artist's gallery. Landscapes he hardly attempted, and his portraits are daubs, lacking all individuality, life, and colour. In that of Moses, which he laboured most, the great leader is little more than a lay-figure rigged out to distribute ecclesiastical upholstery and millinery.2

Very different are the pictures of the patriarchal age bequeathed to us by the author of the Jehovistic document. In purity of outline, lightness and delicacy of touch, and warmth of colouring, they are unsurpassed, perhaps unequalled, in literature. The finest effects are produced by the fewest strokes, because every stroke is that of a master who knows instinctively just what to put in and what to leave out. Thus, while his whole attention seems to be given to the human figures in the foreground, who stand out from the canvas with lifelike truth and solidity, he contrives simultaneously, with a few deft, almost imperceptible touches, to indicate the landscape behind them, and so to complete a harmonious picture which stamps itself indelibly on the memory. The scene, for example, of Jacob and Rachel at the well, with the flocks of sheep lying round it in the noontide heat, is as vivid in the writer's words as it is in the colours of Raphael.

And to this exquisite picturesqueness in the delineation of human life he adds a charming naivety, an antique simplicity, in his descriptions of the divine. He carries us back to the days of old, when no such awful gulf was supposed to yawn between man and the deity. In his pages we read how God moulded the first man out of clay, as a child shapes its mud baby; 1 how he walked in the garden in the cool of the evening and called to the shamefaced couple who had been skulking behind trees;2 how he made coats of skin to replace the too scanty fig-leaves of our first parents;3 how he shut the door behind Noah, when the patriarch had entered into the ark;4 how he sniffed the sweet savour of the burning sacrifice;5 how he came down to look at the tower of Babel,6 apparently because, viewed from the sky, it was beyond his reach of vision; how he conversed with Abraham at the door of his tent, in the heat of the day, under the shadow of the whispering oaks.7 In short, the whole work of this delightful writer is instinct with a breath of poetry, with something of the freshness and fragrance of the olden time, which invests it with an ineffable and immortal charm.8

In the composite narrative of the Great Flood which we possess in Genesis, the separate ingredients contributed by the Jehovistic and the Priestly documents respectively are distinguishable from each other both by verbal and by material differences. To take the verbal differences first, the most striking is that in the Hebrew original the deity is uniformly designated, in the Jehovistic document by the name of Jehovah (Jahweh), and in the Priestly document by the name of Elohim, which in the English version are rendered respectively by the words "Lord" and "God."

In representing the Hebrew Jehovah (Jahweh) by "Lord," the English translators follow the practice of the Jews, who, in reading the Scriptures aloud, uniformly substitute the title Adonai or "Lord" for the sacred name of Jehovah, wherever they find the latter written in the text. Hence the English reader may assume as a general rule that in the passages of the English version, where the title "Lord" is applied to the deity, the name Jehovah stands for it in the written or printed Hebrew text.1 But in the narrative of the flood and throughout Genesis the Priestly writer avoids the use of the name Jehovah and substitutes for it the term Elohim, which is the ordinary Hebrew word for God; and his reason for doing so is that according to him the divine name Jehovah was first revealed by God to Moses,2 and therefore could not have been applied to him in the earlier ages of the world. On the other hand, the Jehovistic writer has no such theory as to the revelation of the name Jehovah; hence he bestows it on the deity without scruple from the creation onwards.

Apart from this capital distinction between the documents, there are verbal differences which do not appear in the English translation. Thus, one set of words is used for "male and female" in the Jehovistic document, and quite a different set in the Priestly.3 Again, the words translated "destroy" in the English version are different in the two documents,4 and similarly with the words which the English translators represent by "die" 5 and "dried." 6

But the material differences between the Jehovistic and the Priestly narratives are still more remarkable, and as they amount in some cases to positive contradictions, the proof that they emanate from separate documents may be regarded as complete. Thus in the Jehovistic narrative the clean animals are distinguished from the unclean, and while seven of every sort of clean animals are admitted to the ark, only a pair of each sort of unclean animals is suffered to enter.7 On the other hand, the Priestly writer makes no such invidious distinction between the animals, but admits them to the ark on a footing of perfect equality, though at the same time he impartially limits them all alike to a single couple of each sort.1 The explanation of this discrepancy is that in the view of the Priestly writer the distinction between clean and unclean animals was first revealed by God to Moses,2 and could not therefore have been known to his predecessor Noah; whereas the Jehovistic writer, untroubled by any such theory, naively assumes the distinction between clean and unclean animals to have been familiar to mankind from the earliest times, as if it rested on a natural difference too obvious to be overlooked by anybody.

Another serious discrepancy between the two writers relates to the duration of the flood. In the Jehovistic narrative the rain lasted forty days and forty nights,3 and afterwards Noah passed three weeks in the ark before the water had subsided enough to let him land.4 On this reckoning the flood lasted sixty-one days. On the other hand, in the Priestly narrative it was a hundred and fifty days before the water began to sink,5 and the flood lasted altogether for twelve months and ten days.6 As the Hebrew months were lunar, twelve of them would amount to three hundred and fifty-four days, and ten days added to them would give a solar year of three hundred and sixty-four days.7 Since the Priestly writer thus assigns to the duration of the flood the approximate length of a solar year, we may safely assume that he lived at a time when the Jews were able to correct the serious error of the lunar calendar by observation of the sun.

Again, the two writers differ from each other in the causes which they allege for the flood; for whereas the Jehovistic writer puts it down to rain only,1 the Priestly writer speaks of subterranean waters bursting forth as well as of sheets of water descending from heaven.2

Lastly, the Jehovistic writer represents Noah as building an altar and sacrificing to God in gratitude for his escape from the flood.3 The Priestly writer, on the other hand, makes no mention either of the altar or of the sacrifice; no doubt because from the stand-point of the Levitical law, which he occupied, there could be no legitimate altar any-where but in the temple at Jerusalem, and because for a mere layman like Noah to offer a sacrifice would have been an unheard-of impropriety, a gross encroachment on the rights of the clergy which he could not for a moment dream of imputing to the respect-able patriarch.

Thus a comparison of the Jehovistic and the Priestly narratives strongly confirms the conclusion of the critics that the two were originally independent, and that the Jehovistic is considerably the older. For the Jehovistic writer is clearly ignorant of the law of the one sanctuary, which forbade the offering of sacrifice anywhere but at Jerusalem; and as that law was first clearly enunciated and enforced by King Josiah in 621 B.C., it follows that the Jehovistic document must have been composed some time, probably a long time, before that date. For a like reason the Priestly document must have been composed some time, probably a considerable time, after that date, since the writer implicitly recog-nizes the law of the one sanctuary by refusing to impute a breach of it to Noah. Thus, whereas the Jehovistic writer betrays a certain archaic simplicity in artlessly attributing to the earliest ages of the world the religious institutions and phraseology of his own time, the Priestly writer reveals the reflection of a later age, which has worked out a definite theory of religious evolution and applies it rigidly to history.

A very cursory comparison of the Hebrew with the Babylonian account of the Deluge may suffice to convince us that the two narratives are not independent, but that one of them must be derived from the other, or both from a common original. The points of resemblance between the two are far too numerous and detailed to be accidental. In both narratives the divine powers resolve to destroy mankind by a great flood; in both the secret is revealed beforehand to a man by a god, who directs him to build a great vessel, in which to save himself and seed of every kind. It is probably no mere acciden-tal coincidence that in the Babylonian story, as reported by Berosus, the hero saved from the flood was the tenth King of Babylon, and that in the Hebrew story Noah was the tenth man in descent from Adam. In both narratives the favoured man, thus warned of God, builds a huge vessel in several stories, makes it water-tight with pitch or bitumen, and takes into it his family and animals of all sorts; in both, the deluge is brought about in large measure by heavy rain, and lasts for a greater or less number of days; in both, all mankind are drowned except the hero and his family; in both, the man sends forth birds, a raven and a dove, to see whether the water of the flood has abated; in both, the dove after a time returns to the ship because it could find no place in which to rest; in both, the raven does not return; in both, the vessel at last grounds on a mountain; in both, the hero, in gratitude for his rescue, offers sacrifice on the mountain; in both, the gods smell the sweet savour, and their anger is appeased.

So much for the general resemblance between the Babylonian story as a whole and the Hebrew story as a whole. But if we take into account the separate elements of the Hebrew story, we shall see that the Jehovistic narrative is in closer agreement than the Priestly with the Babylonian. Alike in the Jehovistic and in the Babylonian narrative special prominence is given to the number seven. In the Jehovistic version, Noah has a seven days' warning of the coming deluge; he takes seven of every sort of clean animals with him into the ark; he allows intervals of seven days to elapse between the successive despatches of the dove from the ark. In the Babylonian version the flood lasts at its greatest height for seven days; and the hero sets out the sacrificial vessels by sevens on the mountain. Again, alike in the Jehovistic and the Babylonian version, special mention is made of shutting the door of the ship or ark when the man, his family, and the animals have entered into it; in both alike we have the picturesque episode of sending forth the raven and the dove from the vessel, and in both alike the offering of the sacrifice, the smelling of it by the gods, and their consequent appeasement. On the other hand, in certain particulars the Priestly narrative in Genesis approaches more closely than the Jehovistic to the Babylonian. Thus, in both the Priestly and the Babylonian version exact directions are given for the construction of the vessel; in both alike it is built in several stories, each of which is divided into numerous cabins; in both alike it is made watertight by being caulked with pitch or bitumen; in both alike it grounds on a mountain; and in both alike on issuing from the vessel the hero receives the divine blessing.

But if the Hebrew and Babylonian narratives are closely related to each other, how is the relation to be explained? The Babylonian cannot be derived from the Hebrew, since it is older than the Hebrew by at least eleven or twelve centuries. Moreover, "as Zimmern has remarked, the very essence of the Biblical narrative presupposes a country liable, like Babylonia, to inundations; so that it cannot be doubted that the story was 'indigenous in Babylonia, and transplanted to Palestine.'"1 But if the Hebrews derived the story of the great flood from Babylonia, when and how did they do so? We have no information on the subject, and the question can only be answered conjecturally. Some scholars of repute have supposed that the Jews first learned the legend in Babylon during the captivity, and that the Biblical narrative is consequently not older than the sixth century before our era."

This view might be tenable if we only possessed the Hebrew version of the Deluge legend in the Priestly recension; for the Priestly Code, as we saw, was probably composed during or after the captivity, and it is perfectly possible that the writers of it acquired a knowledge of the Babylonian tradition either orally or from Babylonian literature during their exile or perhaps after their return to Palestine; for it is reasonable to suppose that the intimate relations which the conquest established between the two countries may have led to a certain diffusion of Babylonian literature in Palestine, and of Jewish literature in Babylonia. On this view some of the points in which the Priestly narrative departs from the Jehovistic and approximates to the Babylonian may conceivably have been borrowed directly by the Priestly writers from Babylonian sources. Such points are the details as to the construction of the ark, and in particular the smearing of it with pitch or bitumen, which is a characteristic product of Babylonia.1 But that the Hebrews were acquainted with the story of the great flood, and that too in a form closely akin to the Babylonian, long before they were carried away into captivity, is abundantly proved by the Jehovistic narrative in Genesis, which may well date from the ninth century before our era and can hardly be later than the eighth.

Assuming, then, that the Hebrews in Palestine were familiar from an early time with the Babylonian legend of the deluge, we have still to ask, how and when did they learn it? Two answers to the question have been given. On the one hand, it has been held that the Hebrews may have brought the legend with them, when they migrated from Babylonia to Palestine about two thousand years before Christ.2 On the other hand, it has been suggested that, after their settlement in Palestine, the Hebrews may have borrowed the story from the native Canaanites, who in their turn may have learned it through the medium of Babylonian literature sometime in the second millennium before our era.3 Which, if either, of these views is the true one, we have at present no means of deciding.

In later times Jewish fancy tricked out the story of the flood with many new and often extravagant details designed apparently to satisfy the curiosity or tickle the taste of a degenerate age, which could not rest satisfied with the noble simplicity of the narrative in Genesis. Among these tawdry or grotesque additions to the ancient legend we read how men lived at ease in the days before the flood, for by a single sowing they reaped a harvest sufficient for the needs of forty years, and by their magic arts they could compel the sun and moon to do them service.   Instead of nine months children were in their mothers' wombs only a few days, and immediately on their birth could walk and talk and set even the demons at defiance. It was this easy luxurious life that led men astray and lured them into the commission of those sins, especially the sins of wantonness and rapacity, which excited the wrath of God and determined him to destroy the sinners by a great flood.

Yet in his mercy he gave them due warning; for Noah, instructed by the deity, preached to them to mend their ways, threatening them with the flood as the punishment of their iniquity;   and this he did for no less than one hundred and twenty years. Even at the end of that period God gave mankind another week's grace, during which, strange to say, the sun rose in the west every morning and set in the east every night. But nothing could move these wicked men to repentance; they only mocked and jeered at the pious Noah when they saw him building the ark. He learned how to make it from a holy book, which had been given to Adam by the angel Raziel and which contained within it all knowledge, human and divine. It was made of sapphires, and Noah enclosed it in a golden casket when he took it with him into the ark, where it served him as a time-piece to distinguish night from day; for so long as the flood prevailed neither the sun nor the moon shed any light on the earth. Now the deluge was caused by the male waters from the sky meeting the female waters which issued forth from the ground. The holes in the sky by which the upper waters escaped were made by God when he removed two stars out of the constellation of the Pleiades; and in order to stop this torrent of rain God had afterwards to bung up the two holes with a couple of stars borrowed from the constellation of the Bear. That is why the Bear runs after the Pleiades to this day: she wants her children back, but she will never get them till after the Last Day.

When the ark was ready, Noah proceeded to gather the animals into it. They came trooping in such numbers that the patriarch could not take them all in, but had to sit at the door of the ark and make a choice; the animals which lay down at the door he took in, and the animals which stood up he shut out. Even after this principle of natural selection had been rigidly enforced, the number of species of reptiles which were taken on board was no less than three hundred and sixty-five, and the number of species of birds thirty-two. No note was taken, at least none appears to have been recorded, of the number of mammals, but many of them were among the passengers, as we shall see presently. Before the flood the unclean animals far outnumbered the clean, but after the flood the proportions were reversed, because seven pairs1 of each of the clean sorts were preserved in the ark, but only two pairs of the unclean. One creature, the reêm, was so huge that there was no room for it in the ark, so Noah tethered it to the outside of the vessel, and the animal trotted behind. The giant Og, king of Bashan, was also much too big to go into the ark, so he sat on the top of it, and in that way escaped with his life. With Noah himself in the ark were his wife Naamah, daughter of Enosh, and his three sons and their wives. An odd pair who also found refuge in the ark were Falsehood and Misfortune. At first Falsehood presented himself alone at the door of the ark, but was refused a passage on the ground that there was no admission except for married couples. So he went away, and meeting with Misfortune induced her to join him, and the pair were received into the ark.

When all were aboard, and the flood began, the sinners gathered some seven hundred thousand strong round about the ark and begged and prayed to be taken in. When Noah sternly refused to admit them, they made a rush at the door as if to break it in, but the wild beasts that were on guard round about the ark fell upon them and devoured some of them, and all that escaped the beasts were drowned in the rising flood. A whole year the ark floated on the face of the waters; it pitched and tossed on the heaving billows, and all inside of it were shaken up like lentils in a pot. The lions roared, the oxen lowed, the wolves howled, and the rest bellowed after their several sorts. But the great difficulty with which Noah had to struggle in the ark was the question of victuals. Long afterwards his son Shem confided to Eliezer, the servant of Abraham, the trouble his father had had in feeding the whole menagerie. The poor man was up and down, up and down, by day and by night. For the daylight animals had to be fed by day and the nocturnal animals by night; and the giant Og had his rations served out to him through a hole in the roof. Though the lion suffered the whole time from a fever, which kept him comparatively quiet, yet he was very surly and ready to fly out on the least provocation. Once when Noah did not bring him his dinner fast enough, the noble animal gave him such a blow with his paw that the patriarch was lame for the rest of his natural life and therefore incapable of serving as a priest. It was on the tenth day of the month Tammuz that Noah sent forth the raven to see and report on the state of the flood. But the raven found a corpse floating on the water and set to work to devour it, so that he quite forgot to return and hand in his report. A week later Noah sent out the dove, which at last, on its third flight, brought back in its bill an olive leaf plucked on the Mount of Olives at Jerusalem; for the Holy Land had not been ravaged by the deluge. When he stepped out of the ark Noah wept to see the widespread devastation wrought by the flood. A thank-offering for his delivery was offered by his son Shem, for the patriarch himself was still suffering from the effects of his encounter with the lion and could not officiate in person.1

From another late account we learn some interesting particulars as to the internal arrangements of the ark and the distribution of the passengers. The beasts and cattle by the battened down in the hold, the middle deck was occupied by the birds, and the promenade deck was reserved for Noah his family. But the men and the women were kept strictly apart. The patriarch and his sons lodged in the east end of the ark, and his wife and his sons' wives lodged in the west end; and between them as a barrier was interposed the dead body of Adam, which was thus rescued from a watery grave. This account, which further favours us with the exact dimensions of the ark in cubits and the exact day of the week and of the month when the passengers got aboard, is derived from an Arabic manuscript found in the library of the Convent of St. Catherine on Mount Sinai. The author would seem to have been an Arab Christian, who flourished about the time of the Mohammedan conquest, though the manuscript is of later date.1

§ 4. Ancient Greek Stories of a Great Flood

Legends of a destructive deluge, in which the greater part of mankind perished, meet us in the literature of ancient Greece. As told by the mythographer Apollodorus, the story runs thus: "Deucalion was the son of Prometheus. He reigned as king in the country about Phthia and married Pyrrha, the daughter of Epimetheus and Pandora, the first woman fashioned by the gods. But when Zeus wished to destroy the men of the Bronze Age, Deucalion by the advice of Prometheus constructed a chest or ark, and having stored in it what was needful he entered into it with his wife. But Zeus poured a great rain from the sky upon the earth and washed down the greater part of Greece, so that all men perished except a few, who flocked to the high mountains near. Then the mountains in Thessaly were parted, and all the world beyond the Isthmus and Peloponnese was overwhelmed. But Deucalion in the ark, floating over the sea for nine days and as many nights, grounded on Parnassus, and there, when the rains ceased, he disembarked and sacrificed to Zeus, the God of Escape. And Zeus sent Hermes to him and allowed him to choose what he would, and he chose men. And at the bidding of Zeus he picked up stones and threw them over his head; and the stones which Deucalion threw became men, and the stones which Pyrrha threw became women. That is why in Greek people are called laoi from laas, 'a stone.'"1

In this form the Greek legend is not older than about the middle of the second century before our era, the time when Apollodorus wrote, but in substance it is much more ancient, for the story was told by Hellanicus, a Greek historian of the fifth century B.C., who said that Deucalion's ark drifted not to Parnassus but to Mount Othrys in Thessaly.2 The other version has the authority of Pindar, who wrote earlier than Hellanicus in the fifth century B.C.; for the poet speaks of Deucalion and Pyrrha descending from Parnassus and creating the human race afresh out of stones.3 According to some, the first city which they founded after the great flood was Opus, situated in the fertile Locrian plain between the mountains and the Euboic Gulf. But Deucalion is reported to have dwelt at Cynus, the port of Opus, distant a few miles across the plain; and there his wife's tomb was shown to travellers down to the beginning of our era. Her husband's dust is said to have rested at Athens.4 The coast of Locris, thus associated with traditions of the great flood, is rich in natural beauties. The road runs at the foot of the mountains, which are of soft and lovely outlines, for the most part covered with forest; while the low hills and glades by the sea are wooded with pines, plane-trees, myrtles, lentisks, and other trees and shrubs, their luxuriant verdure fed by abundant springs. Across the blue waters of the gulf the eye roams to the island of Euboea, with its winding shores and long line of finely cut mountains standing out against the sky. The home of Deucalion was on a promontory jutting into the gulf. On it, and on the isthmus which joins it to the land, may still be seen the mouldering ruins of Cynus; a line of fortification walls, built of sandstone, runs round the edge of the height, and the summit is crowned by the remains of a mediaeval tower. The ground is littered with ancient potsherds.1

It is said that an ancient city on Parnassus was overwhelmed by the rains which caused the deluge, but the inhabitants, guided by the howling of wolves, found their way to the peaks of the mountain, and when the flood had subsided they descended and built a new city, which they called Lycorea or Wolf-town in gratitude for the guidance of the wolves.2 Lucian speaks of Deucalion's ark, with the solitary survivors of the human race, grounding on what was afterwards the site of Wolf-town, while as yet all the rest of the world was submerged.3 But according to another account, the mountain to which Deucalion escaped was a peak in Argolis, which was afterwards called Nemea from the cattle which cropped the greensward on its grassy slopes. There the hero built an altar in honour of Zeus the Deliverer, who had delivered him from the great flood.4 The mountain on which he is said to have alighted is probably the table-mountain, now called Phouka, whose broad flat top towers high above the neighbouring hills and forms a conspicuous landmark viewed from the plain of Argos.5

The Megarians told how, in Deucalion's flood, Megarus, son of Zeus, escaped by swimming to the top of Mount Gerania, being guided by the cries of some cranes, which flew over the rising waters and from which the mountain afterwards received its new name.6 According to Aristotle, writing in the fourth century B.C., the ravages of the deluge in Deucalion's time were felt most sensibly "in ancient Hellas, which is the country about Dodona and the river Achelous, for that river has changed its bed in many places. In those days the land was inhabited by the Selli and the people who were then called Greeks (Graikoi) but are now named Hellenes."7 Some people thought that the sanctuary of Zeus at Dodona was founded by Deucalion and Pyrrha, who dwelt among the Molossians of that country.1 In the fourth century B.C. Plato also mentions, without describing, the flood which took place in the time of Deucalion and Pyrrha, and he represents the Egyptian priests as ridiculing the Greeks for believing that there had been only one deluge, whereas there had been many.2 The Parian chronicler, who drew up his chronological table in the year 265 B.C.,3 dated Deucalion's flood one thousand two hundred and sixty-five years before his own time;4 according to this calculation the cataclysm occurred in the year 1539 B.C.

At a later age the Roman poet Ovid decked out the tradition of the great flood in the pinchbeck rhetoric which betrayed the decline of literary taste. He tells us that Jupiter, weary of the wickedness and impiety of the men of the Iron Age, resolved to destroy the whole of mankind at one fell swoop. His first idea was to overwhelm them under the flaming thunderbolts which he brandished in his red right hand; but on reflection he laid these dangerous weapons aside, lest the upper air and heaven itself should catch fire from the great conflagration which they would kindle on earth; and in this prudent resolution he was confirmed by an imperfect recollection of an old prophecy that the whole world, sky and earth alike, was destined to perish in a grand and final combustion.

Accordingly he decided on the safer course of turning on the celestial taps and drowning the whole wicked race under the tremendous shower bath. So he shut up the North Wind in the cave of Aeolus, to prevent him from sweeping the murky clouds from the blue sky, and he let loose the South Wind, who flew abroad, rigged out in all the stage properties calculated to strike terror into the beholder. He flapped his dripping wings; his dreadful face was veiled in pitchy blackness; mists sat on his forehead, his beard was soaking wet, and water ran down from his hoary hair. In his train the sky lowered, thunder crashed, and the rainbow shone in spangled glory against the dark rain-clouds. To help the sky-god in his onslaught on mankind his sea-blue brother Neptune summoned an assembly of the rivers and bade them roll in flood over the land, while he himself fetched the earth a swashing blow with his trident, causing it to quake like a jelly.

The fountains of the great deep were now opened. The deluge poured over the fields and meadows, whirling away trees, cattle, men and houses. Far and wide nothing was to be seen but a shoreless sea of tossing, turbid water. The farmer now rowed in a shallop over the field where he had lately guided the oxen at the plough-tail, and peering down he could discern his crops and the roof of his farmhouse submerged under the waves. He dropped his anchor on a green meadow, his keel grated on his own vineyard, and he fished for trout in the tops of the tall elms. Seals now lolled and sprawled where goats had lately nibbled the herbage, and dolphins gambolled and plunged in the woods. When at last nothing remained above the waste of waters but the two peaks of Parnassus, toppling over the heaving billows and reaching up above the clouds, Deucalion and his wife drifted in a little boat to the mountain, and landing adored the nymphs of the Corycian cave and the prophetic goddess Themis, who managed the business of the oracle before if was taken over by Apollo. A righteous and godfearing man was Deucalion, and his wife was just such another.

Touched with compassion at the sight of the honest pair, the sole survivors of so many thousands, Jupiter now dispersed the clouds and the deluge, revealing the blue sky and the green earth to each other once more. So Neptune also laid aside his trident, and summoning the bugler Triton, his back blue with the growth of the purple-shell, he ordered him to sound the "Retire." The bugler obeyed, and putting the shell to his lips he blew from his puffed cheeks such a blast that at the sound of it all the waves and rivers fell back and left the land high and dry. This was all very well, but what were Deucalion and Pyrrha to do now, left solitary in a desolate world, where not a sound broke the dreadful silence save the melancholy lapping of the waves on the lonely shore? They shed some natural tears, and then wiping them away they resolved to consult the oracle.

So, pacing sadly by the yellow turbid waters of the Cephisus, they repaired to the temple of the goddess. The sacred edifice presented a melancholy spectacle, its walls still overgrown with moss and sea-weed, its courts still deep in slime; and naturally no fire flamed or smouldered on the defiled altars. However, the goddess was fortunately at home, and in reply to the anxious inquiries of the two suppliants she instructed them, as soon as they had quitted the temple, to veil their heads, unloose their robes, and throw behind their backs the bones of their great parent. This strange answer bewildered them, and for a long time they remained silent. Pyrrha was the first to find her voice, and when at last she broke silence it was to declare respectfully but firmly that nothing would induce her to insult her mother's ghost by flinging her bones about. Her husband, more discerning, said that perhaps by their great parent the goddess meant them to understand the earth, and that by her bones she signified the rocks and stones embedded in the ground. They were not very hopeful of success, but nothing else occurring to them to do, they decided to make the attempt. So they carried out the instructions of the oracle to the letter, and sure enough the stones which Deucalion threw turned into men, and the stones which Pyrrha threw turned into women. Thus was the earth repeopled after the great flood.1

Anyone who compares the laboured ingenuity of this account of the deluge with the majestic simplicity of the corresponding narrative in Genesis is in a position to measure the gulf which divides great literature from its tinsel imitation.

In his account of the catastrophe Ovid so far followed ancient Greek tradition as to represent Deucalion and Pyrrha landing on the peak of Parnassus. Later Roman writers carried the pair much further afield; one of them landed the voyagers on Mount Athos,2 and another conveyed them as far as Mount Etna.3

Various places in Greece, as we have seen, claimed the honour of having been associated in a particular manner with Deucalion and the great flood. Among the claimants, as might have been expected, were the Athenians, who, pluming themselves on the vast antiquity from which they had inhabited the land of Attica, had no mind to be left out in the cold when it came to a question of Deucalion and the deluge. They annexed him accordingly by the simple expedient of alleging that when the clouds gathered dark on Parnassus and the rain came down in torrents on Lycorea where Deucalion reigned as king, he fled for safety to Athens, and on his arrival founded a sanctuary of Rainy Zeus, and offered thank-offerings for his escape.1 In this brief form of the legend there is no mention of a ship, and we seem to be left to infer that the hero escaped on foot. Be that as it may, he is said to have founded the old sanctuary of Olympian Zeus and to have been buried in the city. Down to the second century of our era the local Athenian guides pointed with patriotic pride to the grave of the Greek Noah near the later and far statelier temple of Olympian Zeus, whose ruined columns, towering in solitary grandeur above the modern city, still attract the eye from far, and bear silent but eloquent witness to the glories of ancient Greece.2

Nor was this all that the guides had to show in memory of the tremendous cataclysm. Within the great precinct overshadowed by the vast temple of Olympian Zeus they led the curious traveller to a smaller precinct of Olympian Earth, where they pointed to a cleft in the ground a cubit wide. Down that cleft, they assured him, the waters of the deluge ran away, and down it every year they threw cakes of wheaten meal kneaded with honey.3 These cakes would seem to have been soul-cakes destined for the consumption of the poor souls who perished in the great flood; for we know that a commemoration service or requiem mass was celebrated every year at Athens in their honour. It was called the Festival of the Water-bearing,4 which suggests that charitable people not only threw cakes but poured water down the cleft in the ground to slake the thirst as well as to stay the hunger of the ghosts in the nether world.

Another place where the great flood was commemorated by a similar ceremony was Hierapolis on the Euphrates. There down to the second century of our era the ancient Semitic deities were worshipped in the old way under a transparent disguise imposed on them, like modern drapery on ancient statues, by the nominally Greek civilization which the conquests of Alexander had spread over the East. Chief among these aboriginal divinities was the great Syrian goddess Astarte, who to her Greek worshippers masqueraded under the name of Hera. Lucian has bequeathed to us a very valuable description of the sanctuary and the strange rites performed in it.1 He tells us that according to the general opinion the sanctuary was founded by Deucalion, in whose time the great flood took place. This gives Lucian occasion to relate the Greek story of the deluge, which according to him ran as follows. The present race of men, he says, are not the first of human kind; there was another race which perished wholly. We are of the second breed, which multiplied after the time of Deucalion. As for the folk before the flood, it is said that they were exceedingly wicked and lawless; for they neither kept their oaths, nor gave hospitality to strangers, nor respected suppliants, wherefore the great calamity befell them.

So the fountains of the deep were opened, and the rain descended in torrents, the rivers swelled, and the sea spread far over the land, till there was nothing but water, water everywhere, and all men perished. But Deucalion was the only man who, by reason of his prudence and piety, survived and formed the link between the first and the second race of men; and the way in which he was saved was this. He had a great ark, and into it he entered with his wives and children; and as he was entering there came to him pigs, and horses, and lions, and serpents, and all other land animals, all of them in pairs.

He received them all, and they did him no harm; nay, by God's help there was a great friendship between them, and they all sailed in one ark so long as the flood prevailed on the earth. Such says Lucian, is the Greek story of Deucalion's deluge; but the people of Hierapolis, he goes on, tell a marvellous thing. They say that a great chasm opened in their country, and all the water of the flood ran away down it.

And when that happened, Deucalion built altars and founded a holy temple of Hera beside the chasm. "I have seen the chasm," he proceeds, "and a very small one it is under the temple. Whether it was large of old and has been reduced to its present size in course of time, I know not, but what I saw is undoubtedly small. In memory of this legend they perform the following ceremony; twice a year water is brought from the sea to the temple. It is brought not by the priests only, but by all Syria and Arabia, by and from beyond the Euphrates many men go to the sea, and all of them bring water. The water is poured into the chasm, and though the chasm is small yet it receives a mighty deal of water. In doing this they say that they comply with the custom which Deucalion instituted in the sanctuary for a memorial at once of calamity and of mercy." 1 Moreover, at the north gate of the great temple there stood two tall columns, or rather obelisks, each about three hundred and sixty feet high; and twice a year a man used to ascend one of them and remain for seven days in that airy situation on the top of the obelisk. Opinions differed as to why he went there, and what he did up aloft. Most people thought that at that great height he was within hail of the gods in heaven, who were near enough to hear distinctly the prayers which he offered on behalf of the whole land of Syria. Others, however, opined that he clambered up the obelisk to signify how men had ascended to the tops of mountains and of tall trees in order to escape from the waters of Deucalion's flood.2

In this late Greek version of the deluge legend the resemblances to the Babylonian version are sufficiently close; and a still nearer trait is supplied by Plutarch, who says that Deucalion let loose a dove from the ark in order to judge by its return or its flight whether the storm still continued or had abated.1 In this form the Greek legend of the great flood was unquestionably coloured, if not moulded, by Semitic influence, whether the colours and the forms were imported from Israel or from Babylon.

But Hierapolis on the Euphrates was not the only place in Western Asia which Greek tradition associated with the deluge of Deucalion. There was, we are told, a certain Nannacus, king of Phrygia, who lived before the time of Deucalion, and, foreseeing the coming catastrophe, gathered his people into the sanctuaries, there to weep and pray. Hence "the age of Nannacus" became a proverbial expression for great antiquity or loud lamentations.2 According to another account Nannacus or Annacus, the Phrygian, lived over three hundred years, and when his neighbours, apparently tired of the old man, inquired of the oracle how much longer he might be expected to live, they received the discouraging reply that when the patriarch died, all men would perish with him. So the Phrygians lamented bitterly, which gave rise to the old proverb about "weeping for Nannacus." 3 The Greek satyric poet Herodas puts the proverb in the mouth of a mother, who brings her brat to the schoolmaster to receive a richly deserved thrashing; and in so doing she refers sorrowfully to the cruel necessity she was under of paying the school fees, even though she were to "weep like Nannacus." 4

When the deluge had swept away the whole race of mankind, and the earth had dried up again, Zeus commanded Prometheus and Athena to fashion images of mud, and then summoning the winds he bade them breathe into the mud images and make them live. So the place was called Iconium after the images (eikones) which were made there.5 Some have thought that the patriarchal Nannacus or Annacus was no other than the Biblical Enoch or Hanoch,6 who lived before the flood for three hundred and sixty-five years and was then removed from the world in a mysterious fashion.1 But against this identification it is to be said that the name Nannacus would seem to be genuine Greek, since it occurs in Greek inscriptions of the island of Cos.2

Another city of Asia Minor which appears to have boasted of its connexion with the great flood was Apamea Cibotos in Phrygia. The surname of Cibotos, which the city assumed, is the Greek word for chest or ark 3; and on coins of the city, minted in the reigns of Severus, Macrinus, and Philip the Elder, we see the ark floating on water with two passengers in it, whose figures appear from the waist upwards; beside the ark two other human figures, one male and the other female, are represented standing; and lastly, on the top of the chest are perched two birds, one of them said to be a raven and the other a dove carrying an olive-branch. As if to remove all doubt as to the identification of the legend, the name Noe, the Greek equivalent of Noah, is inscribed on the ark. No doubt, the two human figures represent Noah and his wife twice over, first in the ark, and afterwards outside of it.4 These coin types prove unquestionably that in the third century of our era the people of Apamea were acquainted with the Hebrew tradition of the Noachian deluge in the form in which the story is narrated in the Book of Genesis.

They may easily have learned it from their Jewish fellow-citizens, who in the first century before our era were so numerous or so wealthy that on one occasion they contributed no less than a hundred pounds weight of gold to be sent as an offering to Jerusalem.1 Whether at Apamea the tradition of the deluge was purely Jewish in origin, or whether it was grafted upon an old native legend of a great flood, is a question on which scholars are not agreed.2 Though the deluge associated with the name of Deucalion was the most familiar and famous, it was not the only one recorded by Greek tradition. Learned men, indeed, distinguished between three such great catastrophes, which had befallen the world at different epochs. The first, we are told, took place in the time of Ogyges, the second in the time of Deucalion, and the third in the time of Dardanus.3 Ogyges or Ogygus, as the name is also spelled, is said to have founded and reigned over Thebes in Boeotia,4 which, according to the learned Varro, was the oldest city in Greece, having been built in antediluvian times before the earliest of all the floods.5 The connection of Ogyges with Boeotia in general and with Thebes in particular is further vouched for by the name Ogygian which was bestowed on the land,6 on the city,7 and on one of its gates.8

Yet the Athenians, jealous of the superior antiquity which this tradition assigned to their hated rival, claimed the ancient Boeotian hero as an aboriginal of their country;1

one tradition describes Ogyges as a king of Attica,2 and another represents him as the founder and king of Eleusis.3 So great was the devastation wrought in Attica by the flood that the country remained without kings from the time of Ogyges down to the reign of Cecrops.4 If we may trust the description of a rhetorical poet, the whole earth was submerged by the deluge, even the lofty peaks of Thessaly were covered, and the snowy top of Parnassus itself was lashed by the snowy billows.5 With regard to the date of the catastrophe, some writers of antiquity profess to give us more or less exact information. The learned Roman scholar Varro tells us that the Boeotian Thebes was built about two thousand one hundred years before the time when he was writing, which was in or about the year 36 B.C.; and as the deluge, according to him, took place in the lifetime of Ogyges but after he had founded Thebes, we infer that in Varro's opinion the great flood occurred in or soon after the year 2136 B.C.6 Still more precise is the statement of Julius Africanus, a Christian author who drew up a chronicle of the world from the Creation down to the year 221 A.D. He affirms that the deluge of Ogyges happened just one thousand and twenty years before the first Olympiad, from which the Greeks dated their exact reckoning; and as the first Olympiad fell in the year 776 B.C., we arrive at the year 1796 B.C. as the date to which the Christian chronicler referred the great Ogygian flood. It happened, he tells us, in the reign of Phoroneus, king of Argos.

He adds for our further information that Ogyges, who survived the deluge to which he gave his name, was a contemporary of Moses and flourished about the time when that great prophet led the children of Israel out of Egypt; and he clinches his chain of evidence by observing that at a time when God was visiting the land of Egypt with hailstorms and other plagues, it was perfectly natural that distant parts of the earth should simultaneously" feel the effects of the divine anger, and in particular it was just and right that Attica should smart beneath the rod, since according to some people, including the historian Theopompus, the Athenians were in fact colonists from Egypt and therefore shared the guilt of the mother-country.1 According to the Church historian Eusebius, the great flood in the time of Ogyges occurred about two thousand two hundred years after the Noachian deluge and two hundred and fifty years before the similar catastrophe in the days of Deucalion.2 It would seem indeed to have been a point of honour with the early Christians to claim for the flood recorded in their sacred books an antiquity far more venerable than that of any flood described in mere profane writings. We have seen that Julius Africanus depresses Ogyges from the age of Noah to that of Moses; and Isidore, the learned bishop of Seville at the beginning of the seventh century, heads his list of floods with the Noachian deluge, while the second and third places in order of time are assigned to the floods of Ogyges and Deucalion respectively; according to him, Ogyges was a contemporary of the patriarch Jacob, while Deucalion lived in the days of Moses. The bishop was, so far as I am aware, the first of many writers who have appealed to fossil shells imbedded in remote mountains as witnesses to the truth of the Noachian tradition.2

If Ogyges was originally, as seems probable, a Boeotian rather than an Attic hero, the story of the deluge in his time may well have been suggested by the vicissitudes of the Copaic Lake which formerly occupied a large part of Central Boeotia.1 For, having no outlet above ground, the lake depended for its drainage entirely on subterranean passages or chasms which the water had hollowed out for itself in the course of ages through the limestone rock, and according as these passages were clogged or cleared the level of the lake rose or fell. In no lake, perhaps, have the annual changes been more regular and marked than in the Copaic; for while in winter it was a reedy mere, the haunt of thousands of wild fowl, in summer it was a more or less marshy plain, where cattle browsed and crops were sown and reaped. So well recognized were the vicissitudes of the seasons that places on the bank of the lake such as Orchomenus, Lebadea, and Copae, had summer roads and winter roads by which they communicated with each other, the winter roads following the sides of the hills, while the summer roads struck across the plain. With the setting in of the heavy autumnal rains in November the lake began to rise and reached its greatest depth in February or March, by which time the mouths of the emissories were completely submerged and betrayed their existence only by swirls on the surface of the mere. Yet even then the lake presented to the eye anything but an unbroken sheet of water.

Viewed from a height, such as the acropolis of Orchomenus, it appeared as an immense fen, of a vivid green colour, stretching away for miles and miles, overgrown with sedge, reeds, and canes, through which the river Cephisus or Melas might be seen sluggishly oozing, while here and there a gleam of sunlit water, especially towards the northeast corner of the mere, directed the eye to what looked like ponds in the vast green swamp. Bare grey mountains on the north and east, and the beautiful wooded slopes of Helicon on the south, bounded the fen. In spring the water began to sink. Isolated brown patches, where no reeds grew, were the first to show as islands in the mere; and as the season advanced they expanded more and more till they met. By the middle of summer great stretches, especially in the middle and at the edges, were bare. In the higher parts the fat alluvial soil left by the retiring waters was sown by the peasants and produced crops of corn, rice, and cotton; while the lower parts, overgrown by rank grass and weeds, were grazed by herds of cattle and swine. In the deepest places of all, the water often stagnated the whole summer, though there were years when it retreated even from these, leaving behind it only a bog or perhaps a stretch of white clayey soil, perfectly dry, which the summer heat seamed with a network of minute cracks and fissures. By the end of August the greater part of the basin was generally dry, though the water did not reach its lowest point till October. At that time what had lately been a fen was only a great brown expanse, broken here and there by a patch of green marsh, where reeds and other water-plants grew. In November the lake began to fill again fast.

Such was the ordinary annual cycle of changes in the Copaic Lake in modern times, and we have no reason to suppose that it was essentially different in antiquity. But at all times the water of the lake has been liable to be raised above or depressed below its customary level by unusually heavy or scanty rainfall in winter or by the accidental clogging or opening of the chasms. As we read in ancient authors of drowned cities on the margin of the lake,1 so a modern traveller tells of villagers forced to flee before the rising flood, and of vineyards and corn-fields seen under water.2 One such inundation, more extensive and destructive than any of its predecessors, may have been associated ever after with the name of Ogyges.

Among the dead cities whose ruins are scattered in and around the wide plain that was once the Copaic Lake, none is more remarkable or excites our curiosity more keenly than one which bears the modern name of Goulas or Gla. Its ancient name and history are alike unknown; even legend is silent on the subject. The extensive remains occupy the broad summit of a low rocky hill or tableland which rises abruptly on all sides from the dead flat of the surrounding country. When the lake was full, the place must have been an island, divided by about a mile of shallow and weedy water from the nearest point in the line of cliffs which formed the eastern shore of the lake. A fortification wall, solidly built of roughly squared blocks of stone, encircles the whole edge of the table-land, and is intersected by four gates flanked by towers of massive masonry. Within the fortress are the ruins of other structures, including the remains of a great palace constructed in the style, though not on the plan, of the prehistoric palaces of Mycenae and Tiryns. The fortress and palace of Gla would seem to have been erected in the Mycenaean age by a people akin in civilization, if not in race, to the builders of Tiryns and Mycenae, though less skilled in the science of military engineering; for the walls do not exhibit the enormous stones of Tiryns, and the gates are arranged on a plan far less formidable to an assailant than the gates of the two Argive citadels. The scanty remains of pottery and other domestic furniture on the plateau appear to indicate that it was occupied only for a short time, and the traces of fire on the palace point to the conclusion that its end was sudden and violent. Everything within the place bears the imprint of a single plan and a single period; there is no trace of an earlier or a later settlement. Created at a blow, it would seem to have perished at a blow and never to have been inhabited again. In its solitude and silence, remote from all human habitations, looking out from its grey old walls over the vast Copaic plain to the distant mountains which bound the horizon on all sides, this mysterious fortress is certainly one of the most impressive sights in Greece.1

Can it be that this ancient and forgotten town, once lapped on all sides by the waters of the Copaic Lake, was the home of the legendary Ogyges, and that he forsook it, perhaps in consequence of an inundation, to migrate to the higher and drier site which was afterwards known as Thebes? The hypothesis would go some way to explain the legends which gathered round his memory; but it is no more than a simple guess, and as such I venture to hazard it.

The theory which would explain the great flood of Ogyges by an extraordinary inundation of the Copaic Lake, is to some extent supported by an Arcadian parallel. We have seen that in Greek legend the third great deluge was associated with the name of Dardanus. Now according to one account, Dardanus at first reigned as a king in Arcadia, but was driven out of the country by a great flood, which submerged the lowlands and rendered them for a long time unfit for cultivation. The inhabitants retreated to the mountains, and for a while made shift to live as best they might on such food as they could procure; but at last, concluding that the land left by the water was not sufficient to support them all, they resolved to part; some of them remained in the country with Dimas, son of Dardanus, for their king; while the rest emigrated under the leadership of Dardanus himself to the island of Samothrace.1 According to a Greek tradition, which the Roman Varro accepted, the birthplace of Dardanus was Pheneus in north Arcadia.2 The place is highly significant, for, if we except the Copaic area, no valley in Greece is known to have been from antiquity subject to inundations on so vast a scale and for such long periods as the valley of Pheneus.3

The natural conditions in the two regions are substantially alike. Both are basins in a limestone country without any outflow above ground; both receive the rain water which pours into them from the surrounding mountains; both are drained by subterranean channels which the water has worn or which earthquakes have opened through the rock; and whenever these outlets are silted up or otherwise closed, what at other times is a plain becomes converted for the time being into a lake. But with these substantial resemblances are combined some striking differences between the two landscapes. For while the Copaic basin is a vast stretch of level ground little above sea-level and bounded only by low cliffs or gentle slopes, the basin of Pheneus is a narrow upland valley closely shut in on every side by steep frowning mountains, their upper slopes clothed with dark pine woods and their lofty summits capped with snow for many months of the year. The river which drains the basin through an underground channel is the Ladon, the most romantically beautiful of all the rivers of Greece. Milton's fancy dwelt on "sanded Ladon's lilied banks;" even the prosaic Pausanias exclaimed that there was no fairer river either in Greece or in foreign lands;1 and among the memories which I brought back from Greece I recall none with more delight than those of the days I spent in tracing the river from its birthplace in the lovely lake, first to its springs on the far side of the mountain, and then down the deep wooded gorge through which it hurries, brawling and tumbling over rocks in sheets of greenish-white foam, to join the sacred Alpheus. Now the passage by which the Ladon makes its way underground from the valley of Pheneus has been from time to time blocked by an earthquake, with the result that the river has ceased to flow. When I was at the springs of the Ladon in 1895, I learned from a peasant on the spot that three years before, after a violent shock of earthquake, the water ceased to run for three hours, the chasm at the bottom of the pool was exposed, and fish were seen lying on the dry ground. After three hours the spring began to flow a little, and three days later there was a loud explosion, and the water burst forth in immense volume. Similar stoppages of the river have been reported both in ancient and modern times; and whenever the obstruction has been permanent, the valley of Pheneus has been occupied by a lake varying in extent and depth with the more or less complete stoppage of the subterranean outlet.

According to Pliny there had been down to his day five changes in the condition of the valley from wet to dry and from dry to wet, all of them caused by earthquakes.2 In Plutarch's time the flood rose so high that the whole valley was under water, which pious folk attributed to the somewhat belated wrath of Apollo at Hercules, who had stolen the god's prophetic tripod from Delphi and carried it off to Pheneus about a thousand years before.1 However, later in the same century the waters had again subsided, for the Greek traveller Pausanias found the bottom of the valley to be dry land, and knew of the former existence of the lake only by tradition.2 At the beginning of the nineteenth century the basin was a swampy plain, for the most part covered with fields of wheat or barley. But shortly after the expulsion of the Turks, through neglect of the precautions which the Turkish governor had taken to keep the mouth of the subterranean outlet open, the channel became blocked, the water, no longer able to escape, rose in its bed, and by 1830 it formed a deep lake about five miles long by five miles wide. And a broad lake of greenish-blue water it still was when I saw it in the autumn of 1895, with the pine-clad mountains descending steeply in rocky declivities or sheer precipices to the water's edge, except for a stretch of level ground on the north, where the luxuriant green of vineyards and maize-fields contrasted pleasingly with the blue of the lake and the sombre green of the pines. The whole scene presented rather the aspect of a Swiss than of a Greek landscape. A few years later and the scene was changed. Looking down into the valley from a pass on a July afternoon, a more recent traveller beheld, instead of an expanse of sea-blue water, a blaze of golden corn with here and there a white point of light showing where a fustanella'd reaper was at his peaceful toil. The lake had disappeared, perhaps for ever; for we are told that measures have now been taken to keep the subterranean outlets permanently open, and so to preserve for the corn the ground which has been won from the water.3

A permanent mark of the height to which the lake of Pheneus attained in former days and at which, to all appearance, it must have stood for many ages, is engraved on the sides of the mountains which enclose the basin. It is a sharply drawn line running round the contour of the mountains at a uniform level of not less than a hundred and fifty feet above the bottom of the valley. The trees and shrubs extend down the steep slopes to this line and there stop abruptly. Below the line the rock is of a light-yellow colour and almost bare of vegetation; above the line the rock is of a much darker colour. The attention of travellers has been drawn to this conspicuous mark from antiquity to the present day. The ancient traveller Pausanias noticed it in the second century of our era, and he took it to indicate the line to which the lake rose at the time of its highest flood, when the city of Pheneus was submerged.1 This interpretation has been questioned by some modern writers, but there seems to be little real doubt that the author of the oldest extant guide-book to Greece was substantially right; except that the extremely sharp definition of the line and its permanence for probably much more than two thousand years appear to point to a long-continued persistence of the lake at this high level rather than to a mere sudden and temporary rise in a time of inundation. "It is evident," says the judicious traveller Dodwell, "that a temporary inundation could not effect so striking a difference in the superficies of the rock, the colour of which must have been changed from that of the upper parts by the concreting deposit of many ages." 2

In a valley which has thus suffered so many alternations between wet and dry, between a broad lake of sea-blue water and broad acres of yellow corn, the traditions of great floods cannot be lightly dismissed; on the contrary everything combines to confirm their probability. The story, therefore, that Dardanus, a native of Pheneus, was compelled to emigrate by a great inundation which swamped the lowlands, drowned the fields, and drove the inhabitants to the upper slopes of the mountains, may well rest on a solid foundation of fact. And the same may be true of the flood recorded by Pausanias, which rose and submerged the ancient city of Pheneus at the northern end of the lake.1

From his home in the highlands of Arcadia, the emigrant Dardanus is said to have made his way to the island of Samothrace.2 According to one account, he floated thither on a raft;3 but according to another version of the legend, the great flood overtook him, not in Arcadia, but in Samothrace, and he escaped on an inflated skin, drifting on the face of the waters till he landed on Mount Ida, where he founded Dardania or Troy.4 Certainly, the natives of Samothrace, who were great sticklers for their antiquity, claimed to have had a deluge of their own before any other nation on earth. They said that the sea rose and covered a great part of the flat land in their island, and that the survivors retreated to the lofty mountains which still render Samothrace one of the most conspicuous features in the northern Aegean and are plainly visible in clear weather from Troy.5 As the sea still pursued them in their retreat, they prayed to the gods to deliver them, and on being saved they set up landmarks of their salvation all round the island and built altars on which they continued to sacrifice down to later ages. And many centuries after the great flood fishermen still occasionally drew up in their nets the stone capitals of columns, which told of cities drowned in the depths of the sea. The causes which the Samothracians alleged for the inundation were very remarkable. The catastrophe happened, according to them, not through a heavy fall of rain, but through a sudden and extraordinary rising of the sea occasioned by the bursting of the barriers which till then had divided the Black Sea from the Mediterranean. At that time the enormous volume of water dammed up behind these barriers broke bounds, and cleaving for itself a passage through the opposing land created the straits which are now known as the Bosphorus and the Dardanelles, through which the waters of the Black Sea have ever since flowed into the Mediterranean. When the tremendous torrent first rushed through the new opening in the dam, it washed over a great part of the coast of Asia, as well as the flat lands of Samothrace.1

Now this Samothracian tradition is to some extent confirmed by modern geology. "At no very distant period," we are told, "the land of Asia Minor was continuous with that of Europe, across the present site of the Bosphorus, forming a barrier several hundred feet high, which dammed up the waters of the Black Sea. A vast extent of eastern Europe and of western central Asia thus became a huge reservoir, the lowest part of the lip of which was probably situated somewhat more than 200 feet above the sea-level, along the present southern watershed of the Obi, which flows into the Arctic Ocean. Into this basin, the largest rivers of Europe, such as the Danube and the Volga, and what were then great rivers of Asia, the Oxus and Jaxartes, with all the intermediate affluents, poured their waters. In addition, it received the overflow of Lake Balkash, then much larger; and, probably, that of the inland sea of Mongolia. At that time, the level of the Sea of Aral stood at least 60 feet higher than it does at present. Instead of the separate Black, Caspian, and Aral seas, there was one vast Ponto-Aralian Mediterranean, which must have been prolonged into arms and fiords along the lower valleys of the Danube, and the Volga (in the course of which Caspian shells are now found as far as the Kuma), the Ural, and the other affluent rivers—while it seems to have sent its overflow, northward, through the present basin of the Obi."1

This enormous reservoir or vast inland sea, bounded and held up by a high natural dam joining Asia Minor to the Balkan Peninsula, appears to have existed down to the Pleistocene period; and the erosion of the Dardanelles, by which the pent-up waters at last found their way into the Mediterranean, is believed to have taken place towards the end of the Pleistocene period or later.2 But man is now known for certain to have inhabited Europe in the Pleistocene period; some hold that he inhabited it in the Pliocene or even the Miocene period.3 Hence it seems possible that the inhabitants of Eastern Europe should have preserved a traditional memory of the vast inland Ponto-Aralian sea and of its partial desiccation through the piercing of the dam which divided it from the Mediterranean, in other words, through the opening of the Bosphorus and the Dardanelles. If that were so, the Samothracian tradition might be allowed to contain a large element of historical truth in regard to the causes assigned for the catastrophe.

On the other hand geology seems to lend no support to the tradition of the catastrophe itself. For the evidence tends to prove that the strait of the Dardanelles was not opened suddenly, like the bursting of a dam, either by the pressure of the water or the shock of an earthquake, but that on the contrary it was created gradually by a slow process of erosion which must have lasted for many centuries or even thousands of years ; for the strait "is bounded by undisturbed Pleistocene strata forty feet thick, through which, to all appearance, the present passage has been quietly cut." 1 Thus the lowering of the level of the Ponto-Aralian sea to that of the Mediterranean can hardly have been sudden and catastrophic, accompanied by a vast inundation of the Asiatic and European coasts ; more probably it was effected so slowly and gradually that the total amount accomplished even in a generation would be imperceptible to ordinary observers or even to close observers unprovided with instruments of precision.

Hence, instead of assuming that Samothracian tradition preserved a real memory of a widespread inundation consequent on the opening of the Dardanelles, it seems safer to suppose that this story of a great flood is nothing but the guess of some early philosopher, who rightly divined the origin of the straits without being able to picture to himself the extreme slowness of the process by which nature had excavated them. As a matter of fact, the eminent physical philosopher Strata, who succeeded Theophrastus as head of the Peripatetic school in 287 B.C., actually maintained this view on purely theoretical grounds, not alleging it as a tradition which had been handed down from antiquity, but arguing in its favour from his observations of the natural features of the Black Sea. He pointed to the vast quantities of mud annually washed down by great rivers into the Euxine, and he inferred that but for the outlet of the Bosphorus the basin of that sea would in time be silted up. Further, he conjectured that in former times the same rivers had forced for themselves a passage through the Bosphorus, allowing their collected waters to escape first to the Propontis, and then from it through the Dardanelles to the Mediterranean. Similarly he thought that the Mediterranean had been of old an inland sea, and that its junction with the Atlantic was effected by the dammed up water cutting for itself an opening through the Straits of Gibraltar.1 Accordingly we may conclude that the cause which the Samothracians alleged for the great flood was derived from an ingenious speculation rather than from an ancient tradition.

There are some grounds for thinking that the flood story which the Greeks associated with the names of Deucalion and Pyrrha may in like manner have been, not so much a reminiscence of a real event, as an inference founded on the observation of certain physical facts. We have seen that in one account the mountains of Thessaly are said to have been parted by the deluge in Deucalion's time, and that in another account the ark, with Deucalion in it, is reported to have drifted to Mount Othrys in Thessaly.

These references seem to indicate Thessaly as the original seat of the legend; and the indication is greatly strengthened by the view which the ancients took of the causes that had moulded the natural features of the country. Thus Herodotus relates a tradition that in ancient times Thessaly was a great lake or inland sea, shut in on all sides by the lofty mountains of Ossa and Pelion, Olympus, Pindus, and Othrys, through which there was as yet no opening to allow the pent-up waters of the rivers to escape. Afterwards, according to the Thessalians, the sea-god Poseidon, who causes earthquakes, made an outlet for the lake through the mountains, by cleaving the narrow gorge of Tempe, through which the river Peneus has ever since drained the Thessalian plain. The pious historian intimates his belief in the truth of this local tradition. "Whoever believes," says he, "that Poseidon shakes the earth, and that chasms caused by earthquakes are his handiwork, would say, on seeing the gorge of the Peneus, that Poseidon had made it. For the separation of the mountains, it seems to me, is certainly the effect of an earthquake." [1] The view of the father of history was substantially accepted by later writers of antiquity,[2] though one of them would attribute the creation of the gorge and the drainage of the lake to the hero Hercules, among whose beneficent labours for the good of mankind the construction of waterworks on a gigantic scale was commonly reckoned.[3] More cautious or more philosophical authors contented themselves with referring the origin of the defile to a simple earthquake, without expressing any opinion as to the god or hero who may have set the tremendous disturbance in motion.[4]

Yet we need not wonder that popular opinion in this matter should incline to the theory of divine or heroic agency, for in truth the natural features of the pass of Tempe are well fitted to impress the mind with a religious awe, with a sense of vast primordial forces which, by the gigantic scale of their operations, present an overwhelming contrast to the puny labours of man. The traveller who descends at morning into the deep gorge from the west, may see, far above him, the snows of Olympus flushed with a golden glow under the beams of the rising sun, but as he pursues the path downwards the summits of the mountains disappear from view, and he is confronted on either hand only by a stupendous wall of mighty precipices shooting up in prodigious grandeur and approaching each other in some places so near that they almost seem to meet, barely leaving room for the road and river at their foot, and for a strip of blue sky overhead. The cliffs on the side of Olympus, which the traveller has constantly before his eyes, since the road runs on the south or right bank of the river, are indeed the most magnificent and striking in Greece, and in rainy weather they are rendered still more impressive by the waterfalls that pour down their sides to swell the smooth and steady current of the stream.

112

The grandeur of the scenery culminates about the middle of the pass, where an enormous crag rears its colossal form high in air, its soaring summit crowned with the ruins of a Roman castle. Yet the sublimity of the landscape is tempered and softened by the richness and verdure of the vegetation. In some parts of the defile the cliffs recede sufficiently to leave little grassy flats at their foot, where thickets of evergreens—the laurel, the myrtle, the wild olive, the arbutus, the agnus castus—are festooned with wild vines and ivy, and variegated with the crimson bloom of the oleander and the yellow gold of the jasmine and laburnum, while the air is perfumed by the luscious odours of masses of aromatic plants and flowers. Even in the narrowest places the river bank is overshadowed by spreading plane-trees, which stretch their roots and dip their pendent boughs into the stream, their dense foliage forming so thick a screen as almost to shut out the sun. The scarred and fissured fronts of the huge cliffs themselves are tufted with dwarf oaks and shrubs, wherever these can find a footing, their verdure contrasting vividly with the bare white face of the limestone rock; while breaks here and there in the mountain wall open up vistas of forests of great oaks and dark firs mantling the steep declivities. The overarching shade and soft luxuriance of the vegetation strike the traveller all the more by contrast if he comes to the glen in hot summer weather after toiling through the dusty, sultry plains of Thessaly, without a tree to protect him from the fierce rays of the southern sun, without a breeze to cool his brow, and with little variety of hill and dale to relieve the dull monotony of the landscape.1 No wonder that speculation should have early busied itself with the origin of this grand and beautiful ravine, and that primitive religion and science alike should have ascribed it to some great primeval cataclysm, some sudden and tremendous outburst of volcanic energy, rather than to its true cause, the gradual and agelong erosion of water.2

Hence we may with some confidence conclude that the cleft in the Thessalian mountains, which is said to have been rent by Deucalion's flood, was no other than the gorge of Tempe. Indeed, without being very rash, we may perhaps go farther and conjecture that the story of the flood itself was suggested by the desire to explain the origin of the deep and narrow defile. For once men had pictured to themselves a great lake dammed in by the circle of the Thessalian mountains, the thought would naturally occur to them, what a vast inundation must have followed the bursting of the dam, when the released water, rushing in a torrent through the newly opened sluice, swept over the subjacent lowlands carrying havoc and devastation in its train! If there is any truth in this conjecture, the Thessalian story of Deucalion's flood and the Samothracian story of the flood of Dardanus stood exactly on the same footing; both were mere inferences drawn from the facts of physical geography; neither of them contained any reminiscences of actual events. In short, both were what Sir Edward Tylor has called myths of observation rather than historical traditions.1

§ 5 Other European Stories of a Great Flood

Apart from the ancient Greek stories of a great flood, it is remarkable that very few popular traditions of a universal or widespread deluge have been recorded in Europe.

An Icelandic version of the tradition occurs in the Younger Edda, the great collection of ancient Norse myths and legends which was put together by Snorri Sturluson about 1222

A.D.2 We there read how the god Bor had three divine sons, Odin, Wili, and We, and how these sons slew the giant Ymir. From the wounds of the dying giant there gushed such a stream of blood that it drowned all the other giants except one, named Bergelmir, who escaped with his wife in a boat, and from whom the later race of giants is descended. Afterwards the sons of Bor took the carcase of the giant Ymir and fashioned the world out of it, for down to that time the world, as we see it now, did not exist. Out of his flowing blood they made the ocean, the seas, and all waters; out of his flesh the earth; out of his bones the mountains; out of his teeth and broken bones the rocks and stones; and out of his skull the vault of the sky, which they set up on four horns, with a dwarf under each horn to prop it up.1 However, this Norse tale differs from the Babylonian, the Hebrew, and the Greek in dating the great flood before the creation of the world and of mankind; it hardly therefore belongs to the same class of legends.2 In it the formation of the world out of the body and blood of a giant has been compared to the Babylonian cosmogony recorded by Berosus, according to which the god Bel made the world by splitting a giantess in two and converting one half of her into the earth and the other half of her into the sky, after which he cut off his own head, and from the flowing blood mingled with earth the other gods moulded the human race.3 The resemblance between the two cosmogonies is fairly close, but whether, as some think, this proves a direct Babylonian influence on the Norse legend may be doubted.4 A Welsh legend of a deluge runs thus. Once upon a time the lake of Llion burst and flooded all lands, so that the whole human race was drowned, all except Dwyfan and Dwyfach, who escaped in a naked or mastless ship and re-peopled the island of Prydain (Britain). The ship also contained a male and a female of every sort of living creature, so that after the deluge the animals were able to propagate their various kinds and restock the world.5

A Lithuanian story of a great flood is also reported. One day it chanced that the supreme god Pramzimas was looking out of a window of his heavenly house, and surveying the world from this coign of vantage he could see nothing but war and injustice among mankind. The sight so vexed his righteous soul that he sent two giants, Wandu and Wejas, down to the sinful earth to destroy it. Now the two giants were no other than Water and Wind, and they laid about them with such hearty good will, that after twenty nights and twenty days there was very little of the world left standing. The deity now looked out of the window again to see how things were progressing, and, as good luck would have it, he was eating nuts at the time. As he did so, he threw down the shells, and one of them happened to fall on the top of the highest mountain, where animals and a few pairs of human beings had sought refuge from the flood. The nutshell came, in the truest sense of the word, as a godsend; everybody clambered into it, and floated about on the surface of the far-spreading inundation. At this critical juncture the deity looked out of the window for the third time, and, his wrath being now abated, he gave orders for the wind to fall and the water to subside. So the remnant of mankind were saved, and they dispersed over the earth. Only a single couple remained on the spot, and from them the Lithuanians are descended. But they were old and naturally a good deal put out by their recent experience; so to comfort them God sent the rainbow, which advised them to jump over the bones of the earth nine times. The aged couple did as they were bid; nine times they jumped, and nine other couples sprang up in consequence, the ancestors of the nine Lithuanian tribes.1

The gipsies of Transylvania are reported to tell the following legend of a deluge. There was a time, they say, when men lived for ever, and knew neither trouble nor cold, neither sickness nor sorrow. The earth brought forth the finest fruits; flesh grew on many trees, and milk and wine flowed in many rivers. Men and animals lived happily with each other, and they had no fear of death.

But one day it happened that an old man came into the country and begged a cottager to give him a night's lodging. He slept in the cottage and was well entertained by the cottager's wife. Next day, on taking his leave, the old man gave his host a small fish in a little vessel, and said, "Keep this fish and do not eat it. In nine days I will return, and if you give me the fish back, I will reward you." Then away he went. The housewife looked at the little fish and said to her husband, "Goodman, how would it be if we roasted the fish?" Her husband answered, "I promised the old man to give him back the fish. You must swear to me to spare the fish and to keep it till the old man returns." The wife swore, saying, "I will not kill the fish, I will keep it, so help me God!" After two days the woman thought, "The little fish must taste uncommonly well, since the old man sets such store on it, and will not let it be roasted, but carries it with him about the world." She thought about it a long time, till at last she took the little fish out of the vessel, and threw it on the hot coals. Hardly had she done so than the first flash of lightning came down from heaven and struck the woman dead. Then it began to rain. The rivers overflowed their beds and swamped the country. On the ninth day the old man appeared to his host and said, "Thou hast kept thine oath and not killed the fish. Take thee a wife, gather thy kinsfolk together, and build thee a boat in which ye can save yourselves. All men and all living things must be drowned, but ye shall be saved. Take with thee also animals and seeds of trees and herbs, that ye may afterwards people the earth again." Then the old man disappeared, and the man did as he was bidden. It rained for a whole year, and nothing was to be seen but water and sky. After a year the water sank, and the man, with his wife and kinsfolk, and the animals, disembarked. They had now to work, tilling and sowing the earth, to gain a living. Their life was now labour and sorrow, and worse than all came sickness and death. So they multiplied but slowly, and many, many thousands of years passed before mankind was as numerous as they had been before the flood, and as they are now.1 The incident of the fish in this story reminds us of the fish which figures prominently in the ancient Indian legend of a great flood;2 and accordingly it seems possible that, as Dr. H. von Wlislocki believes,3 the ancestors of the gipsies brought the legend with them to Transylvania from their old home in India.

A story of a great flood has also been recorded among the Voguls, a people of the Finnish or Ugrian stock, who inhabit the country both on the east and the west of the Ural Mountains, and who therefore belong both to Asia and Europe.4 The story runs thus. After seven years of drought the Great Woman said to the Great Man, "It has rained elsewhere. How shall we save ourselves? The other giants are gathered in a village to take counsel. What shall we do?" The Great Man answered, "Let us cut a poplar in two, hollow it out, and make two boats. Then we shall weave a rope of willow roots five hundred fathoms long. We shall bury one end of it in the earth and fasten the other to the bow of our boats. Let every man with children embark in the boat with his family, and let them be covered in with a tarpaulin of cowhide, let victuals be made ready for seven days and seven nights and put under the tarpaulin. And let us place pots of melted butter in each boat." Having thus provided for their own safety, the two giants ran about the villages, urging the inhabitants to build boats and weave ropes. Some did not know how to set about it, and the giants showed them how it should be done.

Others preferred to seek a place of refuge, but they sought in vain, and the Great Man, to whom they betook themselves because he was their elder, told them that he knew no place of refuge large enough to hold them. "See," said he, "the holy water will soon be on us; for two days we have heard the rumble of its waves. Let us embark without delay." The earth was soon submerged, and the people who had not built boats perished in the hot water. The same fate befell the owners of boats whose ropes were too short, and likewise those who had not provided themselves with liquid butter wherewith to grease the rope as it ran out over the gunwale. On the seventh day the water began to sink, and soon the survivors, set foot on dry ground. But there were neither trees nor plants on the face of the earth; the animals had perished; even the fish had disappeared. The survivors were on the point of dying of hunger, when they prayed to the great god Numi-târom to create anew fish, animals, trees, and plants, and their prayer was heard.1

Some curious relics of the great flood are still pointed out in Savoy. Here and there a huge iron or bronze ring may be seen fixed into a steep rock in some apparently inaccessible position. Tradition runs that when the water of the deluge had covered all the low-lying parts of Savoy, such persons as were lucky enough to own boats fastened them to these rings, which afforded them a temporary security. There are three of these rings in the Mont de Salève, which overlooks Julien in the Haute-Savoie, and there is another in the mountains of Voirons. Again, in the Passo del Cavollo there is a well-known stone bearing great hoof-marks. These, the peasants say, were made by a horse, for which Noah could find no room in the ark. When the flood rose, the animal leaped on to this rock, which was the highest he could see; and as fast as the drowning people tried to clamber up it, the horse beat them off, till the water overwhelmed him also.2

§ 6. Supposed Persian Stories of a Great Flood

Some scholars have held that in ancient Persian literature they can detect the elements of diluvial traditions. Thus in the Bundahis, a Pahlavi work on cosmogony, mythology, and legendary history, we read of a conflict which the angel Tistar, an embodiment of the bright star Sirius, waged with the Evil Spirit apparently in the early ages of the world. When the sun was in the sign of Cancer, the angel converted himself successively into the forms of a man, a horse, and a bull, and in each form he produced rain for ten days and nights, every drop of the rain being as big as a bowl; so that at the end of the thirty days the water stood at the height of a man all over the world, and all noxious creatures, the breed of the Evil Spirit, were drowned in the caves and dens of the earth. It is the venom of these noxious creatures, diffused in the water, which has made the sea salt to this day.1 But this story has all the appearance of being a cosmogonic myth devised to explain why the sea is salt; it is certainly not a diluvial tradition of the ordinary type, since nothing is said in it about mankind; indeed we are not even given to understand that the human race had come into existence at the time when the angelic battle with the principle of evil took place.2

Another ancient Persian story recorded in the Zend-Avesta, has sometimes been adduced as a diluvial tradition. We read that Yima was the first mortal with whom the Creator Ahura Mazda deigned to converse, and to whom the august deity revealed his law. For nine hundred winters the sage Yima, under the divine superintendence, reigned over the world, and during all that time there was neither cold wind nor hot wind, neither disease nor death; the earth was replenished with flocks and herds, with men and dogs and birds, and with red blazing fires. But as there was neither disease nor death mankind and animals increased at such an alarming rate that on two occasions, at intervals of three hundred years, it became absolutely necessary to enlarge the earth in order to find room for the surplus population. The necessary enlargement was successfully carried out by Yima with the help of two instruments, a golden ring and a gold-inlaid dagger, which he had received as insignia of royalty at the hands of the Creator. However, after the third enlargement it would seem that either the available space of the universe or the patience of the Creator was exhausted; for he called a council of the celestial gods, and as a result of their mature deliberations he informed Yima that "upon the material world the fatal winters are going to fall, that shall bring the fierce, foul frost; upon the material world the fatal winters are going to fall, that shall make snow-flakes fall thick, even an aredvi deep on the highest tops of mountains. And all the three sorts of beasts shall perish, those that live in the wilderness, and those that live on the tops of the mountains, and those that live in the bosom of the dale, under the shelter of stables."

Accordingly the Creator warned Yima to provide for himself a place of refuge in which he could find safety from the threatened calamity. He was told to make a square enclosure (Vara), as long as a riding-ground on every side, and to convey into it the seeds of sheep and oxen, of men, of dogs, of birds, and of red blazing fires. "There thou shalt establish dwelling places, consisting of a house with a balcony, a courtyard, and a gallery. Thither thou shalt bring the seeds of men and women, of the greatest, best, and finest kinds on this earth; thither thou shalt bring the seeds of every kind of cattle, of the greatest, best, and finest kinds on this earth. Thither thou shalt bring the seeds of every kind of tree, of the greatest, best, and finest kinds on this earth; thither thou shalt bring the seeds of every kind of fruit, the fullest of food and sweetest of odour. All those seeds shalt thou bring, two of every kind, to be kept inexhaustible there, so long as those men shall stay in the enclosure (Vara). There shall be no humpbacked, none bulged forward there; no impotent, no lunatic; no Poverty, no lying; no meanness, no jealousy; no decayed tooth, no leprous to be confined, nor any of the brands wherewith Angra Mainyu stamps the bodies of mortals." Yima obeyed the divine command, and made the enclo-

117

sure, and gathered into it the seeds of men and animals, of trees and fruits, the choicest and the best. On that blissful abode the sun, moon, and stars rose only once a year, but on the other hand a whole year seemed only as one day. Every fortieth year to every human couple were born two children, a male and a female, and so it was also with every sort of cattle. And the men in Yima's enclosure lived the happiest life.1

In all this it is hard to see any vestige of a flood story. The destruction with which the animals are threatened is to be the effect of severe winters and deep snow, not of a deluge; and nothing is said about repeopling the world after the catastrophe by means of the men and animals who had been preserved in the enclosure. It is true that the warning given by the Creator to Yima, and the directions to bestow himself and a certain number of animals in a place of safety, resemble the warning given by God to Noah and the directions about the building and use of the ark. But in the absence of any reference to a deluge we are not justified in classing this old Persian story with diluvial traditions.2

§ 7. Ancient Indian Stories of a Great Flood

No legend of a great flood is to be found in the Vedic hymns, the most ancient literary monuments of India, which appear to have been composed at various dates between 1500 and 1000 B.C., while the Aryans were still settled in the Punjab and had not yet spread eastward into the valley of the Ganges. But in the later Sanscrit literature a well-marked story of a deluge repeatedly occurs in forms which combine a general resemblance with some variations of detail. The first record of it meets us in the Satapatha Brahmana, an important prose treatise on sacred ritual, which is believed to have been written not long before the rise of Buddhism, and therefore not later than the sixth century before Christ. The Aryans then occupied the upper valley of the Ganges as well as the valley of the Indus; but they were probably as yet little affected by the ancient civilizations of Western Asia and Greece. Certainly the great influx of Greek ideas and Greek art came centuries later with Alexander's invasion in 326 B.C.1 As related in the Satapatha Brahmana the story of the great flood runs as follows :—

"In the morning they brought to Manu water for washing, just as now also they are wont to bring water for washing the hands. When he was washing himself, a fish came into his hands. It spake to him the word, 'Rear me, I will save thee!'

'Wherefrom wilt thou save me?'

'A flood will carry away all these creatures: from that I will save thee!'

'How am I to rear thee?'

It said, 'As long as we are small, there is great destruction for us; fish devours fish. Thou wilt first keep me in a jar. When I outgrow that, thou wilt dig a pit and keep me in it. When I outgrow that, thou wilt take me down to the sea, for then I shall be beyond destruction.' It soon became a ghasha (a large fish); for that grows largest of all fish. Thereupon it said, 'In such and such a year that flood will come. Thou shalt then attend to me by preparing a ship; 1 and when the flood has risen thou shalt enter into the ship, and I will save thee from it.' After he had reared it in this way, he took it down to the sea. And in the same year which the fish had indicated to him, he attended to the advice of the fish by preparing a ship;2 and when the flood had risen, he entered into the ship. The fish then swam up to him, and to its horn he tied the rope of the ship, and by that means he passed swiftly up to yonder northern mountain. It then said, 'I have saved thee. Fasten the ship to a tree; but let not the water cut thee off, whilst thou art on the mountain. As the water subsides, thou mayest gradually descend!' Accordingly he gradually descended, and hence that slope of the northern mountain is called 'Manu's descent.' The flood then swept away all these creatures, and Manu alone remained here.

"Being desirous of offspring, he engaged in worshipping and austerities. During this time he also performed a pâka-sacrifice; he offered up in the waters clarified butter, sour milk, whey, and curds. Thence a woman was produced in a year; becoming quite solid she rose; clarified butter gathered in her footprint. Mitra and Varuna met her. They said to her, 'Who art thou?'

'Manu's daughter,' she replied.

'Say thou art ours,' they said.

'No,' she said, 'I am the daughter of him who begat me.'

They desired to have a share in her. She either agreed or did not agree, but passed by them. She came to Manu. Manu said to her, 'Who art thou?'

'Thy daughter,' she replied.

'How, illustrious one, art thou my daughter?' he asked.

She replied, 'Those offerings of clarified butter, sour milk, whey, and curds, which thou madest in the waters, with them thou hast begotten me. I am the blessing; make use of me at the sacrifice! If thou wilt make use of me at the sacrifice, thou wilt become rich in offspring and cattle. Whatever blessing thou shalt invoke through me, all that shall be granted to thee!'

He accordingly made use of her as the benediction in the middle of the sacrifice; for what is intermediate between the fore-offerings and the after-offerings, is the middle of the sacrifice. With her he went on worshipping and performing austerities, wishing for offspring. Through her he generated this race, which is this race of Manu; and whatever blessing he invoked through her, all that was granted to him." 1

The next record of the flood legend in Sanscrit literature meets us in the Mahabharata, the vast Indian epic, which, in the form in which we now possess it, is about eight times as long as the Iliad and Odyssey put together. The nucleus of this huge compilation may date from the fifth century before Christ; through successive expansions it attained its present enormous bulk in the early centuries of our era. The evidence of inscriptions proves that by the year 500 A.D. the poem was complete.2 As told in the epic, the legend runs thus :—

"There was a great sage [rishi] Manu, son of Vivasvat, majestic, in lustre equal to Prajâpati. In energy, fiery vigour, prosperity, and austere fervour he surpassed both his father and his grandfather. Standing with uplifted arm, on one foot, on the spacious Badari, he practised intense austere fervour. This direful exercise he performed, with his head downwards, and with unwinking eyes, for ten thousand years. Once, when, clad in dripping rags, with matted hair, he was so engaged, a fish came to him on the banks of the Chîrinî, and spake: 'Lord, I am a small fish; I dread the stronger ones, and from them you must save me. For the stronger fish devour the weaker; this has been immemorially ordained as our means of subsistence. Deliver me from this flood of apprehension in which I am sinking, and I will requite the deed.' Hearing this, Manu, filled with compassion, took the fish in his hand, and bringing him to the water threw him into a jar bright as a moonbeam. In it the fish, being excellently tended, grew; for Manu treated him like a son. After a long time he became very large, and could not be contained in the jar.

Then, seeing Manu, he said again, 'In order that I may thrive, remove me elsewhere.' Manu then took him out of the jar, brought him to a large pond, and threw him in. There he continued to grow for very many years. Although the pond was two yojanas long, and one yojana broad, the lotus-eyed fish found in it no room to move; and again said to Manu, 'Take me to Ganga, the dear queen of the ocean-monarch; in her I shall dwell; or do as thou thinkest best, for I must contentedly submit to thy authority, as through thee I have exceedingly increased.' Manu accordingly took the fish and threw him into the river Ganga. There he waxed for some time, when he again said to Manu, 'From my great bulk I cannot move in the Ganga; be gracious and remove me quickly to the ocean.' Manu took him out of the Ganga; and cast him into the sea. Although so huge, the fish was easily borne, and pleasant to touch and smell, as Manu carried him. When he had been thrown into the ocean he said to Manu, 'Great lord, thou hast in every way preserved me; now hear from me what thou must do when the time arrives. Soon shall all these terrestrial objects, both fixed and moving, be dissolved. The time for the purification of the worlds has now arrived. I therefore inform thee what is for thy greatest good.

'The period dreadful for the universe, moving and fixed, has come. Make for thyself a strong ship, with a cable attached; embark in it with the seven sages [rishis], and stow in it, carefully preserved and assorted, all the seeds which have been described of old by Brahmanas. When embarked in the ship, look out for me; I shall come recognizable by my horn. So shalt thou do; I greet thee and depart. These great waters cannot be crossed over without me. Distrust not my word.'

Manu replied, 'I shall do as thou hast said.' After taking mutual leave they departed each on his own way. Manu then, as enjoined, taking with him the seeds, floated on the billowy ocean in the beautiful ship. He then thought on the fish, which, knowing his desire, arrived with all speed, distinguished by a horn. When Manu saw the horned leviathan, lofty as a mountain, he fastened the ship's cable to the horn. Being thus attached, the fish dragged the ship with great rapidity, transporting it across the briny ocean which seemed to dance with its waves and thunder with its waters. Tossed by the tempests, the ship whirled like a reeling and intoxicated woman. Neither the earth, nor the quarters of the world appeared; there was nothing but water, air, and sky. In the world thus confounded, the seven sages [rishis], Manu, and the fish were beheld.

So, for very many years, the fish, unwearied, drew the ship over the waters; and brought it at length to the highest peak of Himavat. He then, smiling gently, said to the sages, 'Bind the ship without delay to this peak.' They did so accordingly. And that highest peak of Himavat is still known by the name of Naubandhana ('the Binding of the Ship'). The friendly fish (or god, animisha) then said to the sages, 'I am the Prajapati Brahma, than whom nothing higher can be reached. In the form of a fish I have delivered you from this great danger. Manu shall create all living beings, gods, demigods [asuras] men, with all worlds, and all things moving and fixed. By my favour and through severe austere fervour, he shall attain perfect insight into his creative work, and shall not become bewildered.' Having thus spoken, the fish in an instant disappeared. Manu, desirous to call creatures into existence and bewildered in his work, performed a great act of austere fervour; and then began visibly to create all living beings. This which I have narrated is known as the Matsyaka Purana (or 'Legend of the Fish')."1

In this latter version Manu is not a common man but a great seer, who by his religious austerities and the favour of the Supreme Being is promoted to the dignity of Creator of the world and of all living things, including gods and men.

The same legend is repeated, with minor variations, in the later class of Sanscrit books known as the Puranas. These are epic works, didactic in character and sectarian in Purpose, generally designed to recommend the worship of Vishnu, though some of them inculcate the religion of Siva. So far as they deal with the legends of ancient days, they derive their materials mainly from the Mahabharata. The Vayu Purana, which may be the oldest of them, is believed to date from about 320 A.D.1 In the Matsyu ("Fish") Purana the legend of the deluge runs thus:—

"Formerly a heroic king called Manu, the patient son of the Sun, endowed with all good qualities, indifferent to pain and pleasure, after investing his son with royal authority, practised intense austere fervour, in a certain region of Malaya (Malabar), and attained to transcendent union with the Deity (yoga). When a million years had elapsed, Brahma became pleased and disposed to bestow a boon, which he desired Manu to choose. Bowing before the father of the world the monarch said, 'I desire of thee this one incomparable boon, that when the dissolution of the universe arrives I may have the power to preserve all existing things, whether moving or stationary.'

'So be it,' said the Soul of all things, and vanished on the spot; when a great shower of flowers, thrown down by the gods, fell from the sky. Once as, in his hermitage, Manu offered the oblation to the Manes, there fell upon his hands, along with some water, a S'aphari fish (a carp), which the kind-hearted king perceiving, strove to preserve in his water-jar. In one day and night the fish grew to the size of sixteen fingers, and cried, 'Preserve me, preserve me.' Manu then took and threw him into a large pitcher, where in one night he increased three cubits, and again cried, with the voice of one distressed, to the son of Vivasvat, 'Preserve me, preserve me, I have sought refuge with thee.' Manu next put him into a well, and when he could not be contained even in that, he was thrown into a lake, where he attained to the size of a yojana; but still cried in humble tones, 'Preserve me, preserve me.' When, after being flung into the Ganga, he increased there also, the king threw him into the ocean. When he filled the entire ocean, Manu said, in terror, 'Thou art some god, or thou art Vasudeva; how can any one else be like this? Whose body could equal two hundred thousand yojanas?'

'Thou art recognised under this form of a fish, and thou tormentest me, Kesava; reverence be to thee, Hrishlkesa, lord of the world, abode of the universe!'

Thus addressed, the divine Janardana, in the form of a fish, replied: 'Thou hast well spoken, and hast rightly known me.

'In a short time the earth with its mountains, groves, and forests, shall be submerged in the waters. This ship has been constructed by the company of all the gods for the preservation of the vast host of living creatures. Embarking in it all living creatures, both those engendered from moisture and from eggs, as well as the viviparous, and plants, preserve them from calamity. When driven by the blasts at the end of the yuga?1 the ship is swept along, thou shalt bind it to this horn of mine. Then at the close of the dissolution thou shalt be the Prajapati (lord of creatures) of this world, fixed and moving. When this shall have been done, thou, the omniscient, patient sage [rishi], and lord of the Manvantara"2 shalt be an object of worship to the gods.' 2nd Adhyaya Suta said: Being thus addressed, Manu asked the slayer of the Asura, ' In how many years shall the (existing) Man-vantara2 come to an end? And how shall I preserve the living creatures? or how shall I meet again with thee?' The fish answered: 'From this day forward a drought shall visit the earth for a hundred years and more, with a tormenting famine. Then the seven direful rays of the sun, of little power, destructive, shall rain burning charcoal. At the close of the yuga the submarine fire shall burst forth, while the poisonous flame issuing from the mouth of Sankarshana (shall blaze) from Patala, and the fire from Mahadeva's third eye shall issue from his forehead.

Thus kindled the world shall become confounded. When, consumed in this manner, the earth shall become like ashes, the aether too shall be scorched with heat. Then the world, together with the gods and planets, shall be destroyed. The seven clouds of the period of dissolution, called Samvartta, Bhimanada, Drona, Chanda, Balahaka, Vidyutpataka, and Sonambu, produced from the steam of the fire, shall inundate the earth. The seas agitated, and joined together, shall reduce these entire three worlds to one ocean. Taking this celestial ship, embarking on it all the seeds, and through contemplation fixed on me fastening it by a rope to my horn, thou alone shalt remain, protected by my power, when even the gods are burnt up. The sun and moon, I, Brahma, with the four worlds, the holy river Narmada [Nerbudda], the great sage Markandeya, Mahadeva, the Vedas, the Purana, with the sciences—these shall remain with thee at the close of the Manvantara. The world having thus become one ocean at the end of the Chakshusha manvantara, I shall give currency to the Vedas at the commencement of thy creation.'

Suta continued: Having thus spoken, the divine Being vanished on the spot; while Manu fell into a state of contemplation (yoga) induced by the favour of Vasudeva. When the time announced by Vasudeva had arrived, the predicted deluge took place in that very manner. Then Janardana appeared in the form of a horned fish; (the serpent) Ananta came to Manu in the shape of a rope. Then he who was skilled in duty (i.e. Manu) drew towards himself all creatures by contemplation (yoga) and stowed them in the ship, which he then attached to the fish's horn by the serpent-rope, as he stood upon the ship, and after he had made obeisance to Janardana. I shall now declare the Purana which, in answer to an enquiry from Manu, was uttered by the deity in the form of the fish, as he lay in a sleep of contemplation till the end of the universal inundation: Listen." The Matsya Purana says nothing more about the progress and results of the deluge.1

Another ancient Indian work of the same class, the Bhagavata Purana, gives the same story with variations as follows :—

"At the close of the past Kalpa2 there occurred an occasional dissolution of the universe arising from Brahma's nocturnal repose, in which the Bhurloka and other worlds were submerged in the ocean.

When the creator, desirous of rest, had under the influence of time been overcome by sleep, the strong Hayagriva coming near, carried off the Vedas which had issued from his mouth. Discovering this deed of the prince of the Danavas, the divine Hari, the Lord, took the form of a S'apharl fish. At that time a certain great royal sage [rishi], called Satyavrata, who was devoted to Narayana, practised austere fervour, subsisting on water. He was the same who in the present great Kalpa is the son of Visvasvat, called S'raddhadeva,1 and was appointed by Hari to the office of Manu. Once, as in the river Kritamala he was offering the oblation of water to the Pitris [ancestral spirits], a S'aphari fish came into the water in the hollow of his hands. The lord of Dravida, Satyavrata, cast the fish in his hands with the water into the river. The fish very piteously cried to the merciful king, 'Why dost thou abandon me poor and terrified to the monsters who destroy their kindred in this river?

Satyavrata then took the fish from the river, placed it in his waterpot, and as it grew larger and larger, threw it successively into a larger vessel, a pond, various lakes, and at length into the sea. The fish objects to be left there on the plea that it would be devoured; but Manu replies that it can be no real fish, but Vishnu himself; and with various expressions of devotion enquires why he had assumed this disguise.

The god replies: 'On the seventh day after this the three worlds Bhurloka, etc., shall sink beneath the ocean of the dissolution. When the universe is dissolved in that ocean, a large ship, sent by me, shall come to thee. Taking with thee the plants and various seeds, surrounded by the seven sages [rishis] and attended by all existences, thou shalt embark on the great ship, and shalt without alarm move over the one dark ocean, by the sole light of the sages [rishis]. When the ship shall be vehemently shaken by the tempestuous wind, fasten it by the great serpent to my horn—for I shall come near. So long as the night of Brahma lasts, I shall draw thee with the sages [rishis] and the ship over the ocean.'

[The god then disappears after promising that Satyavrata shall practically know his greatness and experience his kindness, and Satyavrata awaits the predicted events.]

Then the sea, augmenting as the great clouds poured down their waters, was seen overflowing its shores and everywhere inundating the earth. Meditating on the injunctions of the deity, Satyavrata beheld the arrival of the ship, on which he embarked with the Brahmans, taking along with him the various kinds of plants. Delighted, the Munis said to him, 'Meditate on Kesava; he will deliver us from this danger, and grant us prosperity.' Accordingly when the king had meditated on him, there appeared on the ocean a golden fish, with one horn, a million yojanas long. Binding the ship to his horn with the serpent for a rope, as he had been before commanded by Hari, Satyavrata landed Madhusudana. [The hymn follows.] When the king had thus spoken, the divine primeval Male, in the form of a fish, moving on the vast ocean declared to him the truth; the celestial collection of Puranas, with the Sankhya, Yoga, the ceremonial, and the mystery of the soul. Seated on the ship with the sages [rishis], Satyavrata heard the true doctrine of the soul, of the eternal Brahma, declared by the god. When Brahma arose at the end of the past dissolution, Hari restored to him the Vedas, after slaying Hayagriva. And King Satyavrata, master of all knowledge, sacred and profane, became, by the favour of Vishnu, the son of Vivasvat, the Manu in this Kalpa" 1

Yet another ancient Indian version of the deluge legend meets us in the Agni Purana: it runs thus:—

"Vasishtha said: 'Declare to me Vishnu, the cause of the creation, in the form of a Fish and his other incarnations; and the Puranic revelation of Agni, as it was originally heard from Vishnu.'

Agni replied: 'Hear O Vasishtha, I shall relate to thee the Fish-incarnation of Vishnu, and his acts when so incarnate for the destruction of the wicked, and protection of the good. At the close of the past Kalpa there occurred an occasional dissolution of the universe caused by Brahma's sleep, when the Bhurloka and other worlds were inundated by the ocean. Manu, the son of Vivasvat, practised austere fervour for the sake of worldly enjoyment as well as final liberation. Once, when he was offering the libation of water to the Pitris [ancestral spirits] in the river Kritamala, a small fish came into the water in the hollow of his hands, and said to him when he sought to cast it into the stream, 'Do not throw me in, for I am afraid of alligators and other monsters which are here.' On hearing this Manu threw it into a jar. Again, when grown, the Fish said to him, 'Provide me a large place.' Manu then cast it into a larger vessel. When it increased there, it said to the king, 'Give me a wide space.' When, after being thrown into a pond, it became as large as its receptacle, and cried out for greater room, he flung it into the sea. In a moment it became a hundred thousand yojanas in bulk.

Beholding the wonderful fish, Manu said in astonishment: 'Who art thou? Art thou Vishnu? Adoration be paid to thee, O Narayana. Why, O Janardana, dost thou bewilder me by thy illusion?'

The Fish, which had become incarnate for the welfare of this world and the destruction of the wicked, when so addressed, replied to Manu, who had been intent upon its preservation, 'Seven days after this the ocean shall inundate the world. A ship shall come to thee, in which thou shalt place the seeds, and accompanied by the sages [rishis] shalt sail during the night of Brahma. Bind it with the great serpent to my horn, when I arrive.'

Having thus spoken the Fish vanished. Manu awaited the promised period, and embarked on the ship when the sea overflowed its shores. (There appeared) a golden Fish, a million yojanas long, with one horn, to which Manu attached the ship, and heard from the Fish the Matsya Purana, which takes away sin, together with the Veda. Kesava then slew the Danava Hayagriva who had snatched away the Vedas, and preserved its mantras and other portions." 1

§ 8. Modern Indian Stories of a Great Flood

The Bhils, a wild jungle tribe of Central India, relate that once upon a time a pious man (dhobi), who used to wash his clothes in a river, was warned by a fish of the approach of a great deluge. The fish informed him that, out of gratitude for his humanity in always feeding the fish, he had come to give him this warning, and to urge him to prepare a large box in which he might escape. The pious man accordingly made ready the box and embarked in it with his sister and a cock. After the deluge Rama sent out his messenger to inquire into the state of affairs. The messenger heard the crowing of the cock and so discovered the box. Thereupon Rama had the box brought before him, and asked the man who he was and how he had escaped. The man told his tale. Then Rama made him face in turn north, east, and west, and swear that the woman with him was his sister. The man stuck to it that she was indeed his sister. Rama next turned him to the south, whereupon the man contradicted his former statement and said that the woman was his wife. After that, Rama inquired of him who it was that told him to escape, and on learning that it was the fish, he at once caused the fish's tongue to be cut out for his pains; so that sort of fish has been tongueless ever since.

Having executed this judgment on the fish for blabbing, Rama ordered the man to repeople the devastated world. Accordingly the man married his sister and had by her seven sons and seven daughters. The firstborn received from Rama the present of a horse, but, being unable to ride, he left the animal in the plain and went into the forest to cut wood. So he became a woodman, and woodmen his descendants the Bhils have been from that day to this.1

In this Bhil story the warning of the coming flood given by the fish to its human benefactor resembles the corresponding incident in the Sanscrit story of the flood too closely to be independent. It may be questioned whether the Bhils borrowed the story from the Aryan invaders, or whether on the contrary the Aryans may not have learned it from the aborigines whom they encountered in their progress through the country. In favour of the latter view it may be pointed out that the story of the flood does not occur in the most ancient Sanscrit literature, but only appears in books written long after the settlement of the Aryans in India.

The Kamars, a small Dravidian tribe of the Raipur District and adjoining States, in the Central Provinces of India, tell the following story of a great flood. They say that in the beginning God created a man and woman, to whom in their old age two children were born, a boy and a girl. But God sent a deluge over the world in order to drown a jackal which had angered him. The old couple heard of the coming deluge, so they shut up their children in a hollow piece of wood with provision of food to last them till the flood should subside. Then they closed up the trunk, and the deluge came and lasted for twelve years. The old couple and all other living things on earth were drowned, but the trunk floated on the face of the waters. After twelve years God created two birds and sent them to see whether his enemy the jackal had been drowned. The birds flew over all the corners of the world, and they saw nothing but a log of wood floating on the surface of the water. They perched on it, and soon heard low and feeble voices coming from inside the log. It was the children saying to each other that they had only provisions for three days left. So the birds flew away and told God, who then caused the flood to subside, and taking out the children from the log of wood he heard their story. Thereupon he brought them up, and in due time they were married, and God gave the name of a different caste to every child who was born to them, and from them all the inhabitants of the world are descended.1 In this story the incident of the two birds suggests a reminiscence of the raven and the dove in the Biblical legend, which may have reached the Kamars through missionary influence.

The Hos or Larka Kols, an aboriginal race who inhabit Singbhum, in south-western Bengal, say that after the world was first peopled mankind grew incestuous and paid no heed either to God or to their betters. So Sirma Thakoor, or Sing Bonga, the Creator, resolved to destroy them all, and he carried out his intention, some say by water, others say by fire. However, he spared sixteen people, and from them presumably the present race of mortals is descended.2 A fuller version of this legend is reported to be current among the Mundaris or Mundas, a tribe of Kols akin to the Hos who inhabit the tableland of Chota Nagpur to the north of Singbhum. According to the Mundas, God created mankind out of the dust of the ground. But soon mankind grew wicked; they would not wash themselves, or work, or do anything but dance and sing perpetually. So it repented Sing Bonga that he had made them, and he resolved to destroy them by a great flood. For that purpose he sent down a stream of fire-water (Sengle-Daa) from heaven, and all men died. Only two, a brother and a sister, were saved by hiding under a tiril tree; hence the wood of a tiril tree is black and charred with fire to this day. But God thought better of it, and to stop the fiery rain he created the snake Lurbing, which puffed its soul up into the shape of a rainbow, thereby holding up the showers. So when the Mundaris see a rainbow they say, "It will rain no more. Lurbing has destroyed the rain." 1

The Santals, another aboriginal race of Bengal, have also a legend that in the early ages of the world almost the whole human race was destroyed by fire from heaven. There are various traditions concerning this great calamity. Some say that it occurred soon after the creation of the first man and woman. Others assign it to a later period, and mention different places as the scene of the catastrophe. Different reasons, too, are alleged for the visitation. Some say it was sent by God as a punishment for the sins of the people; others affirm that two discontented members of the Marndi tribe invoked the vengeance of the Creator Thakur upon those who had offended them. The account which dates the event immediately after the creation makes no reference to the causes which operated to bring it about. It runs as follows. When Pilchu Haram and Pilchu Budhi, the first man and woman, had reached adolescence, it rained fire-rain for seven days and seven nights.

They sought refuge from the burning liquid in a cave in a rock, from which, when the flood was over, they came forth unscathed. Jaher-era then came and inquired of them where they had been. They answered, "We were underneath a rock." The following verse, we are told, completes the description :—

"Seven days and seven nights it rained fire-rain, Where were you, ye two human beings; Where did you pass the time?"

The other Santal story, which explains the fire-flood by the discontent of the Marndi tribe, is as follows. When the different social distinctions and duties were assigned to the various tribes, the Marndis were overlooked. Two members of the tribe, by name Ambir Singh and Bir Singh, who dwelt on Mount Here, were incensed at the slight thus put upon their fellows, and they prayed that fire from heaven might descend and destroy the other tribes. Their prayer was answered; one half of the country was destroyed, and one half of the population perished. The house in which Ambir Singh and Bir Singh lived was of stone, with a door of the same material. It therefore resisted the fire which was devastating the country far and wide, and the two inmates escaped unhurt. At this point the reciter of the tale sings the following verses :—

"Thou art shut in with a stone door, Ambir Singh, thou art shut in with a stone door, Ambir Singh, the country is burning, Ambir Singh, the country is burnt up"

When Kisku Raj heard of what had happened, he inquired who had done it. They told him it was the work of Ambir Singh and Bir Singh. He at once ordered them into his presence and asked why they had brought such a disaster upon the people. They answered, "In the distribution of distinctions and offices all were considered but ourselves."

127

To that Kisku Raj replied, "Yes, yes, do not act thus, and you also shall receive an office." Then they caused the fire to be extinguished. So Kisku Raj, addressing them, said, "I appoint you treasurers and stewards over all the property and possessions of all kings, princes, and nobles. All the rice and the unhusked rice will be under your charge. From your hands will all the servants and dependents receive their daily portion." Thus was the fire-flood stayed, and thus did the Marndi tribe attain to its present rank.

Yet a third Santal version of the fire-flood story has it that, while the people were at Khojkaman, their iniquity rose to such a pitch that Thakur Jiu, the Creator, punished them by sending fire-rain upon earth. Out of the whole race two individuals alone escaped destruction by hiding in a cave on Mount Haradata.1

The Lepchas of Sikhim have a tradition of a great flood during which a couple escaped to the top of a mountain called Tendong, near Darjeeling.2 Captain Samuel Turner, who went on an embassy from India to the court of the Teshoo Lama at the close of the eighteenth century, reports that according to a native legend Tibet was long ago almost totally inundated, until a deity of the name of Gya, whose chief temple is at Durgeedin, took compassion on the survivors, drew off the waters through Bengal, and sent teachers to civilize the wretched inhabitants, who were destined to repeople the land, and who up to that time had been very little better than monkeys.3 The Singphos of Assam relate that once on a time mankind was destroyed by a flood because they omitted to offer the proper sacrifices at the slaughter of buffaloes and pigs. Only two men, Khun litang and Chu liyang, with their wives, were saved, and being appointed by the gods to dwell on Singrabhum hill, they became the progenitors of the present human race.4 The Lushais of Assam have a legend that the king of the water demons fell in love with a woman named Ngai-ti (Loved One), but she rejected his addresses and ran away, so he pursued her, and surrounded the whole human race with water on the top of a hill called Phunlubuk, which is said to be far away to the north-east. As the water continued to rise, the people took Ngai-ti and threw her into the flood, which thereupon receded. In flowing away, the water hollowed out the deep valleys and left standing the high mountains which we see to this day, for down to the time of the great flood the earth had been level.1 Again, the Anals of Assam say that once upon a time the whole world was flooded. All the people were drowned except one man and one woman, who ran to the highest peak of the Leng hill, where they climbed up a high tree and hid themselves among the branches. The tree grew near a large pond, which was as clear as the eye of a crow. They spent the night perched on the tree, and in the morning, what was their astonishment to find that they had been changed into a tiger and a tigress! Seeing the sad plight of the world, the Creator, whose name is Pathian, sent a man and a woman from a cave on a hill to repeople the drowned world. But on emerging from the cave, the couple were terrified at the sight of the huge tiger and tigress, and they said to the Creator, "O Father, you have sent us to repeople the world, but we do not think that we shall be able to carry out your intention, as the whole world is under water, and the only spot on which we could make a place of rest is occupied by two ferocious beasts, which are waiting to devour us; give us strength to slay these animals." After that, they killed the tigers, and lived happily, and begat many sons and daughters, and from them the drowned world was repeopled.2

A long story of a great flood is told by the Ahoms of Assam, a branch of the great Shan race of Indo-China, from which their ancestors crossed over the Patkoi mountains about 1228 A.D. to settle in their present abode.3 The Ahom, or rather Shan, legend runs as follows:—

Long, long ago there were many worlds beneath the sky, but in the world of men, the middle world, there was as yet no race of kings (the Shans). The earth was like a wild mountainous jungle. On a time, bamboos cracked and opened, and from them came forth animals. They lived in deep forests, far from the haunts of men. Thereafter, a king and queen from heaven, Hpi-pok and Hpi-mot, came down to earth and found their way to Möng-hi on the Cambodia River's banks. They were the ancestors of the kingly race of Shans. But a time came when they made no sacrificial offerings to their gods. Therefore the storm-god, Ling-lawn, was angry at their impiety, and he sent down great cranes to eat them up. The cranes came, but could not eat all the people up, because there were so many of them. Then the storm-god sent down great tawny lions, but they too found more Shans than they could devour. Next he sent down great serpents to swallow the whole impious race, but all the people, from palace to hamlet, from the oldest to the youngest, attacked the serpents with their swords, and killed them. The storm-god was enraged, he snorted threateningly, and the battle was not over.

The old year passed, and from the first to the third month of the new year, which was the nineteenth of the cycle, there was a great drought. In the fourth month (March, well on in the dry season) the parched earth cracked open in wide seams, and many people died of thirst and famine. But in whatever country they were, there they must stay. There was no water, and they could not pass from one country to another. The water dried up in the deepest ponds and in the broadest rivers; where elephants had bathed, the people now dug wells for drinking water. What had been their watering-places, where many people had gathered together like swarms of bees in their search for water, now stank with the bodies of the dead.

Then Ling-lawn, the storm-god, called his counsellors, Kaw-hpa and Hseng-kio, old Lao-hki, Tai-long and Bak-long, and Ya-hseng-hpa, the smooth talker, and many others. At his court they gathered together. Entering his palace they bowed down to worship. Over the head of the god was an umbrella, widely spread and beautiful as a flower. They talked together in the language of men (Shan), and they took counsel to destroy the human race. "Let us send for Hkang-hkak," said they. He was the god of streams and of ponds, of crocodiles and of all water animals. Majestically came he in, and the storm-god gave him instructions, saying, "Descend with the clouds. Tarry not. Straightway report to Lip-long the distinguished lord."

Soon thereafter the water-god Hkang-hkak appeared before the sage Lip-long, who had been consulting his chicken bones. The omens were evil. When the sage came down from his house, the sky was dry as an oven. He knew that some great calamity was impending. On meeting the water-god, therefore, the sage was not surprised to hear him

129

say that Ling-lawn, the storm-god, was about to send a flood to overwhelm the earth. The divine messenger declared that the people of every land would be destroyed, that trees would be uprooted and houses submerged or float bottom up on the water. Even great cities would be overwhelmed. None could escape. Every living thing would be drowned. But against the coming of the flood the sage was commanded to make a strong raft, binding it firmly together with ropes. A cow, too, he was to take with him on the raft, and though all things else should be destroyed, yet would he and the cow escape. He might not even warn his loving wife and dear children of the coming destruction.

Musing on the water-god's sad instructions, the sage went homeward with bowed head in deep dejection. He caught up his little son in his arms and wept aloud. He longed to tell his eldest son, but he feared the cruel vengeance of the gods. Too sore at heart to eat, he went down in the morning hungry and bent to the river's bank. There he toiled day by day, gathering the parts of his raft and firmly binding them side by side. Even his own wife and children jeered at his finished but futile task. From house to house the scoffers mocked and railed. "Quit it, thou fool, thou ass," they cried; "if this come to the ear of the governors, they will put thee out of the way; if it come to the ear of the king, he will command thy death." Over the great kingdoms then reigned Hkun Chao and Hkun Chu.

A few days more and the flood came, sweeping on and increasing in violence like the onward rush of a forest fire. Fowls died in their coops. The crying of children was hushed in death. The bellowing of bulls and the trumpeting of elephants ceased as they sank in the water. There was confusion and destruction on every side. All animals were swept away, and the race of men perished. There was no one left in the valleys or on the mountains. The strong raft, bearing the sage Lip-long and the cow, alone floated safe upon the water. Drifting on, he saw the dead bodies of his wife and children. He caught and embraced them, and let them fall back again into the water. As he cast them from him into the deep he wept bitterly; bitterly did he lament that the storm-god had not given him leave to warn them of the impending doom. Thus perished the kingly race (the Shans). Paying their ferry-hire, their spirits passed over to the mansions of heaven. There they heard the reverberations of the celestial drums. They came by tens of thousands, and eating cold crab they were refreshed. When they reached the spirit-world they looked round and said, "Spirit-land is as festive and charming as a city of wine and women."

But now the stench of dead bodies, glistering in the sun, filled the earth. The storm-god Ling-lawn sent down serpents innumerable to devour them, but they could not, so many were the corpses. The angry god would have put the serpents to death, but they escaped by fleeing into a cave. Then he sent down nine hundred and ninety-nine thousand tigers, but even they could make little headway in the consumption of the corpses and retired discomfited. More angry than ever, the god hurled showers of thunderbolts at the retreating tigers, but they too fled into caves, growling so fiercely that the very sky might have fallen. Then the storm-god sent down Hsen-htam and Hpa-hpai, the god of fire. As they descended, riding their horses, they viewed all the country round. Alighting on a mountain they could see but three elevations of land. They sent forth a great conflagration, scattering their fire everywhere. The fire swept over all the earth, and the smoke ascended in clouds to heaven.

When he saw the fire coming, the sage Lip-long snatched up a stick and knocked down the cow at one blow. With his sword he ripped up her belly and crawled in. There he saw seed of the gourd plant, white as leavened bread. The fire swept over the dead cow, roaring as it went. When it was gone, Lip-long came forth, the only living man beneath the sun. He asked the great water-god Hkang-hkak what he should do, and the god bade him plant the seed of the gourd on a level plot of ground. He did so, and one gourd-vine climbed up a mountain and was scorched by the fierce rays of the sun. Another vine ran downward, and, soaked in the water of the flood, it rotted and died. A third vine, springing upwards with clinging tendrils, twined about the bushes and trees. News of its rapid growth reached the ears of Ling-lawn, the storm-god, and he sent down his gardener to care for the vine. The gardener made haste and arrived in the early morning at cock-crow. He dug about and manured the vine. He trailed up its branches with his own hand. When the rainy season came, the vine grew by leaps and bounds. It spread far and wide, coiling itself like a serpent about the shrubs and trees. It blossomed and bore fruit, great gourds such as no man may see again.

Then Ling-lawn, the rain-god, sent down Sao-pang, the god of the clear sky, to prepare the earth for human habitation. From him went forth waves of heat to dry up what remained of the flood. When the earth was dry once more and fit for habitation, the storm-god threw thunderbolts to break the gourds in pieces. A bolt struck and broke open a gourd. The people within the gourd cried out, "What is this? a bolt from a clear sky; let us go forth to till the land." Stooping low, they came forth. Again, another bolt struck another gourd, breaking it open, and the Shans therein said, "What shall we do, lord?" He replied, "You shall come forth to rule many lands." Thus the thunderbolts struck gourd after gourd, and from them came rivers of water, animals, both tame and wild, domestic fowls and birds of the air, and every useful plant. So was the earth filled again with life in all its varied forms.1

According to another version of the Shan legend, the persons who survived the deluge were seven men and seven women, who were more righteous than their neighbours and escaped death by crawling into the dry shell of a gigantic gourd, which floated on the face of the waters. On emerging from this ark of safety, they were fruitful and replenished the drowned earth.1

The secluded Alpine valley of Cashmeer, which by its delightful climate and beautiful scenery, at once luxuriant and sublime, has earned for itself the title of the Earthly Paradise of India, is almost completely surrounded by the lofty mountain-ranges of the Himalayas, their sides belted with magnificent forests, above which extend rich Alpine pastures close up to the limit of eternal snow. A native tradition, recorded by the early chroniclers of Cashmeer, relates that the whole of the valley was once occupied by a great lake. One of the oldest of these annals, called the Nilamata Purana, claims to give the sacred legends regarding the origin of the country, together with the special ordi-

131

nances which Nila, the lord of the Cashmeerian Nagas, laid down for the regulation of its religious worship and ceremonies. In this chronicle, which may date from the sixth or seventh century of our era, we read how at the beginning of the present Kalpa, or great era of the world, the valley was filled by a lake called Satisaras, that is, the Lake of Sati. Now in the period of the seventh Manu, a certain demon named Jalodbhava or "waterborn," resided in the lake and caused great distress to all neighbouring countries by the devastations which he spread far and wide. But it so happened that the wise Kasyapa, the father of all Nagas, went on pilgrimage to the holy places of northern India, and there he learned of the ravages of the demon from his son Nila, the king of the Cashmeerian Nagas.

The sage promised to punish the evil-doer, and accordingly repaired to the seat of the great god Brahman to implore his help. His prayer was granted. At Brahman's command, the whole host of gods set off for the lake and took up their posts on the lofty peaks of the Naubandhana Mountain, overlooking the lake; that is, on the very same mountain on which, according to the Mahabharata, Manu anchored his ship after the great flood. But it was vain to challenge the demon to single combat; for in his own element he was invincible, and he was too cunning to quit it and come forth. In this dilemma the god Vishnu called upon his brother Balabhadra to drain the lake. His brother did so by piercing the mountains with his weapon, the ploughshare; the water drained away, and in the dry bed of the lake the demon, now exposed to the assaults of his enemies, was attacked by Vishnu, and after a fierce combat was slain by the deity with his war-disc. After that King Kasyapa settled the land of Cashmeer, which had thus been born of the waters. The gods also took up their abode in it, and the various goddesses adorned the country in the shape of rivers.1 And a land of rivers and lakes it has been from that day to this. The same legend is told in a briefer form by the Cashmeerian chronicler Kalhana, who wrote in the middle of the twelfth century of our era, and whose work displays an extremely accurate knowledge both of the topography of the valley and of the popular legends still current among the natives.2 And the same story is told, in nearly the same form, by the Mohammedan writers Beddia and Dien; 3 it is alluded to, in a Buddhistic setting, by the famous Chinese pilgrim of the sixth century, Hiuen Tsiang, who lived as an honoured guest for two full years in the happy valley; 4 and it survives to this day in popular tradition.5

Now there are physical facts which seem at first sight to support the belief that in comparatively late geological times the valley of Cashmeer was wholly or in great part occupied by a vast lake, for undoubted lacustrine deposits are to be seen on some of the tablelands of the valley.6 Moreover, "the aspect of the province confirms the truth of the legend, the subsidence, of the waters being distinctly defined by horizontal lines on the face of the mountains. It is also not at all unlikely to have been the scene of some great convulsion of nature, as indications of volcanic action are not unfrequent; hot springs are numerous; at particular seasons the ground in various places is sensibly hotter than the atmosphere, and earthquakes are of common occurrence."

Are we then to suppose that a tradition of the occupation of the Vale of Cashmeer by a great lake has survived among the inhabitants from late geological times to the present day? It is true that in Cashmeer the popular local traditions appear to be peculiarly tenacious of life and to outlive the written traditions of the learned. From the experience gained on his antiquarian tours, Sir Marc Aurel Stein is convinced that, when collected with caution and critically sifted, these local legends may safely be accepted as supplements to the topographical information of our written records, and their persistence he attributes in large measure to the secluded position of the valley and to the naturally conservative habits of life and thought, which mountain barriers and consequent isolation tend everywhere to foster in Alpine countries. Certainly for ages Cashmeer remained, like Tibet, a hermit land, little known to the outer world and jealously exclusive of strangers. The army of Alexander, on its victorious march through India, passed almost within sight of the gates of Cashmeer, yet the great captain, thirsting for new worlds to conquer, seems to have heard no whisper of the earthly paradise that lay beyond these snowcapped mountains.2

Yet we may reasonably doubt whether any memory of an event so remote as the comparative desiccation of the valley of Cashmeer should survive in human tradition even under circumstances so favourable to its preservation. It is far more likely that the legend owes its origin to a natural inference, based partly on observation of the general features of the country, partly on a knowledge of the drainage operations, which within the memory of man have extended the area of arable land and reduced the area covered by lakes and marshes.

"To any one, however ignorant of geology, but acquainted with the latter fact," says Sir Marc Aurel Stein, "the picture of a vast lake originally covering the whole valley might naturally suggest itself. It would be enough for him to stand on a hillside somewhere near the Volur, to look down on the great lake and the adjoining marshes, and to glance then beyond towards that narrow gorge of Baramula where the mountains scarcely seem to leave an opening. It is necessary to bear in mind the singular flights of Hindu imagination as displayed in the Puranas, Mdhdtmyas and similar texts. Those acquainted with them will, I think, be ready to allow that the fact of that remarkable gorge being the single exit for the drainage of the country might alone even have sufficed as a starting-point for the legend." 1

Thus we may fairly conclude that, like the Samothracian legend of a great flood caused by the bursting of the Black Sea and its consequent union with the Mediterranean, the Cashmeer legend furnishes no evidence of human tradition stretching back into the mists of geological time, but is simply the shrewd guess of intelligent observers, who used their wits to supplement the evidence of their eyes. However, it is to be observed that the Cashmeer story hardly falls under the head of flood legends, since it recounts the desiccation rather than the inundation of a mountain basin. No doubt if the event really happened as it is said to have done, it must have caused a tremendous flood in the lowlands beyond the valley; but as the disastrous consequences can only have concerned other people, the Cashmeerians naturally say nothing about it.

133

§ 9. Stories of a Great Flood in Eastern Asia

According to the Karens of Burma the earth was of old deluged with water, and two brothers saved themselves from the flood on a raft. The waters rose till they reached to heaven, when the younger brother saw a mango-tree hanging down from the celestial vault. With great presence of mind he clambered up it and ate of the fruit, but the flood, suddenly subsiding, left him suspended in the tree. Here the narrative breaks off abruptly, and we are left to conjecture how he extricated himself from his perilous position.1 The Chingpaws or Singphos of Upper Burma, like their brethren in Assam, have a tradition of a great flood. They say that when the deluge came, a man Pawpaw Nan-chaung and his sister Chang-hko saved themselves in a large boat. They had with them nine cocks and nine needles. After some days of rain and storm they threw overboard one cock and one needle to see whether the waters were falling. But the cock did not crow and the needle was not heard to strike bottom. They did the same thing day after day, but with no better result, till at last on the ninth day the last cock crew and the last needle was heard to strike on a rock. Soon after the brother and sister were able to leave their boat, and they wandered about till they came to a cave inhabited by two elves or fairies (nats), a male and a female. The elves bade them stay and make themselves useful in clearing the jungle, tilling the ground, hewing wood, and drawing water. The brother and sister did so, and soon after the sister gave birth to a child.

While the parents were away at work, the old elfin woman, who was a witch, used to mind the baby and whenever the infant squalled, the horrid wretch would threaten, if it did not stop bawling, to make mince meat of it at a place where nine roads met. The poor child did not understand the dreadful threat and persisted in giving tongue, till one day the old witch in a fury snatched it up, hurried it to the meeting-place of nine roads, and there hewed it in pieces, and sprinkled the blood and strewed the bits all over the roads and the country round about. But some of the titbits she carried back to her cave and made into a savoury curry. Moreover, she put a block of wood into the baby's empty cradle. And when the mother came back from her work in the evening and asked for her child, the witch said, "It is asleep. Eat your rice." So the mother ate the rice and curry, and then went to the cradle, but in it she found nothing but a block of wood. When she asked the witch where the child was, the witch replied tartly, "You have eaten it." The poor mother fled from the house, and at the crossroads she wailed aloud and cried to the Great Spirit to give her back her child or avenge its death. The Great Spirit appeared to her and said, "I cannot piece your baby together again, but instead I will make you the mother of all nations of men."

And then from one road there sprang up the Shans, from another the Chinese, from others the Burmese, and the Bengalees, and all the races of mankind; and the bereaved mother claimed them all as her children, because they all sprang from the scattered fragments of her murdered babe.1

The Bahnars, a primitive tribe of Cochin China, tell how once on a time the kite quarrelled with the crab, and pecked the crab's skull so hard that he made a hole in it, which may be seen down to this very day. To avenge this injury to his skull, the crab caused the sea and the rivers to swell till the waters reached the sky, and all living beings perished except two, a brother and a sister, who were saved in a huge chest. They took with them into the chest a pair of every sort of animal, shut the lid tight, and floated on the waters for seven days and seven nights. Then the brother heard a cock crowing outside, for the bird had been sent by the spirits to let our ancestors know that the flood had abated, and that they could come forth from the chest. So the brother let all the birds fly away, then he let loose the animals, and last of all he and his sister walked out on the dry land. They did not know how they were to live, for they had eaten up all the rice that was stored in the chest. However, a black ant brought them two grains of rice : the brother planted them, and next morning the plain was covered with a rich crop. So the brother and sister were saved.1

A legend of a deluge has been recorded by a French missionary among the Bannavs, one of the savage tribes which inhabit the mountains and tablelands between Cochin China, Laos, and Cambodia. "If you ask them respecting the origin of mankind, all they tell you is, that the father of the human race was saved from an immense inundation by means of a large chest in which he shut himself up; but of the origin or creator of this father they know nothing. Their traditions do not reach beyond the Deluge; but they will tell you that in the beginning one grain of rice sufficed to fill a saucepan and furnish a repast for a whole family. This is a souvenir of the first age of the world, that fugitive period of innocence and happiness which poets have called the golden age." 2 The tradition is probably only an abridged form of the deluge legend which, as we have just seen, is recorded by another French missionary among the Bahnars, who may be supposed to be the same with the Bannavs. As to the racial affinity of the tribe, the missionary writes: "To what race do the Bannavs belong? That is the first question I asked myself on arriving here, and I must confess that I cannot yet answer it; all I can say is, that in all points they differ from the Annamites and Chinese; neither do they resemble the Laotians or Cambodians, but appear to have a common origin with the Cédans, Halangs, Reungao, and Giaraïe, their neighbours. Their countenances, costumes, and belief are nearly the same and the language, although it differs in each tribe, has yet many words common to all; the construction, moreover, is perfectly identical. I have not visited the various tribes of the south, but from all I have heard I conclude that these observations apply to them also, and that all the savages inhabiting the vast country lying between Cochin China, Laos, and Cambodia, belong to the same great branch of the human family." 1

The Benua-Jakun, a primitive aboriginal tribe of the Malay Peninsula, in the State of Johor, say that the ground on which we stand is not solid, but is merely a skin covering an abyss of water. In ancient times Pirman, that is the deity, broke up this skin, so that the world was drowned and destroyed by a great flood. However, Pirman had created a man and a woman and put them in a ship of pulai wood, which was completely covered over and had no opening. In this ship the pair floated and tossed about for a time, till at last the vessel came to rest, and the man and woman, nibbling their way through its side, emerged on dry ground and beheld this our world stretching away on all sides to the horizon. At first all was very dark, for there was neither morning nor evening, because the sun had not yet been created. When it grew light, they saw seven small shrubs of rhododendron and seven clumps of the grass called sambau. They said one to another, "Alas, in what a sad plight are we, without either children or grandchildren!" But some time afterwards the woman conceived in the calves of her legs, and from her right calf came forth a male, and from her left calf came forth a female. That is why the offspring of the same womb may not marry. All mankind are the descendants of the two children of the first pair.2

In Kelantan, a district of the Malay Peninsula, they say that one day a feast was made for a circumcision, and all manner of beasts were pitted to fight against one another. There were fights between elephants, and fights between buffaloes, and fights between bullocks, and fights between goats; and at last there were fights between dogs and cats. And when the fights took place between dogs and cats, a great flood came down from the mountains, and overwhelmed the people that dwelt in the plains. And they were all drowned in that flood, save only some two or three menials who had been sent up into the hills to gather firewood. Then the sun, moon, and stars were extinguished, and there was a great darkness. And when light returned, there was no land but a great sea, and all the abodes of men had been overwhelmed.1

The legend of a great flood plays an important part in the traditionary lore of the Lolos, an aboriginal race who occupy the almost impregnable mountain fastnesses of Yunnan and other provinces of South-western China, where they have succeeded in maintaining their independence against the encroachments of the Chinese. A robust and warlike people, they not only make raids into Chinese territory for the purpose of levying black-mail and carrying off prisoners, whom they hold to ransom, but they actually maintain a large population of slaves entirely composed of Chinese captives. Yet in spite of their hostility to the Chinese, with whom they never intermarry, they appear to belong to the same race; at least they speak a monosyllabic language of extreme simplicity, which belongs to the Tibeto-Burman branch of the Tibeto-Chinese family.

They are so far from being savages that they have even invented a mode of writing, pictographic in origin, in which they have recorded their legends, songs, genealogies, and religious ritual. Their manuscripts, copied and recopied, have been handed down from generation to generation.2 They bear family surnames, which are said always to signify a plant or an animal; the members of each family believe that they are descended from the species of animal or plant whose name they bear, and they will neither eat nor even touch it. These facts suggest the existence of totemism among the Lolos. At the same time the Lolos believe in patriarchs who now live in the sky, but who formerly dwelt on earth, where they attained to the great ages of six hundred and sixty and even nine hundred and ninety years, thereby surpassing Methusaleh himself in longevity. Each family, embracing the persons united by a common surname, pays its devotions to a particular patriarch.

136

The most famous of these legendary personages is a certain Tse-gu-dzih, who enjoys many of the attributes of divinity. He it was who brought death into the world by opening the fatal box which contained the seeds of mortality; and he too it was who caused the deluge. The catastrophe happened thus. Men were wicked, and Tse-gu-dzih sent down a messenger to them on earth, asking for some flesh and blood from a mortal. No one would give them except only one man, Du-mu by name. So Tse-gu-dzih in wrath locked the rain gates, and the waters mounted to the sky. But Du-mu, who complied with the divine injunction, was saved, together with his four sons, in a log hollowed out of a Pieris tree; and with them in the log were likewise saved otters, wild ducks and lampreys. From his four sons are descended the civilized peoples who can write, such as the Chinese and the Lolos. But the ignorant races of the world are the descendants of the wooden figures whom Du-mu constructed after the deluge in order to repeople the drowned earth. To this day the ancestral tablets which the Lolos worship on set days of the year and on all the important occasions of life, are made out of the same sort of tree as that in which their great forefather found safety from the waters of the deluge, and nearly all the Lolo legends begin with some reference to him or to the great flood. In considering the origin of this flood legend it should be mentioned that the Lolos generally keep a Sabbath of rest every sixth day, when ploughing is forbidden, and in some places women are not allowed to sew or wash clothes. Taken together with this custom, the Lolo traditions of the patriarchs and of the flood appear to betray Christian influence; and Mr. A. Henry may well be right in referring them all to the teaching of Nestorian missionaries, for Nestorian churches existed in Yunnan in the thirteenth century when Marco Polo travelled in the country, and the Nestorian Alopen is said to have arrived in China as early as 635 A.D.1

The Chinese have a tradition of a great flood which happened in the reign of the emperor Yao, who reigned in the twenty-fourth century before our era. In his distress the emperor addressed his prime minister, saying, "Ho! President of the Four Mountains, destructive in their overflow are the waters of the inundation. In their vast extent they embrace the hills and overtop the great heights, threatening the heavens with their floods, so that the lower people groan and murmur! Is there a capable man to whom I can assign the correction of this calamity?"

All the court replied to the emperor, saying, "Is there not Khwan?"

But the emperor answered, "Alas! how perverse is he! He is disobedient to orders, and tries to injure his peers."

The prime minister rejoined, "Well, but try whether he can accomplish the work."

So the emperor employed Khwan, and said to him, "Go, and be reverent!" Thus put on his mettle Khwan worked assiduously for nine years, but he laboured in vain, for at the end of the nine years the work was still unaccomplished, the floods were still out. Yet did his son Yu afterwards cope successfully with the inundation, accomplishing all that he had undertaken and showing his superiority to other men.2 This Chinese tradition has been by some people forcibly identified with the Biblical account of the Noachian deluge, but in truth it hardly belongs to the class of diluvial legends at all, since it obviously records merely a local, though widespread, inundation, not a universal cataclysm in which the greater part of mankind perished. The event it describes may well have been a real flood caused by the Yellow River, a great and very rapid stream, partially enclosed by artificial and ill-constructed banks and dykes, which in modern times have often burst and allowed the water to spread devastation over the surrounding country. Hence the river is a source of perpetual anxiety and expense to the Chinese Government; and it is the opinion of a modern observer that a repetition of the great flood of Yao's time might still occur and lay the most fertile and populous plains of China under water.1

That the Chinese were totally unacquainted with traditions of a universal deluge may be affirmed on the high authority of a Chinese emperor. In the ninth century of our era an Arab traveller, named Ibn-Wahab, of Koraishite origin, of the family of Habbar Ben el-Aswad, made his way by sea from Bassorah to India and thence to China. Arrived there, he sought an interview with the Chinese emperor, alleging as part of his credentials that he was of the family of the Prophet Mohammed. The emperor caused inquiries to be instituted on this point, and being satisfied as to the truth of the allegation, he admitted the traveller to his presence and held a long conversation with him through an interpreter. The Arab has recorded at some length what passed between him and his august interlocutor. Amongst other things the emperor asked him, through the interpreter, whether he could recognize his Lord, that is to say, the Prophet Mohammed, if he should see him.

"How can I see him?" said the Arab, "he is with God."

"I do not mean it literally," replied the emperor, "but in a representation."

The Arab answered that he could. The emperor then ordered a box to be brought and when it was before him, he took a casket out of it, and said to the interpreter, "Show him his Lord."

The Arab looked. "And I saw," he tells us, " in the casket, the images of the prophets. My lips muttered benedictions upon them. The king did not know that I knew them; hence, he said to the interpreter, 'Ask him why he moves his lips.' He interrogated me, and I answered him that I was pronouncing benedictions upon the prophets.

He asked me further how I recognized them, and I told him that I knew them by the attributes with which they were represented. 'This,' I exclaimed, 'is Núh in the ark; he has been saved with those who were with him whilst God submerged the whole earth, and all that was on it.'

He smiled and said, 'It is Núh, as thou sayest, but it is not true that the whole earth was inundated. The flood occupied only a part of the globe, and did not reach our country.

Your traditions are correct, as far as that part of the earth is concerned which you inhabit; but we, the inhabitants of China, of India, of es-Sind, and other nations, do not agree with your account; nor have our forefathers left us a tradition agreeing with yours on this head. As to thy belief that the whole earth was covered with water, I must remark that this would be so remarkable an event that the terror would keep up its recollection, and all the nations would have handed it down to their posterity.' I endeavoured to answer him, and to bring forth arguments against his assertion in defence of my statement."1

The Arab has not reported the arguments with which he maintained the truth of the Noachian tradition, but we may surmise that they did not succeed in shaking the incredulity of the sceptical emperor.

The Kamchadales have a tradition of a great flood which covered the whole land in the early days of the world. A remnant of the people saved themselves on large rafts made of tree-trunks bound together; on these they loaded their property and provisions, and on these they drifted about, dropping stones tied to straps instead of anchors in order to prevent the flood from sweeping them away out to sea. When at last the water of the deluge sank, it left the people and their rafts stranded high and dry on the tops of the mountains.1

In a Chinese Encyclopaedia there occurs the following passage : "Eastern Tartary.— In travelling from the shore of the Eastern Sea toward Che-lu, neither brooks nor ponds are met with in the country, although it is intersected by mountains and valleys. Nevertheless there are found in the sand very far away from the sea, oyster-shells and the shields of crabs. The tradition of the Mongols who inhabit the country is, that it has been said from time immemorial that in remote antiquity the waters of the deluge flooded the district, and when they retired, the places where they had been made their appearance covered with sand." 2

10. Stories of a Great Flood in the Indian Archipelago

The Battas or Bataks of Sumatra say that in the beginning of time the earth rested on the head, or rather on the three horns, of Naga Padoha, a monster who is described as a serpent with the horns of a cow, but who appears to have been also provided with hands and feet. When Naga Padoha grew weary of supporting the earth on his horns, he shook his head, and the earth sank into the water. Thereupon the high god Batara Guru set about recovering it from the watery abyss. For that purpose he sent down his daughter Puti-orla-bulan; indeed she requested to be despatched on this beneficent mission. So down she came, riding on a white owl and accompanied by a dog. But she found all the nether world so covered with water that there was no ground for the soles of her feet to rest upon. In this emergency her divine father Batara Guru came to the rescue of his child, and let Mount Bakarra fall from heaven to be an abode for her. It may be seen in the land of the Battas to this day, and from it gradually sprang all the rest of the habitable earth. Batara Guru's daughter had afterwards three sons and three daughters, from whom the whole of mankind are descended, but who the father of them all may have been is not revealed by the legend. The restored earth was again supported on the horns of Naga Padoha and from that time forward there has been a constant struggle between him and Batara Guru, the monster always trying to rid himself of his burden, and the deity always endeavouring to prevent him from so doing.

Hence come the frequent earthquakes, which shake the world in general and the island of Sumatra in particular. At last, when the monster proved obstreperous, Batara Guru sent his son Layang-layang mandi (which means the diving swallow1) to tie Naga Padoha's hands and feet. But even when he was thus fettered, the monster continued to shake his head, so that earthquakes have not ceased to happen. And he will go on shaking himself till he snaps his fetters. Then the earth will again sink into the sea, and the sun will approach to within an ell of this our world. The men of that time will, according to their merit, either be transported to heaven or cast into the flaming cauldron in which Batara Guru torments the wicked until they have expiated their sins. At the destruction of the world, the fire of the cauldron will join with the fire of the sun to consume the material universe.2

A less grandiose version of the Batta belief, which in the preceding form unites the reminiscence of a universal flood with the prophecy of a future destruction of the earth by water and fire, is recorded by a modern traveller, who visited the Battas in their mountain home. According to him, the people say that, when the earth grew old and dirty, the Creator, whom they call Debata, sent a great flood to destroy every living thing. The last human pair had taken refuge on the top of the highest mountain, and the waters of the deluge had already reached to their knees, when the Lord of All repented of his resolution to make an end of mankind. So he took a clod of earth, kneaded it into shape, tied it to a thread, and laid it on the rising flood, and the last pair stepped on it and were saved. As the descendants of the couple multiplied, the clod increased in size till it became the earth which we all inhabit at this day.1

The natives of Nias, an island to the west of Sumatra, say that in days of old there was a strife between the mountains of their country as to which of them was the highest. The strife vexed their great ancestor Balugu Luomewona, and in his vexation he went to the window and said, "Ye mountains, I will cover you all!" So he took a golden comb and threw it into the sea, and it became a huge crab, which stopped up the sluices whereby the waters of the sea usually run away. The consequences of the stoppage were disastrous. The ocean rose higher and higher till only the tops of two or three mountains in Nias still stood above the heaving billows. All the people who with their cattle had escaped to these mountains were saved, and all the rest were drowned. That is how the great ancestor of the islanders settled the strife between the mountains, and the strife is proverbial among his descendants to the present day.2

The natives of Engano, another island to the west of Sumatra, have also their story of a great flood. Once on a time, they say, the tide rose so high that it overflowed the island and every living being was drowned, except one woman. She owed her preservation to the fortunate circumstance that, as she drifted along on the tide, her hair caught in a thorny tree, to which she was thus enabled to cling. When the flood sank, she came down from the tree, and saw with sorrow that she was left all alone in the world. Beginning to feel the pangs of hunger, she wandered inland in the search for food, but finding nothing to eat, she returned disconsolately to the beach, where she hoped to catch a fish. A fish, indeed, she saw but when she tried to catch it, the creature glided into one of the corpses that were floating on the water or weltering on the shore. Not to be balked, the woman picked up a stone and struck the corpse a smart blow therewith. But the fish leaped from its hiding-place and made off in the direction of the interior. The woman followed, but hardly had she taken a few steps when, to her great surprise, she met a living man. When she asked him what he did there, seeing that she herself was the sole survivor of the flood, he answered that somebody had knocked on his dead body, and that in consequence he had returned to life. The woman now related to him her experiences, and together they resolved to try whether they could not restore all the other dead to life in like manner by knocking on their corpses with stones. No sooner said than done. The drowned men and women revived under the knocks, and thus was the island repeopled after the great flood.1

The Ibans or Sea Dyaks of Sarawak, in Borneo, are fond of telling a story which relates how the present race of men survived a great deluge, and how their ancestress discovered the art of making fire. The story runs thus. Once upon a time some Dyak women went to gather young bamboo shoots for food. Having got them, they walked through the jungle till they came to what they took to be a great fallen tree. So they sat down on it and began to pare the bamboo shoots, when to their astonishment the trunk of the tree exuded drops of blood at every cut of their knives. Just then up came some men, who saw at once that what the women were sitting on was not a tree but a gigantic boa-constrictor in a state of torpor. They soon killed the serpent, cut it up, and carried the flesh home to eat. While they were busy frying the pieces, strange noises were heard to issue from the frying-pan, and a torrential rain began to fall and never ceased falling till all the hills, except the highest, were submerged and the world was drowned, all because these wicked men had killed and fried the serpent.

Men and animals all perished in the flood, except one woman, a dog, a rat, and a few small creatures, who fled to the top of a very high mountain. There, seeking shelter from the pouring rain, the woman noticed that the dog had found a warm place under a creeper; for the creeper was swaying to and fro in the wind and was warmed by rubbing against the trunk of the tree. She took the hint, and rubbing the creeper hard against a piece of wood she produced fire for the first time. That is how the art of making fire by means of the fire-drill was discovered after the great flood. Having no husband the woman took the fire-drill for her mate, and by its help she gave birth to a son called Simpang-impang, who, as his name implies, was but half a man, since he had only one arm, one leg, one eye, one ear, one cheek, half a body, and half a nose. These natural defects gave great offence to his playmates the animals, and at last he was able to supply them by striking a bargain with the Spirit of the Wind, who had carried off some rice which Simpang-impang had spread out to dry. At first, when Simpang-impang demanded compensation for this injury, the Spirit of the Wind flatly refused to pay him a farthing but being vanquished in a series of contests with Simpang-impang, he finally consented, instead of paying him in gongs or other valuables, of which indeed he had none, to make a whole man of him by supplying him with the missing parts and members. Simpang-impang gladly accepted the proposal, and that is why mankind have been provided with the usual number of arms and legs ever since.1

Another Dyak version of the story relates how, when the flood began, a certain man called Trow made a boat out of a large wooden mortar, which had hitherto served for pounding rice. In this vessel he embarked with his wife, a dog, a pig, a fowl, a cat, and other live creatures, and so launched out on the deep. The crazy ship outrode the storm, and when the flood had subsided, Trow and his wife and the animals disembarked. How to repeople the earth after the destruction of nearly the entire human race was now the problem which confronted Trow, and in order to grapple with it he had recourse to polygamy, fashioning for himself new wives out of a stone, a log, and anything else that came to hand. So he soon had a large and flourishing family, who learned to till the ground and became the ancestors of various Dyak tribes.1 The Ot-Danoms, a tribe of Dutch Borneo in the valley of the Barito, tell of a great deluge which drowned many people. Only one mountain peak rose above the water, and the few people who were able to escape to it in boats dwelt on it for three months, till the flood subsided and the dry land appeared once more.2

The Bare'e-speaking Toradjas of Central Celebes also tell of a flood which once covered the highest mountains, all but the summit of Mount Wawo Pebato, and in proof of their story they point to the sea-shells which are to be found on the tops of hills two thousand feet and more above the level of the sea. Nobody escaped the flood except a pregnant woman and a pregnant mouse, who saved themselves in a pig's trough and floated about, paddling with a pot-ladle instead of an oar, till the waters sank down and the earth again became habitable. Just then the woman, looking about for rice to sow, spied a sheaf of rice hanging from an uprooted tree, which drifted ashore on the spot where she was standing. With the help of the mouse, who climbed up the tree and brought down the sheaf, she was able to plant rice again. But before she fetched down the sheaf, the mouse stipulated that as a recompense for her services mice should thenceforth have the right to eat up part of the harvest. That is why the mice come every year to fetch the reward of their help from the fields of ripe rice; only they may not strip the fields too bare. As for the woman, she in due time gave birth to a son, whom she took, for want of another, to be her husband. By him she had a son and daughter, who became the ancestors of the present race of mankind.3 In Minahassa, a district of northern Celebes, there is a mountain called Lankooe, and the natives say that on the top of that mountain the dove which Noah sent out of the ark plucked the olive-branch which she brought back to the patriarch.1 The story is clearly due to Mohammedan or Christian influence. In a long Malay poem, taken down in the island of Sunda, we read how Noah and his family were saved in the ark from the great flood, which lasted forty days, and during the prevalence of which all mountains were submerged except Goonoong Padang and Goonoong Galoonggoong.2

142

The Alfoors of Ceram, a large island between Celebes and New Guinea, relate that after a great flood, which overwhelmed the whole world, the mountain Noesakoe appeared above the sinking tide, its sides clothed with great trees, of which the leaves were shaped like the female organs of generation. Only three persons survived on the top of the mountain, but the sea-eagle brought them tidings that other mountain peaks had emerged from the waters. So the three persons went thither, and by means of the remarkable leaves of the trees they repeopled the world.3 The inhabitants of Rotti, a small island to the south-west of Timor, say that in former times the sea flooded the earth, so that all men and animals were drowned and all plants and herbs beaten down to the earth. Not a spot of dry ground was left. Even the high mountains were submerged, only the peak of Laki-mola, in Bilba, still rose solitary over the waves. On that mountain a man and his wife and children had taken refuge. After some months the tide still came creeping up and up the mountain, and the man and his family were in great fear, for they thought it would soon reach them. So they prayed the sea to return to his old bed. The sea answered "I will do so, if you give me an animal whose hairs I cannot count." The man thereupon heaved first a pig, then a goat, then a dog, and then a hen into the flood, but all in vain; the sea could number the hairs of every one of them, and it still came on. At last he threw in a cat: this was too much for the sea, it could not do the sum, and sank abashed accordingly. After that the osprey appeared and sprinkled some dry earth on the waters, and the man and his wife and children descended the mountain to seek a new home. Thereupon the Lord commanded the osprey to bring all kinds of seed to the man, such as maize, millet, rice, beans, pumpkins, and sesame, in order that he might sow them and live with his family on the produce. That is the reason why in Rotti, at the end of harvest, people set up a sheaf of rice on the open place of the village as an offering to Mount Lakimola. Everybody cooks rice, and brings it with betel-nuts, coco-nuts, tobacco, bananas, and breadfruit as an oblation to the mountain; they feast and dance all kinds of dances to testify their gratitude, and beg him to grant a good harvest next year also, so that the people may have plenty to eat.1

The Nages, in the centre of the East Indian island of Flores, say that Dooy, the forefather of their tribe, was saved in a ship from the great flood. His grave is under a stone platform, which occupies the centre of the public square at Boa Wai, the tribal capital. The harvest festival, which is attended not only by the villagers but also by people from far and near, takes place round this grave of their great ancestor. The people dance round the grave, and sacrifices of buffaloes are offered. The spirits of all dead members of the tribe, wherever they may be, whether in the air, or in the mountains, or in the caves and dens of the earth, are invited to attend the festival and are believed to be invisibly present at it. On this occasion the civil chief of the tribe is gorgeously arrayed in golden jewellery, and on his head he wears the golden model of a ship with seven masts in memory of the escape of their great ancestor from the flood.1

Stories of a great flood are told also by some of the wild tribes of Mindanao, one of the Philippine Islands. One such tale is said to be current among the Atás of the Davao District, who are supposed to be descendants of an invading people that intermarried with the Negritoes and other aboriginal tribes. Their legend of the deluge runs thus. The greatest of all the spirits is Manama, who made the first men from blades of grass, weaving them together until they assumed the human form. In this manner he created eight persons, male and female, who later became the ancestors of the Atás and all the neighbouring tribes. Long afterwards the water covered the whole earth, and all the Atás were drowned except two men and a woman. The waters carried them far away, and they would have perished if a great eagle had not come to their aid. The bird offered to carry them on its back to their homes. One of the men refused, but the other man and the woman accepted the offer and returned to Mapula.2 Another version of the story is told by the Mandayas, another wild tribe of the same district, who inhabit a rugged, densely wooded region, where the mountains descend almost to the water's edge, forming high sheer cliffs at their base. They say that many generations ago a great flood happened, which drowned all the inhabitants of the world except one pregnant woman. She prayed that her child might be a boy. Her prayer was answered, and she gave birth to a boy whose name was Uacatan. When he grew up, he took his mother to wife, and from their union all the Mandayas are descended.3

Further, stories of a great flood are current among the wild tribes which occupy the central mountains and eastern coasts of Formosa and, as these tribes apparently belong by race and language to the Malayan family,1 their traditions of a deluge may appropriately find a place here, though the large island which is their home lies off the coast of China. The stories have been recorded by a Japanese gentleman, Mr. Shinji Ishii, who resided for some years in Formosa for the sake of studying the natives. He has very kindly placed his unpublished manuscripts at my disposal for the purposes of this work.

One of the tribes which inhabit the eastern coast of Formosa are the Ami. They are supposed to have been the last to arrive in this part of the island. Unlike the rest of the aborigines, they trace the descent of blood and property through their mothers instead of through their fathers, and they have a peculiar system of age-grades, that is, they classify all members of the tribe in a series of ranks according to their respective ages.2 Among these people Mr. Ishii discovered the story of a great flood in several different versions. One of them, recorded at the village of Kibi, runs as follows :—

In ancient times there existed the god Kakumodan Sappatorroku and the goddess Budaihabu. They descended to a place called Taurayan, together with two children, the boy Sura and the girl Nakao. At the same time they brought with them a pig and a chicken, which they reared. But one day it happened that two other gods, named Kabitt and Aka, were hunting near by, and seeing the pig and the chicken they coveted them. So they went up to the house and asked Kakumodan to give them the creatures, but having nothing to offer in exchange they met with a flat refusal. That angered them, and to avenge the affront they plotted to kill Kakumodan. To assist them in carrying out this nefarious design they called in a loud voice on the four sea-gods, Mahahan, Mariyaru, Marimokoshi, and Kosomatora, who readily consented to bear a hand. "In five days from now," they said, "when the round moon appears, the sea will make a booming sound, then escape to a mountain, where there are stars."

So on the fifth day, without waiting for the sound, Kabitt and Aka fled to the mountain where there were stars. When they reached the summit, the sea suddenly began to make the sound and rose higher and higher, till soon Kakumodan's house was flooded. But Kakumodan and his wife escaped from the swelling tide, for they climbed up a ladder to the sky. Yet so urgent was the danger and so great their haste, that they had no time to rescue their two children. Accordingly, when they had reached their place of safety up aloft, they remembered their offspring, and feeling great anxiety on their account they called them in a loud voice, but no voice answered. However, the two children, Sura and Nakao, were not drowned. For when the flood overtook them, they embarked in a wooden mortar, which chanced to be lying in the yard of the house, and in that frail vessel they floated safely to the Ragasan mountain. The brother and sister now found themselves alone in the world ; and though they feared to offend the ancestral gods by contracting an incestuous marriage, they nevertheless became man and wife, and their union was blest with five children, three boys and two girls, whose names are recorded. Yet the pair sought to mitigate or avert the divine wrath by so regulating their conjugal intercourse that they came into contact with each other as little as possible and for that purpose they interposed a mat between them in the marriage bed. The first gram of millet was produced from the wife's ear during her first pregnancy, and in due time husband and wife learned the proper ritual to be observed in the cultivation of that cereal.

At the village of Baran a somewhat different version of the story was recorded by Mr. Ishii. According to this latter version the great flood was due not to a rising of the sea, but to an earthquake, followed by the bursting forth of hot subterranean waters. They say that at that time the mountains crumbled down, the earth gaped, and from the fissure a hot spring gushed forth, which flooded the whole face of the earth. Many people were drowned; indeed few living things survived the ravages of the inundation. However, two sisters and a brother escaped in a wooden mortar, which floated with them southward along the coast to a place called Rarauran. There they landed and climbed to the top of Mount Kaburugan to survey the country round about. Then they separated, the sisters going to the south and the brother to the west, to search for a good land but, finding none they returned once more to Rarauran. Again they ascended the mountain, and the brother and his younger sister reached the summit, but the elder sister was so tired that she remained behind half-way up. When her brother and her younger sister searched for her, they found to their sorrow that she was turned into a stone. After that they desired to return to their native land, from which they had drifted in the wooden mortar. But when they came to examine the mortar, they found it so rotten and leaky that they dared not venture to put to sea in it again. So they wandered away on foot. One day the forlorn wanderers were alarmed by the sight of smoke rising at a distance. Expecting nothing less than a second eruption and a second flood, they hurried away, the brother taking his sister by the hand to hasten her steps. But she was so weary with wandering that she could not go a step farther and fell to the ground. So there they were forced to stay for many days. Meantime the symptoms which had alarmed them had ceased to threaten, and they resolved to settle on the spot.

But they were now all alone in the land, and they reflected with apprehension on the misery of the childless old age which seemed in store for them. In this dilemma, as there was nobody else for them to marry, they thought they had better marry each other. Yet they felt a natural delicacy at doing so, and in their perplexity they resolved to submit their scruples to the judgment of the sun. So next morning, when the sun was rising out of the sea, the brother inquired of it in a loud voice whether he might marry his sister. The sun answered, apparently without hesitation, that he might. The brother was very glad to hear it, and married his sister accordingly. A few months afterwards the wife conceived, and, with her husband's help, gathered china-grass, spun it into yarn, and wove the yarn into clothes for the expected baby. But when her time came, to the bitter disappointment of both parents, she was delivered of two abortions that were neither girl nor boy. In their vexation they tore up the baby-linen and threw it, with the abortions, into the river. One of the abortions swam straight down the river, and the other swam across the river; the one became the ancestor of fish, and the other the ancestor of crabs. Next morning the brother inquired of the moon why fish and crabs should thus be born from human parents. The moon made answer, "You two are brother and sister, and marriage between you is strictly prohibited. As neither of you can find another spouse, you must place a mat between you in the marriage bed." The advice was accepted, and soon afterwards the wife gave birth to a stone. They were again painfully surprised, and said, "The moon is mocking us. Who ever heard of a woman giving birth to a stone?" In their impatience they were about to heave the stone into the river, when the moon appeared and checked them, saying, "Although it is a stone, you must take great care of it." They obeyed the injunction and kept the stone very carefully.

Afterwards they descended the mountain and settled in a rich fat land called Arapanai. In time the husband died, and the wife was left with no other companion than the white stone to which she had given birth. But the moon, pitying her loneliness and grief, informed the woman that soon she would have a companion. And sure enough, only five days later, the stone swelled up, and four children came forth from it, some of them wearing shoes and others barefooted. Those that wore shoes were probably the ancestors of the Chinese.

A third version of the Ami story was recorded by Mr. Ishii at the village of Pokpok. Like the preceding versions, it relates how a brother and sister escaped in a wooden mortar from a destructive deluge, in which almost all living beings perished; how they landed on a high mountain, married, begat offspring, and founded the village of Pokpok in a hollow of the hills, where they thought they would be secure against another deluge.

The Tsuwo, a tribe of head-hunters in the mountainous interior of Formosa, have also a story of a great flood, which they told to Mr. Ishii at the village of Paichana. When their ancestors were living dispersed in all directions, there occurred a mighty inundation whereby plain and mountains alike were covered with water.

Then all the people fled and took refuge on the top of Mount Niitaka-yama, and there they stayed until the flood subsided, and the hills and valleys emerged once more from the watery waste. After that the survivors descended in groups from the mountains and took their several ways over the land as chance or inclination prompted them. They say that it was while they dwelt on the top of the mountain, during the great flood, that they first conceived the idea of hunting for human heads. At first they resorted to it simply as a pastime, cutting off the head of a bad boy and hoisting it on the point of a bamboo, to the great amusement of the bystanders. But afterwards, when they had descended from the mountain and settled in separate villages, the young men of each village took arms and went out to decapitate their neighbours in grim earnest. That, they say, was the origin of the practice of head-hunting.

The Tsuwo of the same village also tell how they obtained fire during the great flood. For in their hurried retreat to the mountain they had no time to take fire with them, and for a while they were hard put to it by the cold. Just then some one spied a sparkle like the twinkling of a star on the top of a neighbouring mountain. So the people said, "Who will go thither and bring fire for us?" Then a goat came forward and said, "I will go and bring back the fire." So saying, the noble animal plunged into the swelling flood and swam straight for the mountain, guided by the starlike twinkling of the fire on its top. The people awaited its return in great anxiety. After a while it reappeared from out the darkness, swimming with a burning cord attached to its horns. Nearer and nearer it drew to the shore, but at the same time lower and lower burned the fire on the cord. Would the goat reach the bank before the flame had burned itself out ? The excitement among the people was intense, but none dared to dive into the angry surges and swim to the rescue of the animal. Tired with its long and strenuous exertions, the goat swam more and more feebly, till at last it drooped its head, the water closed over it, and the fire was out. After that the people despatched a taoron (?) on the same errand, and it succeeded in bringing the fire safe to land. So pleased were the people at its success, that they all gathered round the animal and patted it. That is why the creature has such a shiny skin and so tiny a body to this day.

Further, the Tsuwo of the same village relate how the great flood was drained by the disinterested exertions of a wild pig, and how the natural features of the country were artificially moulded when all the water had run away. They say that they tried various plans for draining the water, but all in vain, until a large wild pig came forward and said, "I will go into the water, and by breaking a bank in a lower reach of the river, I may cause the flood to abate. In case I should be drowned in the river I would beg you, of your kindness, to care for my orphan children, and to give them potatoes every day. If you consent to this proposal, I am willing to risk my life in your service." The people gladly closed with this generous offer; the pig plunged into the water, and swimming with the current, disappeared in the distance. The efforts of the animal were crowned with success, for very soon afterwards the water of the flood suddenly sank, and the crests of the mountains began to appear above it. Rejoiced at their escape, the people resolved to make a river with the help of the animals, apparently for the purpose of preventing a recurrence of the great flood.

As they descended from Mount Niitaka-yama, where they had taken refuge, a great snake offered to act as their guide, and by gliding straight down the slope he hollowed out a bed for the stream. Next thousands of little birds, at the word of command, came each with a pebble in its beak, and by depositing the pebbles in the channel of the river they paved it, as we see it to this day. But the banks of the river had still to be formed, and for this purpose the services of the animals were enlisted. By treading with their feet and working with a will all together, they soon fashioned the river banks and valleys. The only bird that did not help in this great work was the eagle; instead of swooping down he flew high in air, and as a punishment he has never since been allowed to drink of the river water, but is obliged to slake his thirst at the puddles in the hollow trunks of trees. In this way the valleys and rivers were fashioned, but there was as yet no plain. Then the goddess Hipararasa came from the south and made a plain by crushing the mountains. She began in the south and worked up along the western part, levelling the mountains as she went. But when she came to the central range she was confronted by an angry bear, which said, "We are fond of the mountains. If you make them into a plain, we shall lose our dwelling-places." With that he bit and wounded the child of the goddess. Surprised by this attack, the goddess desisted from her work of destruction in order to tend her wounded child. Meantime the earth hardened, so that not even the power of God could level the mountains. That is why the central range still stands in Formosa.

The Bunun, another tribe in the interior of Formosa, whose territory borders on that of the Tsuwo to the east, tell stories of a great flood in which a gigantic snake and crab figure prominently. They say that once upon a time, in the land where their ancestors lived there fell a heavy rain for many days, and to make matters worse a huge snake lay across the river, blocking up the current, so that the whole land was flooded. The people escaped to the top of the highest mountain, but such was the strength of the rising tide that they trembled at the sight of it. Just then a crab appeared opportunely and cut the body of the snake clean through with its nippers. So the flood soon subsided but many people were drowned and few survived. In another version of the Bunun story the cause of the flood is related somewhat differently. A gigantic crab tried to devour a big snake, clutching it fast in its nippers. But the snake contrived to shake off its assailant and escape to the sea. At once a great flood occurred; the waves washed the mountains, and the whole world was covered with water. The ancestors of the Bunun took refuge on Mount Usabeya (Niitaka-yama) and Mount Shinkan, where they made shift to live by hunting, till the water subsided and they returned to their former abode. There they found that their fields and gardens had been washed away but, fortunately, a stalk of millet had been preserved, the seeds' were planted, and on the produce the people subsisted. They say that many mountains and valleys were formed by the great flood, for before that time the land had been quite flat.

The primitive inhabitants of the Andaman Islands, in the Bay of Bengal, have a legend of a great flood, which may be related here, though their islands do not strictly belong to the Indian Archipelago. They say that some time after they had been created, men grew disobedient and regardless of the commands which the Creator had given them at their creation. So in anger he sent a great flood which covered the whole land, except perhaps Saddle Peak where the Creator himself resided. All living creatures, both men and animals, perished in the waters, all save two men and two women, who, having the good luck to be in a canoe at the time when the catastrophe occurred, contrived to escape with their lives. When at last the waters sank, the little company landed, but they found themselves in a sad plight, for all other living creatures were drowned. However, the Creator, whose name was Puluga, kindly helped them by creating animals and birds afresh for their use. But the difficulty remained of lighting a fire, for the flood had extinguished the flames on every hearth, and all things were of course very damp.

Hereupon the ghost of one of their friends, who had been drowned in the deluge, opportunely came to the rescue. Seeing their distress he flew in the form of a kingfisher to the sky, where he found the Creator seated beside his fire. The bird made a dab at a burning brand, intending to carry it off in his beak to his fireless friends on earth, but in his haste or agitation he dropped it on the august person of the Creator himself, who, incensed at the indignity and smarting with pain, hurled the blazing brand at the bird. It missed the mark and whizzing past him dropped plumb from the sky at the very spot where the four people were seated moaning and shivering. That is how mankind recovered the use of fire after the great flood. When they had warmed themselves and had leisure to reflect on what had happened, the four survivors began to murmur at the Creator for his destruction of all the rest of mankind and their passion getting the better of them they even plotted to murder him. From this impious attempt they were, however, dissuaded by the Creator himself, who told them, in very plain language, that they had better not try, for he was as hard as wood, their arrows could make no impression on him, and if they dared so much as to lay a finger on him, he would have the blood of every mother's son and daughter of them. This dreadful threat had its effect; they submitted to their fate, and the mollified Creator condescended to explain to them, in milder terms, that men had brought the great flood on themselves by wilful disobedience to his commands, and that any repetition of the offence in future would be visited by him with condign punishment. That was the last time that the Creator ever appeared to men and conversed with them face to face; since then the Andaman Islanders have never seen him, but to this day they continue to do his will with fear and trembling.1

§ 11. Stories of a Great Flood in Australia

The Kurnai, an aboriginal Australian tribe of Gippsland, in Victoria, say that a long time ago there was a very great flood; all the country was under water, and all the black people were drowned except a man and two or three women, who took refuge in a mud island near Port Albert. The water was all round them. Just then the pelican, or Bunjil Borun, as the Kurnai call the bird, came sailing by in his canoe, and seeing the distress of the poor people he went to help them. One of the women was so beautiful that he fell in love with her. When she would have stepped into the canoe, he said, "Not now, next time," so that after he had ferried all the rest, one by one, across to the mainland, she was left to the last. Afraid of being alone with the ferryman, she did not wait his return on his last trip, but swam ashore and escaped. However, before quitting the island, she dressed up a log in her opossum rug and laid it beside the fire, so that it looked just like herself. When the pelican arrived to ferry her over, he called, "Come on, now." The log made no reply, so the pelican flew into a passion, and rushing up to what he took to be the woman, he lunged out with his foot at her and gave the log a tremendous kick. Naturally he only hurt his own foot, and what with the pain and the chagrin at the trick that had been played him, he was very angry indeed and began to paint himself white in order that he might fight the husband of the impudent hussy who had so deceived him. He was still engaged in these warlike preparations, and had only painted white one half of his black body, when another pelican came up, and not knowing what to make of such a strange creature, half white and half black, he pecked at him with his beak and killed him. That is why pelicans are now black and white; before the flood they were black all over.1

According to the aborigines about Lake Tyers, in Victoria, the way in which the great flood came about was this. Once upon a time all the water in the world was swallowed by a huge frog, and nobody else could get a drop to drink. It was most inconvenient, especially for the fish, who flapped about and gasped on the dry land. So the animals laid their heads together and came to the conclusion that the only way of making the frog disgorge the waters was to tickle his fancy so that he should laugh. Accordingly they gathered before him and cut capers and played pranks that would have caused any ordinary person to die of laughing. But the frog did not even smile. He sat there in gloomy silence, with his great goggle eyes and his swollen cheeks, as grave as a judge. As a last resort the eel stood up on its tail and wriggled and danced about, twisting itself into the most ridiculous contortions. This was more than even the frog could bear. His features relaxed, and he laughed till the tears ran down his cheeks and the water poured out of his mouth. However, the animals had now got more than they had bargained for, since the waters disgorged by the frog swelled into a great flood in which many people perished. Indeed the whole of mankind would have been drowned, if the pelican had not gone about in a canoe picking up the survivors and so saving their lives.1

Another legend of a deluge current among the aborigines of Victoria relates how, many long ages ago, the Creator Bundjel was very angry with black people because they did evil. So he caused the ocean to swell by the same process by which Strepsiades in Aristophanes supposed that Zeus made rain to fall from the clouds;2 and in the rising flood all black people were drowned, except those whom Bundjel loved and, catching up from the water, fixed as stars in the sky. Nevertheless one man and one woman escaped the deluge by climbing a high tree on a mountain; so they lived and became the ancestors of the present human race.3 The Narrinyeri of South Australia say that once on a time a man's two wives ran away from him. He pursued them to Encounter Bay, and there seeing them at a distance he cried out in anger, "Let the waters arise and drown them." On that a terrible flood swept over the hills and overtaking the fugitives overwhelmed them, so that they died. To such a height did the waters rise that a certain man named Nepelle, who lived at Rauwoke, was obliged to drag his canoe to the top of the hill which is now called Point Macleay. The dense part of the Milky Way is said to be his canoe floating in the sky.4

The natives about Mount Elliot, on the coast of Queensland, say that in the time of their forefathers there happened a great flood, which drowned most of them; only a few were saved who contrived to escape to the top of a very high mountain, called Bibbiringda, which rises inland from the northern bay of Cape Cleveland.5

12.   Stories of a Great Flood in New Guinea and Melanesia In the Kabadi district of British New Guinea the natives have a tradition that once on a time a certain man Lohero and his younger brother were angry with the people about them, and they put a human bone into a small stream. Soon the great waters came forth, forming a sea, flooding all the low land, and driving the people back to the mountains, till step by step they had to escape to the tops of the highest peaks. There they lived till the sea receded, when some of them descended to the lowlands, while others remained on the ridges and there built houses and formed plantations.1 The Valmans of Berlin Harbour, on the northern coast of New Guinea, tell how one day the wife of a very good man saw a great fish swimming to the bank. She called to her husband, but at first he could not see the fish. So his wife laughed at him and hid him behind a banana-tree, that he might peep at it through the leaves. When he did catch sight of it at last, he was horribly afraid, and sending for his family, a son and two daughters, he forbade them to catch and eat the fish. But the other people took bow and arrow and a cord, and they caught the fish and drew it to land. Though the good man warned them not to eat of the fish, they did it notwithstanding. When the good man saw that, he hastily drove a pair of animals of every sort up into the trees, and then he and his family climbed up into a coco-nut tree. Hardly had the wicked men consumed the fish than water burst from the ground with such violence that nobody had time to save himself. Men and animals were all drowned. When the water had mounted to the top of the highest tree, it sank as rapidly as it had risen. Then the good man came down from the tree with his family and laid out new plantations.2

The natives of the Mamberano River, in Dutch New Guinea, are reported to tell a story of a great flood, caused by the rising of the river, which overwhelmed Mount Vanessa, and from which only one man and his wife escaped, together with a pig, a cassowary, a kangaroo, and a pigeon. The man and his wife became the ancestors of the present race of men; the beasts and birds became the ancestors of the existing species. The bones of the drowned animals still lie on Mount Vanessa.1

On the subject of deluge legends in New Guinea the following remarks of a judicious and well-informed writer deserve to be borne in mind. "New Guinea," he says, "is the classic land of earthquakes, and ten years never pass without the occurrence somewhere of a tremendous convulsion, such as the sinking of whole districts or the inroad of destructive flood-waves. Thus, for example, the sea is said to have formerly reached to the top of Saddle Mountain. Stories of a flood are therefore common in New Guinea, and have originated in the country itself under the impression of these natural phenomena. Now the Papuan hears the Biblical story of the flood, in which his fancy is particularly taken by the many great animals, of each of which a pair was saved. The terrestrial animals of his own country are hardly worth the saving, and the birds can escape from the flood without the help of man. But since in the Biblical flood large animals were saved, of which pictures are shown to the native, animals which afford much better eating than wretched rats and mice, the black man modifies his own flood legends accordingly. It cannot surprise us, therefore, that legends with a Biblical colouring already existed in New Guinea when the first mission settled there in 1886; for the neighbourhood of the Malay Archipelago, where missionaries had been much longer resident, facilitated the importation of the stories. Besides, a mission had been established in the island of Rook as early as about the middle of the nineteenth century and Rook has been in constant communication with the mainland of New Guinea by means of the neighbouring Siassi Islands. The Bismarck Archipelago also, where missionaries have long been at work, deserves to be considered with reference to the importation of Biblical stories into Northern New Guinea (Kaiser-Wilhelmsland; for a perpetual intercourse of ideas is kept up between the two countries by the seafaring Siassi and Tami." 1

The Fijians have a tradition of a great deluge, which they call Walavu-levu; some say that the flood was partial, others that it was universal. The way in which the catastrophe came about was this. The great god Ndengei had a monstrous bird called Turukawa, which used to wake him punctually by its cooing every morning. One day his two grandsons, whether by accident or design, shot the bird dead with their bows and arrows, and buried the carcase in order to conceal the crime. So the deity overslept himself, and being much annoyed at the disappearance of his favourite fowl, he sent out his messenger Uto to look for it everywhere. The search proved fruitless. The messenger reported that not a trace of the bird was to be found. But a second search was more successful, and laid the guilt of the murder at the door of the god's grandsons. To escape the rage of their incensed grandfather the young scapegraces fled to the mountains and there took refuge with a tribe of carpenters, who willingly undertook to build a stockade strong enough to keep Ndengei and all his catchpolls at bay. They were as good as their word, and for three months the god and his minions besieged the fortress in vain. At last, in despair of capturing the stockade by the regular operations of war, the baffled deity disbanded his army and meditated a surer revenge.

At his command the dark clouds gathered and burst, pouring torrents of rain on the doomed earth. Towns, hills, and mountains were submerged one after the other, yet for long the rebels, secure in the height of their town, looked down with unconcern on the rising tide of waters. At last when the surges lapped their wooden walls and even washed through their fortress, they called for help to a god, who, according to one account, instructed them to form a float out of the fruit of the shaddock; according to others, he sent two canoes for their use, or taught them how to build a canoe for themselves and thus ensure their own safety. It was Rokoro, the god of carpenters, who with his foreman Rokola came to their rescue. The pair sailed about in two large double canoes, picking up the drowning people and keeping them on board till the flood subsided. Others, however, will have it that the survivors saved themselves in large bowls, in which they floated about. Whatever the minor variations may be in the Fijian legend, all agree that even the highest places were covered by the deluge, and that the remnant of the human race was saved in some kind of vessel, which was at last left high and dry by the receding tide on the island of Mbengha. The number of persons who thus survived the flood was eight. Two tribes were completely destroyed by the waters; one of them consisted entirely of women, the members of the other had tails like those of dogs. Because the survivors of the flood landed on their island, the natives of Mbengha claimed to rank highest of all the Fijians, and their chiefs always acted a conspicuous part in Fijian history; they styled themselves "Subject to heaven alone" (Ngali-duva-ki-langi). It is said that formerly the Fijians always kept great canoes ready for use against another flood, and that the custom was only discontinued in modern times.1

The Melanesians of the New Hebrides say that their great legendary hero Qat disappeared from the world in a deluge. They show the very place from which he sailed away on his last voyage. It is a broad lake in the centre of the island of Gaua. In the days of Qat the ground now occupied by the lake was a spacious plain clothed with forest. Qat felled one of the tallest trees in the wood and proceeded to build himself a canoe out of the fallen trunk. While he was at work on it, his brothers would come and jeer at him, as he sat or stood there sweating away at his unfinished canoe in the shadow of the dense tropical forest. "How will you ever get that huge canoe through the thick woods to the sea?" they asked him mockingly.

"Wait and see," was all he deigned to answer.

When the canoe was finished, he gathered into it his wife and his brothers and all the living creatures of the island, down to the smallest ants, and shut himself and them into the vessel, which he provided with a covering. Then came a deluge of rain; the great hollow of the island was filled with water, which burst through the circle of the hills at the spot where the great waterfall of Gaua still descends seaward, with a thunderous roar, in a veil of spray. There the canoe swept on the rushing water through the barrier of the hills, and driving away out to sea was lost to view. The natives say that the hero Qat took away the best of everything with him when he thus vanished from sight, and still they look forward to his joyful return. When Bishop Patteson and his companions first landed on Mota, the happy natives took him for the long-lost Qat and his brethren. And some years afterwards, when a small trading vessel was one day seen standing in for the island of Gaua and making apparently for the channel down which the water of the great cascade flows to mingle with the sea, the old people on the island cried out joyfully that Qat was come again, and that his canoe knew her own way home. But alas! the ship was cast away on the reef, and Qat has not yet come home.1

§ 13. Stories of a Great Flood in Polynesia and Micronesia

Legends of a great flood in which a multitude of people perished are told by the natives of those groups of islands which under the general names of Polynesia and Micronesia are scattered widely over the Pacific. "The principal facts," we are told, "are the same in the traditions prevailing among the inhabitants of the different groups, although they differ in several minor particulars. In one group the accounts state, that in ancient times Taaroa, the principal god (according to their mythology, the creator of the world), being angry with men on account of their disobedience to his will, overturned the world into the sea, when the earth sank in the waters, excepting a few aurus, or projecting points, which, remaining above its surface, constituted the principal cluster of

islands. The memorial preserved by the inhabitants of Eimeo states, that after the inundation of the land, when the water subsided, a man landed from a canoe near Tiataepua,
in their island, and erected an altar, or marae, in honour of his god." 1

In Tahiti the legend ran as follows. Tahiti was destroyed by the sea; no man, nor hog,
nor fowl, nor dog survived. The groves of trees and the stones were carried away by the
wind. They were destroyed, and the deep was over the land. But two persons, a husband
and a wife, were saved. When the flood came, the wife took up her young chicken, her
young dog, and her kitten; the husband took up his young pig. [These were
all the animals formerly known to the natives; and as the term fanaua, 'young,' is both
singular and plural, it may apply to one or more than one chicken, etc.]. The husband
proposed that they should take refuge on Mount Orofena, a high mountain in Tahiti, saying that it was lofty and would not be reached by the sea. But his wife said that the sea
would reach to Mount Orofena, and that they had better go to Mount O Pitohito, where
they would be safe from the flood. So to Mount O Pitohito they went; and she was right,
for Orofena was overwhelmed by the sea, but O Pitohito rose above the waste of waters
and became their abode. There they watched ten nights, till the sea ebbed, and they saw
the little heads of the mountains appearing above the waves.

When the sea retired, the land remained without produce, without man, and the fish
were putrid in the caves and holes of the rocks. They said, "Dig a hole for the fish in the
sea." The wind also died away, and when all was calm, the stones and the trees began to
fall from the heavens, to which they had been carried up by the wind. For all the trees of
the land had been torn up and whirled aloft by the hurricane. The two looked about, and
the woman said, "We two are safe from the sea, but death, or hurt, comes now in these
stones that are falling. Where shall we abide?" So the two dug a hole, lined it with grass,
and covered it over with stones and earth. Then they crept into the hole, and sitting there
they heard with terror the roar and crash of the stones falling down from the sky. By and
by the rain of stones abated, till only a few stones fell at intervals, and then they dropped
one by one, and finally ceased altogether. The woman said, "Arise, go out, and see
whether the stones are still falling." But her husband said, "Nay, I go not out, lest I die." A
day and a night he waited, and in the morning he said, "The wind is truly dead, and the
stones and the trunks of trees cease to fall, neither is there the sound of the stones." They
went out, and like a small mountain was the heap of fallen stones and tree trunks. Of the
land there remained the earth and the rocks, but the shrubs were destroyed by the sea.
They descended from the mountain, and gazed with astonishment; there were no houses,
nor coco-nuts, nor palm-trees, nor bread-fruit, nor hibiscus, nor grass; all was destroyed
by the sea. The two dwelt together. The woman brought forth two children; one was a
son, the other a daughter. They grieved that there was no food for their children. Again
the mother brought forth, but still there was no food; then the breadfruit bore fruit, and
the coco-nut, and every other kind of food. In three days the land was covered with food
and in time it swarmed with men also, for from those two persons, the father and the
mother, all the people are descended.1

In Raiatea, one of the Leeward Islands in the Tahitian group, tradition ran that shortly after the peopling of the world by the descendants of Taata, the sea-god Ruahatu was reposing among groves of coral in the depths of ocean, when his repose was rudely interrupted. A fisherman, paddling his canoe overhead, in ignorance or forgetfulness of the divine presence, let down his hooks among the branching corals at the bottom of the clear translucent water, and they became entangled in the hair of the sleeping god.

With great difficulty the fisherman wrenched the hooks out of the ambrosial locks and began pulling them up hand-overhand. But the god, enraged at being disturbed in his nap, came also bubbling up to the surface, and popping his head out of the water up-braided the fisherman for his impiety, and threatened in revenge to destroy the land. The affrighted fisherman prostrated himself before the sea-god, confessed his sin, and implored his forgiveness, beseeching that the judgment denounced might be averted, or at least that he himself might escape. Moved by his penitence and importunity, Ruahatu bade him return home for his wife and child and go with them to Toamarama, a small island situated within the reefs on the eastern side of Raiatea. There he was promised security amid the destruction of the surrounding islands. The man hastened home, and taking with him his wife and child he repaired to the little isle of refuge in the lagoon. Some say that he took with him also a friend, who was living under his roof, together with a dog, a pig, and a pair of fowls, so that the refugees numbered four souls, together with the only domesticated animals which were then known in the islands. They reached the harbour of refuge before the close of day, and as the sun set the waters of the ocean began to rise, and the inhabitants of the adjacent shore left their dwellings and fled to the mountains. All that night the waters rose, and next morning only the tops of the high mountains appeared above the widespread sea. Even these were at last covered, and all the inhabitants of the land perished. Afterwards the waters retired, the fisherman and his companions left their retreat, took up their abode on the mainland, and became the progenitors of the present inhabitants.1

The coral islet in which these forefathers of the race found refuge from the great flood is not more than two feet at the highest above the level of the sea, so that it is difficult to understand how it could have escaped the inundation, while the lofty mountains which tower up thousands of feet from the adjacent shore were submerged. This difficulty, however, presents no stumbling-block to the faith of the natives; they usually decline to discuss such sceptical doubts, and point triumphantly for confirmation of their story to the coral, shells, and other marine substances which are occasionally found near the surface of the ground on the tops of their highest mountains. These must, they insist, have been deposited there by the waters of the ocean when the islands were submerged.1

It is significant, as we shall see later on, that in these Tahitian legends the flood is ascribed solely to the rising of the sea, and not at all to heavy rain, which is not even mentioned. On this point the Rev. William Ellis, to whom we owe the record of these legends, makes the following observations : "I have frequently conversed with the people on the subject, both in the northern and southern groups, but could never learn that they had any accounts of the windows of heaven having been opened, or the rain having descended. In the legend of Ruahatu, the Toamarama of Tahiti, and the Kai of Kahinarii in

Hawaii, the inundation is ascribed to the rising of the waters of the sea. In each account, the anger of the god is considered as the cause of the inundation of the world, and the destruction of its inhabitants." 2

When Mr. Ellis preached in the year 1822 to the natives of Hawaii on the subject of Noah's deluge, they told him of a similar legend which had been handed down among them. "They said they were informed by their fathers, that all the land had once been overflowed by the sea, except a small peak on the top of Mouna-Kea, where two human beings were preserved from the destruction that overtook the rest, but they said they had never before heard of a ship, or of Noah, having been always accustomed to call it kai a Kahinárii (sea of Kahinárii)." 3

A somewhat later version of the Hawaiian legend runs thus. "A tradition of the flood likewise exists, which states that all the land, except the summit of Mauna-kea, was over-flowed by copious rains and risings of the waters. Some of the inhabitants preserved themselves in a canoe, which finally rested upon that mountain, after which the waters fell, and the people went forth, and again dwelt in the land. This flood is called Kaiakahnialii, the great deluge of Hinalii." 1 In this later version there are two not unim-portant variations from the earlier. First, the deluge is said to have been partly caused by rain, whereas in the earlier version there is no mention of rain, and in it the flood is attributed to the rising of the sea alone. Second, in the later version the survivors are reported to have saved themselves in a canoe, whereas in the earlier version no canoe is mentioned, the survivors being merely said to have escaped to the mountain. In both points the later version agrees with the Biblical legend and has probably been influ-enced by it.

Mangaia, one of the Hervey Group, is an island which rises from deep water as a ring of live coral. The unbroken reef which surrounds it is covered by the sea at half tide. Inward from this ring of live coral rises a second ring of dead coral, from one to two miles wide, which falls away perpendicularly on the landward side, thus forming a sort of cyclopean wall which runs right round the island. The interior of the island is composed of dark volcanic rock and red clay, which descend in low hills from a flat-topped centre known as the Crown of Mangaia. There is no lagoon. The streams, after fertilizing thou-sands of taro plantations, find their way to the sea by subterranean channels through the inner ring of dead coral.2 Such is Mangaia at the present time. But the natives say that it was not always so. Originally, if we may believe them, the surface of the island was ev-erywhere a gentle uniform slope from the centre to the sea without a single hollow or valley. The process by which the island was transformed into the present shape is said to have been as follows.

Aokeu, a son of Echo, disputed warmly with Ake who should perform the most won-derful thing. Ake's home is the ocean, and his constant employment is to tread down its flooring; thus he ever deepens its vast basin, and enables it to hold more of his favourite element. Ake was confident that he could easily beat Aokeu, who was ignobly born of the continual drippings of purest water from the stalactite roof of a narrow cavern. His name means "Red Circle," and he is so called because after heavy rains the water washes down the red clay and tinges the ocean round the island with a crimson band.

To make sure of success Ake summoned to his help Raka, the god of the winds, who drove a fearful hurricane over sea and land, as if he would bury the island in the depths. The two twin children of the blustering storm-god also lent their aid. One of them, Tikokura, is seen in the line of huge curling, foaming billows, which break in thunder on the reef, threatening to dash the solid coral itself into shivers. The other twin-child of the wind-god is Tane-ere-tue; he manifests himself in the great storm-wave, which is rarely seen, but never without striking terror into the beholder. On rushed these mighty monsters, secure of victory. They swamped the rocks near the sea to the height of a hundred feet above the level of the sea. In proof of it you may see to this day numberless clam and other shells, as well as "coral-borers" (ungakoa) imbedded in the solid rock, which is burrowed and worn, even at its highest points, into a thousand fantastic shapes by the action of the sea.

Meantime, Aokeu on his side had not been idle. He caused the rain—his favourite element—to fall in sheets for five days and nights without intermission. The red clay and small stones were washed down into the ocean, discolouring its waters a long way from the land. On every side the channels deepened until the narrow valleys were formed; but still the wind howled and the rain poured incessantly, till the deep valleys, walled in on the seaward side by perpendicular rocks, where the principal taro-grounds may now be seen, gradually assumed their present dimensions. The flat summit of the central hill, Rangimotia, the Crown of Mangaia, alone rose above the water, to mark the original height of the island.

At the outset, Rangi, the first ruler of Mangaia, had been warned of the desperate strife of the elements which was about to take place and, with his few people, awaited at Rangimotia the issue of the contest. With deep concern he saw on the one hand the wild ocean covering the belt of rocks which surrounds the island, and, on the other hand, a vast lake of fresh water rising rapidly and rushing tumultuously to meet the advancing ocean. Everywhere an immense expanse of water met the eye of Rangi, save only the long narrow strip of level soil upon which he and his people tremblingly stood. Already the rising tide lapped their feet. What if it should rise a little higher? Rangi resolved to appeal to the great god Rongo to save him and his beloved island from destruction. To reach the temple (marae) of the god, which faced the rising sun, Rangi had to wade through the waters, which reached to his chin, along a ridge of hills to a point called Teunu, lying due east. Just there is a spot called "the standing-place of Rongo," because that god hearkened to his grandson's prayer, and looking at the war of waters—the flood from the land meeting and battling with the flood from the sea—he cried, "It is enough (A tira)!" The eye of Vatea, the Sun, opened at the same moment above the scene of conflict; the god saw and pitied mankind. Then the sea sullenly sank to its former level, the rain ceased to fall, the waters of the interior were drained away, and the island assumed its present agreeable diversity of hill and vale. Hence the proud title of the high god of Mangaia, "Rongo, the warder-off of mad billows" (Rongo arai kea).

Mankind were saved, and the land became better adapted than ever to their abode. Aokeu, lord of rain, was acknowledged victor for the ocean had expended its fury in vain on the rocky heights near the sea, they still stood firm, and in vain had the twin-sons of the wind-god sought to storm the heights of the island. But the turbid floods, rushing down from the hills, flowed far away into the ocean, everywhere marking their triumphant progress with the red clay of the mountains of Mangaia. So real was this war of the elements to the men of former days that they disputed as to the route which Rangi took in wading through the flood to the temple of Rongo, some holding that he took the straight road, others that he followed a more circuitous path to avoid a dip in the hills.1

This story of a great flood is interesting, because it appears to be a simple myth invented to explain the peculiar physical features of the island. Had the writer who records the tale not also described the aspect of the island, with which he was familiar, we should probably have failed to perceive the purely local origin of the story, and might have been tempted to derive it from some distant source, perhaps even to find in it a confused reminiscence of Noah and the ark. It is allowable to conjecture that many other stories of a great flood could similarly be resolved into merely local myths, if we were better acquainted with those natural features of the country which the tales were invented to explain.

A somewhat different story of a great flood is told in Rakaanga, an outlying island of the Hervey Group. They say that once on a time a certain chief named Taoiau was greatly incensed with his people for not bringing him the sacred turtle. So in his wrath he roused all the mighty sea-gods, on whose good-will the islands depend for their existence. Amongst them in particular was one who sleeps at the bottom of mid-ocean, but who on that occasion, moved by the king's prayer, stood up in anger like a vast upright stone. A dreadful hurricane burst forth; the ocean rose and swept over the whole island of Rakaanga. The few inhabitants of those days escaped destruction by taking refuge on a mound, which was pointed out to the missionary who has recorded the tale. There was no mountain to which they could fly for safety, since the island is a low atoll covered with forests of coco-nut palms. The memorable event was long known as "the overwhelming of Taoiau." 1

In Samoa it is, or used to be, a universal belief that of old the fish swam where the land now is and tradition adds that when the waters abated, many of the fish of the sea were left on the land and were afterwards changed into stones. Hence, they say, in the bush and on the mountains there are stones in plenty which were once sharks and other inhabitants of the deep.2 According to another Samoan tradition the only survivor of the deluge was a certain Pili, who was either a man or a lizard, and by marriage with a bird, the stormy petrel, begat offspring whose names are recorded.3 The natives of Nanumanga or Hudson's Island, in the South Pacific, also tell of a deluge, and how it was dispelled by the sea-serpent, who, as a woman, married the earth as a man, and by him became the ancestress of the present race of mortals.1 The Maoris of New Zealand have a long legend of the deluge. They say that when men multiplied on the earth and there were many

158

great tribes, evil prevailed everywhere, the tribes quarrelled and made war on each other. The worship of the great god Tane, who had created man and woman, was neglected and his doctrines openly denied. Two great prophets, indeed, there were who taught the true doctrine concerning the separation of heaven and earth, but men scoffed at them, saying that they were false teachers and that heaven and earth had been from the beginning just as we see them now. The names of these two wise prophets were Para-whenua-mea and Tupu-nui-a-uta. They continued to preach till the tribes cursed them, saying, "You two can eat the words of your history as food for you, and you can eat the heads of the words of that history." That grieved the prophets, when men said the wicked words "Eat the heads," and they grew angry. So they took their stone axes and cut down trees, and dragged the trunks to the source of the Tohinga River, and bound them together with vines and ropes, and made a very wide raft. Moreover, they built a house on the raft, and put much food in it, fern-root, and sweet potatoes, and dogs. Then they recited incantations and prayed that rain might descend in such abundance as would convince men of the existence and power of the god Tane, and would teach them the need of worship for life and for peace.

After that the two prophets embarked on the raft, along with two men called Tiu and Reti and a woman named Wai-puna-hau. But there were other women also on the raft. Now Tiu was the priest on the raft, and he prayed and uttered incantations for rain. So it rained in torrents for four or five days, and then the priest repeated incantations to make the rain cease, and it ceased. But still the flood rose; next day it reached the settlement, and on the following day the raft was lifted up by the waters, and floated down the River Tohinga. Great as a sea was now the inundation, and the raft drifted to and fro on the face of the waters. When they had tossed about for seven moons, the priest Tiu said to his companions, "We shall not die, we shall land on the earth," and in the eighth month he said moreover, "The sea has become thin; the flood has begun to subside." The two prophets asked him, " By what do you know?" He answered, "By the signs of my staff." For he had kept his altar on one side of the deck, and there he performed his ceremonies, and repeated his incantations, and observed his staff. And he understood the signs of his staff, and he said again to his companions, "The blustering winds of the past moons have fallen, the winds of this month have died away, and the sea is calm." In the eighth month the raft no longer rolled as before; it now pitched as well as rolled, so the priest knew that the sea was shallow, and that they were drawing near to land. He said to his companions, "This is the moon in which we shall land on dry earth, for by the signs of my staff I know that the sea is becoming less deep."

All the while they floated on the deep they repeated incantations and performed ceremonies in honour of the god Tane. At last they landed on dry earth at Hawaiki. They thought that they might find some of the inhabitants of the world still alive, and that the earth would look as it had looked before the flood. But all was changed. The earth was cracked and fissured in some places, and in others it had been turned upside down and confounded by reason of the flood. And not one soul was left alive in the world. They who came forth from the raft were the solitary survivors of all the tribes of the earth. When they landed, the first thing they did was to perform ceremonies and repeat incantations.

They worshipped Tane, and the Heaven (Rangi), and Rehua, and all the gods; and as they worshipped them they offered them seaweed, a length of the priest's two thumbs for each god. Each god was worshipped in a different place, and for each there was an altar, where the incantations were recited. The altar was a root of grass, a shrub, a tree, or a flax-bush. These were the altars of the gods at that time and now, if any of the people of the tribes go near to such altars, the food they have eaten in their stomachs will swell and kill them. The chief Priest alone may go to such holy spots. If common folk were to go to these sacred places and afterwards cook food in their village, the food would kill all who ate it. It would be cursed by the sin of the people in desecrating the sanctity of the altars, and the punishment of the eaters would be death. When the persons who were saved on the raft had performed all the ceremonies needful for removing the taboo under which they laboured, they procured fire by friction at one of the sacred places. And with the fire the priest kindled bundles of grass, and he put a bundle of burning grass on each altar beside the piece destined for the god, and the priests presented the seaweed to the gods as a thank-offering for the rescue of the people from the flood and for the preservation of their lives on the raft.[1]

Other Maori stories of a great flood associate the catastrophe with a certain legendary hero called Tawhaki. They say that once upon a time two of his brothers-in-law attacked and wounded him and left him for dead. But he recovered from his wounds and quitted the place where his wicked brothers-in-law lived. Away he went with all his own warriors and their families, and he built a fortified village upon the top of a very lofty mountain, where he could easily defend himself, and there they all dwelt secure. " Then he called aloud to the gods, his ancestors, for revenge, and they let the floods of heaven descend, and the earth was overwhelmed by the waters and all human beings perished, and the name given to that event was ' The overwhelming of the Mataaho,' and the whole of that race perished."[2] Some say that Tawhaki was a man, who went up to the top of a mountain, and, having there transfigured himself by putting off his earthly raiment and put on a garment of lightning, was worshipped as a god, and all the tribes chanted incantations and offered sacrifices to him. In his divine character he once, in a fit of anger, stamped on the floor of heaven, so that it cracked and the celestial waters burst through and flooded the earth.[3] Others say that it was Tawhaki's mother who caused the deluge by weeping so copiously that her tears, falling on the earth, inundated it and drowned all men.[1]

In Micronesia as well as Polynesia the story of a great flood has been recorded. The Pelew Islanders say that once on a time a man went up into the sky, whence the gods with their shining eyes, which are the stars, look down every night upon the earth. The cunning fellow stole one of these bright eyes and brought it home with him, and all the money of the Pelew Islanders has been made out of that starry eye ever since. But the gods were very angry at the theft, and down they came to earth to reclaim their stolen property and to punish the thief. They disguised themselves in the likeness of ordinary men, and begged for food and lodging from door to door. But men were churlish and turned them away without a bite or a sup. Only one old woman received them kindly in her cottage, and set before them the best she had to eat and drink. So when they went away they warned the old woman to make a raft of bamboo ready against the next full moon, and when the night of the full moon came she was to lie down on the raft and sleep. She did as she was bidden. Now with the full moon came a dreadful storm and rain, and the sea rose higher and higher, and flooded the islands, rent the mountains, and destroyed the abodes of men, and people knew not how to save themselves, and they all perished in the rising flood. But the good old dame, fast asleep on the raft, was borne on the face of the waters and drifted till her hair caught in the boughs of a tree on the top of Mount Armlimui. There she lay, while the flood ebbed and the water sank lower and lower down the sides of the mountain. Then the gods came down from the sky to seek for the good old woman whom they had taken under their protection, but they found her dead. So they summoned one of their women-folk from heaven, and she entered into the dead body of the old woman and made her live. After that the gods begat five children by the resuscitated old wife, and having done so they left the earth and returned to heaven; the goddess who had kindly reanimated the corpse the ancient dame also went back to her mansion in the sky. But the five children of the divine fathers and the human mother repeopled the Pelew Islands, and from them the present inhabitants are descended.1

§ 14. Stories of a Great Flood in South America

At the time of their discovery the Indians of Brazil, in the neighbourhood of what was afterwards Rio de Janeiro, had a legend of a universal deluge in which only two brothers with their wives were saved. According to one account, the flood covered the whole earth and all men perished except the ancestors of those Indians, who escaped by climbing up into high trees ;2 others, however, thought that the survivors were saved in a canoe.3

As reported by the Frenchman André Thevet, who travelled in Brazil about the middle of the sixteenth century, the story related by the Indians about Cape Frio ran thus. A certain great medicine-man, by name Sommay, had two sons called Tamendonare and Ariconte. Tamendonare tilled the ground and was a good father and husband, and he had a wife and children. But his brother Ariconte cared for none of these things. He busied himself only with war, and his one desire was to subdue neighbouring peoples and even his own righteous brother. One day this truculent warrior, returning from a battle, brought to his peaceful brother the amputated arm of a slain foe, and as he did so he said proudly to his brother, "Away with you, coward that you are. I'll have your wife and children, for you are not strong enough to defend them."

The good man, grieved at his brother's pride, answered with stinging sarcasm, "If you are as valiant as you say, why did not you bring the whole carcass of your enemy?"

Indignant at the taunt, Ariconte threw the arm at the door of his brother's house. At the same moment the village in which they dwelt was transported to the sky, but the two brothers remained on earth. Seeing that, in astonishment or anger Tamendonare stamped on the ground so forcibly that a great fountain of water sprang from it and rose so high that it out-topped the hills and seemed to mount above the clouds, and the water continued to spout till it had covered the whole earth. On perceiving their danger, the two brothers hastened to ascend the highest mountains, and there sought to save themselves by climbing the trees, along with their wives.

Tamendonare climbed one tree, called pindona, of which the French traveller saw two sorts, one of them with larger fruit and leaves than the other. In his flight from the rising flood he dragged up one of his wives with him, while his brother with his wife climbed another tree called geniper. While they were all perched among the boughs, Ariconte gave some of the fruit of the tree to his wife, saying, "Break off some of the fruit and let it fall." She did so, and they perceived by the splash that the water was still high, and that it was not yet time for them to descend into the valley. The Indians believe that in this flood all men and women were drowned, except the two brothers and their wives, and that from these two pairs after the deluge there came forth two different peoples, to wit, the Tonnasseares, surnamed Tupinambo, and the Tonnaitz Hoyanans, surnamed Tominu, who are at perpetual feud and war with each other. The Tupinambo, wishing to exalt themselves and to make themselves out better than their fellows and neighbours, say, " We are descended from Tamendonare, while you are descended from Ariconte," by which they imply that Tamendonare was a better man than Ariconte.1

A somewhat different version of the same legend was recorded by the Jesuit Simon de Vasconcellos. In it only a single family is said to have been saved, and no mention is made of the bad brother. Once upon a time, so runs the tale, there was a clever medicine-man or sorcerer named Tamanduare. To him the great god Tupi revealed the coming of a great flood which would swamp the earth, so that even the high trees and mountains would be submerged. Only one lofty peak would rise above the waters, and on its top would be found a tall palm-tree with a fruit like a coco-nut. To that palm the sorcerer was warned to turn for refuge with his family in the hour of need. Without delay Tamanduare and his family betook themselves to the top of the lofty peak. When they were safely there, it began to rain, and it rained and rained till all the earth was covered. The flood even crept up the mountain and washed over the summit, and the man and his family climbed up into the palm-tree and remained in the branches so long as the inundation lasted, and they subsisted by eating the fruit of the palm. When the water subsided, they descended, and being fruitful they proceeded to repeople the drowned and devastated world.1

The Caingangs, or Coroados, an Indian tribe of Rio Grande do Sul, the most southerly province of Brazil, have a tradition of a great flood which covered the whole earth inhabited by their forefathers. Only the top of the coastal range called Serra do Mar still appeared above the water. The members of three Indian tribes, namely the Caingangs, the Cayurucres, and the Cames, swam on the water of the flood toward the mountains, holding lighted torches between their teeth. But the Cayurucres and the Cames grew weary, they sank under the waves and were drowned, and their souls went to dwell in the heart of the mountain. However, the Caingangs and a few of the Curutons made shift to reach the mountain, and there they abode, some on the ground, and some on the branches of trees. Several days passed, and yet the water did not sink, and they had no food to eat.

They looked for nothing but death, when they heard the song of the saracuras, a species of waterfowl, which flew to them with baskets of earth. This earth the birds threw into the water, which accordingly began slowly to sink. The people cried to the birds to hurry, so the birds called the ducks to their help, and working together they soon cleared enough room and to spare for all the people, except for such as had climbed up the trees; these latter were turned into monkeys. When the flood subsided, the Caingangs descended and settled at the foot of the mountain. The souls of the drowned Cayurucres and Cames contrived to burrow their way out from the bowels of the mountain in which they were imprisoned and when they had crept forth they kindled a fire, and out of the ashes of the fire one of the Cayurucres moulded jaguars, and tapirs, and ant-bears, and bees, and animals of many other sorts, and he made them live and told them what they should eat. But one of the Cames imitated him by fashioning pumas, and poisonous snakes, and wasps, all in order that these creatures should fight the other animals which the Cayurucres had made, as they do to this day.1

A story of a great flood is told also by the Carayas, a tribe of Brazilian Indians, who inhabit the valley of the Araguaya River, which, with the Tocantins, forms the most easterly of the great southern tributaries of the Amazon. The tribe is said to differ from all its neighbours in manners and customs as well as in physical characteristics, while its language appears to be unrelated to any other known language spoken by the Indians of Brazil.2 The Caraya story of a deluge runs thus. Once upon a time the Carayas were out hunting wild pigs and drove the animals into their dens. Thereupon they began to dig them out, killing each pig as it was dragged forth. In doing so they came upon a deer, then a tapir, and then a white deer. Digging still deeper, they laid bare the feet of a man. Horrified at the discovery, they fetched a mighty magician, who knew all the beasts of the forest, and he contrived to draw the man out of the earth. The man thus unearthed was named Anatiua, and he had a thin body but a fat paunch. He now began to sing, "I am Anatiua. Bring me tobacco to smoke."

But the Carayas did not understand what he said. They ran about the wood, and came back with all kinds of flowers and fruits, which they offered to Anatiua. But he refused them all, and pointed to a man who was smoking. Then they understood him and offered him tobacco. He took it and smoked till he fell to the ground senseless.

So they carried him to the canoe and brought him to the village. There he awoke from his stupor and began to dance and sing. But his behaviour and his unintelligible speech frightened the Carayas, and they decamped, bag and baggage. That made Anatiua very angry, and he turned himself into a great piranha and followed them, carrying with him many calabashes full of water. He called to the Carayas to halt, but they paid no heed, and in his rage he smashed one of the calabashes which he was carrying. The water at once began to rise, but still the Carayas pursued their flight. Then he broke another calabash, and then another and another, and higher and higher rose the water, till the whole land was inundated, and only the mountains at the mouth of Tapirape River projected above the flood.

The Carayas took refuge on the two peaks of that range. Anatiua now called all fish together to drag the people down into the water. The jaku, the pintado, and the pacu tried to do so, but none of them succeeded. At last the bicudo (a fish with a long beak-like snout) contrived to scale the mountain from behind and to tear the Carayas down from its summit. A great lagoon still marks the spot where they fell. Only a few persons remained on the top of the mountain, and they descended when the water of the flood had run away.1

On this story the writer who records it remarks that "though in general regularly re-curring inundations, as on the Araguaya, do not give rise to flood stories, as Andree has rightly pointed out,1 yet the local conditions are here favourable to the creation of such a story. The traveller, who, after a long voyage between endless low river-banks, sud-denly comes in sight of the mighty conical mountains on the Tapirape River, towering abruptly from the plain, can easily understand how the Carayas, who suffer much from inundations, came to tell their story of the flood. Perhaps on some occasion when the inundation rose to an unusual height, these mountains may really have served as a last refuge to the inhabitants of the surrounding district." And he adds, "As in most South American legends of a flood, this particular flood is said to have been caused, not by rain, but by the breaking of vessels full of water." 2

The Ipurina, a warlike tribe on the Purus River, one of the great rivers which flow into the Upper Amazon from the south, tell of a destructive deluge of hot water. They say that formerly there was a great kettle of boiling water in the sun. About it perched or flut-tered a countless flock of storks. Some of the birds flew over the world collecting every-thing that mouldered or decayed to throw it into the kettle. Only the hard, indestructible parukuba wood they left alone. The storks surrounded the kettle and waited till some-thing appeared on the surface of the boiling water, whereupon they snapped it up. Now the chief of the storks, indeed the creator of all birds, was Mayuruberu. When the water in the kettle was getting low, he cast a round stone into it. The kettle was upset, the hot liquid poured down on earth and burned everything up, including the woods and even the water. Mankind indeed survived, but of the vegetable world nothing escaped but the cassia. The ancestor of the Ipurina was the sloth. He climbed the cassia-tree to fetch down the fruits, for men had nothing else to subsist upon. On earth it was very dark, for the sun and moon were hidden. The sloth plucked the fruit and threw down the kernels. The first kernel fell on hard earth, the second in water, the third in deep water, and so on. At the fall of the first kernel, the sun appeared again but still very small, hardly an inch across; at the fall of the second, it was larger; at the fall of the third, it measured a span across; and so on until it expanded to its present dimensions. Next the sloth begged Mayuruberu to give him seeds of useful fruits. So Mayuruberu appeared with a great basketful of plants, and the Ipurina began to till their fields. He who would not work was eaten by Mayuruberu. Every day Mayuruberu received a man to devour. Thus the world gradually became such as it is at the present time. The kettle still stands in the sun, but it is empty.1

Again, the Pamarys, Abederys, and Kataushys, on the river Purus, relate that once on

164

a time people heard a rumbling above and below the ground. The sun and moon, also, turned red, blue, and yellow, and the wild beasts mingled fearlessly with men. A month later they heard a roar and saw darkness ascending from the earth to the sky, accompanied by thunder and heavy rain, which blotted out the day and the earth. Some people lost themselves, some died, without knowing why for everything was in a dreadful state of confusion. The water rose very high, till the earth was sunk beneath the water and only the branches of the highest trees still stood out above the flood. Thither the people had fled for refuge, and there, perched among the boughs, they perished of cold and hunger; for all the time it was dark and the rain fell. Then only Uassu and his wife were saved. When they came down after the flood they could not find a single corpse, no, not so much as a heap of bleached bones.

After that they had many children, and they said one to the other, "Go to, let us build our houses on the river, that when the water rises, we too may rise with it." But when they saw that the land was dry and solid, they thought no more about it. Yet the Pamarys build their houses on the river to this day. The Jibaros, an Indian tribe on the upper waters of the Amazon, in the territories of Peru and Ecuador, have also a tradition, more or less confused, of a great deluge which happened long ago. They say that a great cloud fell from heaven, which turned into rain and caused the death of all the inhabitants of the earth; only an old man and his two sons were saved, and it was they who repeopled the earth after the deluge, though how they contrived to do so without the assistance of a woman is a detail about which our authority does not deign to enlighten us. However that may be, one of the two sons who survived was cursed by his father, and the Jibaros are descended from him. The curse may be a reminiscence of the story of Noah and his sons recorded in Genesis, of which the Jibaros may have heard through missionaries. The difficulty of propagating the human species without the help of the female sex would seem to have struck the acuter minds among the Jibaros, for according to some of them the survivors of the deluge were a man and a woman, who took refuge in a cave on a high mountain, together with samples of all the various species of the animal kingdom. This version provides, with commendable foresight, for the restoration of animals as well as of men after the great flood. Yet another version of the story told by the Jibaros solves the problem of population in a more original manner. Nobody, they say, escaped the flood but two brothers, who found refuge in a mountain which, strange to tell, rose higher and higher with the rise of the waters. When the flood had subsided, the two brothers went out to search for food, and on their return to the hut what was their surprise to find victuals set forth ready for them! To clear up the mystery, one of the brothers hid himself, and from his place of concealment he saw two parrots with the faces of women enter the hut and prepare the meal.

Darting out from his ambush he seized one of the birds and married it or her, and from this marriage sprang three boys and three girls, who became the ancestors of the Jibaros.1

The Muratos, a branch of the Jibaros in Ecuador, have their own version of the deluge story. They say that once on a time a Murato Indian went to fish in a lagoon of the Pastaza River; a small crocodile swallowed his bait, and the fisherman killed the young animal.

165

The crocodile's mother, or rather the mother of crocodiles in general, was angry and lashed the water with her tail, till the water overflowed and flooded all the neighbourhood of the lagoon. All the people were drowned except one man, who climbed a palm-tree and stayed there for many days. All the time it was as dark as night. From time to time he dropped a fruit of the palm, but he always heard it splash in the water. At last one day the fruit which he let fall dropped with a simple thud on the ground; there was no splash, so he knew that the flood had subsided. Accordingly he descended from the tree, built a house, and set about to till a field. He was without a wife, but he soon provided himself with one by cutting off a piece of his own body and planting it in the ground, for from the earth thus fertilized there sprang up a woman, whom he married.1

The incident of a moving mountain, which meets us in the Jibaro story of the flood, recurs in another Indian narrative of the great catastrophe. The Araucanians of Chili have a tradition of a great deluge, in which only a few persons were saved. These fortunate survivors took refuge on a high mountain called Thegtheg, the thundering, or the sparkling, which had three points and possessed the property of floating on water. "From hence," says the Spanish historian, "it is inferable that this deluge was in consequence of some volcanic eruption, accompanied by terrible earthquakes, and is probably very different from that of Noah. Whenever a violent earthquake occurs, these people fly for safety to those mountains which they fancy to be of a similar appearance, and which of course, as they suppose, must possess the same property of floating on the water, assigning as a reason, that they are fearful after an earthquake that the sea will again return and deluge the world. On these occasions, each one takes a good supply of provisions, and wooden plates to protect their heads from being scorched, provided the Thegtheg, when raised by the waters, should be elevated to the sun. Whenever they are told that plates made of earth would be much more suitable for this purpose than those of wood, which are liable to be burned, their usual reply is, that their ancestors did so before them." 1

The Ackawois of British Guiana tell a story of the great flood which is enriched by a variety of details. They say that in the beginning of the world the great spirit Makonaima created birds and beasts and set his son Sigu to rule over them. Moreover, he caused to spring from the earth a great and very wonderful tree, which bore a different kind of fruit on each of its branches, while round its trunk bananas, plantains, cassava, maize, and corn of all kinds grew in profusion; yams, too, clustered round its roots and, in short, all the plants now cultivated on earth flourished in the greatest abundance on or about or under that marvellous tree. In order to diffuse the benefits of the tree all over the world, Sigu resolved to cut it down and plant slips and seeds of it everywhere, and this he did with the help of all the beasts and birds, all except the brown monkey, who, being both lazy and mischievous, refused to assist in the great work of transplantation. So to keep him out of mischief Sigu set the animal to fetch water from the stream in a basket of open-work, calculating that the task would occupy his misdirected energies for some time to come. In the meantime, proceeding with the labour of felling the miraculous tree, he discovered that the stump was hollow and full of water in which the fry of every sort of fresh-water fish was swimming about.

The benevolent Sigu determined to stock all the rivers and lakes on earth with the fry on so liberal a scale that every sort of fish should swarm in every water. But this generous intention was unexpectedly frustrated. For the water in the cavity, being connected with the great reservoir somewhere in the bowels of the earth, began to overflow, and to arrest the rising flood, Sigu covered the stump with a closely woven basket. This had the desired effect. But unfortunately the brown monkey, tired of his fruitless task, stealthily returned, and his curiosity being aroused by the sight of the basket turned upside down, he imagined that it must conceal something good to eat. So he cautiously lifted it and peeped beneath, and out poured the flood, sweeping the monkey himself away and inundating the whole land. Gathering the rest of the animals together Sigu led them to the highest point of the country, where grew some tall coco-nut palms. Up the tallest of these trees he caused the birds and climbing animals to ascend, and as for the animals that could not climb and were not amphibious, he shut them up in a cave with a very narrow entrance, and having sealed up the mouth of it with wax he gave the animals inside a long thorn with which to pierce the wax and so ascertain when the water had subsided. After taking these measures for the preservation of the more helpless species, he and the rest of the creatures climbed up the palm-tree and ensconced themselves among the branches. During the darkness and storm which followed, they all suffered intensely from cold and hunger; the rest bore their sufferings with stoical fortitude, but the red howling monkey uttered his anguish in such horrible yells that his throat swelled and has remained distended ever since; that, too, is the reason why to this day he has a sort of bony drum in his throat.

Meanwhile Sigu from time to time let fall seeds of the palm into the water to judge of its depth by the splash. As the water sank, the interval between the dropping of the seed and the splash in the water grew longer; and at last, instead of a splash, the listening Sigu heard the dull thud of the seeds striking the soft earth. Then he knew that the flood had subsided, and he and the animals prepared to descend. But the trumpeter-bird was in such a hurry to get down that he flopped straight into an ants' nest, and the hungry insects fastened on his legs and gnawed them to the bone. That is why the trumpeter-bird has still such spindle shanks. The other creatures profited by this awful example and came down the tree cautiously and safely. Sigu now rubbed two pieces of wood together to make fire, but just as he produced the first spark, he happened to look away, and the bush-turkey, mistaking the spark for a firefly, gobbled it up and flew off. The spark burned the greedy bird's gullet, and that is why turkeys have red wattles on their throats to this day. The alligator was standing by at the time, doing no harm to anybody; but as he was for some reason an unpopular character, all the other animals accused him of having stolen and swallowed the spark. In order to recover the spark from the jaws of the alligator Sigu tore out the animal's tongue, and that is why alligators have no tongue to speak of down to this very day.1

The Arawaks of British Guiana believe that since its creation the world has been twice destroyed, once by fire and once by flood. Both destructions were brought on it by Aiomun Kondi, the great "Dweller on High," because of the wickedness of mankind. But he announced beforehand the coming catastrophe, and men who accepted the warning prepared to escape from the great fire by digging deep into a sand-reef and there making for themselves a subterranean chamber with a roof of timber supported on massive pillars of the same material. Over it all they spread layers of earth and a thick upper coating of sand. Having carefully removed everything combustible from the neighbourhood, they retired to this underground dwelling and there stayed quietly till the roaring torrent of flame, which swept across the earth's surface, had passed over them. Afterwards, when the destruction of the world by a deluge was at hand, a pious and wise chief named Marerewana was informed of the coming flood and saved himself and his family in a large canoe. Fearing to drift away out to sea or far from the home of his fathers, he had made ready a long cable of bush-rope, with which he tied his bark to the trunk of a great tree. So when the waters subsided he found himself not far from his former abode.2

The Macusis of British Guiana say that in the beginning the good spirit Makunaima, whose name means "He who works in the night," created the heaven and the earth. When he had stocked the earth with plants and trees, he came down from his celestial mansion, climbed up a tall tree, and chipped off the bark with a big stone axe. The chips fell into the river at the foot of the tree and were changed into animals of all kinds. When he had thus provided for the creation of animals, the good spirit next created man, and when the man had fallen into a sound sleep he awoke to find a woman standing at his side. Afterwards the evil spirit got the upper hand on earth, so the good spirit Makunaima sent a great flood. Only one man escaped in a canoe; he sent out a rat to see whether the water had abated, and the rat returned with a cob of maize. When the deluge had retreated, the man repeopled the earth, like Deucalion and Pyrrha, by throwing stones behind him.1 In this story the special creation of woman, the mention of the evil spirit, and the incident of the rat sent out to explore the depth of the flood, present suspicious resemblances to the Biblical narrative and may be due to missionary, or at all events European, influence. Further, the mode in which, after the flood, the survivors create mankind afresh by throwing stones behind them, resembles so exactly the corresponding incident in the Greek story of Deucalion and Pyrrha, that it is difficult to regard the two as independent.

Legends of a great flood are current also among the Indians of the Orinoco. On this subject Humboldt observes : "I cannot quit this first chain of the mountains of Encamarada without recalling a fact which was not unknown to Father Gili, and which was often mentioned to me during our stay among the missions of the Orinoco. The aborigines of these countries have preserved a belief that at the time of the great flood, while their fathers were forced to betake themselves to canoes in order to escape the general inundation, the waves of the sea broke against the rocks of Encamarada. This belief is not found isolated among a single people, the Tamanaques; it forms part of a system of historical traditions of which scattered notices are discovered among the Maypures of the great cataracts, among the Indians of the Rio Erevato, which falls into the Caura, and among almost all the tribes of the Upper Orinoco. When the Tamanaques are asked how the human race escaped this great cataclysm, 'the Age of Water,' as the Mexicans call it, they say that one man and one woman were saved on a high mountain called Tamanacu, situated on the banks of the Asiveru, and that on casting behind them, over their heads, the fruits of the Mauritia palm, they saw springing from the kernels of these fruits men and women, who repeopled the earth." 1 This they did in obedience to a voice which they heard speaking to them as they descended the mountain full of sorrow at the destruction of mankind by the flood. The fruits which the man threw became men, and the fruits which the woman threw became women.2

The Muyscas or Chibchas of Bogota, in the high Andes of Colombia, say that long ago their ancestors offended Chibchachum, a deity of the second rank, who had hitherto been their special patron and protector. To punish them, Chibchachum created the torrents of Sopo and Tibito, which, pouring down from the hills, flooded the whole plain and rendered cultivation impossible. The people fled to the mountains, but even there the rising waters of the inundation threatened to submerge them. In despair they prayed to the great god Bochica, who appeared to them seated on a rainbow and holding a golden wand in his hand. "I have heard your prayers," said he, "and I will punish Chibchachum. I shall not destroy the rivers, which he has created, because they will be useful to you in time of drought, but I will open a passage for the waters." With these words he threw his golden wand at the mountain, split it from top to bottom at the spot where the river Funzha now forms the famous waterfall of Tequendama. So all the waters of the deluge flowed away down this new opening in the circle of mountains which encloses the high upland tableland of Bogota, and thus the plain became habitable again. To punish Chibchachum, the great god Bochica condemned him to bear on his shoulders the whole weight of the earth, which before that time was supported on massive pillars of wood. When the weary giant tries to get a little ease by shifting his burden from one shoulder to another, he causes an earthquake.3

This tradition is in so far well founded as the evidence of geology appears to prove that for ages the mountain-girt plain of Bogota was occupied by a lake, and that the pent up waters at last found vent and flowed away through a fissure suddenly cleft by a great earthquake in the sandstone rocks. The cleft in the rocky dam may be seen to this day. It is near the meeting of the rivers Bogota and Muño. Here the wall of sandstone is broken by a sort of natural gateway formed by a beetling crag on one side and a mass of shattered, crumbling rocks on the other. The scene is one well fitted to impress the mind and excite the imagination of primitive man, who sees in the sublime works of nature the handiwork of awful and mysterious beings. The sluggish current of the tawny river flows in serpentine windings towards the labyrinth of rocks and cliffs where it takes its leap into the tremendous abyss. As you near the fall, and the hollow sound of its tumbling waters grows louder and louder, a great change comes over the landscape. The bare monotonous plain of Bogota is left behind, and you seem to be entering on enchanted land. On every side rise hills of varied outline mantled to their tops with all the luxuriant vegetation of the tropics, from the grasses which carpet the ground to the thickets and tall forest trees which spread over the whole a dense veil of green. At their foot the river hurries in a series of rapids, between walls of rock, to the brink of the fall, there to vanish in a cloud of mist and spray, lit up by all the gay colours of the rainbow, into the dark and dizzy chasm below, while the thunderous roar of the cataract breaks the stillness of the lonely hills. The cascade is thrice as high as Niagara; and by a pardonable exaggeration the river is said to fall perpendicularly from the temperate to the tropical zone.1

The Cañaris, an Indian tribe of Ecuador, in the ancient kingdom of Quito, tell of a great flood from which two brothers escaped to a very high mountain called Huaca-yñan. As the waters rose, the hill rose with them, so that the flood never reached the two brothers on the summit. When the water sank and their store of provisions was consumed, the brothers descended and sought their food in the hills and valleys. They built a small house, where they dwelt, eking out a miserable subsistence on herbs and roots, and suffering much from hunger and fatigue. One day, after the usual weary search, they returned home, and there found food to eat and chicha to drink without knowing who could have prepared or brought it. This happened for ten days, and after that they laid their heads together to find out who it was that did them so much good in their time of need. So the elder brother hid himself, and presently he saw two macaws approaching, dressed like Cañaris. As soon as the birds came to the house, they began to prepare the food which they had brought with them. When the man saw that they were beautiful and had the faces of women, he came forth from his hiding-place ; but at sight of him the birds were angry and flew away, leaving nothing to eat. When the younger brother came home from his search for food, and found nothing cooked and ready as on former days, he asked his elder brother the reason, and they were both very angry. Next day the younger brother resolved to hide and watch for the coming of the birds. At the end of three days the two macaws reappeared and began to prepare the food. The two men waited till the birds had finished cooking and then shut the door on them. The birds were very angry, at being thus trapped, and while the two brothers were holding the smaller bird, the larger one escaped. Then the two brothers took the smaller macaw to wife, and by her they had six sons and daughters, from whom all the Cañaris are descended. Hence the hill Huaca-yñan, where the macaw lived as the wife of the brothers, is looked upon as a sacred place by the Indians, and they venerate macaws and value their feathers highly for use at their festivals.1

The Indians of Huarochiri, a province of Peru in the Andes to the east of Lima, say that once on a time the world nearly came to an end altogether. It happened thus. An Indian was tethering his llama in a place where there was good pasture, but the animal resisted, showing sorrow and moaning after its manner. The master said to the llama, "Fool why do you moan and refuse to eat? Have I not put you where there is good food ?" The llama answered, "Madman, what do you know about it ? Learn that I am not sad without due cause; for within five days the sea will rise and cover the whole earth, destroying all there is upon it." Wondering to hear the beast speak, the man asked whether there was any way in which they could save themselves. The llama bade him take food for five days and to follow him to the top of a high mountain called Villca-coto, between the parish of San Damian and the parish of San Geronimo de Surco. The man did as he was bid, carrying the load of food on his back and leading the llama. On reaching the top of the mountain he found many kinds of birds and animals there assembled. Hardly had he reached this place of refuge when the sea began to rise, and it rose till the water flooded all the valleys and covered the tops of the hills, all but the top of Villca-coto, and even there the

170

waves washed so high that the animals had to crowd together in a narrow space, and some of them could hardly find foothold. The tail of the fox was dipped in the flood, and that is why the tips of foxes' tails are black to this day. At the end of five days the waters began to abate, and the sea returned to its former bounds; but all the people in the world were drowned except that one man, and from him all the nations of the earth are descended.1

A similar story of the flood is told by the Indians of Ancasmarca, a province five leagues from Cuzco. They say that a month before the flood came, their sheep displayed much sadness, eating no food by day and watching the stars by night. At last their shepherd asked them what ailed them, and they answered that the conjunction of stars foreshadowed the coming destruction of the world by water. So the shepherd and his six children took counsel, and gathered together all the food and sheep they could get, and with these they betook themselves to the top of an exceeding great mountain called Ancasmarca. They say that as the water rose, the mountain still rose higher, so that its top was never submerged, and when the flood sank, the mountain sank also. Thus the six children of that shepherd returned to repeople the province after the great flood.1

The Incas of Peru had also a tradition of a deluge. They said that the water rose above the highest mountains in the world, so that all people and all created things perished. No living thing escaped except a man and a woman, who floated in a box on the face of the waters and so were saved. When the flood subsided, the wind drifted the box with the two in it to Tiahuanacu, about seventy leagues from Cuzco. There the Creator commanded them to dwell, and there he himself set to work to raise up the people who now inhabit that country. The way in which he did so was this. He fashioned each nation out of clay and painted on each the dresses they were to wear. Then he gave life and soul to every one of the painted clay figures and bade them pass under the earth. They did so, and then came up at the various places where the Creator had ordered the different nations to dwell. So some of them came out of caves, others issued from hills, others from fountains, and others from the trunks of trees. And because they came forth from these various places, the Indians made various idols (huacas) and places of worship in memory of their origin; that is why the idols (huacas) of the Indians are of diverse shapes.2

The Peruvian legends of a great flood are told more summarily by the Spanish historian Herrera as follows. "The ancient Indians reported, they had received it by tradition from their ancestors, that many years before there were any Incas, at the time when the country was very populous, there happened a great flood, the sea breaking out beyond its bounds, so that the land was covered with water, and all the people perished. To this the Guancas inhabiting the vale of Xauxa, and the natives of Chiquito in the province of Collao, add, that some persons remained in the hollows and caves of the highest mountains, who again peopled the land. Others of the mountain people affirm that all perished in the deluge, only six persons being saved on a float, from whom descended all the inhabitants of that country. That there had been some particular flood may be credited, because all the several provinces agree in it." 1

The Chiriguanos, a once powerful Indian tribe of southeastern Bolivia, tell the following story of a great flood. They say that a certain potent but malignant supernatural being, named Aguara-Tunpa, declared war against the true god Tunpaete, the Creator of the Chiriguanos. His motive for this declaration of war is unknown, but it is believed to have been pure spite or the spirit of contradiction. In order to vex the true god, Aguara-Tunpa set fire to all the prairies at the beginning or middle of autumn, so that along with the plants and trees all the animals perished on which in those days the Indians depended for their subsistence, for as yet they had not begun to cultivate maize and other cereals, as they do now. Thus deprived of food the Indians nearly died of hunger. However, they retreated before the flames to the banks of the rivers, and there, while the earth around still smoked from the great conflagration, they made shift to live on the fish which they caught in the water. Seeing his human prey likely to escape him, the baffled Aguara-Tunpa had recourse to another device in order to accomplish his infernal plot against mankind. He caused torrential rain to fall, hoping to drown the whole Chiriguano tribe in the water. He very nearly succeeded. But happily the Chiriguanos contrived to defeat his fell purpose.

Acting on a hint given them by the true god Tunpaete, they looked out for a large mate leaf, placed on it two little babies, a boy and a girl, the children of one mother, and allowed the tiny ark with its precious inmates to float on the face of the water. Still the rain continued to descend in torrents; the floods rose and spread over the face of the earth to a great depth, and all the Chiriguanos were drowned; only the two babes on the leaf of mate were saved. At last, however, the rain ceased to fall, and the flood sank, leaving a great expanse of fetid mud behind. The children now emerged from the ark, for if they had stayed there, they would have perished of cold and hunger. Naturally the fish and other creatures that live in the water were not drowned in the great flood; on the contrary they throve on it, and were now quite ready to serve as food for the two babes. But how were the infants to cook the fish which they caught? That was the rub, for of course all fire on earth had been extinguished by the deluge. However, a large toad came to the rescue of the two children. Before the flood had swamped the whole earth, that prudent creature had taken the precaution of secreting himself in a hole, taking with him in his mouth some live coals, which he contrived to keep alight all the time of the deluge by blowing on them with his breath. When he saw that the surface of the ground was dry again, he hopped out of his hole with the live coals in his mouth, and making straight for the two children he bestowed on them the gift of fire. Thus they were able to roast the fish they caught and so to warm their chilled bodies. In time they grew up, and from their union the whole tribe of the Chiriguanos is descended.1

The natives of Tierra del Fuego, in the extreme south of South America, tell a fantastic and obscure story of a great flood. They say that the sun was sunk in the sea, that the waters rose tumultuously, and that all the earth was submerged except a single very high mountain, on which a few people found refuge.2

§ 15. Stories of a Great Flood in Central America and Mexico

The Indians about Panama "had some notion of Noah's flood, and said that when it happened one man escaped in a canoe with his wife and children, from whom all mankind afterwards proceeded and peopled the world." 1 The Indians of Nicaragua believed that since its creation the world had been destroyed by a deluge, and that after its destruction the gods had created men and animals and all things afresh.2

"The Mexicans," says the Italian historian Clavigero, "with all other civilized nations, had a clear tradition, though somewhat corrupted by fable, of the creation of the world, of the universal deluge, of the confusion of tongues, and of the dispersion of the people; and had actually all these events represented in their pictures. They said, that when mankind were overwhelmed with the deluge, none were preserved but a man named Coxcox (to whom others give the name of Teocipactli), and a woman called Xochiquetzal, who saved themselves in a little bark, and having afterwards got to land upon a mountain called by them Colhuacan, had there a great many children; that these children were all born dumb, until a dove from a lofty tree imparted to them languages, but differing so much that they could not understand one another. The Tlascalans pretended that the men who survived the deluge were transformed into apes, but recovered speech and reason by degrees." 3

In the Mexican manuscript known as the Codex Chimal-popoca, which contains a history of the kingdoms of Culhuacan and Mexico from the creation downwards, there is contained an account of the great flood. It runs thus. The world had existed for four hundred years, and two hundred years, and three score and sixteen years, when men were lost and drowned and turned into fishes. The sky drew near to the water; in a single day all was lost, and the day of Nahui-Xochitl or Fourth Flower consumed all our subsistence (all that there was of our flesh). And that year was the year of Ce-Calli or First House, and on the first day, the day of Nahui-Atl, all was lost. The mountains themselves were sunk under the water, and the water remained calm for fifty and two springs. But towards the end of the year Titlaca-huan had warned the man Nata and his wife Nena, saying, "Brew no more wine, but hollow out a great cypress and enter therein when, in the month of Toçoztli, the water shall near the sky." Then they entered into it, and when Titlacahuan had shut the door of it, he said to him, "Thou shalt eat but one sheaf of maize, and thy wife but one also." But when they had finished, they came forth from there, and the water remained calm, for the log moved no more, and opening it they began to see the fishes. Then they lit fire by rubbing pieces of wood together, and they roasted fishes. But the gods Citlallinicue and Citlallotonac at once looked down and said, "O divine Lord, what fire is that they are making there? wherefore do they thus fill the heaven with smoke?" Straightway Titlacahuan Tetzcatlipoca came down, and he grumbled, saying, "What's that fire doing here?" With that he snatched up the fishes, split their tails, modelled their heads, and turned them into dogs.1

In Michoacan, a province of Mexico, the legend of a deluge was also preserved. The natives said that when the flood began to rise, a man named Tezpi, with his wife and children, entered into a great vessel, taking with them animals and seeds of diverse kinds sufficient to restock the world after the deluge. When the waters abated, the man sent forth a vulture, and the bird flew away, but finding corpses to fatten on, it did not return. Then the man let fly other birds, but they also came not back. At last he sent forth a humming-bird, and it returned with a green bough in its beak.1 In this story the messenger birds seem clearly to be reminiscences of the raven and the dove in the Noachian legend, of which the Indians may have heard through missionaries.

The Popol Vuh, a book which contains the legendary history of the Quiches of Guatemala, describes how the gods made several attempts to create mankind, fashioning them successively out of clay, out of wood, and out of maize. But none of their attempts were successful, and the various races moulded out of these diverse materials had all, for different reasons, to be set aside. It is true that the wooden race of men begat sons and daughters and multiplied upon the earth, but they had neither heart nor intelligence, they forgot their Creator, and they led a useless life, like that of the animals. Even regarded from the merely physical point of view, they were very poor creatures. They had neither blood nor fat, their cheeks were wizened, their feet and hands were dry, their flesh was languid. "So the end of this race of men was come, the ruin and destruction of these wooden puppets; they also were put to death. Then the waters swelled by the will of the Heart of Heaven, and there was a great flood which rose over the heads of these puppets, these beings made of wood." A rain of thick resin fell from the sky. Men ran hither and thither in despair. They tried to climb up into the houses, but the houses crumbled away and let them fall to the ground; they essayed to mount up into the trees, but the trees shook them afar off; they sought to enter into the caves, but the caves shut them out. Thus was accomplished the ruin of that race of men; they were all given up to destruction and contempt. But they say that the posterity of the wooden race may still be seen in the little monkeys which live in the woods, for these monkeys are very like men, and like their wooden ancestors their flesh is composed of nothing but wood.2

The Huichol Indians, who inhabit a mountainous region near Santa Catarina in Western Mexico, have also a legend of a deluge. By blood the tribe is related to the Aztecs, the creators of that semi-civilized empire of Mexico which the Spanish invaders destroyed but, secluded in their mountain fastnesses, the Huichols have always remained in a state of primitive barbarism. It was not until 1722 that the Spaniards succeeded in subduing them, and the Franciscan missionaries, who followed the Spanish army into the mountains, built a few churches and converted the wild Indians to Christianity. But the conversion was hardly more than nominal. It is true that the Huichols observe the principal Christian festivals, which afford them welcome excuses for lounging, guzzling, and swilling, and they worship the saints as gods. But in their hearts they cling to their ancient beliefs, customs, and ceremonies; they jealously guard their country against the encroachments of the whites; not a single Catholic priest lives among them and all the churches are in ruins.1

The Huichol story of the deluge runs thus. A Huichol was felling trees to clear a field for planting. But every morning he found, to his chagrin, that the trees which he had felled the day before had grown up again as tall as ever. It was very vexatious and he grew tired of labouring in vain. On the fifth day he determined to try once more and to go to the root of the matter.

Soon there rose from the ground in the middle of the clearing an old woman with a staff in her hand. She was no other than Great-grandmother Nakawe, the goddess of earth, who makes every green thing to spring forth from the dark underworld. But the man did not know her. With her staff she pointed to the south north, west, and east, above and below, and all the trees which the young man had felled immediately stood up again. Then he understood how it came to pass that in spite of all his endeavours the clearing was always covered with trees. So he said to the old woman angrily, "Is it you who are undoing my work all the time ?"

" Yes," she said, "because I wish to talk to you." Then she told him that he laboured in vain. "A great flood," said she, "is coming. It is not more than five days off. There will come a wind, very bitter, and as sharp as chile, which will make you cough. Make a box from the salate (fig) tree, as long as your body, and fit it with a good cover. Take with you five grains of corn of each colour, and five beans of each colour; also take the fire and five squash-stems to feed it, and take with you a black bitch."

The man did as the woman told him. On the fifth day he had the box ready and placed in it the things she had told him to take with him. Then he entered the box with the black bitch and the old woman put on the cover, and caulked every crack with glue, asking the man to point out any chinks. Having made the box thoroughly water-tight and air-tight, the old woman took her seat on the top of it, with a macaw perched on her shoulder. For five years the box floated on the face of the waters. The first year it floated to the south, the second year it floated to the north, the third year it floated to the west, the fourth year it floated to the east, and in the fifth year it rose upward on the flood, and all the world was filled with water.

The next year the flood began to abate, and the box settled on a mountain near Santa Cantarina, where it may still be seen. When the box grounded on the mountain, the man took off the cover and saw that all the world was still under water. But the macaws and the parrots set to work with a will; they pecked at the mountains with their beaks till they had hollowed them out into valleys, down which the water all ran away and was separated into five seas. Then the land began to dry, and trees and grass sprang up. The old woman turned into wind and so vanished away. But the man resumed the work of clearing the field which had been interrupted by the flood. He lived with the bitch in a cave, going forth to his labour in the morning and returning home in the evening. But the bitch stayed at home all the time. Every evening on his return the man found cakes baked ready against his coming, and he was curious to know who it was that baked them. When five days had passed, he hid himself behind some bushes near the cave to watch. He saw the bitch take off her skin, hang it up, and kneel down in the likeness of a woman to grind the corn for the cakes. Stealthily he drew near her from behind, snatched the skin away, and threw it on the fire. "Now you have burned my tunic!" cried the woman and began to whine like a dog. But he took water mixed with the flour she had prepared, and with the mixture he bathed her head. She felt refreshed and remained a woman ever after. The two had a large family, and their sons and daughters married. So was the world repeopled, and the inhabitants lived in caves.1

The Cora Indians, a tribe of nominal Christians whose country borders that of the Huichols on the west, tell a similar story of a great flood, in which the same incidents occur of the woodman who was warned of the coming flood by a woman, and who after the flood cohabited with a bitch transformed into a human wife. But in the Cora version of the legend the man is bidden to take into the ark with him the woodpecker, the sand-piper, and the parrot, as well as the bitch. He embarked at midnight when the flood began. When it subsided, he waited five days and then sent out the sandpiper to see if it were possible to walk on the ground. The bird flew back and cried, "Ee-wee-wee!" from which the man understood that the earth was still too wet. He waited five days more, and then sent out the woodpecker to see if the trees were hard and dry. The woodpecker thrust his beak deep into the tree, and waggled his head from side to side but the wood was still so soft with the water that he could hardly pull his beak out again, and when at last with a violent tug he succeeded he lost his balance and fell to the ground. So when he returned to the ark he said, "Chu-ee, chu-ee!" The man took his meaning and waited five days more, after which he sent out the spotted sandpiper. By this time the mud was so dry that, when the sandpiper hopped about, his legs did not sink into it, so he came back and reported that all was well. Then the man ventured out of the ark stepping very gingerly till he saw that the land was dry and flat.1

In another fragmentary version of the deluge story, as told by the Cora Indians, the survivors of the flood would seem to have escaped in a canoe. When the waters abated, God sent the vulture out of the canoe to see whether the earth was dry enough. But the vulture did not return, because he devoured the corpses of the drowned. So God was angry with the vulture, and cursed him, and made him black instead of white, as he had been before; only the tips of his wings he left white, that men might know what their colour had been before the flood. Next God commanded the ringdove to go out and see whether the earth was yet dry. The dove reported that the earth was dry, but that the rivers were in spate. So God ordered all the beasts to drink the rivers dry, and all the beasts and birds came and drank, save only the weeping dove (Paloma llorona), which would not come. Therefore she still goes every day to drink water at nightfall, because she is ashamed to be seen drinking by day, and all day long she weeps and wails.2 In these Cora legends the incident of the birds, especially the vulture and the raven, seems clearly to reflect the influence of missionary teaching.

A somewhat different story of a deluge is told by the Tarahumares, an Indian tribe who inhabit the mountains of Mexico farther to the north than the Huichols and Coras. The greater part of the Tarahumares are nominal Christians, though they seem to have learned little more from their teachers than the words Señor San Jose and Maria Santissima, and the title of Father God (Tata Dios), which they apply to their ancient deity the sun-god.1 They say that when all the world was water-logged, a little boy and a little girl climbed up a mountain called Lavachi (gourd) to the south of Panalachic, and when the flood subsided the two came down again. They brought three grains of corn and three beans with them. So soft were the rocks after the flood that the feet of the little boy and girl sank into them, and their footprints may be seen there to this day. The two planted corn and slept and dreamed a dream, and afterwards they harvested, and all the Tarahumares are descended from them.2 Another Tarahumare version of the deluge legend runs thus. The Tarahumares were fighting among themselves, and Father God (Tata Dios) sent much rain, and all the people perished. After the flood God despatched three men and three women to repeople the earth. They planted corn of three kinds, soft corn, hard corn, and yellow corn, and these three sorts still grow in the country.3

The Caribs of the Antilles had a tradition that the Master of Spirits, being angry with their forefathers for not presenting to him the offerings which were his due, caused such a heavy rain to fall for several days that all the people were drowned; only a few contrived to save their lives by escaping in canoes to a solitary mountain. It was this deluge, they say, which separated their islands from the mainland and formed the hills and pointed rocks or sugar-loaf mountains of their country.4

§ 16. Stories of a Great Flood in North America

The Papagos of south-western Arizona say that the Great Spirit made the earth and all living creatures before he made man. Then he came down to earth, and digging in the ground found some potter's clay. This he took back with him to the sky, and from there let it fall into the hole which he had dug. Immediately there came out the hero Montezuma, and with his help there also issued forth all the Indian tribes in order. Last of all appeared the wild Apaches, who ran away as fast as they were created. Those first days of the world were happy and peaceful. The sun was then nearer the earth than he is now; his rays made all the seasons equable and clothing superfluous. Men and animals talked together; a common language united them in the bonds of brotherhood. But a terrible catastrophe put an end to those golden days. A great flood destroyed all flesh wherein was the breath of life; Montezuma and his friend the coyote alone escaped. For before the waters began to rise, the coyote prophesied the coming of the flood, and Montezuma took warning, and hollowed out a boat for himself, and kept it ready on the top of Santa Rosa. The coyote also prepared an ark for himself for he gnawed down a great cane by the river bank, entered it, and caulked it with gum. So when the waters rose, Montezuma and the coyote floated on them and were saved, and when the flood retired, the man and the animal met on dry land. Anxious to discover how much dry land was left, the man sent out the coyote to explore, and the animal reported that to the west, the south, and the east there was sea, but that to the north he could find no sea, though he had journeyed till he was weary. Meanwhile the Great Spirit, with the help of Montezuma, had restocked the earth with men and animals.1

The Pimas, a neighbouring tribe, related to the Papagos, say that the earth and mankind were made by a certain Chiowotmahke, that is to say Earth-prophet.

Now the Creator had a son called Szeukha, who, when the earth began to be tolerably peopled, lived in the Gila valley. In the same valley there dwelt at that time a great prophet, whose name has been forgotten. One night, as the prophet slept, he was wakened by a noise at the door. When he opened, who should stand there but a great eagle. And the eagle said, "Arise, for behold, a deluge is at hand." But the prophet laughed the eagle to scorn, wrapt his robe about him, and slept again. Again, the eagle came and warned him, but again he would pay no heed. A third time the long-suffering bird warned the prophet that all the valley of the Gila would be laid waste with water, but still the foolish man turned a deaf ear to the warning. That same night came the flood, and next morning there was nothing alive to be seen but one man, if man indeed he was, for it was Szeukha, the son of the Creator, who had saved himself by floating on a ball of gum or resin. When the waters of the flood sank, he landed near the mouth of the Salt River and dwelt there in a cave on the mountain; the cave is there to this day, and so are the tools which Szeukha used when he lived in it. For some reason or other Szeukha was very angry with the great eagle, though that bird had warned the prophet to escape for his life from the flood. So with the help of a rope-ladder he climbed up the face of the cliff where the eagle re-sided, and finding him at home in his eyrie he killed him. In and about the nest he discov-ered the mangled and rotting bodies of a great multitude of people whom the eagle had carried off and devoured. These he raised to life and sent them away to repeople the earth.1

Another version of the Pima legend runs as follows. In the early days of the world the Creator, whom the Indians call Earth Doctor, made the earth habitable by fashioning the mountains, the water, the trees, the grass, and the weeds; he made the sun also and the moon, and caused them to pursue their regular courses in the sky. When he had thus prepared the world for habitation, the Creator fashioned all manner of birds and creep-ing things, and he moulded images of clay, and commanded them to become animated human beings, and they obeyed him, and they increased and multiplied, and spread over the earth. But in time the increase of population outran the means of subsistence; food and even water became scarce, and as sickness and death were as yet unknown, the steady multiplication of the species was attended by ever growing famine and dis-tress. In these circumstances the Creator saw nothing for it but to destroy the creatures he had made, and this he did by pulling down the sky on the earth and crushing to death the people and all other living things. After that he restored the broken fabric of the world and created mankind afresh, and once more the human race increased and multi-plied.

It was during this second period of the world that the earth gave birth to one who has since been known as Siuuhû or Elder Brother. He came to Earth Doctor, that is, to the Creator, and spoke roughly to him, and the Creator trembled before him. The popula-tion was now increasing, but Elder Brother shortened the lives of the people, and they did not overrun the earth as they had done before. However, not content with abridging the natural term of human existence, he resolved to destroy mankind for the second time altogether by means of a great flood. So he began to fashion a jar, in which he intended to save himself from the deluge, and when the jar should be finished, the flood would come. He announced his purpose of destruction to the Creator, and the Creator called his people together and warned them of the coming deluge. After describing the calamity that would befall them, he chanted the following staves :—

"Weep, my unfortunate people!

All this you will see take place. Weep, my unfortunate people!

For the waters will overwhelm the land. Weep, my unhappy relatives!

You will learn all. The waters will overwhelm the mountains."

Also he thrust his staff into the ground, and with it bored a hole right through to the other side of the earth. Some people took refuge in the hole for fear of the coming flood, and others appealed for help to Elder Brother, but their appeal was unheeded. Yet the assistance which Elder Brother refused to mankind he vouchsafed to the coyote or prairie wolf; for he told that animal to find a big log and sit on it, and so sitting he would float safely on the surface of the water along with the driftwood. The time of the deluge was now come, and accordingly Elder Brother got into the jar which he had been making against the great day, and as he closed the opening of the jar behind him he sang—

" Black house! Black house! hold me safely in;

Black house! Black house! hold me safely in,

As I journey to and fro, to and fro."

And as he was borne along on the flood he sang—

" Running water, running water, herein resounding,

As on the clouds I am carried to the sky.

Running water, running water, herein roaring,

As on the clouds I am carried to the sky."

The jar in which Elder Brother ensconced himself is called by him in the song the Black House, because it was made of black gum. It bobbed up and down on the face of the waters and drifted along till it came to rest beyond Sonoita, near the mouth of the Colorado River. There the jar may be seen to this day; it is called the Black Mountain, after the colour of the gum out of which the jar was moulded. On emerging from the jar Elder Brother sang—

"Here I come forth! Here I come forth!

With magic powers I emerge. Here I come forth!

Here I come forth! With magic powers I emerge.

I stand alone! Alone !

Who will accompany me? My staff and my crystal

They shall bide with me."

The Creator himself, or Earth Doctor, as the Indians call him, also escaped destruction by enclosing himself in his reed staff, which floated on the surface of the water. The coyote, too, survived the great flood, for the log on which he had taken refuge floated southward with him to the place where all the driftwood of the deluge was gathered together. Of all the birds that had been before the flood only five of different sorts survived; they clung with their beaks to the sky till a god took pity on them and enabled them to make nests of down from their own breasts, and in these nests they floated on the waters till the flood went down. Among the birds thus saved from the deluge were the flicker and the vulture. As for the human race, some people were saved in the deep hole which the Creator had bored with his staff, and others were saved in a similar hole which a powerful personage, called the South Doctor, had in like manner made by thrusting his cane into the earth. Yet others in their distress resorted to the Creator, but he told them that they came too late, for he had already sent all whom he could save down the deep hole and through to the other side of the earth. However, he held out a hope to them that they might still be saved if they would climb to the top of Crooked Mountain, and he directed South Doctor to assist the people in their flight to this haven of refuge. So South Doctor led the people to the summit of the mountain, but the flood rose apace behind them. Yet by his enchantments did South Doctor raise the mountain and set bounds to the angry water, for he traced a line round the hill and chanted an incantation, which checked the rising flood. Four times by his incantations did he raise the mountain above the waters; four times did he arrest the swelling tide. At last his power was exhausted; he could do no more, and he threw his staff into the water, where it cracked with a loud noise. Then turning, he saw a dog near him, and sent the animal to see how high the tide had risen. The dog turned towards the people and said, "It is very near the top." At these words the anxious watchers were transformed into stone; and there to this day you may see them standing in groups, just as they were at the moment of transformation, some of the men talking, some of the women cooking, and some crying.1

This Pima legend of the flood contains, moreover, an episode which bears a certain reminiscence to an episode in the Biblical narrative of the great catastrophe. In Genesis we read how in the days immediately preceding the flood, "the sons of God came in unto the daughters of men, and they bare children to them; the same were the mighty men which were of old, the men of renown." 2 In like manner the Pimas relate that when Elder Brother had determined to destroy mankind, he began by creating a handsome youth, whom he directed to go among the Pimas, to wed their women, and to beget children by them. He was to live with his first wife "until his first child was born, then leave her and go to another, and so on until his purpose was accomplished. His first wife gave birth to a child four months after marriage and conception. The youth then went and took a second wife, to whom a child was born in less time than the first. The period was yet shorter in the case of the third wife, and with her successors it grew shorter still, until at last the child was born from the young man at the time of the marriage. This was the child that caused the flood which destroyed the people and fulfilled the plans of Elder Brother. Several years were necessary to accomplish these things, and during this time the people were amazed and frightened at the signs of Elder Brother's power and at the deeds of his agent."1 How the child of the young man's last wife caused the flood is not clearly explained in the story, though we are told that the screams of the sturdy infant shook the earth and could be heard at a great distance.2 Indeed, the episode of the handsome youth and his many wives is, like the corresponding episode in the Biblical narrative, fitted very loosely into the story of the flood. It may be that both episodes were originally independent of the diluvial tradition, and that in its Indian form the tale of the fair youth and his human spouses is a distorted reminiscence of missionary teaching.

The Indians of Zuñi, a pueblo village of New Mexico, relate that once upon a time a great flood compelled them to quit their village in the valley and take refuge on a lofty and conspicuous tableland, which towers like an island from the flat, with steep or precipitous sides of red and white sandstone. But the waters rose nearly to the summit of the tableland, and the Indians, fearing to be swept off the face of the earth, resolved to offer a human sacrifice in order to appease the angry waters. So a youth and a maiden, the children of two Priests of the Rain, were dressed in their finest robes, decked with many precious beads, and thrown into the swelling flood. Immediately the waters began to recede, and the youth and maiden were turned into stone. You may still see them in the form of two great pinnacles of rock rising from the tableland.1

The Acagchemem Indians, near St. Juan Capistrano in California, "were not entirely destitute of a knowledge of the universal deluge, but how, or from whence, they received the same, I could never understand. Some of their songs refer to it and they have a tradition that, at a time very remote, the sea began to swell and roll in upon the plains and fill the valleys, until it had covered the mountains, and thus nearly all the human race and animals were destroyed, excepting a few, who had resorted to a very high mountain which the waters did not reach. But the songs give a more distinct relation of the same, and they state that the descendants of Captain Ouiot asked of Chinigchinich vengeance upon their chief—that he appeared unto them, and said to those endowed with the power, 'Ye are the ones to achieve vengeance—ye who cause it to rain! Do this, and so inundate the earth, that every living being will be destroyed.'The rains commenced, the sea was troubled, and swelled in upon the earth, covering the plains, and rising until it had overspread the highest land, excepting a high mountain, where the few had gone with the one who had caused it to rain, and thus every other animal was destroyed upon the face of the earth. These songs were supplications to Chinigchinich to drown their enemies. If their opponents heard them, they sang others in opposition, which in substance ran thus:

181

'We are not afraid, because Chinigchinich does not wish to, neither will he destroy the world by another inundation.' Without doubt this account has reference to the universal deluge, and the promise God made, that there should not be another." 2

The Luiseño Indians of Southern California also tell of a great flood which covered all the high mountains and drowned most of the people. But a few were saved, who took refuge on a little knoll near Bonsall. The place was called Mora by the Spaniards, but the Indians call it Katuta. Only the knoll remained above water when all the rest of the country was inundated. The survivors stayed there till the flood went down. To this day you may see on the top of the little hill heaps of sea-shells and seaweed, and ashes and stones set together, marking the spot where the Indians cooked their food. The shells are those of the shell-fish which they ate, and the ashes and stones are the remains of their fire-places. The writer who relates this tradition adds that "the hills near Del Mar and other places along the coast have many such heaps of sea-shells, of the species still found on the beaches, piled in quantities." The Luiseños still sing a Song of the Flood, in which mention is made of the knoll of Katuta.1

An Indian woman of the Smith River tribe in California gave the following account of the deluge. At one time there came a great rain. It lasted a long time and the water kept rising till all the valleys were submerged, and the Indians retired to the high land. At last they were all swept away and drowned except one pair, who escaped to the highest peak and were saved. They subsisted on fish, which they cooked by placing them under their arms. They had no fire and could not get any, as everything was far too wet. At last the water sank, and from that solitary pair all the Indians of the present day are descended. As the Indians died, their spirits took the forms of deer, elks, bears, snakes, insects, and so forth, and in this way the earth was repeopled by the various kinds of animals as well as men. But still the Indians had no fire, and they looked with envious eyes on the moon, whose fire shone so brightly in the sky. So the Spider Indians and the Snake Indians laid their heads together and resolved to steal fire from the moon. Accordingly the Spider Indians started off for the moon in a gossamer balloon, but they took the precaution to fasten the balloon to the earth by a rope which they paid out as they ascended. When they arrived at the moon, the Indians who inhabited the lunar orb looked askance at the newcomers, divining their errand. To lull their suspicions the Spider Indians assured them that they had come only to gamble, so the Moon Indians were pleased and proposed to begin playing at once. As they sat by the fire deep in the game, a Snake Indian dexterously climbed up the rope by which the balloon was tethered, and before the Moon Indians knew what he was about he had darted through the fire and escaped down the rope again. When he reached the earth he had to travel over every rock, stick, and tree; everything he touched from that time forth contained fire, and the hearts of the Indians were glad. But the Spider Indians were long kept prisoners in the moon, and when they were at last released and had returned to earth, expecting to be welcomed as the benefactors of the human race, ungrateful men killed them lest the Moon Indians should wish to take vengeance for the deceit that had been practised on them.1

The Ashochimi Indians of California say that long ago there was a mighty flood which prevailed over all the land and drowned every living creature save the coyote alone. He set himself to restore the population of the world as follows. He collected the tail-feathers of owls, hawks, eagles, and buzzards, tied them up in a bundle, and journeyed with them over the face of the earth. He sought out the sites of all the Indian villages, and wherever a wigwam had stood before the flood, he planted a feather. In due time the feathers sprouted, took root, and flourished greatly, at last turning into men and women; and thus the world was repeopled.2

The Maidu Indians of California say that of old the Indians abode tranquilly in the Sacramento Valley, and were happy. All on a sudden there was a mighty and swift rushing of waters, so that the whole valley became like the Big Water, which no man can measure. The Indians fled for their lives, but many were overtaken by the waters and drowned. Also, the frogs and the salmon pursued swiftly after them, and they ate many Indians. Thus all the Indians perished but two, who escaped to the hills. But the Great Man made them fruitful and blessed them, so that the world was soon repeopled. From these two there sprang many tribes, even a mighty nation, and one man was chief over all this nation—a chief of great renown. Then he went out on a knoll, overlooking the wide waters, and he knew that they covered fertile plains once inhabited by his ancestors. Nine sleeps he lay on the knoll without food, revolving in his mind the question, 'How did this deep water cover the face of the world?' And at the end of nine sleeps he was changed, for now no arrow could wound him. Though a thousand Indians should shoot at him, not one flint-pointed arrow would pierce his skin. He was like the Great Man in heaven, for none could slay him henceforth. Then he spoke to the Great Man, and commanded him to let the water flow off from the plains which his ancestors had inhabited. The Great Man obeyed; he rent open the side of the mountain, and the water flowed away into the Big Water.1

According to Du Pratz, the early French historian of Louisiana, the tradition of a great flood was current among the Natchez, an Indian tribe of the Lower Mississippi. He tells us that on this subject he questioned the guardian of the temple, in which the sacred and perpetual fire was kept with religious care. The guardian replied that "the ancient word taught all the red men that almost all men were destroyed by the waters except a very small number, who had saved themselves on a very high mountain; that he knew nothing more regarding this subject except that these few people had repeopled the earth." And Du Pratz adds, "As the other nations had told me the same thing, I was assured that all the natives thought the same regarding this event, and that they had not preserved any memory of Noah's ark, which did not surprise me very much, since the Greeks, with all their knowledge, were no better informed, and we ourselves, were it not for the Holy Scriptures, might perhaps know no more than they." 2 Elsewhere he reports the tradition somewhat more fully as follows. "They said that a great rain fell on the earth so abundantly and during such a long time that it was completely covered except a very high mountain where some men saved themselves; that all fire being extinguished on the earth, a little bird named Coüy-oüy, which is entirely red (it is that which is called in Louisiana the cardinal bird), brought it from heaven. I understood by that that they had forgotten almost all the history of the deluge." 1

The Mandan Indians had a tradition of a great deluge in which the human race perished except one man, who escaped in a large canoe to a mountain in the west. Hence the Mandans celebrated every year certain rites in memory of the subsidence of the flood, which they called Mee-nee-ro-ka-ha-sha, "the sinking down or settling of the waters." The time for the ceremony was determined by the full expansion of the willow leaves on the banks of the river, for according to their tradition "the twig that the bird brought home was a willow bough and had full-grown leaves on it;" and the bird which brought the willow bough was the mourning-or turtle-dove. These doves often fed on the sides of their earth-covered huts, and none of the Indians would destroy or harm them; even their dogs were trained not to molest the birds. In the Mandan village a wooden structure was carefully preserved to represent the canoe in which the only man was saved from the flood. "In the centre of the Mandan village," says the painter Catlin, "is an open, circular area of a hundred and fifty feet diameter, kept always clear, as a public ground, for the display of all their feasts, parades, etc., and around it are their wigwams placed as near to each other as they can well stand, their doors facing the centre of this public area. In the middle of this ground, which is trodden like a hard pavement, is a curb (somewhat like a large hogshead standing on its end) made of planks and bound with hoops, some eight or nine feet high, which they religiously preserve and protect from year to year, free from mark or scratch, and which they call the 'big canoe': it is undoubtedly a symbolic representation of a part of their traditional history of the Flood; which it is very evident, from this and numerous other features of this grand ceremony, they have in some way or other received, and are here endeavouring to perpetuate by vividly impressing it on the minds of the whole nation.

This object of superstition, from its position as the very centre of the village, is the rallying-point of the whole nation. To it their devotions are paid on various occasions of feasts and religious exercises during the year."

On the occasion when Catlin witnessed the annual ceremony commemorative of the flood, the first or only man (Nu-mohk-muck-a-nah) who escaped the flood was personated by a mummer dressed in a robe of white wolf-skins, which fell back over his shoulders, while on his head he wore a splendid covering of two ravens' skins and in his left hand he carried a large pipe. Entering the village from the prairie he approached the medicine or mystery lodge, which he had the means of opening, and which had been strictly closed during the year except for the performance of these religious rites.

All day long this mummer went through the village, stopping in front of every hut and crying, till the owner of the hut came out and asked him who he was and what was the matter. To this the mummer replied by relating the sad catastrophe which had happened on the earth's surface through the overflowing of the waters, saying that "he was the only person saved from the universal calamity; that he landed his big canoe on a high mountain in the west, where he now resides; that he had come to open the medicine-lodge, which must needs receive a present of some edged tool from the owner of every wigwam, that it may be sacrificed to the water; for he says, 'If this is not done, there will be another flood, and no one will be saved, as it was with such tools that the big canoe was made.'" Having visited every wigwam in the village during the day, and having received from each a hatchet, a knife, or other edged tool, he deposited them at evening in the medicine lodge, where they remained till the afternoon of the last day of the ceremony. Then as the final rite they were thrown into a deep pool in the river from a bank thirty feet high in presence of the whole village; "from whence they can never be recovered, and where they were, undoubtedly, sacrificed to the Spirit of the Water." Amongst the ceremonies observed at this spring festival of the Mandans was a bull dance danced by men disguised as buffaloes and intended to procure a plentiful supply of buffaloes in the ensuing season; further, the young men underwent voluntarily a series of excruciating tortures in the medicine lodge for the purpose of commending themselves to the Great Spirit. But how far these quaint and ghastly rites were connected with the commemoration of the Great Flood does not appear from the accounts of our authorities.1

This Mandan festival went by the name of O-kee-pa and was "an annual religious ceremony, to the strict observance of which those ignorant and superstitious people attributed not only their enjoyment in life, but their very existence, for traditions, their only history, instructed them in the belief that the singular forms of this ceremony produced the buffaloes for their supply of food, and that the omission of this annual ceremony, with its sacrifices made to the waters, would bring upon them a repetition of the calamity which their traditions say once befell them, destroying the whole human race, excepting one man, who landed from his canoe on a high mountain in the West. This tradition, however, was not peculiar to the Mandan tribe, for amongst one hundred and twenty different tribes that I have visited in North and South and Central America, not a tribe exists that has not related to me distinct or vague traditions of such a calamity, in which one, or three, or eight persons were saved above the waters, on the top of a high mountain. Some of these, at the base of the Rocky Mountains and in the plains of Venezuela, and the Pampa del Sacramento in South America, make annual pilgrimages to the fancied summits where the antediluvian species were saved in canoes or otherwise, and, under the mysterious regulations of their medicine (mystery) men, tender their prayers and sacrifices to the Great Spirit, to ensure their exemption from a similar catastrophe." 2

The Cherokee Indians are reported to have a tradition that the water once prevailed over the land until all mankind were drowned except a single family. The coming of the calamity was revealed by a dog to his master. For the sagacious animal went day after day to the banks of a river, where he stood gazing at the water and howling piteously. Being rebuked by his master and ordered home, the dog opened his mouth and warned the man of the danger in which he stood. "You must build a boat," said he, "and put in it all that you would save, for a great rain is coming that will flood the land." The animal concluded his prediction by informing his master that his salvation depended on throwing him, the dog, into the water, and for a sign of the truth of what he said he bade him look at the back of his neck. The man did so, and sure enough, the back of the dog's neck was raw and bare, the flesh and bone appearing. So the man believed, and following the directions of the faithful animal he and his family were saved, and from them the whole of the present population of the globe is lineally descended.1

Stories of a great flood are widely spread among Indians of the great Algonquin stock, and they resemble each other in some details. Thus the Delawares, an Algonquin tribe whose home was about Delaware Bay, told of a deluge which submerged the whole earth, and from which few persons escaped alive. They saved themselves by taking refuge on the back of a turtle, which was so old that his shell was mossy like the bank of a rivulet. As they were floating thus forlorn, a loon flew their way, and they begged him to dive and bring up land from the depth of the waters. The bird dived accordingly, but could find no bottom. Then he flew far away and came back with a little earth in his bill. Guided by him, the turtle swam to the place, where some dry land was found. There they settled and repeopled the country.2

The Montagnais, a group of Indian tribes in Canada who also belong to the great Algonquin stock,1 told an early Jesuit missionary that a certain mighty being, whom they called Messou, repaired the world after it had been ruined by the great flood. They said that one day Messou went out to hunt, and that the wolves which he used instead of hounds entered into a lake and were there detained. Messou sought them everywhere, till a bird told him that he saw the lost wolves in the middle of the lake. So he waded into the water to rescue them, but the lake overflowed, covered the earth, and overwhelmed the world. Greatly astonished, Messou sent the raven to search for a clod of earth out of which he might rebuild that element, but no earth could the raven find. Next Messou sent an otter, which plunged into the deep water, but brought back nothing. Lastly, Messou despatched a musk-rat, and the rat brought back a little soil, which Messou used to re-fashion the earth on which we live. He shot arrows at the trunks of trees, and the arrows were changed into branches; he took vengeance on those who had detained his wolves in the lake, and he married a musk-rat, by which he had children, who repeopled the world.2

In this legend there is no mention of men, and but for the part played in it by the animals we might have supposed that the deluge took place in the early ages of the world before the appearance of life on the earth. However, some two centuries later, another Catholic missionary tells us that the Montagnais of the Hudson Bay Territory have a tradition of a great flood which covered the world, and from which four persons, along with animals and birds, escaped alive on a floating island.3 Yet another Catholic missionary reports the Montagnais legend more fully as follows. God, being angry with the giants, commanded a man to build a large canoe. The man did so, and when he had embarked in it, the water rose on all sides, and the canoe with it, till no land was anywhere to be seen. Weary of beholding nothing but a heaving mass of water, the man threw an otter into the flood, and the animal dived and brought up a little earth. The man took the earth or mud in his hand and breathed on it, and at once it began to grow. So he laid it on the surface of the water and prevented it from sinking. As it continued to grow into an island, he desired to know whether it was large enough to support him.

Accordingly he placed a reindeer upon it, but the animal soon made the circuit of the island and returned to him, from which he concluded that the island was not yet large enough. So he continued to blow on it till the mountains, the lakes, and the rivers were formed. Then he disembarked.1 The same missionary reports a deluge legend current among the Crees, another tribe of the Algonquin stock in Canada, but this Cree story bears clear traces of Christian influence, for in it the man is said to have sent forth from the canoe, first a raven, and second a wood-pigeon. The raven did not return, and as a punishment for his disobedience the bird was changed from white to black; the pigeon returned with his claws full of mud, from which the man inferred that the earth was dried up, so he landed.2

The genuine old Algonquin legend of the flood appears to have been first recorded at full length by a Mr. H. E. MacKenzie, who passed much of his early life with the Salteaux or Chippeway Indians, a large and powerful branch of the Algonquin stock. He communicated the tradition to Lieutenant W. H. Hooper, R.N., at Fort Norman, near Bear Lake, about the middle of the nineteenth century. In substance the legend runs as follows.

Once upon a time there were certain Indians and among them a great medicine-man named Wis-kay-tchach. With them also were a wolf and his two sons, who lived on a footing of intimacy with the human beings. Wis-kay-tchach called the old wolf his brother and the young ones his nephews, for he recognized all animals as his relations. In the winter time the whole party began to starve, so in order to find food the parent wolf announced his intention of separating with his children from the band. Wis-kay-tchach offered to bear him company, so off they set together. Soon they came to the track of a moose. The old Wolf and the medicine-man Wis (as we may call him for short) stopped to smoke, while the young wolves pursued the moose. After a time, the young ones not returning, Wis and the old Wolf set off after them, and soon found blood on the snow, whereby they knew that the moose was killed. Soon they came up with the young wolves, but no moose was to be seen, for the young wolves had eaten it up. They bade Wis make a fire, and when he had done so, he found the whole of the moose restored and already quartered and cut up. The young wolves divided the spoil into four portions, but one of them retained the tongue and the other the mouffle (upper lip), which are the chief delicacies of the animal. Wis grumbled, and the young wolves gave up these dainties to him. When they had devoured the whole, one of the young wolves said he would make marrow fat, which is done by breaking up the bones very small and boiling them. Soon this resource was also exhausted, and they all began to hunger again. So they agreed to separate once more. This time Old Wolf went off with one of his sons, leaving Wis and the other young wolf to hunt together.

The story now leaves the Old Wolf and follows the fortunes of Wis and his nephew, one of the two young wolves. The young wolf killed some deer and brought them home in his stomach, disgorging them as before on his arrival. At last he told his uncle that he could catch no more, so Wis sat up all night making medicine or using enchantments. In the morning he bade his nephew go a-hunting, but warned him to be careful at every valley and hollow place to throw a stick over before he ventured to jump himself, or else

187

some evil would certainly befall him. So away went the young wolf, but in pursuing a deer he forgot to follow his uncle's directions, and in attempting to leap a hollow he fell plump into a river and was there killed and devoured by water-lynxes. What kind of a beast a water-lynx is, the narrator did not know. But let that be. Enough that the young wolf was killed and devoured by these creatures. After waiting long for his nephew, Wis set off to look for him, and coming to the spot where the young wolf had leaped, he guessed rightly that the animal had neglected his warning and fallen into the stream. He saw a kingfisher sitting on a tree and gazing fixedly at the water. Asked what he was looking at so earnestly, the bird replied that he was looking at the skin of Wis's nephew, the young wolf, which served as a door-mat to the house of the water-lynxes; for not content with killing and devouring the nephew, these ferocious animals had added insult to injury by putting his skin to this ignoble use. Grateful for the information, Wis called the kingfisher to him, combed the bird's head, and began to put a ruff round his neck, but before he had finished his task, the bird flew away, and that is why down to this day kingfishers have only part of a ruff at the back of their head. Before the kingfisher flew away, he gave Wis a parting hint, that the water-lynxes often came ashore to lie on the sand, and that if he wished to be revenged on them he must turn himself into a stump close by, but must be most careful to keep perfectly rigid and on no account to let himself be pulled down by the frogs and snakes, which the water-lynxes would be sure to send to dislodge him. On receiving these directions Wis returned to his camp and resorted to enchantments; also he provided all things necessary, among others a large canoe to hold all the animals that could not swim.

Before daylight broke, he had completed his preparations and embarked all the aforesaid animals in the big canoe. He then paddled quietly to the neighbourhood of the lynxes, and having secured the canoe behind a promontory, he landed, transformed himself into a stump, and awaited, in that assumed character, the appearance of the water-lynxes. Soon the black one crawled out and lay down on the sand, and then the grey one did the same. Last of all the white one, which had killed the young wolf, popped his head out of the water, but espying the stump, he grew suspicious, and called out to his brethren that he had never seen that stump before. They answered carelessly that it must have been always there, but the wary white lynx, still suspicious, sent frogs and snakes to pull it down. Wis had a severe struggle to keep himself upright, but he succeeded, and the white lynx, his suspicions now quite lulled to rest, lay down to sleep on the sand. Wis waited a little, then resuming his natural shape he took his spear and crept softly to the white lynx. He had been warned by the kingfisher to strike at the animal's shadow or he would assuredly be balked, but in his eagerness he forgot the injunction, and striking full at his adversary's body he missed his mark. The creature rushed towards the water, but Wis had one more chance and aiming this time at the lynx's shadow he wounded grievously the beast itself. However, the creature contrived to escape into the river, and the other lynxes with it. Instantly the water began to boil and rise, and Wis made for his canoe as fast as he could run. The water continued flowing, until land, trees, and hills were all covered. The canoe floated about on the surface, and Wis, having before taken on board all animals that could not swim, now busied himself in picking up all that could swim only for a short time and were now struggling for life in the water around him.

But in his enchantments to meet the great emergency, Wis had overlooked a necessary condition for the restoration of the world after the flood. He had no earth, not even a particle, which might serve as a nucleus for the new lands which were to rise from the waste of waters. He now set about obtaining it. Tying a string to the leg of a loon he ordered the bird to try for soundings and to persevere in its descent even if it should perish in the attempt; for, said he, "If you are drowned, it is no matter; I can easily restore you to life." Encouraged by this assurance, the bird dropped like a stone into the water, and the line ran out fast. When it ceased to run, Wis hauled it up, and at the end of the line was the loon dead. Being duly restored to life, the bird informed Wis that he had found no bottom. So Wis next despatched an otter on the same errand, but he fared no better than the loon. After that Wis tried a beaver, which after being drowned and resuscitated in the usual way, reported that he had seen the tops of trees, but could sink no deeper. Last of all Wis let down a rat fastened to a stone; down went the rat and the stone, and presently the line slackened. Wis hauled it up and at the end of it he found the rat dead but clutching a little earth in its paws. Wis had now all that he wanted. He restored the rat to life and spread out the earth to dry; then he blew upon it till it swelled and grew to a great extent. When he thought it large enough, he sent out a wolf to explore, but the animal soon returned, saying that the world was small. Thereupon Wis again blew on the earth for a long time, and then sent forth a crow. When the bird did not return, Wis concluded that the world was now large enough for all, so he and the animals disembarked from the canoe.1

A few years later, in September 1855, a German traveller obtained another version of the same legend from an old Ojibway woman, the mother of a half-caste. In this Ojibway version the story turns on the doings of Menaboshu, a great primeval hero, who, if he did not create the world, is generally believed by the Ojibways to have given to the earth its present form, directing the flow of the rivers, moulding the beds of the lakes, and cleaving the mountains into deep glens and ravines. He lived on very friendly terms with the animals, whom he regarded as his kinsfolk and with whom he could converse in their own language. Once he pitched his camp in the middle of a solitary wood. The times were bad; he had no luck in the chase, though he fasted and hungered. In his dire distress he went to the wolves and said to them, "My dear little brothers, will you give me something to eat ?" The wolves said, "That we will," and they gave him of their food. He found it so good that he begged to be allowed to join them in the chase, and they gave him leave. So Menaboshu hunted with the wolves, camped with them, and shared their booty.

This they did for ten days, but on the tenth day they came to a cross-road. The wolves wished to go one way, and Menaboshu wished to go another, and as neither would give way, it was resolved to part company. But Menaboshu said that at least the youngest wolf must go with him, for he loved the animal dearly and called him his little brother. The little wolf also would not part from him, so the two went one way, while all the rest of the wolves went the other. Menaboshu and the little wolf camped in the middle of the wood and hunted together, but sometimes the little wolf hunted alone. Now Menaboshu was anxious for the safety of the little wolf, and he said to him, "My dear little brother, have you seen that lake which lies near our camp to the west? Go not thither, never tread the ice on it! Do you hear?" This he said because he knew that his worst enemy, the serpent-king, dwelt in the lake and would do anything to vex him. The little wolf promised to do as Menaboshu told him, but he thought within himself, "Why does Menaboshu forbid me to go on the lake? Perhaps he thinks I might meet my brothers the wolves there! After all I love my brothers!" Thus he thought for two days, but on the third day he went on the lake and roamed about on the ice to see whether he could find his brothers. But just as he came to the middle of the lake, the ice broke, and he fell in and was drowned.

All that evening Menaboshu waited for his little brother, but he never came. Menaboshu waited for him the next day, but still he came not. So he waited five days and five nights. Then he began to weep and wail, and he cried so loud after his little brother, that his cries could be heard at the end of the wood. All the rest of the melancholy winter he passed in loneliness and sorrow. Well he knew who had killed his brother; it was the serpent-king, but Menaboshu could not get at him in the winter. When spring came at last, he went one bright warm day to the lake in which his little brother had perished. All the long winter he could not bear to visit the fatal spot. But now on the sand, where the snow had melted, he saw the footprints of his lost brother, and when he saw them he broke into lamentations so loud that they were heard far and near.

The serpent-king heard them also, and curious to know what was the matter, he popped his head out of the water. "Ah, there you are," said Menaboshu to himself, wiping away the tears with the sleeve of his coat, "you shall pay for your misdeed." He turned himself at once into a tree-stump and stood in that likeness stiff and stark on the water's edge. The serpent-king and all the other serpents, who popped out after him, looked about very curiously to discover who had been raising this loud lament, but they could discover nothing but the tree-stump, which they had never seen there before. As they were sniffing about it, "Take care," said one of them, "there's more there than meets the eye. Maybe it is our foe, the sly Menaboshu, in disguise." So the serpent-king commanded one of his attendants to go and search the matter out. The gigantic serpent at once coiled itself round the tree-stump and squeezed it so hard, that the bones in Menaboshu's body cracked, but he bore the agony with stoical fortitude, not betraying his anguish by a single sound. So the serpents were easy in their minds and said, "No, it is not he. We can sleep safe. It is only wood !" And the day being warm, they all lay down on the sandy beach of the lake and fell fast asleep.

Scarcely had the last snake closed his eyes, when Menaboshu slipped from his ambush, seized his bow and arrows, and shot the serpent-king dead. Three also of the serpent-king's sons he despatched with his arrows. At that the other serpents awoke, and glided back into the water, crying, "Woe! woe! Menaboshu is among us! Menaboshu is killing us !" They made a horrible noise all over the lake and lashed the water with their long tails. Those of them who had the most powerful magic brought forth their medicine-bags, opened them, and scattered the contents all around on the banks and the wood and in the air. Then the water began to run in whirlpools and to swell. The sky was overcast with clouds, and torrents of rain fell. First the neighbourhood, then half the earth, then the whole world was flooded. Frightened to death, Menaboshu fled away, hopping from mountain to mountain like a squirrel, but finding no rest for the soles of his feet, for the swelling waves followed him everywhere. At last he escaped to a very high mountain, but soon the water rose even over its summit. On the top of the mountain grew a tall fir-tree, and Menaboshu climbed up it to its topmost bough. Even there the flood pursued him and had risen to his mouth, when it suddenly stood still. In this painful position, perched on the tree-top and surrounded by the heaving waters of the flood, Menaboshu remained five days and five nights, wondering how he could escape. At last he saw a solitary bird, a loon, swimming on the face of the water. He called the bird and said, "Brother loon, thou skilful diver, be so good as to dive into the depths and see whether thou canst find any earth, without which I cannot live." Again and again the loon dived, but no earth could he find. Menaboshu was almost in despair. But next day he saw the dead body of a drowned musk-rat drifting; towards him. He caught it, took it in his hand, breathed on it, and brought it to life again. Then he said to the rat "Little brother rat, neither you nor I can live without earth. Dive into the water and bring me up a little earth. If it be only three grains of sand, yet will I make something out of it for you and me." The rat dived and after a long time reappeared on the surface. It was dead, but Menaboshu caught it and examined its paws. On one of the fore-paws he found two grains of sand or dust. So he took them, dried them on his hand in the sun, and blew them away over the water. Where they fell they grew into little islands, and these united into larger ones, till at last Menaboshu was able to jump down from the tree-top on one of them. On it he floated about as on a raft, and helped the other islands to grow together, until at last they formed lands and continents. Then Menaboshu walked from place to place, restoring nature to its former beauty and variety. He found little roots and tiny plants which he planted, and they grew into meadows, shrubs, and forests. Many of the dead bodies of animals had drifted ashore. Menaboshu gathered them and blew on them, and they came to life. Then he said, "Go each of you to his own place." So they went all of them to their places. The birds nested in the trees. The fishes and beavers chose for themselves the little lakes and rivers, and the bears and other four-footed beasts roamed about on the dry land. Moreover, Menaboshu walked to and fro with a measuring-line, determining the length of the rivers, the depth of the lakes, the height of the mountains, and the form of the lands. The earth thus restored by Menaboshu was the first land in the world to be inhabited by the Indians ; the earlier earth which was overwhelmed by the flood was inhabited only by Menaboshu and the wolves and the serpent-king and his satellites. So at least said the old Ojibway woman who told the story of the flood to the German traveller.1

Another version of the same story has been recorded more briefly, with minor variations, among the Ojibways of south-eastern Ontario. It runs thus. Nenebojo was living with his brother in the woods. Every day he went out hunting, while his brother stayed at home. One evening when he returned he noticed that his brother was not at home, so he went out to look for him. But he could find him nowhere. Next morning he again started in search of his brother. As he walked by the shore of a lake, what should he see but a kingfisher sitting on a branch of a tree that drooped over the water. The bird was looking at something intently in the water below him. "What are you looking at?" asked Nenebojo. But the kingfisher pretended not to hear him. Then Nenebojo said again, "If you will tell me what you are looking at, I will make you fair to see. I will paint your feathers." The bird gladly accepted the offer, and as soon as Nenebojo had painted his feathers, the kingfisher said, "I am looking at Nenebojo's brother, whom the water-spirits have killed and whose skin they are using as a door-flap." Then Nenebojo asked again, "Where do these water-spirits come to the shore to sun themselves? "The kingfisher answered, "They always sun themselves over there at one of the bays, where the sand is quite dry."

Then Nenebojo left the kingfisher. He resolved to go over to the sandy beach indicated to him by the bird, and there to wait for the first chance of killing the water-spirits. He first pondered what disguise he should assume in order to approach them unawares. Said he to himself, "I will change myself into an old rotten stump." No sooner said than done; the transformation was effected by a long rod, which Nenebojo always carried with him. When the lions came out of the water to sun themselves, one of them noticed the stump and said to one of his fellows, "I never saw that old stump there before. Surely it can't be Nenebojo." But the lion he spoke to said, "Indeed, I have seen that stump before." Then a third lion came over to peer and make sure. He broke a piece off and saw that it was rotten. So all the lions were easy in their minds and lay down to sleep. When Nenebojo thought they were fast asleep he struck them on their heads with his stick. As he struck them the water rose from the lake. He ran away, but the waves pursued him. As he ran he met a woodpecker, who showed him the way to a mountain where grew a tall pine-tree. Nenebojo climbed up the tree and began to build a raft. By the time he had finished the raft the water reached to his neck. Then he put on the raft two animals of all the kinds that existed, and with them he floated about.

When they had drifted for a while, Nenebojo said, "I believe that the water will never subside, so I had better make land again." Then he sent an otter to dive to the bottom of the water and fetch up some earth; but the otter came back without any. Next he sent the beaver on the same errand, but again in vain. After that Nenebojo despatched the musk-rat to bring up earth out of the water. When the musk-rat returned to the surface his paws were tightly closed. On opening them Nenebojo found some little grains of sand, and he discovered other grains in the mouth of the musk-rat. So he put all the grains together, dried them, and then blew them into the lake with the horn which he used for calling the animals. In the lake the grains of sand formed an island. Nenebojo enlarged the island, and sent out a raven to find out how large it was. But the raven never returned. So Nenebojo decided to send out the hawk, the fleetest of all birds on the wing. After a while the hawk returned, and being asked whether he had seen the raven anywhere, he said he had seen him eating dead bodies by the shore of the lake. Then Nenebojo said, "Henceforth the raven will never have anything to eat but what he steals." Yet another interval, and Nenebojo sent out the caribou to explore the size of the island. The animal soon returned, saying that the island was not large enough. So Nenebojo blew more sand into the water, and when he had done so he ceased to make the earth.1

The same story is told, with variations, by the Timagami Ojibways of Canada. They speak of a certain hero named Nenebuc, who was the son of the Sun by a mortal woman. One day, going about with his bow and arrows, he came to a great lake with a beautiful sandy shore, and in the lake he saw lions. They were too far off to shoot at, so he waited till, feeling cold in the water, the lions came ashore to sun and dry themselves on the sandy beach. In order to get near them unseen, he took some birch-bark from a rotten stump, rolled it into a hollow cylinder and set it, like a wigwam, near the shore. Then he ensconced himself in it, making a little loophole in the bark, through which he could see and shoot the lions. The lions were curious as to this new thing on the shore, and they sent a great snake to spy it out. The snake coiled itself round the cylinder of bark and tried to upset it, but it could not, for Nenebuc inside of it stood firm. Then the lions them-selves approached, and Nenebuc shot an arrow and wounded a lioness, the wife of the lion chief. She was badly hurt, but contrived to crawl away to the cave in which she lived. The cave may be seen to this day. It is in a high bluff on the west shore of Smoothwater Lake. Disguised in the skin of a toad, and pretending to be a medicine-woman, Nenebuc was admitted to the presence of the wounded lioness in the cave; but instead of healing her, as he professed to do, he thrust the point of the arrow still deeper into the wound, so that she died. No sooner did she expire than a great torrent of water poured out of the cave, and the lake began to rise. "That is going to flood the world and be the end of all things," said Nenebuc. So he cut down trees and made a raft. And hardly was the raft ready, when the flood was upon him. It rose above the trees, bearing the raft with it, and wherever he looked he could see nothing but water everywhere. All kinds of animals were swimming about in it; they made for his raft, and he took them in. For he wished to save them in order that, when the flood subsided, the earth should be stocked with the same kinds of animals as before. They stayed with him on the raft for a longwhile. After a time he made a rope of roots, and tying it to the beaver's tail, he bade him dive down to the land below the water. The beaver dived, but came up again, saying that he could find no bottom. Seven days afterwards Nenebuc let the musk-rat try whether he could not bring up some earth. The musk-rat plunged into the water and remained down a long time. At last he came up dead, but holding a little earth in his paws. Nenebuc dried the earth, but not entirely. That is why in some places there are swamps to this day. So the animals again roamed over the earth, and the world was remade.1

The Blackfoot Indians, another Algonquin tribe, who used to range over the eastern slopes of the Rocky Mountains and the prairies at their foot, tell a similar tale of the great primeval deluge. "In the beginning," they say, "all the land was covered with water, and Old Man and all the animals were floating around on a large raft. One day Old Man told the beaver to dive and try to bring up a little mud. The beaver went down, and was gone a long time, but could not reach the bottom. Then the loon tried, and the otter, but the water was too deep for them. At last the muskrat dived, and he was gone so long that they thought he had been drowned, but he finally came up, almost dead, and when they pulled him on to the raft, they found, in one of his paws, a little mud. With this, Old Man formed the world, and afterwards he made the people." 2

The Ottawa Indians, another branch of the Algonquin stock,3 tell a long fabulous story, which they say has been handed down to them from their ancestors. It contains an ac-

193

count of a deluge which overwhelmed the whole earth, and from which a single man, by name Nana-boujou, escaped by floating on a piece of bark.4 The missionary who reports this tradition gives us no further particulars concerning it, but from the similarity of the name Nanaboujou to the names Nenebojo, Nenebuc, and Menaboshu, we may surmise that the Ottawa version of the deluge legend closely resembled the Ojibway versions which have already been narrated.1

Certainly similar stories appear to be widely current among the Indian tribes of North-Western Canada. They are not confined to tribes of the Algonquin stock, but occur also among their northern neighbours, the Tinnehs or Denes, who belong to the great Athapascan family, the most widely distributed of all Indian linguistic families in North America, stretching as it does from the Arctic coast far into Mexico, and extending from the Pacific to Hudson's Bay, and from the Rio Colorado to the mouth of the Rio Grande.2 Thus the Crees, who are an Algonquin tribe,3 relate that in the beginning there lived an old magician named Wissaketchak, who wrought marvels by his enchantments. However, a certain sea monster hated the old man and sought to destroy him. So when the magician was paddling in his canoe, the monster lashed the sea with his tail till the waves rose and engulfed the land. But Wissaketchak built a great raft and gathered upon it pairs of all animals and all birds, and in that way he saved his own life and the lives of the other creatures. Nevertheless the great fish continued to lash his tail and the water continued to rise, till it had covered not only the earth but the highest mountains, and not a scrap of dry land was to be seen. Then Wissaketchak sent the diver duck to plunge into the water and bring up the sunken earth, but the bird could not dive to the bottom and was drowned. Thereupon Wissaketchak sent the musk-rat, which, after remaining long under water, reappeared with its throat full of slime.

Wissaketchak took the slime, moulded it into a small disk, and placed it on the water, where it floated. It resembled the nests which the musk-rats make for themselves on the ice. By and by the disk swelled into a hillock. Then Wissaketchak blew on it, and the more he blew on it the more it swelled, and being baked by the sun it became a solid mass. As it grew and hardened, Wissaketchak sent forth the animals to lodge upon it, and at last he himself disembarked and took possession of the land thus created, which is the world we now inhabit.1 A similar tale is told by the Dogrib and Slave Indians, two Tinneh tribes,2 except that they give the name of Tchapewi to the man who was saved from the great flood, and they say that when he was floating on the raft with couples of all sorts of animals, which he had rescued, he caused all the amphibious animals, one after the other, including the otter and the beaver, to dive into the water, but none of them could bring up any earth except the musk-rat, who dived last of all and came up panting with a little mud in his paw. That mud Tchapewi breathed on till it grew into the earth as we now see it. So Tchapewi replaced the animals on it, and they lived there as before; and he propped the earth on a stout stay, making it firm and solid.3 The Hareskin Indians, another Tinneh tribe,4 say that a certain Kunyan, which means Wise Man, once upon a time resolved to build a great raft. When his sister, who was also his wife, asked him why he would build it, he said, "If there comes a flood, as I foresee, we shall take refuge on the raft." He told his plan to other men on the earth, but they laughed at him, saying,

"If there is a flood, we shall take refuge on the trees." Nevertheless the Wise Man made a great raft, joining the logs together by ropes made of roots. All of a sudden there came a flood such that the like of it had never been seen before. The water seemed to gush forth on every side. Men climbed up in the trees, but the water rose after them, and all were drowned. But the Wise Man floated safely on his strong and well-corded raft. As he floated he thought of the future, and he gathered by twos all the herbivorous animals, and all the birds, and even all the beasts of prey he met with on his passage. "Come up on my raft," he said to them, "for soon there will be no more earth." Indeed, the earth disappeared under the water, and for a long time nobody thought of going to look for it. The first to plunge into the depth was the musk-rat, but he could find no bottom, and when he bobbed up on the surface again he was half drowned. "There is no earth!" said he. A second time he dived, and when he came up, he said, "I smelt the smell of the earth, but I could not reach it." Next it came to the turn of the beaver. He dived and remained a long time under water. At last he reappeared, floating on his back, breathless and unconscious. But in his paw he had a little mud, which he gave to the Wise Man. The Wise Man placed the mud on the water, breathed on it, and said, "I would there were an earth again!" At the same time he breathed on the handful of mud, and lo! it began to grow. He put a small bird on it, and the patch of mud grew still bigger. So he breathed, and breathed, and the mud grew and grew. Then the man put a fox on the floating island of mud, and the fox ran round it in a single day. Round and round the island ran the fox, and bigger and bigger grew the island. Six times did the fox make the circuit of the island, but when he made it for the seventh time, the land was complete even as it was before the flood.

Then the Wise Man caused all the animals to disembark and landed them on the dry ground. Afterwards he himself disembarked with his wife and son, saying, "It is for us that this earth shall be repeopled." And repeopled it was, sure enough. Only one difficulty remained with which the Wise Man had to grapple. The floods were still out, and how to reduce them was the question. The bittern saw the difficulty and came to the rescue. He swallowed the whole of the water, and then lay like a log on the bank, with his belly swollen to a frightful size. This was more than the Wise Man had bargained for; if there had been too much water before, there was now too little. In his embarrassment the Wise Man had recourse to the plover. "The bittern," he said, "is lying yonder in the sun with his belly full of water. Pierce it." So the artful plover made up to the unsuspecting bittern. "My grandmother," said he, in a sympathizing tone, "has no doubt a pain in her stomach." And he passed his hand softly over the ailing part of the bittern as if to soothe it. But all of a sudden he put out his claws and clawed the swollen stomach of the bittern. Such a scratch he gave it! There was a gurgling, guggling sound, and out came the water from the stomach bubbling and foaming. It flowed away into rivers and lakes, and thus the world became habitable once more.1

Some Tinneh Indians affirm that the deluge was caused by a heavy fall of snow in the month of September. One old man alone foresaw the catastrophe and warned his fellows, but all in vain. "We will escape to the mountains," said they. But they were all drowned. Now the old man had built a canoe, and when the flood came, he sailed about in it, rescuing from the water all the animals he fell in with. Unable long to support this manner of life, he caused the beaver, the otter, the musk-rat, and the arctic duck to dive into the water in search of the drowned earth. Only the arctic duck came back with a little slime on its claws, and the man spread the slime on the water, caused it to grow by his breath, and for six days disembarked the animals upon it. After that, when the ground had grown to the size of a great island, he himself stepped ashore. Other Tinnehs say that the old man first sent forth a raven, which gorged itself on the floating corpses and came not back. Next he sent forth a turtle-dove, which flew twice round the world and returned. The third time she came back at evening, very tired, with a budding twig of fir in her mouth.2 The influence of Christian teaching on this last version of the story is manifest.

The Tinneh Indians in the neighbourhood of Nulato tell a story of a great flood which happened thus. In a populous settlement there lived a rich youth and his four nephews. Far away across the sea there dwelt a fair damsel, whom many men had wooed in vain. The rich young man resolved to seek her hand, and for that purpose he sailed to her village across the sea with his nephews in their canoes. But she would not have him. So next morning he was preparing to return home. He was already in his canoe down on the beach; his nephews had packed up everything, and were about to shove off from the shore. Many of the villagers had come out of their houses to witness the departure of the strangers, and among them was a woman with her baby in her arms, an infant not yet weaned. Speaking to her baby, the fond mother said, "And what of this little girl? If they want a little girl, why not take this one of mine?" The rich young man heard the words, and holding out his paddle to the woman, he said, "Put her upon this, the little one you speak of." The woman put the baby on the paddle, and the young man drew the child in and placed it behind him in the canoe. Then he paddled away and his nephews after him. Meanwhile the girl whom he had asked to marry him came down to get water. But as she stepped on the soft mud at the water's edge she began to sink into it. "Oh!" she cried, "here I am sinking up to my knees." But the young man answered, "It is your own fault." She sank still deeper and cried, "Oh! now I am in up to my waist!" But he said again, "It is your own fault." Deeper yet she sank and cried, "Oh! I am in up to my neck!"

And again he answered, "It is your own fault." Then she sank down altogether and disappeared.

But the girl's mother saw what happened, and angry at the death of her daughter, she brought down some tame brown bears to the edge of the water, and laying hold of their tails she said to them, "Raise a strong wind," for thus she hoped to drown the young man who had left her daughter to perish. The bears now began to dig the bottom in a fury, making huge waves. At the same time the water rose exceedingly and the billows ran high. The young man's four nephews were drowned in the storm, and all the inhabitants of that village perished in the waters, all except the mother of the baby and her husband; these two were the only people that survived. But the young man himself escaped, for he possessed a magical white stone, and when he threw it ahead it clove a smooth passage for his canoe through the angry water; so he rode out the storm in safety. Still all around him was nothing but the raging sea. Then he took a harpoon and threw it and hit the crest of a wave. Soon after he found himself in a forest of spruce-trees. The land had been formed again. The wave he struck with his harpoon had become a mountain, and rebounding from the rock the harpoon had shot up into the sky and there stuck fast. The harpoon is there to this day, though only the medicine-men can see it. After that the young man turned to the baby girl behind him in the canoe. But he found her grown into a beautiful woman with a face as bright as the sun. So he married her, and their offspring repeopled the drowned earth. But the man and the woman who had been saved from the waters in his wife's village became the ancestors of the people beyond the sea.1

The Sarcees, another Indian tribe belonging to the great Tinneh stock, were formerly a powerful nation, but are now reduced to a few hundreds. Their reserve, a fine tract of prairie land, adjoins that of the Blackfeet in Alberta, a little south of the Canadian Pacific Railway. They have a tradition of a deluge which agrees in its main features with that of the Ojibways, Crees, and other Canadian tribes. They say that when the world was flooded, only one man and woman were left alive, being saved on a raft, on which they also collected animals and birds of all sorts. The man sent a beaver down to dive to the bottom. The creature did so and brought up a little mud, which the man moulded in his hands to form a new world. At first the world was so small that a little bird could walk round it, but it kept growing bigger and bigger. "First," said the narrator, "our father took up his abode on it, then there were men, then women, then animals, and then birds. Our father next created the rivers, the mountains, the trees, and all the things as we now see them." At the conclusion of the story the white man, who reports it, observed to the Sarcees that the Ojibway tradition was very like theirs, except that in the Ojibway tradition it was not a beaver but a musk-rat that brought up the earth from the water. The remark elicited a shout of approval from five or six of the tribe, who were squatting around in the tent. "Yes! yes!" they cried in chorus. "The man has told you lies. It was a musk-rat! it was a musk-rat!"1

A different story of a great flood is told by the Loucheux or Dindjies, the most northerly Indian tribe of the great Tinneh family which stretches from Alaska to the borders of Arizona. They say that a certain man, whom they call the Mariner (Etroetchokren), was the first person to build a canoe. One day, rocking his canoe from side to side, he sent forth such waves on all sides that the earth was flooded and his canoe foundered. Just then a gigantic hollow straw came floating past, and the man contrived to scramble into it and caulk up the ends. In it he floated about safely till the flood dried up. Then he landed on a high mountain, where the hollow straw had come to rest. There he abode many days, wherefore they call it the Place of the Old Man to this day. It is the rocky peak which you see to the right of Fort MacPherson in the Rocky Mountains. Farther down the Yukon River the channel contracts, and the water rushes rapidly between two high cliffs. There the Mariner took his stand, straddlewise, with one foot planted on each cliff, and with his hands dipping in the water he caught the dead bodies of men as they floated past on the current, just as you might catch fish in a bag-net. But of living men he could find not one.

The only live thing within sight was a raven, who, gorged with food, sat perched on the top of a lofty rock fast asleep. The Mariner climbed up the rock, surprised the raven in his nap, and thrust him without more ado into a bag, intending to make short work of Master Raven. But the raven said, "I beg and entreat that you will not cast me down from this rock. For if you do, be sure that I will cause all the men who yet survive to disappear, and you will find yourself all alone in the world." Undeterred by this threat, the man let the raven in the bag drop, and the bird was dashed to pieces at the foot of the mountain. However, the words of the raven came true, for though the man travelled far and wide, not a single living wight could he anywhere discover. Only a loach and a pike did he see sprawling on the mud and warming themselves in the sun. So he bethought him of the raven, and returned to the spot where the mangled body, or rather the bones, of the bird lay bleaching at the foot of the mountain. For he thought within himself, "Maybe the raven will help me to repeople the earth." So he gathered the scattered bones, fitted them together as well as he could, and by blowing on them caused the flesh and the life to return to them. Then the man and the raven went together to the beach, where the loach and the pike were still sleeping in the sun. "Bore a hole in the stomach of the pike," said the raven to the man, "and I will do the same by the loach." The man did bore a hole in the pike's stomach, and out of it came a crowd of men. The raven did likewise to the loach, and a multitude of women came forth from the belly of the fish. That is how the world was repeopled after the great flood.1

In the religion and mythology of the Tlingits or Thlin-keets, an important Indian tribe of Alaska, Yehl or the Raven plays a great part. He was not only the ancestor of the Raven clan but the creator of men ; he caused the plants to grow, and he set the sun, moon, and stars in their places. But he had a wicked uncle, who had murdered Yehl's ten elder brothers either by drowning them or, according to others, by stretching them on a board and sawing off their heads with a knife. To the commission of these atrocious crimes he was instigated by the passion of jealousy, for he had a young wife of whom he was very fond, and he knew that according to Tlingit law his nephews, the sons of his sister, would inherit his widow whenever he himself should depart from this vale of tears.

So when Yehl grew up to manhood, his affectionate uncle endeavoured to dispose of him as he had disposed of his ten elder brothers, but all in vain. For Yehl was not a common child. His mother had conceived him through swallowing a round pebble which she found on the shore at ebb tide, and by means of another stone she contrived to render the infant invulnerable. So when his uncle tried to saw off his head in the usual way, the knife made no impression at all on Yehl. Not discouraged by this failure, the old villain attempted the life of his virtuous nephew in other ways. In his fury he said, "Let there be a flood," and a flood there was which covered all the mountains. But Yehl assumed his wings and feathers, which he could put off and on at pleasure, and spreading his pinions he flew up to the sky, and there remained hanging by his beak for ten days, while the water of the flood rose so high that it lapped his wings. When the water sank, he let go and dropped like an arrow into the sea, where he fell soft on a bank of seaweed and was rescued from his perilous position by a sea otter, which brought him safe to land. What happened to mankind during the flood is not mentioned in this version of the Tlingit legend.1

Another Tlingit legend tells how Raven caused a great flood in a different way. He had put a woman under the world to attend to the rising and falling of the tides. Once he wished to learn about all that goes on under the sea, so he caused the woman to raise the water, in order that he might go there dry-shod. But he thoughtfully directed her to heave the ocean up slowly, so that when the flood came people might have time to load their canoes with the necessary provisions and get on board. So the ocean rose gradually, bearing on its surface the people in their canoes.

As they rose up and up the sides of the mountains, they could see the bears and other wild beasts walking about on the still unsubmerged tops. Many of the bears swam out to the canoes, wishing to scramble on board ; then the people who had been wise enough to take their dogs with them were very glad of it, for the noble animals kept off the bears Some people landed on the tops of the mountains, built walls round them to dam out the water, and tied their canoes on the inside. They could not take much firewood up with them ; there was not room for it in the canoes. It was a very anxious and dangerous time. The survivors could see trees torn up by the roots and swept along on the rush of the waters; large devil-fish, too, and other strange creatures floated past on the tide-race. When the water subsided, the people followed the ebbing tide down the sides of the mountains, but the trees were all gone, and having no firewood they perished of cold. When Raven came back from under the sea, and saw the fish lying high and dry on the mountains and in the creeks, he said to them, "Stay there and be turned to stones." So stones they became. And when he saw people coming down he would say in like manner, " Turn to stones just where you are." And turned to stones they were. After all mankind had been destroyed in this way, Raven created them afresh out of leaves. Because he made this new generation out of leaves, people know that he must have turned into stone all the men and women who survived the great flood. And that, too,is why to this day so many people die in autumn with the fall of the leaf; when flowers and leaves are fading and falling, we also pass away like them.1 According to yet another account, the Tlingits or Kolosh, as the Russians used to call them, speak of a universal deluge, during which men were saved in a great floating ark which, when the water sank, grounded on a rock and split in two, and that, in their opinion, is the cause of the diversity of languages. The Tlingits represent one-half of the population, which was shut up in the ark, and all the remaining peoples of the earth represent the other half.2 This last legend may be of Christian origin, for it exhibits a sort of blend of Noah's ark with the tower of Babel.

The Haida Indians of Queen Charlotte Islands say that very long ago there was a great flood by which all men and animals were destroyed, with the exception of a single raven. This creature was not, however, exactly an ordinary bird, but—as with all animals in the old Indian stories— possessed the attributes of a human being to a great extent. His coat of feathers, for instance, could be put on or taken off at will, like a garment. It is even related in one version of the story that he was born of a woman who had no husband, and that she made bows and arrows for him. When old enough, with these he killed birds, and of their skins she sewed a cape or blanket. The birds were the little snow-bird with black head and neck, the large black and red, and the Mexican woodpeckers. The name of this being was Ne-kil-stlas. When the flood had gone down Ne-kil-stlas looked about, but could find neither companions nor a mate, and became very lonely. At last he took a cockle (Cardium Nuttalli) from the beach, and marrying it, he constantly continued to brood and think earnestly of his wish for a companion. By and by in the shell he heard a very faint cry, like that of a newly born child, which gradually became louder, and at last a little female child was seen, which growing by degrees larger and larger, was finally married by the raven, and from this union all the Indians were produced and the country peopled." 1

The Tsimshians, an Indian tribe who inhabit the coast of British Columbia, opposite to the Queen Charlotte Islands, have a tradition of a great flood which was sent by heaven as a punishment for the ill-behaviour of man. First, all people, except a few, were destroyed by a flood, and afterwards they were destroyed by fire. Before the flood the earth was not as it is now, for there were no mountains and no trees. These were created by a certain Leqa after the deluge.2 Once when a clergyman, in a sermon preached at Observatory Inlet, referred to the great flood, a Tsimshian chief among his hearers told him the following story: "We have a tradition about the swelling of the water a long time ago. As you are going up the river you will see the high mountain to the top of which a few of our forefathers escaped when the waters rose, and thus were saved. But many more were saved in their canoes, and were drifted about and scattered in every direction. The waters went down again; the canoes rested on the land and the people settled themselves in the various spots whither they had been driven. Thus it is the Indians are found spread all over the country; but they all understand the same songs and have the same customs, which shows that they are one people." 1

The Bella Coola Indians of British Columbia tell a different story of the flood. They say that the great Masmasalanich, who made men, fastened the earth to the sun by a long rope in order to keep the two at a proper distance from each other and to prevent the earth from sinking into the sea. But one day he began to stretch the rope, and the consequence naturally was that the earth sank deeper and deeper, and the water rose higher and higher, till it had covered the whole earth and even the tops of the mountains. A terrible storm broke out at the same time, and many men, who had sought safety in boats, were drowned, while others were driven far away. At last Masmasalanich hauled in the rope, the earth rose from the waves, and mankind spread over it once more. It was then that the diversity of tongues arose, for before the flood all men had been of one speech.2

The Kwakiutl, who inhabit the coast of British Columbia to the south of the Bella Coola, have also their legend of a deluge. "Very long ago," they say, "there occurred a great flood, during which the sea rose so as to cover everything with the exception of three mountains. Two of these are very high, one near Bella-Bella, the other apparently to the north-east of that place. The third is a low but prominent hill on Don Island, named Ko-Kwus by the Indians; this they say rose at the time of the flood so as to remain above the water. Nearly all the people floated away in various directions on logs and trees. The people living where Kit-Katla now is, for instance, drifted to Fort Rupert, while the Fort Ruperts drifted to Kit-Katla. Some of the people had small canoes, and by anchoring them managed to come down near home when the water subsided. Of the Hailtzuk there remained only three individuals; two men and a woman, with a dog. One of the men landed at Kâ-pa, a second at another village site, not far from Bella-Bella, and the woman and dog at Bella-Bella. From the marriage of the woman with the dog, the Bella-Bella Indians originated. When the flood had subsided there was no fresh water to be found, and the people were very thirsty. The raven, however, showed them how, after eating, to chew fragments of cedar (Thuya) wood, when water came into the mouth. The raven also advised them where, by digging in the ground, they could get a little water, but soon a great rain came on, very heavy and very long, which filled all the lakes and rivers so that they have never been dry since. The water is still, however, in some way understood to be connected with the cedar, and the Indians say if there were no cedar trees there would be no water. The converse would certainly hold good." J

The Lillooet Indians of British Columbia say that in former times, while they lived together around Green Lake and below it on the Green River, there came a great and continuous rain, which made all the lakes and rivers overflow their banks and deluge the surrounding country. A man called Ntcinemkin had a very large canoe, in which he took refuge with his family. The other people fled to the mountains, but the water soon covered them too, and in their distress the people begged Ntcinemkin to save at least their children in his canoe. But the canoe was too small to hold all the children, so Ntcinemkin took one child from each family, a male from one, a female from the next, and so on. But still the rain fell and the water rose till all the land was submerged, except the peak of the high mountain called Split (Ncikato), which rises on the west side of the Lower Lillooet Lake, its pinnacle consisting of a huge precipice cleft in two from top to bottom. The canoe drifted about on the flood until the waters sank and it grounded on Smimelc Mountain. Each stage in the sinking of the water is marked by a flat terrace on the side of the mountain, which can be seen there to this day.1

The Thompson Indians of British Columbia say that once there was a great flood which covered the whole country, except the tops of some of the highest mountains. The Indians think, though they are not quite sure, that the flood was caused by three brothers called Qoaqlqal, who in those days travelled all over the country working miracles and transforming things, till the transformers were themselves transformed into stones. Be that as it may, everybody was drowned in the great flood except the coyote and three men; the coyote survived because he turned himself into a piece of wood and so floated on the water, and the men escaped with their lives by embarking in a canoe, in which they drifted to the Nzukeski Mountains. There they were afterwards, with their canoe, transformed into stones, and there you may see them sitting in the shape of stones down to this day. As for the coyote, when the flood subsided, he was left high and dry on the shore in the likeness of the piece of wood into which, at the nick of time, he had cleverly transformed himself. So he now resumed his natural shape and looked about him. He found he was in the Thompson River country.

He took trees to him to be his wives, and from him and the trees together the Indians of the present day are descended. Before the flood there were neither lakes nor streams in the mountains, and therefore there were no fish. When the waters of the deluge receded, they left lakes in the hollows of the mountains, and streams began to flow down from them towards the sea. That is why we now find lakes in the mountains, and fish in the lakes. Thus the deluge story of the Thompson River Indians appears to have been invented to explain the presence of lakes in the mountains; the primitive philosopher accounted for them by a great flood which, as it retired, left the lakes behind it in the hollows of the hills, just as the ebbing tide leaves pools behind it in the hollows of the rocks on the sea-shore.

The Kootenay Indians, who inhabit the south-eastern part of British Columbia, say that once upon a time a chicken-hawk (Accipiter Cooperi) forbade his wife, a small grey bird, to bathe in a certain lake. One day, after picking berries on the mountain in the hot sun, she was warm and weary, and seeing the lake so cool and tempting she plunged into it, heedless of her husband's warning. But the water rose, a giant rushed forth, and ravished the bird, or rather the woman, for in these Indian tales no sharp line of distinction is drawn between the animal and the human personages. Her angry husband came to the rescue and discharged an arrow which struck the giant in the breast. To be revenged, the monster swallowed all the waters, so that none remained for the Indians to drink. But the injured wife plucked the arrow from the giant's breast, and the pent-up waters gushed forth and caused a flood. The husband and his wife took refuge on a mountain, and remained there till the flood subsided. In another version of this Kootenay story, a big fish takes the place of the giant and is killed by the injured husband; the spouting blood of the fish causes the deluge, and the man, or the hawk, escapes from it by climbing up a tree. The scene of the story is laid on the Kootenay River near Fort Steele.1

Legends of a great flood appear to have been current among the Indian tribes of Washington State. Thus the Twanas, on Puget Sound, say that once on a time the people were wicked and to punish them a great flood came, which overflowed all the land except one mountain. The people fled in their canoes to the highest mountain in their country—a peak of the Olympic range—and as the water rose above it they tied their canoes with long ropes to the highest tree, but still the water rose above it. Then some of the canoes broke from their moorings and drifted away to the west, where the descendants of the persons saved in them now live, a tribe who speak a language like that of the Twanas. That, too, they say, is why the present number of the tribe is so small. In their language this mountain is called by a name which means "Fastener," because they fastened their canoes to it at that time. They also speak of a pigeon which went out to view the dead.1

The Clallam Indians of Washington State, whose country adjoins that of the Twanas, also have a tradition of a flood, but some of them believe that it happened not more than a few generations ago. Indeed about the year 1878 an old man asserted that his grandfather had seen the man who was saved from the flood, and that he was a Clallam Indian. Their Ararat, too, is a different mountain from that on which the Twana Noah and his fellows found refuge. The Lummi Indians, who live near the northern boundary of Washington State, also speak of a great flood, but no particulars of their tradition are reported. The Puyallop Indians, near Tacoma, say that the deluge overspread all the country except one high mound near Steilacoom, and this mound is still called by the Indians "The Old Land," because it was not submerged.2

"Do you see that high mountain over there?" said an old Indian to a mountaineer about the year 1860, as they were riding across the Cascade Mountains. "I do," was the reply. "Do you see that grove to the right?" the Indian next asked. "Yes," answered the white man. "Well," said the Indian, "a long time ago there was a flood, and all the country was overflowed. There was an old man and his family on a boat or raft, and he floated about, and the wind blew him to that mountain, where he touched bottom. He stayed there for some time, and then sent a crow to hunt for land, but it came back without finding any. After some time it brought a leaf from that grove, and the old man was glad, for he knew that the water was abating."1

When the earliest missionaries came among the Spokanas, Nez Perces, and Cayuses, who, with the Yakimas, used to inhabit the eastern part of Washington State, they found that these Indians had their own tradition of a great flood, in which one man and his wife were saved on a raft. Each of these three tribes, together with the Flathead tribes, had its own separate Ararat on which the survivors found refuge.2

The story of a great flood is also told by the Indians of Washington State who used to inhabit the lower course of the Columbia River and speak the Kathlamet dialect of Chinook.3 In one respect their tale resembles the Algonquin legend. They say that a certain maiden was advised by the blue-jay to marry the panther, who was an elk-hunter and the chief of his town to boot. So away she hied to the panther's town, but when she came there she married the beaver by mistake instead of the panther. When her husband the beaver came back from the fishing, she went down to the beach to meet him, and he told her to take up the trout he had caught But she found that they were not really trout at all, but only willow branches. Disgusted at the discovery, she ran away from him, and finally married the panther, whom she ought to have married at first. Thus deserted by the wife of his bosom, the beaver wept for five days, till all the land was flooded with his tears. The houses were overwhelmed, and the animals took to their canoes. When the flood reached nearly to the sky, they bethought them of fetching up earth from the depths, so they said to the blue-jay, "Now dive, blue-jay !" So the blue-jay dived, but he did not go very deep, for his tail remained sticking out of the water. After that, all the animals tried to dive. First the mink and next the otter plunged into the vasty deep, but came up again without having found the bottom. Then it came to the turn of the musk-rat. He said, "Tie the canoes together." So they tied the canoes together and laid planks across them.

Thereupon the musk-rat threw off his blanket, sang his song five times over, and without more ado dived into the water, and disappeared. He was down a long while. At last flags came up to the surface of the water. Then it became summer, the flood sank, and the canoes with it, till they landed on dry ground. All the animals jumped out of the canoes, but as they did so, they knocked their tails against the gunwale and broke them off short. That is why the grizzly bears and the black bears have stumpy tails down to this day. But the otter, the mink, the musk-rat, and the panther returned to the canoe, picked up their missing tails, and fastened them on the stumps. That is why these animals have still tails of a decent length, though they were broken off short at the flood.1 In this story little is said of the human race, and how it escaped from the deluge. But the tale clearly belongs to that primitive type of story in which no clear distinction is drawn between man and beast, the lower creatures being supposed to think, speak, and act like human beings, and to live on terms of practical equality with them. This community of nature is implicitly indicated in the Kathlamet story by the marriage of a girl, first to a beaver, and then to a panther, and it appears also in the incidental description of the beaver as a man with a big belly.2 Thus in describing how the animals survived the deluge, the narrator may have assumed that he had sufficiently explained the survival of mankind also.

In North America legends of a great flood are not confined to the Indian tribes; they are found also among the Eskimo and their kinsfolk the Greenlanders. At Oro-wignarak, in Alaska, Captain Jacobsen was told that the Eskimo have a tradition of a mighty inundation which, simultaneously with an earthquake, swept over the land so rapidly that only a few persons were able to escape in their skin canoes to the tops of the highest mountains.1 Again, the Eskimo of Norton Sound, in Alaska, say that in the first days the earth was flooded, all but a very high mountain in the middle. The water came up from the sea and covered the whole land except the top of this mountain. Only a few animals escaped to the mountain and were saved, and a few people made a shift to survive by floating about in a boat and subsisting on the fish they caught till the water subsided. As the flood sank and the mountains emerged from the water, the people landed from the canoe on these heights, and gradually followed the retreating flood to the coast. The animals which had escaped to the mountains also descended and replenished the earth after their kinds.2

Again, the Tchiglit Eskimo, who inhabit the coast of the Arctic Ocean from Point Barrow on the west to Cape Bathurst on the east, tell of a great flood which broke over the face of the earth and, driven by the wind, submerged the dwellings of men. The Eskimo tied several boats together so as to form a great raft, and on it they floated about on the face of the great waters, huddling together for warmth under a tent which they had pitched, but shivering in the icy blast and watching the uprooted trees drifting past on the waves. At last a magician named An-odjium, that is, Son of the Owl, threw his bow into the sea, saying, "Enough, wind, be calm!" After that he threw in his earrings, and that sufficed to cause the flood to subside.3

The Central Eskimo say that long ago the ocean suddenly began to rise and continued rising until it had inundated the whole land. The water even covered the tops of the mountains, and the ice drifted over them. When the flood had subsided, the ice stranded and ever since forms an ice-cap on the top of the mountains. Many shell-fish, fish, seals, and whales were left high and dry, and their shells and bones may be seen there to this day. Many Eskimo were then drowned, but many others, who had taken to their boats when the flood began to rise, were saved.1

With regard to the Greenlanders their historian Crantz tells us that "almost all heathen nations know something of Noah's Flood, and the first missionaries found also some pretty plain traditions among the Greenlanders; namely, that the world once overset, and all mankind, except one, were drowned, but some were turned into fiery spirits. The only man that escaped alive, afterwards smote the ground with his stick, and out sprang a woman, and these two repeopled the world. As a proof that the deluge once overflowed the whole earth, they say that many shells, and relics of fishes, have been found far within the land where men could never have lived, yea that bones of whales have been found upon a high mountain." 2 Similar evidence in support of the legend was adduced to the traveller C. F. Hall by the Innuits or Eskimo with whom he lived. He tells us that "they have a tradition of a deluge which they attribute to an unusually high tide. On one occasion when I was speaking with Tookoolito concerning her people, she said, 'Innuits all think this earth once covered with water.' I asked her why they thought so. She answered, 'Did you never see little stones, like clams and such things as live in the sea, away up on mountains?'"3

An Eskimo man once informed a traveller, that he had often wondered why all the mammoths are extinct. He added that he had learned the cause from Mr. Whittaker, the missionary at Herschel Island. The truth is, he explained, that when Noah entered into the ark and invited all the animals to save themselves from the flood by following his example, the sceptical mammoths declined to accept the kind invitation, on the ground that they did not believe there would be much of a flood, and that even if there were, they thought their legs long enough to keep their heads above water. So they stayed outside and perished in their blind unbelief, but the caribou and the foxes and the wolves are alive to this day, because they believed and were saved.1

§ 17. Stories of a Great Flood in Africa

It is curious, that while legends of a universal flood are widely spread over many parts of the world, they are hardly to be found at all in Africa. Indeed, it may be doubted whether throughout that vast continent a single genuinely native tradition of a great flood has been recorded. Even traces of such traditions are rare. None have as yet been discovered in the literature of ancient Egypt.2 In Northern Guinea, we are told, there is "a tradition of a great deluge which once overspread the face of the whole earth, but it is coupled with so much that is marvellous and imaginative, that it can scarcely be identified with the same event recorded in the Bible."3 As the missionary who reports this gives no details, we cannot judge how far the tradition is native and how far borrowed from Europeans. Another missionary has met with a reference to a great flood in the traditions of the natives of the Lower Congo. "The sun and moon once met together, they say, and the sun plastered some mud over a part of the moon, and thus covered up some of the light, and that is why a portion of the moon is often in shadow. When this meeting took place there was a flood, and the ancient people put their porridge (luku) sticks to their backs and turned into monkeys. The present race of people is a new creation. Another statement is that when the flood came the men turned into monkeys, and the women into lizards; and the monkey's tail is the man's gun. One would think from this that the transformation took place, in their opinion, in very recent times; but the Congo native has no legend concerning the introduction of the gun into their country, nor any rumours of the time when hunting and fighting were carried on with spears, shields, bows and arrows, and knives."4 The Bapedi, a Basuto tribe of South Africa, are said to have a legend of a great flood which destroyed nearly all mankind.1

The experienced missionary Dr. Robert Moffat made fruitless inquiries concerning legends of a deluge among the natives of South Africa; one native who professed to have received such a legend from his forefathers was discovered to have learned it from a missionary named Schmelen. "Stories of a similar kind," adds Dr. Moffat, "originally obtained at a missionary station, or from some godly traveller, get, in course of time, so mixed up and metamorphosed by heathen ideas, that they look exceedingly like native traditions." 2 After recording a legend as to the formation of Lake Dilolo in Angola, in which a whole village with its inhabitants, its fowls, and its dogs is said to have perished, Dr. Livingstone remarks, "This may be a faint tradition of the Deluge, and it is remark-able as the only one I have met with in this country." 3 My experienced missionary friend, the Rev. John Roscoe, who spent about twenty-five years in intimate converse with the natives of Central Africa, particularly the Uganda Protectorate, tells me that he has found no native legend of a flood among the tribes with which he is acquainted.

Traditions of a great flood have, however, been discovered by German writers among the natives of East Africa, but the stories are plainly mere variations of the Biblical narra-tive, which has penetrated to these savages through Christian or possibly Mohammedan influence. One such tradition has been recorded by a German officer among the Masai. It runs as follows :—

Tumbainot was a righteous man whom God loved. He married a wife Naipande, who bore him three sons, Oshomo, Bartimaro, and Barmao. When his brother Lengerni died, Tumbainot, in accordance with Masai custom, married the widow Nahaba-logunja, whose name is derived from her high narrow head, that being a mark of beauty among the Masai. She bore her second husband three sons ; but in consequence of a domestic jar, arising from her refusal to give her husband a drink of milk in the evening, she withdrew from his homestead and set up one of her own, fortifying it with a hedge of thorn-bushes against the attacks of wild beasts. In those days the world was thickly peopled, but men were not good. On the contrary they were sinful and did not obey God's commands. However, bad as they were, they refrained from murder. But at last, one unlucky day, a certain man named Nambija knocked another man named Suage on the head. This was more than God could bear, and he resolved to destroy the whole race of mankind.

Only the pious Tumbainot found grace in the eyes of God, who commanded him to build an ark of wood, and go into it, with his two wives, his six sons, and their wives, taking with him some animals of every sort. When they were all safely aboard, and Tumbainot had laid in a great stock of provisions, God caused it to rain so heavily and so long that a great flood took place, and all men and beasts were drowned, except those which were in the ark; for the ark floated on the face of the waters. Tumbainot longed for

206

the end of the rain, for the provisions in the ark began to run short. At last the rain stopped. Anxious to ascertain the state of the flood, Tumbainot let a dove fly out of the ark. In the evening she came back tired, so Tumbainot knew that the flood must still be high, and that the dove could have found no place to rest. Several days later he let a vulture fly out of the ark, but before doing so he took the precaution to fasten an arrow to one of its tail-feathers, calculating that if the bird perched to eat, it would trail the arrow behind it, and that the arrow, hitching on to something as it was dragged over the ground, would stick fast and be lost. The event answered his expectation, for in the evening the vulture returned to the ark without the arrow and the tail-feather. So Tumbainot inferred that the bird had lighted on carrion, and that the flood must be abating. When the water had all run away, the ark grounded on the steppe, and men and animals disembarked. As he stepped out of the ark, Tumbainot saw no less than four rainbows, one in each of the four quarters of the sky, and he took them as a sign that the wrath of God was over.[1]

Another version of the flood story is reported by a German missionary from the same region. He obtained it at the mission-station of Mkulwe, on the Saisi or Momba river, about twenty miles from where the river flows into Lake Rukwa. His informant professed to have had it from his grandfather, and stoutly asserted that it was a genuine old tradition of the country and not borrowed from foreigners. His statement was corroborated by another truth-loving native, who only differed from his fellow in opining that the African Noah sent out two doves instead of one. The story runs thus:—

Long ago, the rivers came down in flood. God said to the two men, "Go into the ship. Also take into it seeds of all sorts and all animals, male and female." They did so. The flood rose high, it overtopped the mountains, the ship floated on it. All animals and all men died. When the water dried up, the man said, "Let us see. Perhaps the water is not yet dried up." He sent out a dove, she came back to the ship. He waited and sent out a hawk, but she did not return, because the water was dried up. The men went out of the ship, they also let out all animals and all seeds.[1]

§ 18. The Geographical Diffusion of Flood Stories

The foregoing survey of diluvial traditions suffices to prove that this type of story, whether we call it legendary or mythical, has been widely diffused throughout the world. Before we inquire into the relation in which the traditions stand to each other, and the cause or causes which have given rise to them, it may be well to recapitulate briefly the regions in which they have been found. To begin with Asia, we have found examples of them in Babylonia, Palestine, Syria, Phrygia, ancient and modern India, Burma, Cochin China, the Malay Peninsula, and Kamtchatka. Roughly speaking, therefore, the traditions prevail in Southern Asia, and are conspicuously absent from Eastern, Central, and Northern Asia. It is particularly remarkable that neither of the great civilized peoples of Eastern Asia, the Chinese and the Japanese, should, so far as I know, have preserved in their voluminous and ancient literatures any native legends of a great flood of the sort we are here considering, that is, of a universal inundation in which the whole or the greater part of the human race is said to have perished.

In Europe native diluvial traditions are much rarer than in Asia, but they occurred in ancient Greece, and have been reported in Wales, and among the Lithuanians, the gipsies of Transylvania, and the Voguls of Eastern Russia. The Icelandic story of an inundation of giant's blood hardly conforms to the general type.

In Africa, including Egypt, native legends of a great flood are conspicuously absent; indeed no single clear case of one has yet been reported.

In the Indian Archipelago we find legends of a great flood in the large islands of Sumatra, Borneo, and Celebes, and among the lesser islands in Nias, Engano, Ceram, Rotti, and Flores. Stories of the same sort are told by the native tribes of the Philippine Islands and Formosa, and by the isolated Andaman Islanders in the Bay of Bengal.

In the vast islands, or continents, of New Guinea and Australia we meet with some stories of a great flood, and legends of the same sort occur in the fringe of smaller islands known as Melanesia, which sweeps in a great arc of a circle round New Guinea and Australia on the north and east.

Passing still eastward out into the Pacific, we discover diluvial traditions widely spread among the Polynesians who occupy the scattered and for the most part small islands of that great ocean, from Hawaii on the north to New Zealand on the south. Among the Micronesians a flood legend has been recorded in the Pelew Islands.

In America, South, Central, and North, diluvial traditions are very widespread. They have been found from Tierra del Fuego in the south to Alaska in the north, and in both continents from east to west. Nor do they occur only among the Indian tribes; examples of them have been reported among the Eskimo from Alaska on the west to Greenland on the east.

Such being in general the geographical diffusion of the traditions we have next to ask, how are they related to each other? Are they all genetically connected with each other, or are they distinct and independent? In other words, are they all descended from one common original, or have they originated independently in different parts of the world? Formerly, under the influence of the Biblical tradition, inquirers were disposed to identify legends of a great flood wherever found, with the familiar Noachian deluge, and to suppose that in them we had more or less corrupt and apocryphal versions of that great catastrophe, of which the only true and authentic record is preserved in the Book of Genesis. Such a view can hardly be maintained any longer. Even when we have allowed for the numerous corruptions and changes of all kinds which oral tradition necessarily suffers in passing from generation to generation and from land to land through countless ages, we shall still find it difficult to recognize in the diverse, often quaint, childish, or grotesque stories of a great flood, the human copies of a single divine original. And the difficulty has been greatly increased since modern research has proved the supposed divine original in Genesis to be not an original at all, but a comparatively late copy, of a much older Babylonian or rather Sumerian version. No Christian apologist is likely to treat the Babylonian story, with its strongly polytheistic colouring, as a primitive revelation of God to man, and if the theory of inspiration is inapplicable to the original, it can hardly be invoked to account for the copy.

Dismissing, therefore, the theory of revelation or inspiration as irreconcilable with the known facts, we have still to inquire, whether the Babylonian or Sumerian legend, which is certainly by far the oldest of all diluvial traditions, may not be the one from which all the rest have been derived. The question is one to which a positive answer can hardly be given, since demonstration in such matters is impossible, and our conclusion must be formed from the consideration of a variety of probabilities which different minds will estimate differently. It is no doubt possible to analyse all the stories into their elements, to classify these elements, to count up the number of them which the various versions have in common, and from the sum of the common elements found in any one narrative to calculate the probability of its being a derivative or original version. This, in fact, has been done by one of my predecessors in this department of research,1 but I do not propose to repeat his calculations; readers with a statistical and mathematical turn of mind may either consult them in his work or repeat them for themselves from the data submitted to them in the foregoing pages. Here I shall content myself with stating my general conclusion, leaving the reader to verify, correct, or reject it by reference to the evidence with which I have furnished him.

Apart, then, from the Hebrew legend, which is unquestionably derived from the Babylonian, and from modern instances which exhibit clear traces of late missionary or at all events Christian influence, I do not think that we have decisive grounds for tracing any of the diluvial traditions to the Babylonian as their original. Scholars of repute have, indeed, maintained that both the ancient Greek and the ancient Indian legends are derived from the Babylonian; they may be right, but to me it does not seem that the resemblances between the three are sufficient to justify us in assuming identity of origin. No doubt in the later ages of antiquity the Greeks were acquainted both with the Babylonian and the Hebrew versions of the deluge legend, but their own traditions of a great flood are much older than the conquests of Alexander, which first unlocked the treasuries of Oriental learning to western scholars, and in their earliest forms the Greek traditions exhibit no clear marks of borrowing from Asiatic sources. In the Deucalion legend, for example, which comes nearest to the Babylonian, only Deucalion and his wife are saved from the flood, and after it has subsided they are reduced to the necessity of miraculously creating mankind afresh out of stones, while nothing at all is said about the restoration of animals, which must, presumably have perished in the waters. This is very different from the Babylonian and Hebrew legend, which provides for the regular propagation both of the human and the animal species after the flood by taking a sufficient number of passengers of both sorts on board the ark.

Similarly a comparison of the ancient Indian with the Babylonian version of the legend brings out serious discrepancies between them. The miraculous fish which figures so prominently in all the ancient Indian versions has no obvious parallel in the Babylonian, though some scholars have ingeniously argued that the deity, incarnate in a fish, who warns Manu of the coming deluge in the Indian legend, is a duplicate of Ea, the god who similarly warns Ut-napishtim in the Babylonian legend, for there seems to be no doubt that Ea was a water deity, conceived and represented partly in human and partly in fish form.1 If this suggested parallel between the two legends could be made out, it would certainly forge a strong link between them. On the other hand, in the oldest Indian form of the story, that in the Satapatha Brahmana, Manu is represented as the solitary survivor of the great flood, and after the catastrophe a woman has to be miraculously created out of the butter, sour milk, whey and curds of his sacrifice, in order to enable him to continue the species.

It is only in the later versions of the story that Manu takes a large assortment of animals and plants with him into the ship, and even in them, though the sage appears on shipboard surrounded by a band of brother sages whom he had rescued from a watery grave, nothing whatever is said about rescuing his wife and children. The omission betrays a lack not only of domestic affection but of common prudence on the part of the philosopher, and contrasts forcibly with the practical foresight of his Babylonian counterpart, who under the like distressing circumstances has at least the consolation of being surrounded by the family circle on the stormy waters, and of knowing that as soon as the flood has subsided he will be able, with their assistance, to provide for the continuance of the human race by the ordinary processes of nature. In this curious difference between the two tales is it fanciful to detect the contrast between the worldly prudence of the Semitic mind and the dreamy asceticism of the Indian?1

On the whole, then, there is little evidence to prove that the ancient Indian and Greek legends of a flood are derived from the corresponding Babylonian tradition. When we remember that the Babylonians, so far as we know, never succeeded in handing on their story of a deluge to the Egyptians, with whom they were in direct communication for centuries, we need not wonder if they failed to transmit it to the more distant Greeks and Indians, with whom down to the days of Alexander the Great they had but little intercourse. In later ages, through the medium of Christian literature, the Babylonian legend has indeed gone the round of the world and been echoed in tales told under the palms of coral islands, in Indian wigwams, and amid the Arctic ice and snow;2 but in itself, apart from Christian or Mohammedan agencies, it would seem to have travelled little beyond the limits of its native land and the adjoining Semitic regions.

If, among the many other diluvial traditions which we have passed in review, we look about for evidence of derivation from a common source, and therefore of diffusion from a single centre, we cannot fail to be struck by the manifest tokens of such derivation and diffusion in the Algonquin stories of North America.3 The many flood legends recorded among different tribes of that widely spread stock resemble each other so closely that we cannot but regard them as mere variations of one and the same tradition. Whether in the original story the incident of the various animals diving into the water to fetch up earth is native or based on a reminiscence of the birds in the Noachian story, which has reached the Indians through white men, may be open to question.

Further, we have seen that according to Humboldt a general resemblance may be traced between the diluvial traditions among the Indians of the Orinoco,1 and that according to William Ellis a like resemblance prevails among the Polynesian legends.2 It may be that in both these regions the traditions have spread from local centres, in other words, that they are variations of a common original.

But when we have made allowance for all such cases of diffusion from local centres, it seems probable that there still remain deluge legends which have originated independently.

§ 19. The Origin of Stories of a Great Flood

We have still to ask, What was the origin of diluvial traditions? how did men come so commonly to believe that at some time or other the earth, or at all events the whole inhabited portion of it, had been submerged under the waters of a mighty flood in which almost the entire human race perished? The old answer to the question was that such a catastrophe actually occurred, that we have a full and authentic record of it in the Book of Genesis, and that the many legends of a great flood which we find scattered so widely among mankind embody the more or less imperfect, confused and distorted reminiscences of that tremendous cataclysm. A favourite argument in support of this view was drawn from marine shells and fossils, which were supposed to have been left high and dry in deserts and on mountain-tops by the retiring waters of the Noachian deluge. Seashells found on mountains were adduced by Tertullian as evidence that the waters had once covered the earth, though he did not expressly associate them with the flood recorded in Genesis.1 When excavations made in 1517, for repairing the city of Verona, brought to light a multitude of curious petrifactions, the discovery gave rise to much speculation, in which Noah and the ark of course figured conspicuously. Yet they were not allowed to pass unchallenged, for a philosophical Italian naturalist, Fracastoro, was bold enough to point out difficulties in the popular hypothesis. "That inundation," he observed, "was too transient; it consisted principally of fluviatile waters , and if it had transported shells to great distances, must have strewed them over the surface, not buried them at vast depths in the interior of mountains. His clear exposition of the evidence would have terminated the discussion for ever, if the passions of mankind had not been enlisted in the dispute."2

Towards the end of the seventeenth century the field of geology was invaded by an army of theologians, recruited in Italy, Germany, France, and England, who darkened counsel and left confusion worse confounded. "Henceforward, they who refused to subscribe to the position, that all marine organic remains were proofs of the Mosaic deluge, were exposed to the imputation of disbelieving the whole of the sacred writings. Scarcely any step had been made in approximating to sound theories since the time of Fracastoro, more than a hundred years having been lost, in writing down the dogma that organised fossils were mere sports of nature. An additional period of a century and a half was now destined to be consumed in exploding the hypothesis, that organised fossils had all been buried in the solid strata by Noah's flood. Never did a theoretical fallacy, in any branch of science, interfere more seriously with accurate observation and the systematic classification of facts. In recent times, we may attribute our rapid progress chiefly to the careful determination of the order of succession in mineral masses, by means of their different organic contents, and their regular superposition. But the old diluvialists were induced by their system to confound all the groups of strata together, referring all appearances to one cause and to one brief period, not to a variety of causes acting throughout a long succession of epochs. They saw the phenomena only, as they desired to see them, sometimes misrepresenting facts, and at other times deducing false conclusions from correct data. In short, a sketch of the progress of geology, from the close of the seventeenth to the end of the eighteenth century, is the history of a constant and violent struggle of new opinions against doctrines sanctioned by the implicit faith of many generations, and supposed to rest on scriptural authority." 1

The error thus stigmatized by Sir Charles Lyell died hard. Less than a century ago, when William Buckland was appointed Reader in Geology at Oxford, he could still assure his hearers, in his inaugural address to the University, that "the grand fact of an universal deluge at no very remote period is proved on grounds so decisive and incontrovertible, that had we never heard of such an event from Scripture or any other Authority, Geology of itself must have called in the assistance of some such catastrophe to explain the phenomena of diluvial action."2 And within our own lifetime another eminent geologist wrote and published as follows: "I have long thought that the narrative in Genesis vii. and viii. can be understood only on the supposition that it is a contemporary journal or log of an eye-witness incorporated by the author of Genesis in his work. The dates of the rising and fall of the water, the note of soundings over the hill-tops when the maximum was attained, and many other details, as well as the whole tone of the narrative, seem to require this supposition, which also removes all the difficulties of interpretation which have been so much felt."3 But if the story of the flood in Genesis is the contemporary log-book of an eye-witness, how are we to explain the remarkable discrepancies it contains with regard to the duration of the flood and the number of the animals admitted to the ark? Such a theory, far from solving the difficulties that beset the narrative, would on the contrary render them altogether inexplicable, except on a supposition alike injurious and unjust either to the veracity or to the sobriety of the narrator.1

Nor need we linger long over another explanation of flood stories which has of late years enjoyed a good deal of popularity in Germany. On this view the story of the flood has really nothing to do with water or an ark; it is a myth relating to the sun or the moon or the stars, or all three of them together, for the learned men who have made this surprising discovery, while they are united in rejecting the vulgar terrestrial interpretation, are by no means agreed among themselves as to all the niceties of their high celestial theory. Some of them will have it that the ark is the sun; 1 another thinks that the ark was the moon, that the pitch with which it was caulked is a figurative expression for a lunar eclipse, and that by the three stories in which the vessel was built we must understand the phases of the lunar orb.2 The latest advocate of the lunar theory seeks to reconcile all contradictions in a higher unity by embarking the human passengers on board the moon, while he leaves the animals to do the best they can for themselves among the stars.3 It would be doing such learned absurdities too much honour to discuss them seriously. I have noticed them only for the sake of the hilarity with which they are calculated to relieve the tedium of a grave and prolonged discussion.

But when we have dismissed these fancies to their appropriate limbo, we are still confronted with the question of the origin of diluvial traditions. Are they true or false? Did the flood, which the stories so persistently describe, really happen or did it not? Now so far as the narratives speak of floods which covered the whole world, submerging even the highest mountains and drowning almost all men and animals, we may pronounce with some confidence that they are false for, if the best accredited testimony of modern geology can be trusted, no such cataclysm has befallen the earth during the period of man's abode on it. Whether, as some philosophers suppose, a universal ocean covered the whole surface of our planet long before man had appeared upon it, is quite a different question. Leibnitz, for example, imagined the earth "to have been originally a burning luminous mass, which ever since its creation has been undergoing refrigeration. When the outer crust had cooled down sufficiently to allow the vapours to be condensed, they fell, and formed a universal ocean, covering the loftiest mountains, and investing the whole globe." 1 A similar view of a universal primeval ocean, formed by the condensation of aqueous vapour while the originally molten matter of the planet gradually lost its heat, follows almost necessarily from the celebrated Nebular Hypothesis as to the origin of the stellar universe, which was first propounded by Kant and afterwards developed by Laplace.2 Lamarck, too, "was deeply impressed with a belief prevalent amongst the older naturalists that the primeval ocean invested the whole planet long after it became the habitation of living beings."3 But such speculations, even if they might have occurred to primitive man, are to be clearly distinguished from stories of a deluge which destroyed the majority of mankind, for these stories presuppose the existence of the human race on the earth and therefore can hardly refer to a time earlier than the Pleistocene period.4

But though stories of such tremendous cataclysms are almost certainly fabulous, it is possible and indeed probable that under a mythical husk many of them may hide a kernel of truth; that is, they may contain reminiscences of inundations which really overtook particular districts, but which in passing through the medium of popular tradition have been magnified into world-wide catastrophes. The records of the past abound in instances of great floods which have spread havoc far and wide, and it would be strange indeed if the memory of some of them did not long persist among the descendants of the generation which experienced them. For examples of such disastrous deluges we need go no farther than the neighbouring country of Holland, which has suffered from them again and again. In the thirteenth century "the low lands along the Vlie, often threatened, at last sank in the waves. The German Ocean rolled in upon the inland Lake of Flevo.

The stormy Zuyder Zee began its existence by engulfing thousands of Frisian villages, with all their population, and by spreading a chasm between kindred peoples. The political, as well as the geographical, continuity of the land was obliterated by this tremendous deluge. The Hollanders were cut off from their relatives in the east by as dangerous a sea as that which divided them from their Anglo-Saxon brethren in Britain.1 Again, early in the sixteenth century, a tempest blowing from the north, drove the waters of the ocean on the low coast of Zealand more rapidly than they could be carried off through the Straits of Dover. The dykes of South Beveland burst, the sea swept over the land, hundreds of villages were overwhelmed, and a tract of country, torn from the province, was buried beneath the waves. South Beveland became an island, and the stretch of water which divides it from the continent has ever since been known as "the Drowned Land." Yet at low tide the estuary so formed can be forded by seafaring men who know the ground. During the rebellion which won for Holland its national independence, a column of Spanish troops, led by a daring officer, Colonel Mondragon, waded across the ford by night, with the water breast high, and relieved a garrison which was beleaguered by the rebels in the city of Tergoes.2

Again, "towards the end of the year 1570, still another and a terrible misfortune descended upon the Netherlands. An inundation, more tremendous than any which had yet been recorded in those annals so prolific in such catastrophes, now swept the whole coast from Flanders to Friesland. Not the memorable deluge of the thirteenth century, out of which the Zuyder Zee was born; not that in which the waters of the Dollart had closed for ever over the villages and churches of Gröningen; not one of those perpetually recurring floods by which the inhabitants of the Netherlands, year after year, were recalled to an anxious remembrance of the watery chaos out of which their fatherland had been created, and into which it was in daily danger of resolving itself again, had excited so much terror and caused so much destruction. A continued and violent gale from the north-west had long been sweeping the Atlantic waters into the North Sea, and had now piled them upon the fragile coasts of the provinces.

The dykes, tasked beyond their strength, burst in every direction. The cities of Flanders, to a considerable distance inland, were suddenly invaded by the waters of the ocean. The whole narrow peninsula of North Holland was in imminent danger of being swept away for ever. Between Amsterdam and Meyden, the great Diemer dyke was broken through in twelve places. The Hand-bos, a bulwark formed of oaken piles, fastened with metal clamps, moored with iron anchors, and secured by gravel and granite, was snapped to pieces like packthread. The 'Sleeper,' a dyke thus called, because it was usually left in repose by the elements, except in great emergencies, alone held firm, and prevented the consummation of the catastrophe. Still the ocean poured in upon the land with terrible fury. Dort, Rotterdam, and many other cities were, for a time, almost submerged. Along the coast, fishing vessels, and even ships of larger size, were floated up into the country, where they entangled themselves in groves and orchards, or beat to pieces the roofs and walls of houses. The destruction of life and of property was enormous throughout the maritime provinces, but in Friesland the desolation was complete. There nearly all the dykes and sluices were dashed to fragments; the country, far and wide, converted into an angry sea. The steeples and towers of inland cities became islands of the ocean. Thousands of human beings were swept out of existence in a few

214

hours.

Whole districts of territory, with all their villages, farms and churches, were rent from their places borne along by the force of the waves, sometimes to be lodged in another part of the country, sometimes to be entirely engulfed. Multitudes of men, women, children, of horses, oxen, sheep, and every domestic animal, were struggling in the waves in every direction. Every boat, and every article which could serve as a boat, were eagerly seized upon. Every house was inundated; even the graveyards gave up their dead. The living infant in his cradle, and the long-buried corpse in his coffin, floated side by side. The ancient flood seemed about to be renewed. Everywhere, upon the tops of trees, upon the steeples of churches, human beings were clustered, praying to God for mercy, and to their fellow-men for assistance. As the storm at last was subsiding, boats began to ply in every direction, saving those who were, still struggling in the water, picking fugitives from roofs and tree-tops, and collecting the bodies of those already drowned. Colonel Robles, Seigneur de Billy, formerly much hated for his Spanish or Portuguese blood, made himself very active in this humane work. By his exertions, and those of the troops belonging to Gröningen, many lives were rescued, and gratitude replaced the ancient animosity. It was estimated that at least twenty thousand persons were destroyed in the province of Friesland alone. Throughout the Netherlands, one hundred thousand persons perished. The damage done to property, the number of animals engulfed in the sea, were almost incalculable." 1

On these and other occasions the floods which have laid great tracts of Holland under water have been caused, not by heavy rains, but by risings of the sea. Now it is to be observed that in not a few diluvial traditions the cause alleged for the deluge is in like manner not the fall of rain but an incursion of the ocean. Thus we have found a rising of the sea assigned as the cause of the flood by the natives of the islands of Nias,2 Engano,3 Rotti,4 Formosa,5 Tahiti,6 Hawaii,7 Rakaanga,1 and the Pelew Islands,2 by Indian tribes on the west coast of America from Tierra del Fuego in the south to Alaska in the north,3 and by Eskimo on the shores of the Arctic Ocean.4 The occurrence of such stories far and wide on the coasts and among the islands of the Pacific is very significant, for that ocean is subject from time to time to great earthquake-waves, which have often inundated the very coasts and islands where stories of great floods caused by the rising of the sea are told. Are we not allowed, nay compelled, to trace some at least of these stories to these inundations as their true cause? All the probabilities seem to be in favour of a causal rather than of an accidental connexion between the two things.

To take instances of such earthquake-waves in the Pacific, we may notice the dreadful calamities which have repeatedly overtaken Callao, the seaport of Lima in Peru. One of the most fearful of which we have any account happened on the 20th of October 1687. The earthquake "began at four in the morning, with the destruction of several publick edifices and houses, whereby great numbers of persons perished, but this was little more than a presage of what was to follow, and preserved the greatest part of the inhabitants from being buried under the ruins of the city. The shock was repeated at six in the morning with such impetuous concussions, that whatever had withstood the first, was now laid in ruins, and the inhabitants thought themselves very fortunate in being only spectators of the general devastation from the streets and squares, to which they had directed their flight on the first warning. During this second concussion the sea retired considerably from its bounds, and returning in mountainous waves, totally overwhelmed Callao, and the neighbouring parts, together with the miserable inhabitants."5 The same wave which submerged the city carried ships a league into the country, and drowned man and beast for fifty leagues along the shore.6

Again, on the 28th of October 1746, Callao was over-whelmed by another earthquake and another sea-wave. "At half an hour after ten at night, five hours and three quarters before the full of the moon, the concussions began with such violence, that in little more than three minutes, the greatest part, if not all the buildings, great and small, in the whole city, were destroyed, burying under their ruins those inhabitants who had not made sufficient haste into the streets and squares; the only places of safety in these terrible convulsions of nature. At length the horrible effects of this shock ceased, but the tranquillity was of short duration; concussions returning with such frequent repetitions, that the inhabitants, according to the account sent of it, computed two hundred in the first twenty-four hours. The fort of Callao, at the very same hour, sunk into the like ruins, but what it suffered from the earthquake in its buildings, was inconsiderable, when compared with the terrible catastrophe which followed, for the sea, as is usual on such occasions, receding to a considerable distance, returned in mountainous waves foaming with the violence of the agitation, and suddenly turned Callao, and the neighbouring country, into a sea.

This was not, however, totally performed by the first swell of the waves, for the sea retiring further, returned with still more impetuosity; the stupendous water covering both the walls and other buildings of the place so that whatever had escaped the first, was now totally overwhelmed by those terrible mountains of waves and nothing remained except a piece of the wall of the fort of Santa Cruz, as a memorial of this terrible devastation. There were then twenty-three ships and vessels, great and small, in the harbour, of which nineteen were absolutely sunk, and the other four, among which was a frigate called St. Fermin, carried by the force of the waves to a great distance up the country. This terrible inundation extended to other ports on the coast, as Cavallos and Guanape; and the towns of Chancay, Guara, and the valleys della Baranca, Sape, and Pativilca, underwent the same fate as the city of Lima. The number of persons who perished in the ruin of that city, before the 31st of the same month of October, according to the bodies found, amounted to 1300, besides the maimed and wounded, many of which lived only a short time in torture. At Callao, where the number of inhabitants amounted to about 4000, two hundred only escaped; and twenty-two of these by means of the above-mentioned fragment of a wall. According to an account sent to Lima after this accident, a volcano in Lucanas burst forth the same night and ejected such quantities of water, that the whole country was overflowed and in the mountain near Patas, called Conversiones de Caxamarquilla, three other volcanoes burst, discharging frightful torrents of water."1 From the last part of the foregoing account it appears that a flood of water may be caused by the eruption of a volcano alone.

More recent observations have proved that the oceanic disturbances set up by great earthquakes are not necessarily limited to a short stretch of coast, but that they may be propagated in the form of huge waves across the whole breadth of the Pacific. For example, on the 23rd of December 1854, Simoda in Japan was devastated by an earthquake, and the waves to which it gave rise crossed the North Pacific Ocean and broke on the coast of California. Again, a violent shock of earthquake occurred near Arica, on the coast of Peru, on the 13th of August 1868, and the agitation which it created in the sea was felt north and south along the west coast of America; the waves rose in wild turmoil for several days about the Sandwich Islands, and broke on the Samoan Islands, the east coast of Australia, New Zealand, and the Chatham Islands. The French frigate Néréide, bound at the time for Cape Horn, encountered in latitude 51° S. great packs of jagged icebergs, freshly broken off, which the mighty flood had set free as it penetrated beneath the Antarctic ice.

Again, during the earthquake which befell Iquique in Peru on the 9th of May 1877, the Pacific Ocean rose in great waves on the opposite coast from Kamtchatka and Japan in the north to New Zealand and the Chatham Islands in the south. At the Samoan Islands the waves were from six to twelve feet high; in Japan the sea rose and fell from five to ten feet; in New Zealand the waves varied from three to twenty feet in height.1 Indeed, on the coasts of South America and Japan these earthquake waves are often more destructive and therefore more dreaded than the earthquakes themselves.2 In Japan, which is subject to very frequent movements of the earth, regular calendars of earthquakes are kept, and from them we learn that the eastern coasts of the country have often been devastated by sea waves which have carried off from one thousand to one hundred thousand of the people. On the night of 15th June 1896, for example, such a wave swept over the north-west coast of Nipon for a length of seventy miles, causing a loss of nearly thirty thousand lives. At one place four steamers were carried inland, whilst a hundred and seventy-six vessels of various sorts lined the foot of the hills. Indeed, the ancient capital of Japan, which once numbered a million of inhabitants and included the palace of a Shogun, had to be abandoned in consequence of the inundations which broke over it from the sea in the years 1369 and 1494. The site is now occupied by the quiet village of Kamakura, sheltered by sand dunes and crooked pines. Only a gigantic bronze image of Buddha, fifty feet high, cast more than six centuries ago, rises in solemn majesty and peace to attest the grandeur that has passed away.3

On coasts where the shock of an earthquake is commonly accompanied or followed by an inroad of the sea, it is natural that the first impulse of the natives, on feeling the concussion, should be to take refuge on a height where they may be safe from the dreaded rush of the water.4 Now we have seen that the Araucanian Indians of Chili, who have a tradition of a great deluge and fear a repetition of the disaster, fly for safety to a mountain when they feel a violent shock of earth-quake,5 and that the Fijians, who have likewise a tradition of a calamitous flood, used to keep canoes in readiness against the recurrence of a similar inundation.1 Taking all these facts into account we may accept as reasonable and probable the explanation which the distinguished American ethnologist, Horatio

Hale, gave of the Fijian tradition of a deluge. Commenting on the statement that the Fijians formerly kept canoes ready against a repetition of the flood, he writes as follows :_

"This statement (which we heard from others in the same terms) may induce us to inquire whether there might not have been some occurrence in the actual history of the islands to give rise to this tradition, and the custom here mentioned. On the 7th of November 1837, the Pacific Ocean was traversed from east to west by an immense wave, which, taking its rise with the shock of an earthquake in Chili, was felt as far as the Bonin Islands. At the Sandwich Islands, according to the account given by Mr. Jarvis in his History, p. 21, the water rose, on the east coast of Hawaii, twenty feet above high-water mark, inundated the low lands, swept away several villages, and destroyed many lives. Similar undulations have been experienced at these islands on several occasions. If we suppose (what is no way improbable) that, at some time within the last three or four thousand years, a wave of twice this height crossed the ocean, and swept over the Vitian [Fijian] Islands, it must have submerged the whole alluvial plain on the east side of Vitilevu, the most populous part of the group. Multitudes would no doubt be destroyed. Others would escape in their canoes, and as Mbengga is a mountainous island, in the neighbourhood of this district,it would naturally be the place of refuge for many."[2]

A similar explanation would obviously apply to the other legends of a great flood recorded in the islands of the Pacific, for all these islands have probably suffered in like manner from the invasion of huge earthquake-waves.[3] At least, in the present state of our knowledge, it seems safer to accept provisionally the view of the eminent American ethnologist than to adopt the theory of an eminent German ethnologist, who would explain all these Polynesian traditions as solar, lunar, and stellar myths.[1]

If some of the traditions of a great flood caused by a rising of the sea may thus rest on an historical basis, there can be no reason why some of the traditions of a great flood caused by heavy rain should not be equally well founded. Here in England we who live in flat parts of the country are familiar with local floods produced by this cause; not many years ago, for example, large tracts of Norfolk, including the city of Norwich, were laid under water by a sudden and violent fall of rain, resembling a cloudburst. A similar cause inundated the low-lying parts of Paris a few years ago, creating anxiety and alarm not only among the inhabitants, but among the friends of the beautiful city in all parts of the world. It is easy to understand how among an ignorant and unlettered population, whose intellectual horizon hardly extends beyond the limits of their vision, the memory of a similar catastrophe, orally transmitted, might in the course of a few generations grow into the legend of a universal deluge, from which only a handful of favoured individuals had contrived in one way or another to escape. Even the tradition of a purely local flood, in which many people had been drowned, might unconsciously be exaggerated into vast dimensions by a European settler or traveller, who received it from savages and interpreted it in the light of the Noachian deluge, with which he himself had been familiar from childhood. For instance, we have seen that stories of a great flood are reported to be told by the Indians of Guiana.

On this subject it is well to bear in mind the caution given us by Sir Everard F. Im Thurn, who knows these Indians well. "The calamity to which an Indian is perhaps most exposed is to be driven from his home by a sudden rise in the river and consequent flooding of the whole forest. His way to escape is to get into his canoe with his family and his live stock, and to seek temporarily some higher ground, or, as sometimes happens, if none such can be found, the whole party lives as best they may in the canoe until the waters disappear from the face of the earth. It is well known how in all countries the proverbial 'oldest inhabitant' remembers and tells of the highest flood that ever happened. When therefore the Indian tells in his simple language the tradition of the highest flood which covered all the small world known to him, and tells how the Indians escaped it, it is not difficult to realise that the European hearer, theologically prejudiced in favour of Noah, his flood, and his ark, is apt to identify the two stories with each other, and with many similar stories from many parts of the world."1

In this manner it has been proposed to explain the Babylonian and Hebrew traditions of a great flood by the inundations to which the lower valley of the Euphrates and Tigris is annually exposed by the heavy rains and melting snows in the mountains of Armenia. "The basis of the story," we are told, "is the yearly phenomenon of the rainy and stormy season which lasts in Babylonia for several months and during which time whole districts in the Euphrates Valley are submerged. Great havoc was caused by the rains and storms until the perfection of canal systems regulated the overflow of the Euphrates and Tigris, when what had been a curse was converted into a blessing and brought about that astonishing fertility for which Babylonia became famous. The Hebrew story of the Deluge recalls a particularly destructive season that had made a profound impression, and the comparison with the parallel story found on clay tablets of Ashurbanapal's library confirms this view of the local setting of the tale."2

On this hypothesis, the great flood was brought about by an unusually heavy fall of rain and snow;3 it was only an extraordinary case of an ordinary occurrence, and the widespread devastation which it wrought in the valley imprinted it indelibly on the memory of the survivors and of their descendants. In favour of this view it may be said that in the Babylonian and the oldest form of the Hebrew tradition the only alleged cause of the deluge is heavy rain.1 The theory may also be supported by the dangerous inundations to which the country is still yearly iable through the action of the same natural causes. When Loftus, the first excavator of the ancient city of Erech, arrived in Baghdad, on the 5th of May 1849, he found the whole population in a state of the utmost apprehension and alarm.

In consequence of the rapid melting of the snows on the Kurdish mountains, and the enormous influx of water from the Euphrates through the Seglawiyya canal, the Tigris had risen that spring to the unprecedented height of twenty-two and a half feet; which was about five feet above its highest level in ordinary years and exceeded the great rise of 1831, when the river broke down the walls and destroyed no less than seven thousand dwellings in a single night, at a time when the plague was committing the most fearful ravages among the inhabitants. A few days before the arrival of the English party, the

Turkish pasha of Baghdad had summoned the whole population, as one man, to guard against the general danger by raising a strong high mound completely round the walls. Mats of reeds were placed outside to bind the earth compactly together. The water was thus prevented from devastating the interior of the city, though it filtered through the fine alluvial soil and stood several feet deep in the cellars. Outside the city it reached to within two feet of the top of the bank. On the side of the river the houses alone, many of them very old and frail, prevented the ingress of the flood. It was a critical juncture. Men were stationed night and day to watch the barriers. If the dam or any of the foundations had failed, Baghdad must have been bodily washed away. Happily the pressure was withstood, and the inundation gradually subsided. The country on all sides for miles was under water, so that there was no possibility of proceeding beyond the dyke, except in the boats which were established as ferries to keep up communication across the flood. The city was for a time an island in a vast inland sea, and it was a full month before the inhabitants could ride beyond the walls. As the summer advanced, the evaporation from the stagnant water caused malaria to such an extent that, out of a population of seventy thousand, no less than twelve thousand died of fever.[1]

If the floods caused by the melting of the snow in the Armenian mountains can thus endanger the cities in the river valley down to modern times, it is reasonable to suppose that they did so in antiquity also, and that the Babylonian tradition of the destruction of the city of Shurippak in such an inundation may be well founded. It is true that the city appears to have ultimately perished by fire rather than by water;[2] but this is quite consistent with the supposition that at some earlier time it had been destroyed by a flood and afterwards rebuilt.

However, the theory which would explain the Babylonian and Hebrew tradition of a great flood by the inundations to which the country is annually exposed, may be combated by an argument drawn from the analogy of Egypt. For Egypt from time immemorial has been similarly subject to yearly inundations; yet it has never, so far as we know, either evolved a flood legend of its own or accepted the flood legend of its great Oriental rival. If annual floods sufficed to produce the legend in Babylonia, why, it may be asked, did not the same cause produce the same effect in Egypt?

To meet this difficulty a different explanation of the Babylonian story has been put forward in recent years by an eminent geologist, Professor Eduard Suess of Vienna. Regarding the regular annual changes in the basin of the Euphrates as insufficient to account for the legend, he has recourse to irregular or catastrophic causes. He points out that "there are other peculiarities of the Euphrates valley which may occasionally tend to exacerbate the evils attendant on the inundations. It is very subject to seismic disturbances, and the ordinary consequences of a sharp earthquake shock might be seriously complicated by its effect on a broad sheet of water. Moreover the Indian Ocean lies within the region of typhoons and if, at the height of an inundation, a hurricane from the southeast swept up the Persian Gulf, driving its shallow waters upon the delta and damming back the outflow, perhaps for hundreds of miles up-stream, a diluvial catastrophe, fairly up to the mark of Hasisadra's, might easily result." [1]

Thus Professor Suess would supplement and reinforce the comparatively slow and gentle pressure of rain by the sudden and violent shock of an earthquake and the bursting of a typhoon, and in support of these two catastrophic causes he appeals to two features in the Hebrew version of the flood story, or rather to one feature which actually occurs in that version, and to another which he would import into it by altering the text so as to suit his hypothesis. We will consider each of his arguments separately.

First, in regard to the earthquake, Professor Suess points out that in the Hebrew narrative one cause alleged for the deluge is the breaking out of subterranean waters.2 "This rising of great quantities of water from the deep," he says, "is a phenomenon which is a characteristic accompaniment of earthquakes in the alluvial districts of great rivers. The subterranean water is contained in the recent deposits of the great plains on both sides of the stream, and its upper limit rises to right and left above the mean level of the river, its elevation increasing in proportion to the distance from the river. What lies beneath this limit is saturated and mobile; the ground above it is dry and friable. When seismic oscillations occur in a district of this kind the brittle upper layer of the ground splits open in long clefts, and from these fissures the underground water, either clear or as a muddy mass, is violently ejected, sometimes in great volumes, sometimes in isolated jets several yards high."1 For example, the young alluvial land about the Danube in Wallachia was rent by an earthquake in 1838, and from the fissures water spouted out in many places fathoms high. The same thing happened when the alluvial plain of the Mississippi, a little below the confluence of the Ohio, was convulsed by an earthquake in January 1812: the water that had filled the subterranean cavities forced a passage for itself and blew up the earth with loud explosions, throwing up an enormous quantity of carbonized wood in jets from ten to fifteen feet high, while at the same time the surface of the ground sank, and a black liquid rose as high as a horse's belly. Again, in January 1862 a violent shock of earthquake affected the whole region south of Lake Baikal, and in particular the delta of the river Selenga which flows into the lake. In the town of Kudara the wooden lids of the fountains were shot into the air like corks from champagne bottles, and springs of tepid water rose in places to a height of more than twenty feet. So terrified were the Mongols that they caused the Lamas to perform ceremonies to appease the evil spirits which, as they imagined, were shaking the earth.2

On this it is to be observed that the reference to subterranean waters as one cause of the deluge occurs only in the Hebrew version of the legend, and even there it is found only in the later Priestly narrative; it does not occur in the earlier Jehovistic narrative, nor in the still earlier Babylonian version, 3 nor, finally, is it found in the original Sumerian legend from which both the Babylonian and the Hebrew stories are derived. Accordingly it may be dismissed as a late addition to the legend on which it would be unsafe to build any hypothesis.

So much for the earthquak; next for the typhoon, which Professor Suess would also extract from the Biblical narrative. He supposes that while the valley of the Euphrates was still rocking under an earthquake, a great sea-wave, driven by a hurricane up the

Persian Gulf, suddenly swept over the land, completing the destruction of the doomed cities and their miserable inhabitants. This tremendous effect he produces very simply by altering the vowel-points of the Hebrew text in two passages so as to read "the flood from the sea " instead of "the flood of waters." 1 The textual change, it is true, is very slight, for it extends only to the vowel-points and leaves the consonants unaffected. But though the vowel-points form no part of the original text of the Scriptures, having been introduced into it not earlier than the sixth century of our era, they are not to be lightly altered, since they represent the traditional pronunciation of the sacred words, as it had been handed down with scrupulous care, generation after generation, by a guild of technically trained scholars, the Massorets, as they were called, who "devoted themselves to preserving not only the exact writing of the received consonantal text, but the exact pronunciation and even the musical cadence proper to every word of the sacred text, according to the rules of the synagogal chanting." 2 Hence the proposed emendation in the two verses of Genesis has been rightly rejected by the best recent scholars,1 and with it the appeal to the Hebrew text for evidence of the marine origin of the great flood must be dismissed as unfounded.

It does not of course follow that Professor Suess's theory is false because the arguments by which he supports it are feeble. Fortunately for the world many a sound conclusion is reached from inadequate or even totally irrelevant premises, otherwise it is to be feared that for most men the chances of ever arriving at the truth would be infinitesimal. If the Biblical narrative rests, as seems probable, on a basis of fact, it is quite possible that the great flood which it describes may actually have been produced by an earthquake or a typhoon, or by both combined. But the theory that it was so produced derives extremely little support from the only authorities open to us, the Hebrew, Babylonian, and Sumerian traditions; hence it hardly amounts to more than a plausible conjecture. On a simple calculation of chances, it seems likely that the catastrophe was brought about by forces which are known to act regularly every year on the Euphrates valley, and to be quite capable of producing widespread inundations, rather than by assumed forces which, though certainly capable of causing disastrous floods, are not historically known to have ever done so in that region; for, apart from the supposed references in Semitic tradition, I am aware of no record of a Babylonian deluge caused either by an earthquake-wave or by a typhoon.

On the whole, then, there seems to be good reason for thinking that some and probably many diluvial traditions are merely exaggerated reports of floods which actually occurred, whether as the result of heavy rain, earthquake-waves, or other causes. All such traditions, therefore, are partly legendary and partly mythical; so far as they preserve reminiscences of floods which really happened, they are legendary; so far as they describe universal deluges which never happened, they are mythical. But in our survey of diluvial traditions we found some stories which appear to be purely mythical, that is, to describe inundations which never took place. Such, for example, are the Samothracian and Thessalian stories of great floods which the Greeks associated with the names of Dardanus and Deucalion. The Samothracian story is probably nothing but a false inference from the physical geography of the Black Sea and its outlets, the Bosphorus and

Dardanelles; the Thessalian story is probably nothing but a false inference from the physical geography of the mountain-ringed Thessalian basin and its outlet, the gorge of Tempe.1 In like manner the stories which describe the miraculous desiccation of the upland valleys of Cashmeer and Bogota are probably nothing but false inferences from the natural configuration of these mountain-girt basins.2 Such stories, therefore, are not legendary but purely mythical; they describe catastrophes which never occurred. They are examples of that class of mythical tales which, with Sir Edward Tylor, we may call myths of observation, since they are suggested by a true observation of nature, but err in their interpretation of it.3

Another set of diluvial traditions, of which we have found examples, also falls into the class of myths of observation. These are the stories of a great flood which rest on the observation of marine fossils found on mountains or in other places remote from the sea. Such tales, as we saw, are told by the Mongolians, the Bare'e-speaking people of Celebes, the Tahitians, and the Eskimo and Greenlanders.4 Being based on the false assumption that the sea must formerly have risen above the heights where the fossils are now found, they are mistaken inferences, or myths of observation; whereas if they had assumed the former depression of these heights under the level of the sea, they would have been true inferences, or anticipations of science.

Thus, while there is reason to believe that many diluvial traditions dispersed throughout the world are based on reminiscences of catastrophes which actually occurred, there is no good ground for holding that any such traditions are older than a few thousand years at most; wherever they appear to describe vast changes in the physical configuration of the globe, which must be referred to more or less remote epochs of geologic time, they probably embody, not the record of contemporary witnesses, but the speculation of much later thinkers. Compared with the great natural features of our planet, man is but a thing of yesterday, and his memory a dream of the night.

The Tower of Babel

Among the problems which beset any inquiry into the early history of mankind the question of the origin of language is at the same time one of the most fascinating and one of the most difficult. The writers whose crude speculations on human origins are embodied in the early chapters of Genesis have given us no hint as to the mode in which they supposed man to have acquired the most important of all the endowments which mark him off from the beasts—the gift of articulate speech. On the contrary they seem to have assumed that this priceless faculty was possessed by him from the beginning, nay that it was shared with him by the animals, if we may judge by the example of the talking serpent in Eden. However, the diversity of languages spoken by the various races of men naturally attracted the attention of the ancient Hebrews, and they explained it by the following tale.

In the early days of the world all mankind spoke the same language. Journeying from the east as nomads in one huge caravan, they came to the great plains of Shinar or Babylonia, and there they settled. They built their houses of bricks, bound together with a mortar of slime, because stone is rare in the alluvial soil of these vast swampy flats. But not content with building themselves a city, they proposed to construct out of the same materials a tower so high that its top should reach to heaven; this they did in order to make a name for themselves, and also to prevent the citizens from being scattered over the face of the whole earth. For when any had wandered from the city and lost his way on the boundless plain, he would look back westward and see afar off the outline of the tall tower standing up dark against the bright evening sky, or he would look eastward and behold the top of the tower lit up by the last rays of the setting sun. So he would find his bearings, and guided by the landmark would retrace his steps homeward. Their scheme was good, but they failed to reckon with the jealousy and power of the Almighty. For while they were building away with all their might and main, God came down from heaven to see the city and the tower which men were raising so fast. The sight displeased him, for he said, "Behold, they are one people, and they have all one language, and this is what they begin to do, and now nothing will be withholden from them, which they purpose to do."

Apparently he feared that when the tower reached the sky, men would swarm up it and beard him in his den, a thing not to be thought of. So he resolved to nip the great project in the bud. "Go to," said he to himself, or to his heavenly counsellors, "let us go down, and there confound their language, that they may not understand one another's speech." Down he went accordingly and confounded their language and scattered them over the face of all the earth. Therefore they left off to build the city and the tower and the name of the place was called Babel, that is, Confusion, because God did there confound the language of all the earth.1

On the plain stuff of this narrative later Jewish tradition has embroidered a rich band of picturesque details. From them we learn that the enterprise of the tower was flat rebellion against God, though the rebels were not at one in their aims. Some wished to scale heaven and there wage war with the Almighty in person, or set up their idols to be worshipped in his stead; others limited their ambition to the more modest scheme of damaging the celestial vault by showers of spears and arrows. Many, many years was the tower in building. It reached so high that at last a bricklayer took a whole year to ascend to the top with his hod on his back. If he fell down and broke his neck, nobody minded for the man, but everybody wept for the brick, because it would take a whole year to replace it on the top of the tower.

So eagerly did they work, that a woman would not interrupt her task of brickmaking even to give birth to a child; she would merely tie the baby in a sheet round her body and go on moulding bricks as if nothing had happened. Day and night the work never slackened, and from their dizzy height they shot heavenward arrows, which returned to them dabbled with blood so they cried, "We have slain all who are in heaven." At last the long-suffering deity lost patience, and turning to the seventy angels who encompass his throne, he proposed that they should all go down and confound the language of men. No sooner said than done. The misunderstandings which consequently arose were frequent and painful. One man, for example, would ask for mortar, and the other would hand him a brick, whereupon the first, in a rage, would hurl the brick at his mate's head and kill him. Many perished in this manner, and the rest were punished by God according to the acts of rebellion which they had meditated. As for the unfinished tower, a part of it sank into the earth, and another part was consumed by fire; only one-third of it remained standing. The place of the tower has never lost its peculiar quality. Whoever passes it forgets all he knows.

The scene of the legend was laid at Babylon, for Babel is only the Hebrew form of the name of the city. The popular derivation from a Hebrew verb balal (Aramaic balbel) "to confuse" is erroneous; the true meaning, as shown by the form in which the name is written in inscriptions, seems to be "Gate of God" (Bâb-il or Bâb-ilu).1 The commentators are probably right in tracing the origin of the story to the deep impression produced by the great city on the simple minds of Semitic nomads, who, fresh from the solitude and silence of the desert, were bewildered by the hubbub of the streets and bazaars, dazzled by the shifting kaleidoscope of colour in the bustling crowd, stunned by the din of voices jabbering in strange unknown tongues, and overawed by the height of the buildings, above all by the prodigious altitude of the temples towering up, terrace upon terrace, till their glistering tops of enamelled brick seemed to touch the blue sky. No wonder that dwellers in tents should imagine that they who scaled the pinnacle of such a stupendous pile by the long winding ramp, and appeared at last like moving specks on the summit, must indeed be near the gods.2

Of two such gigantic temples the huge mouldering remains are to be seen at Babylon to this day, and it is probable that to one or other of them the legend of the Tower of Babel was attached. One of them rises among the ruins of Babylon itself, and still bears the name of Babil; the other is situated across the river at Borsippa, some eight or nine miles away to the south-west, and is known as Birs-Nimrud. The ancient name of the temple in the city of Babylon was E-sagil; it was dedicated to Marduk The ancient name of the temple at Borsippa was E-zida; it was dedicated to Nebo. Scholars are not agreed as to which of these ancient edifices was the original Tower of Babel. Local and Jewish tradition identifies the legendary tower with the ruins of Birs-Nimrud at Borsippa.1

The mound of Babil, once the temple of the chief Babylonian god Bel or Marduk, is now merely an oblong mass composed chiefly of unbaked brick, measuring about two hundred yards in length on the longer northern and southern faces, and rising to a height of at least one hundred and ten feet above the plain. The top is broad and flat, but uneven and broken with heaps of rubbish. While the solid core of the structure was built of crude or sun-dried bricks, its outer faces were apparently coated with walls of burnt bricks, some of which, inscribed with the name of King Nebuchadnezzar, have been found on the spot.2 From Herodotus we learn that the temple rose in a series of eight terraces or solid towers, one on the top of the other, with a ramp winding up on the outside, but broken about half-way up by a landing-place, where there were seats for the rest and refreshment of persons ascending to the summit.3 In the ancient Sumerian language the temple was called E-temen-an-ki or "The House of the Foundation of Heaven and Earth."1 Towards the end of the seventh century before our era the temple had fallen into disrepair, if not into ruins, but it was then restored by King Nabopolassar, who reigned 625—604 B.C. In an inscription, which has been preserved, the king describes himself as "the restorer of Esagila and Ezida," and records the restoration of Esagila or Etemenanki as follows:—

"As for Etemenanki, the temple-tower of Babylon, which before my time had become weakened and had fallen in, Marduk the lord commanded me to lay its foundation in the heart of the earth (and) to raise its turrets to heaven. Baskets, spades (?), and U.RU. I made out of ivory, ushu and mismakanna wood; I caused the numerous workmen assembled in my land to carry them. I set to work (?); I made bricks, I manufactured burnt bricks. Like the downpour of heaven, which cannot be measured, like the massive flood, I caused the Arahtu to carry bitumen and pitch. With the co-operation of Ea, with the insight of Marduk, with the wisdom of Nabu and Nisaba, in the broad understanding with which the god, my creator, had endowed me, with my great ingenuity (?), I came to a decision; I gave orders to the skilled workmen. With a nindanaku measure I measured the measurements of the aba ash-lam (?). The architects at first made a survey of the ground plot (?). Afterwards I consulted Shamash, Ramman, and Marduk; to my heart they gave decision, they sanctioned the measurements, the great gods by decree indicated the later stages of the work.

By means of exorcism, in the wisdom of Ea and Marduk, I cleared away that place, (and) on the original site I laid its platform-foundation; gold, silver, stones from mountain and sea in its foundation I set * * * goodly oil, sweet-smelling herbs, and * * * I placed underneath the bricks. An image of my royalty carrying a dupshikku I constructed; in the platform-foundation I placed it. Unto Marduk, my lord, I bowed my neck; I arrayed myself in my gown, the robe of my royalty. Bricks and mortar I carried on my head, a dupshikku of gold and silver I wore and Nebuchadrezzar, the first-born, the chief son, beloved of my heart, I caused to carry mortar mixed with wine, oil, and (other) products along with my workmen. Nabushumlisher, his twin brother, the offspring of my own flesh, the junior, my darling, I ordered to take a basket and spade (?); a dupshikku of gold and silver I placed (on him). Unto Marduk, my lord, as a gift, I dedicated him. I built the temple in front of Esharra with joy and rejoicing, and like a mountain I raised its tower aloft; to Marduk, my lord, as in days of old, I dedicated it for a sight to be gazed at.

"O Marduk, my lord, look with favour upon my goodly deeds! At thy exalted command, which cannot be altered, let the performance of my hands endure for ever! Like the bricks of Etemenanki, which are to remain firm for ever, do thou establish the foundation of my throne for all time! O Etemenanki, grant blessing to the king who has restored thee! When Marduk with joy takes up his abode in thee, O temple, recall to Marduk, my lord, my gracious deeds!"1

Again, the temple was further repaired and adorned by Nabopolassar's son and successor, Nebuchadrezzar the Second, the Nebuchadnezzar of the Bible. To these restorations the great king repeatedly refers in his inscriptions. Thus he says:—

"The temples of Babylon I rebuilt and restored. As for E-temen-an-ki (house of the foundation of heaven and earth) with burnt brick and bright ugnu-stone I raised on high its turrets. To the rebuilding of Esagila my heart incited me; I held it constantly in mind. I selected the best of my cedar trees, which I had brought from Mount Lebanon, the snow-capped forest, for the roofing of E-kua, the shrine of his lordship, and I decorated with brilliant gold the inner sides of the mighty cedar trunks, used in the roofing of E-kua. I adorned the under side of the roof of cedar with gold and precious stones. Concerning the rebuilding of Esagila I prayed every morning to the king of the gods, the lord of lords."1 Again, in another Babylonian inscription King Nebuchadrezzar II says: "In Esagila, the majestic shrine, the temple of heaven and earth, the dwelling-place of royalty, I decorated with shining gold E-kua, the shrine of the lord of the gods, Marduk, Bab-Hili-shud, the home of Çarpanit, (and) Ezida in Esagila, the shrine called 'the king of the gods of heaven and earth,' and I made (them) to shine like the day. E-temen-an-ki, the temple-tower of Babylon, I made anew."2 Again, in another inscription the king declares : "Esagila, the temple of heaven and earth, the dwelling-place of the lord of the gods Marduk, and E-kua, his shrine, I adorned with shining gold like a wall. Ezida I built anew, and with silver, gold, precious stones, bronze, palm-wood, cedar-wood I completed its construction. E-temen-an-ki, the temple-tower of Babylon, I built and completed, and with burnt brick and shining ugnu-stone I raised on high its turrets." 3

The huge pyramidal mound, to which the Arabs give the name of Birs-Nimrud, is a solitary pile rising abruptly from the vast expanse of the desert some eight or nine miles from the ruins of Babylon. Roughly speaking, the mound forms a rectangular oblong, measuring about six hundred and fifty feet on the long sides and four hundred feet on the short sides. The height of its summit above the plain is about one hundred and fifty-three feet. To the ordinary observer at the present time it presents the appearance rather of a natural hill crowned by a ruin than of a structure reared by the hand of man. Yet there appears to be no doubt that the great mound is wholly artificial, being built entirely of bricks, which have to some extent solidified into a single mass. Thirty-seven feet of solid brickwork, looking like a tower, stand exposed at the top, while below this the original building is almost hidden under the masses of rubbish which have crumbled down from the upper portion.

The whole structure, however, is deeply channelled by exposure to the rain, and in places the original brickwork is sufficiently exposed to reveal the true character and plan of the edifice. From the researches carried on by Sir Henry Rawlinson in the year 1854 it appears that the temple, like that of Bel or Marduk in Babylon, was built in a series of receding stages, seven in number, which rose one above the other in a sort of oblique pyramid to a height of about one hundred and fifty-six feet above the plain. The grand entrance was on the north-east, where stood the vestibule, a separate building, of which the remains prolong the mound very considerably in this direction. Such are the mouldering ruins of E-zida, the great temple of Nebo (Nabu, whose shrine probably occupied the summit of the pyramidal or tower-like structure. In its present form the edifice is chiefly the work of King Nebuchadnezzar (Nebuchadrezzar the Second), whose name appears exclusively on the bricks composing it, and on the cylinders deposited at its angles.1 The modern name of Birs-Nimrud preserves in a slightly altered form the first syllable of Borsippa, the ancient name of the city which stood here.2

On two of the cylinders found by Sir Henry Rawlinson at the angles of the temple is engraved an inscription, in which King Nebuchadnezzar (Nebuchadrezzar II.) records his restoration of the edifice, which had fallen into ruins before his time. The inscription runs thus:—

"Behold now the building named 'the Stages of the Seven Spheres,' which was the wonder of Borsippa, had been built by a former king. He had completed forty-two ammas (of the height), but he did not finish its head. From the lapse of time it had become ruined; they had not taken care of the exits of the waters, so the rain and wet had penetrated into the brickwork; the casing of burnt bricks had bulged out, and the terraces of crude brick lay scattered in heaps; (then) Merodach, my great lord, inclined my heart to repair the building. I did not change its site, nor did I destroy its foundation platform but in a fortunate month, and on an auspicious day, I undertook the rebuilding of the crude-brick terraces, and the burnt-brick casing (of the temple). I strengthened its foundation, and I placed a titular record in the part that I had rebuilt. I set my hand to build it up and to finish its summit. As it had been in ancient times, so I built up its structure; as it had been in former days, thus I exalted its head. Nebo, the strengthener of his children, he who ministers to the gods (?), and Merodach, the supporter of sovereignty, may they cause my work to be established for ever! May it last through the seven ages! May the stability of my throne and the antiquity of my empire, secure against strangers and triumphant over many foes, continue to the end of time! "1

From this record we learn that the ancient Babylonian king, who began to build the great temple-tower at Borsippa, had left it incomplete, wanting its top. It may have been the sight of the huge edifice in its unfinished state which gave rise to the legend of the Tower of Babel.

However, there were many more such temple-towers in ancient Babylonia, and the legend in question may have been attached to any one of them. For example, the remains of such a temple still exist at Uru, the Ur of the Chaldees, from which Abraham is said to have migrated to Canaan.2 The place is now known as Mukayyar or Muge-yer; it is situated on the right bank of the Euphrates about a hundred and thirty-five miles southeast of Babylon.3 A series of low mounds, forming an oval, marks the site of the ancient city. The country all around is so flat that often during the annual flood of the Euphrates, from March till June or July, the ruins form an island in a great marsh and can only be approached by boat. Groves of date-palms here line the banks of the river and extend in unbroken succession along its course till it loses itself in the waters of the Persian Gulf. Near the northern end of the site rise the remains of the temple-tower to a height of about seventy feet. The edifice is a rectangular parallelogram, in two stories, with the larger sides facing northeast and southwest, each of them measuring about two hundred feet in length, while the shorter sides measure only one hundred and thirty-three feet.

As in all similar Babylonian buildings, one angle points almost due north. The lower story, twenty-seven feet high, is supported by strong buttresses; the upper story, receding from thirty to forty-seven feet from the edge of the first, is fourteen feet high, surmounted by about five feet of brick rubbish. The ascent was on the northeast. A tunnel driven into the mound proved that the entire edifice was built of sun-dried bricks in the centre, with a thick coating of massive, partially burnt bricks of a light red colour with layers of reeds between them, the whole, to a thickness of ten feet, being cased with a wall of inscribed kiln-burnt bricks. Inscribed cylinders were discovered at the four corners of the building, each standing in a niche formed by the omission of a single brick in the layer. Subsequent excavations seem to prove that commemorative inscriptions, inscribed on cylinders, were regularly deposited by the builders or restorers of Babylonian temples and palaces at the four corners of the edifices.1

The inscriptions on the cylinders found at Ur record the restoration of the temple-tower by Nabonidus, the last king of Babylon (555-538 B.C.), and give us in outline a history of the ancient edifice. One of them runs as follows :—

"Nabonidus, King of Babylon, patron of Esagila and Ezida, who fears the great gods, am I.

"As for E-lugal-(?)-si-di, the temple-tower of E-gish-shir-gal, which is in Ur, which Uruk,

231

a former king, had built, but had not completed—Dun-gi, his son, completed its construction. From the inscriptions of Ur-uk and Dun-gi, his son, I learned that Ur-uk had built this temple-tower, without completing it, and that Dun-gi, his son, had completed its construction. This temple-tower was now old, and upon the old platform-foundation which Ur-uk and Dun-gi, his son, had built, I undertook the reconstruction of this temple-tower, as of old, with bitumen and burnt brick, and for Sin, the lord of the gods of heaven and earth, the king of the gods, the god of gods, who inhabit the great heavens, the lord of E-gish-shir-gal, which is in Ur, my lord, I founded and built (it).

"O Sin, lord of the gods, king of the gods of heaven and earth, the god of gods, who inhabit the great heavens, upon thy joyful entrance into that temple may the good done to Esagila, Ezida (and) E-gish-shir-gal, the temples of thy great divinity, be established on thy lips!

"And do thou implant the fear of thy great divinity in the heart of its people, that they may not sin against thy great divinity, (and) like the heavens may their foundations stand fast!

"As for me, Nabonidus, King of Babylon, save me from sinning against thy great divinity! A life of far-distant days grant me as a present! And as regards Belshazzar, the first-born son, my offspring, do thou implant in his heart the fear of thy great divinity! May he not fall into sin! May he be satisfied with fulness of life! " 1

From this inscription we learn that the name of the city was Ur, and that the temple was dedicated to Sin, the Babylonian moon-god. Further we are informed that King Ur-uk or Urengur, as his name should rather be spelt, who built the temple-tower, left it unfinished, and that the edifice was completed by his son, King Dungi. The reign of King Uruk or Urengur is variously dated about 2700 B.C. or 2300 B.C.2 In either case the foundation of the temple preceded, perhaps by hundreds of years, the date which is usually assigned to the birth of Abraham; 1 so that if the patriarch really migrated from Ur to Canaan, as Hebrew tradition relates, this very building, whose venerable ruins exist on the spot to this day, dominating by their superior height the flat landscape through which the Euphrates winds seaward, must have been familiar to Abraham from childhood, and may have been the last object on which his eyes rested when, setting out in search of the Promised Land, he took a farewell look backward at his native city disappearing behind its palm groves in the distance. It is possible that in the minds of his descendants, the conspicuous pile, looming dim and vast through the mists of time and of distance, may have assumed the gigantic proportions of a heaven-reaching tower, from which in days of old the various nations of the earth set out on their wanderings.

The authors of Genesis say nothing as to the nature of the common language which all mankind spoke before the confusion of tongues, and in which our first parents may be supposed to have conversed with each other, with the serpent, and with the deity in the garden of Eden. Later ages took it for granted that Hebrew was the primitive language of mankind. The fathers of the Church appear to have entertained no doubt on the subject;

and in modern times, when the science of philology was in its infancy, strenuous, but necessarily abortive, efforts were made to deduce all forms of human speech from Hebrew as their original. In this naïve assumption Christian scholars did not differ from the learned men of other religions, who have seen in the language of their sacred writings the tongue not only of our first forefathers but of the gods themselves.

The first in modern times to prick the bubble effectively was Leibnitz, who observed that "there is as much reason for supposing Hebrew to have been the primitive language of mankind, as there is for adopting the view of Goropius, who published a work at Antwerp, in 1580, to prove that Dutch was the language spoken in Paradise."1 Another writer maintained that the language spoken by Adam was Basque, while others, flying clean in the face of Scripture, introduced the diversity of tongues into Eden itself, by holding that Adam and Eve spoke Persian, that the language of the serpent was Arabic, and that the affable archangel Gabriel discoursed with our first parents in Turkish. Yet another eccentric scholar seriously argued that the Almighty addressed Adam in Swedish, that Adam answered his Maker in Danish, and that the serpent conversed with Eve in French.2 We may suspect that all such philological theories were biassed by the national prejudices and antipathies of the philologers who propounded them.

Attempts have been made to arrive at the primitive language of mankind by the experimental method. The first recorded experiment of this nature is said to have been made by Psammetichus, King of Egypt. Desirous of learning what race of man was first created or evolved, he had recourse to the following device. He took two newborn babes, selected at haphazard, and gave them in charge to a goatherd with strict injunctions to rear them in a lonely hut, where they were to be fed on goat's milk and never to hear a word of human speech, for the sagacious monarch calculated that, left to themselves, uncontaminated by oral intercourse with others, the children would in due time yield to the promptings of nature and break out into the primeval language of our first forefathers.

The result seemed to justify his prevision. For when two years had passed, it chanced that one day the goatherd opened the door of the solitary hut as usual to give the two children their daily meal of goat's milk, and no sooner did he do so than the two little ones ran at him, holding out their hands and crying "Bekos"! At first he said nothing, but when the same thing happened day after day, he reported the matter to the king, who on making inquiries discovered that bekos was the Phrygian word for bread. On the strength of that discovery, King Psammetichus concluded that the Phrygians were the most ancient race of mankind, and that the Egyptians must accordingly yield to them the coveted palm of antiquity.1 Such is the tale as told by the Greek historian Herodotus. We may suspect that it is not an Egyptian but a Greek story, invented to flatter Greek vanity by humbling the pride of the Egyptians and transferring the crown of remotest eld from their brows to those of a race akin to the Grecian.2

A later rationalism, accepting the truth of the anecdote, disputed the conclusion drawn from it, by arguing that bekos was nothing but a natural imitation of the bleating of the goats, whose voices the children heard and whose milk they imbibed daily.3 The experiment is said to have been repeated in later ages by several monarchs, including the German emperor Frederick the Second 4 and the Mogul emperor Akbar Khan. Of the latter potentate it is told that, anxious to discover the true religion, and perplexed by the contradictory claims of the rival systems, he hit upon the following device for solving the problem. He took thirty young children and caused them to be brought up by persons who were strictly forbidden to converse with their youthful charges, for he was resolved to adopt the religious faith of that people whose language the infants should spontaneously speak, being apparently satisfied in his own mind that the religion thus authenticated by the voice of nature could be none other than the true one. The result of the experiment was to confirm the philosophic Mogul in his scepticism, for the children, we are informed, spoke no particular language, and the emperor accordingly continued to be of no particular religion.5 In our own country James IV. of Scotland is reported to have shut up two children with a dumb woman in the island of Inchkeith, desiring to know what language the children would speak when they came to the age of perfect speech. Some say that they spoke good Hebrew, but the chronicler seems to have had doubts on the subject.1

Stories which bear a certain resemblance to the legend of the Tower of Babel are reported among several African tribes. Thus, some of the natives of the Zambesi, apparently in the neighbourhood of the Victoria Falls, "have a tradition which may refer to the building of the Tower of Babel, but it ends in the bold builders getting their crowns cracked by the fall of the scaffolding." 2 The story thus briefly referred to by Dr. Livingstone has been more fully recorded by a Swiss missionary. The A-Louyi, a tribe of the Upper Zambesi, say that formerly their god Nyambe, whom they identify with the sun, used to dwell on earth, but that he afterwards ascended up to heaven on a spider's web. From his post up aloft he said to men, "Worship me." But men said, "Come, let us kill Nyambe." Alarmed at this impious threat, the deity fled to the sky, from which it would seem that he had temporarily descended. So men said, "Come", let us make masts to reach up to heaven." They set up masts and added more masts, joining them one to the other, and they clambered up them. But when they had climbed far up, the masts fell down, and all the men on the masts were killed by the fall. That was the end of them.3

The Bambala of the Congo say "that the Wan-gongo once wanted to know what the moon was, so they started to go and see. They planted a big pole in the ground, and a man climbed up it with a second pole which he fastened to the end; to this a third was fixed, and so on. When their Tower of Babel had reached a considerable height, so high in fact that the whole population of the village was carrying poles up, the erection suddenly collapsed, and they fell victims to their ill-advised curiosity. Since that time no one has tried to find out what the moon is." 4 The natives of Mkulwe, in German East Africa, tell a similar tale. According to them, men one day said to each other, "Let us build high, let us reach the moon!" So they rammed a great tree into the earth, and fixed another tree on the top of it, and another on the top of that, and so on, till the trees fell down and the men were killed. But other men said, "Let us not give up this undertaking," and they piled trees one on the top of the other, till one day the trees again fell down and the men were killed. Then the people gave up trying to climb aloft to the moon.1

The Ashantees have a tradition that God of old dwelt among men, but that, resenting an affront put on him by an old woman, he withdrew in high dudgeon to his mansion in the sky. Disconsolate at his departure, mankind resolved to seek and find him. For that purpose they collected all the porridge pestles they could find and piled them up, one on the top of the other. When the tower thus built had nearly reached the sky, they found to their dismay that the supply of pestles ran short. What were they to do? In this dilemma a wise man stood up and said, "The matter is quite simple. Take the lowest pestle of all, and put it on the top, and go on doing so till we arrive at God." The proposal was carried, but when they came to put it in practice, down fell the tower, as indeed you might have expected. However, others say that the collapse of the tower was caused by the white ants, which gnawed away the lowest of the pestles. In whichever way it happened, the communication with heaven was not completed, and men were never able to ascend up to God.2

The Anal clan of the Kuki tribe, in Assam, tell of an attempt made by a man to climb up into the sky, in order to recover his stolen property. The story is as follows. Once upon a time there was a very pious man who devoted much time to worshipping God, and he had a pet bitch. Envious of his noble qualities, the sun and moon resolved to rob him of his virtue. In pursuit of this nefarious design, they promised to give him their virtue, if only he would first entrust them with his. The unsuspecting saint fell into the trap, and the two celestial rogues made off with his virtue. Thus defrauded, the holy man ordered his dog to pursue and catch the thieves. The intelligent animal brought a long pole and climbed up it to reach the fugitives, and the saint swarmed up the pole behind his dumb friend. Unfortunately he ascended so slowly that, before he reached the sky, the white ants had eaten away the lower end of the pole, so he fell down and broke his neck. But the bitch was more agile; before the white ants had gnawed through the wood, she had got a footing in the sky, and there the faithful animal is to this day, chasing the sun and moon round and round the celestial vault. Sometimes she catches them, and when she does so, the sun or moon is darkened, which Europeans call an eclipse. At such times the Anals shout to the bitch, "Release! Release!" meaning, of course, that she is to let go the sun or moon.1

A story like the Biblical narrative of the Tower of Babel is told of the great pyramid of Cholula in Mexico, the vastest work of aboriginal man in all America. This colossal fabric, on which the modern traveller still gazes with admiration, stands near the handsome modern city of Puebla, on the way from Vera Cruz to the capital. In form it resembles, and in dimensions it rivals, the pyramids of Egypt. Its perpendicular height is nearly two hundred feet, and its base is twice as long as that of the great pyramid of Cheops. It had the shape common to the Mexican teocallis, that of a truncated pyramid, facing with its four sides the cardinal points and divided into four terraces. Its original outlines, however, have been effaced by time and the weather, while its surface is now covered by an exuberant growth of shrubs and trees, so that the huge pile presents the aspect of a natural hill rather than of a mound reared by human labour. The edifice is built of rows of bricks baked in the sun and cemented together with mortar, in which are stuck quantities of small stones, potsherds, and fragments of obsidian knives and weapons. Layers of clay are interposed between the courses of brick. The flat summit, which comprises more than an acre of ground, commands a superb prospect over the broad fertile valley away to the huge volcanic mountains which encircle it, their lower slopes covered with grand forests their pinnacles of porphyry bare and arid, the highest of them crowned with eternal snow.1

A legend concerning the foundation of this huge monument is recorded by the Dominican friar Pedro de los Rios. It runs as follows. Before the great flood, which took place four thousand years after the creation of the world, this country was inhabited by giants. All who did not perish in the inundation were turned into fishes, except seven who took refuge in caves. When the waters had retired, one of the seven, by name Xelhua, surnamed the Architect, came to Cholula, where, in memory of the mountain of Tlaloc, on which he and his six brothers had found safety, he built an artificial hill in the shape of a pyramid. He caused the bricks to be made in the province of Tlalmanalco, at the foot of Mount Cocotl, and in order to transport them to Cholula he set a line of men on the road, who passed the bricks from hand to hand. It was his purpose to raise the mighty edifice to the clouds, but the gods, offended at his presumption, hurled the fire of heaven down on the pyramid, many of the workmen perished, and the building remained unfinished. Afterwards it was dedicated to the great god Quetzalcoatl.2

It is said that at the time of the Spanish conquest the inhabitants of Cholula preserved with great veneration a large aerolite, which according to them was the very thunderbolt that fell on the pyramid and set it on fire. A similar tradition, differing somewhat in details, is related by the Spanish historian Duran, who wrote in 1579 "In the beginning," says he, "before the light and sun were created, the earth was in darkness and gloom, void of all created things, quite flat, without hill or dale, encircled by water on every side, without trees and without any other created thing. As soon as the sun and the light were born in the east, some men appeared there, ungainly giants who possessed the land. Wishing to see the rising and the setting of the sun, they agreed to go in search of it; so dividing into two bands they journeyed, the one band toward the west, and the other toward the east. So they journeyed till they were stopped by the sea. Thence they resolved to return to the place from which they had set out, so they came back to the place called Iztacçulin ineminian. Not knowing how to reach the sun, and charmed with its light and beauty, they decided to build a tower so high that its top should reach the sky. In their search for materials with which to carry out their design they found a clay and a very sticky bitumen with which they began in a great hurry to build the tower. When they had reared it as high as they could, so high that it is said to have seemed to reach the sky, the lord of the heights was angry and said to the inhabitants of heaven, 'Have you seen how the inhabitants of the earth have built a tower so high and so proud to climb up here, charmed as they are with the light and beauty of the sun? Come, let us confound them for it is not meet that the people of the earth, who live in bodies of flesh, should mix with us.' In a moment, the inhabitants of heaven, setting out towards the four quarters of the world, overthrew as by a thunderbolt the edifice which the men had built. After that,

236

the giants, scared and filled with terror, separated and scattered in all directions over the earth." 1

In this latter tradition the traces of Biblical influence appear not only in the dispersal of the builders over the face of the earth, but also in the construction of the tower out of clay and bitumen; for while these are the materials out of which the Tower of Babel is said to have been built, bitumen seems never to have been used by the Mexicans for such a purpose and is not found anywhere near Cholula.2 The history of the confusion of tongues seems also to have existed in the country, not long after the Conquest, having very probably been learnt from the missionaries, but it does not seem to have been connected with the Tower-of-Babel legend of Cholula. Something like it at least appears in the Gemelli table of Mexican migrations, reproduced in Humboldt, where a bird in a tree is sending down a number of tongues to a crowd of men standing below."1 On the strength of these suspicious resemblances Tylor may be right in condemning the legend of Cholula "as not genuine, or at least as partly of late fabrication." 2

A like suspicion of spuriousness, or at all events of assimilation to Biblical traditions, must apparently rest on a legend ascribed to the Toltecs of Mexico. "Ixtlil-xochitl writes of this tradition as follows: They say that the world was created in the year Ce Tecpatl, and this time until the deluge they call Atonatiuh, which means the age of the sun of water, because the world was destroyed by the deluge. It is found in the histories of the Toltecs that this age and first world, as they term it, lasted seven hundred and sixteen years; that man and all the earth were destroyed by great showers and by lightnings from heaven, so that nothing remained, and the most lofty mountains were covered up and submerged to the depth of caxtolmoletltli, or fifteen cubits, and here they add other fables of how men came to multiply again from the few who escaped the destruction in a toptlipetlacali; which word very nearly signifies a closed chest; and how, after multiplying, the men built a zacuali of great height, and by this is meant a very high tower, in which to take refuge when the world should be a second time destroyed. After this their tongue became confused, and, not understanding each other, they went to different parts of the world."3 In this legend the coincidences with the Biblical narratives of the flood, the ark, the tower of Babel, and the confusion of tongues seem too numerous to be accidental.

A similar verdict may be pronounced, with even less hesitation, on a tale told by the Karens of Burma, a tribe who display a peculiar aptitude for borrowing Christian legends and disguising them with a thin coat of local colour. Their edition of the Tower of Babel story, as told by the Gaikho section of the tribe, runs as follows. "The Gaikhos trace their genealogy to Adam, and make thirty generations from Adam, to the building of the Tower of Babel, at which time they say they separated from the Red Karens. ... In the days of Pan-dan-man, the people determined to build a pagoda that should reach up to heaven. The place they suppose to be somewhere in the country of the Red Karens, with whom they represent themselves as associated until this event. When the pagoda was half way up to heaven, God came down and confounded the language of the people, so that they could not understand each other. Then the people scattered, and Than-maurai, the father of the Gaikho tribe, came west, with eight chiefs, and settled in the valley of the Sitang."1

The Biblical story of the Tower of Babel and the confusion of tongues reappears also among the Mikirs, one of the many Tibeto-Burman tribes of Assam. They say that in days of old the descendants of Ram were mighty men, and growing dissatisfied with the mastery of the earth they aspired to conquer heaven. So they began to build a tower which should reach up to the skies. Higher and higher rose the building, till at last the gods and demons feared lest these giants should become the masters of heaven, as they already were of earth. So they confounded their speech, and scattered them to the four corners of the world. Hence arose all the various tongues of mankind.2 Again, we find the same old story, in a slightly disguised form, among the Admiralty Islanders. They say that the tribe or family of the Lohi numbered one hundred and thirty souls and had for their chief a certain Muikiu. This Muikiu said to his people, "Let us build a house as high as heaven." So they built it, and when it nearly reached the sky, there came to them from Kali a man named Po Awi, who forbade them to go on with the building. Said he to Muikiu, "Who told you to build so high a house?" Muikiu answered, "I am master of our people the Lohi. I said, ' Let us build a house as high as heaven.' If I had had my way, our houses should have been as high as heaven. But now, thy will is done, our houses will be low." So saying he took water and sprinkled it on the bodies of his people. Then was their language confounded; they understood not each other and dispersed into different lands. Thus every land has now its own speech.1 There can be little doubt that this story is merely an echo of missionary teaching.

Not a few peoples have attempted to explain the diversities of human speech without reference to a Tower of Babel or similar structures. Thus the Greeks had a tradition that for many ages men lived at peace, without cities and without laws, speaking one language, and ruled by Zeus alone. At last Hermes introduced diversities of speech and divided mankind into separate nations. So discord first arose among mortals, and Zeus, offended at their quarrels, resigned the sovereignty and committed it to the hands of the Argive hero Phoroneus, the first king of men.2

The Wa-Sania of British East Africa say that of old all the tribes of the earth knew only one language, but that during a severe famine the people went mad and wandered in all directions, jabbering strange words, and so the different languages arose.3

A different explanation of the diversities of language is given by the Kachcha Nagas, a hill tribe of Assam. According to them, at the creation all men were of one race, but they were destined soon afterwards to be broken up into different nations. The king of the men then on earth had a daughter named Sitoylê. She was wondrous fleet of foot, and loved to roam the jungle the livelong day, far from home, thereby causing much anxiety to her parents, who feared lest she should be devoured by wild beasts. One day her father conceived a plan for keeping her at home. He sent for a basket of linseed, and upsetting it on the ground he ordered his daughter to put the seeds back, one by one, into the basket, counting them as she did so. Then thinking that the task he had set her

238

would occupy the maiden the whole day, he withdrew. But by sunset his daughter had counted all the seeds and put them back in the basket, and no sooner had she done so than away she hurried to the jungle. So when her parents returned, they could find no trace of their missing daughter. After searching for days and days, however, they at last came across a monster python lying gorged in the shade of the trees. All the men being assembled, they attacked the huge reptile with spear and sword. But even as they struck at the snake, their appearance changed, and they found themselves speaking various dialects. The men of the same speech now drew apart from the rest and formed a separate band, and the various bands thus created became the ancestors of the different nations now existing on earth.1 But what became of the princess, whether she was restored to her sorrowing parents, or whether she had been swallowed by the python, the story does not relate.

The Kukis of Manipur, another hill race of Assam, account for the diversity of languages in their tribes by saying, that once on a time the three grandsons of a certain chief were all playing together in the house, when their father bade them catch a rat. But while they were busy hunting the animal, they were suddenly smitten with a confusion of tongues and could not understand each other, so the rat escaped. The eldest of the three sons now spoke the Lamyang language; the second spoke the Thado language, and as for the third, some say that he spoke the Waiphie language, but others think it was the Manipur tongue which he spoke. At all events the three lads became the ancestors of three distinct tribes.2

The Encounter Bay tribe of South Australia trace the origin of languages to an ill-tempered old woman, who died long ago. Her name was Wurruri, she lived towards the east, and generally walked about with a big stick in her hand to scatter the fires round which other people were sleeping. When at last she died, her people were so glad to be rid of her, that they sent messengers in all directions to announce the good news of her death. Men, women, and children accordingly assembled, not to mourn but to rejoice over the decease and to celebrate it by a cannibal banquet. The Raminjerar were the first who fell upon the corpse and commenced to devour the flesh, and no sooner did they do so than they began to speak intelligibly. The other tribes to the eastward, arriving later, ate the contents of the intestines, which caused them to speak a language slightly different. Last of all came the northern tribes, and having consumed the intestines and all that remained of the corpse, they spoke a language which differed still more from that of the Raminjerar.1

The Maidu Indians of California say that down to a certain time everybody spoke the same language. But once, when the people were having a burning, and everything was ready for the next day, suddenly in the night everybody began to speak in a different tongue, except that each husband and wife talked the same language. That night the Creator, whom they call Earth-Initiate, appeared to a certain man named Kuksu, told him what had happened, and instructed him how to proceed next day when the Babel of tongues would commence. Thus prepared, Kuksu summoned all the people together, for he could speak all the languages. He taught them the names of the different animals and so forth in their various dialects, showed them how to cook and to hunt, gave them their laws, and appointed the times for their dances and festivals. Then he called each tribe by name, and sent them off in different directions, telling them where they were to dwell.2

We have seen that the Tlingits of Alaska explain the diversity of tongues by the story of a great flood, which they may have borrowed from Christian missionaries or traders.1

The Quiches of Guatemala told of a time, in the early ages of the world, when men lived together and spoke but one language, when they invoked as yet neither wood nor stone, and remembered naught but the word of the Creator, the Heart of heaven and of earth. However, as years went on the tribes multiplied, and leaving their old home came to a place called Tulan. It was there, according to Quiché tradition, that the language of the tribes changed and the diversity of tongues originated; the people ceased to understand each other's speech and dispersed to seek new homes in different parts of the world.2

These last stories, in attempting to account for the diversities of language, make no reference to a Tower of Babel, and accordingly they may, with the possible exception of the Tlingit tale, be accepted as independent efforts of the human mind to grapple with that difficult problem, however little they succeed in solving it.

241

www.ingramcontent.com/pod-product-compliance
Lightning Source LLC
Chambersburg PA
CBHW080527090426
42733CB00015B/2512